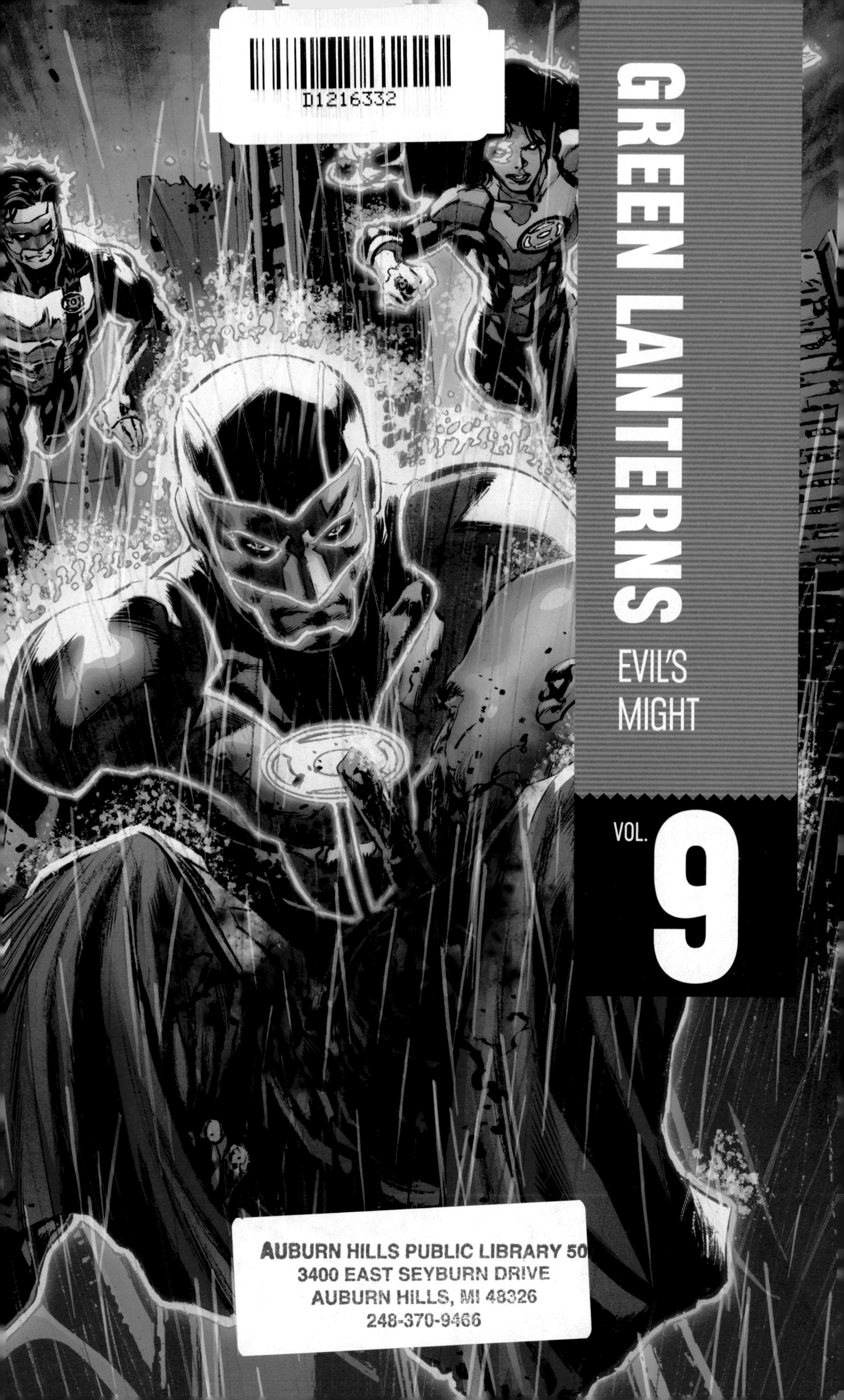

GREEN LANTERNS

EVIL'S MIGHT

VOL. 9

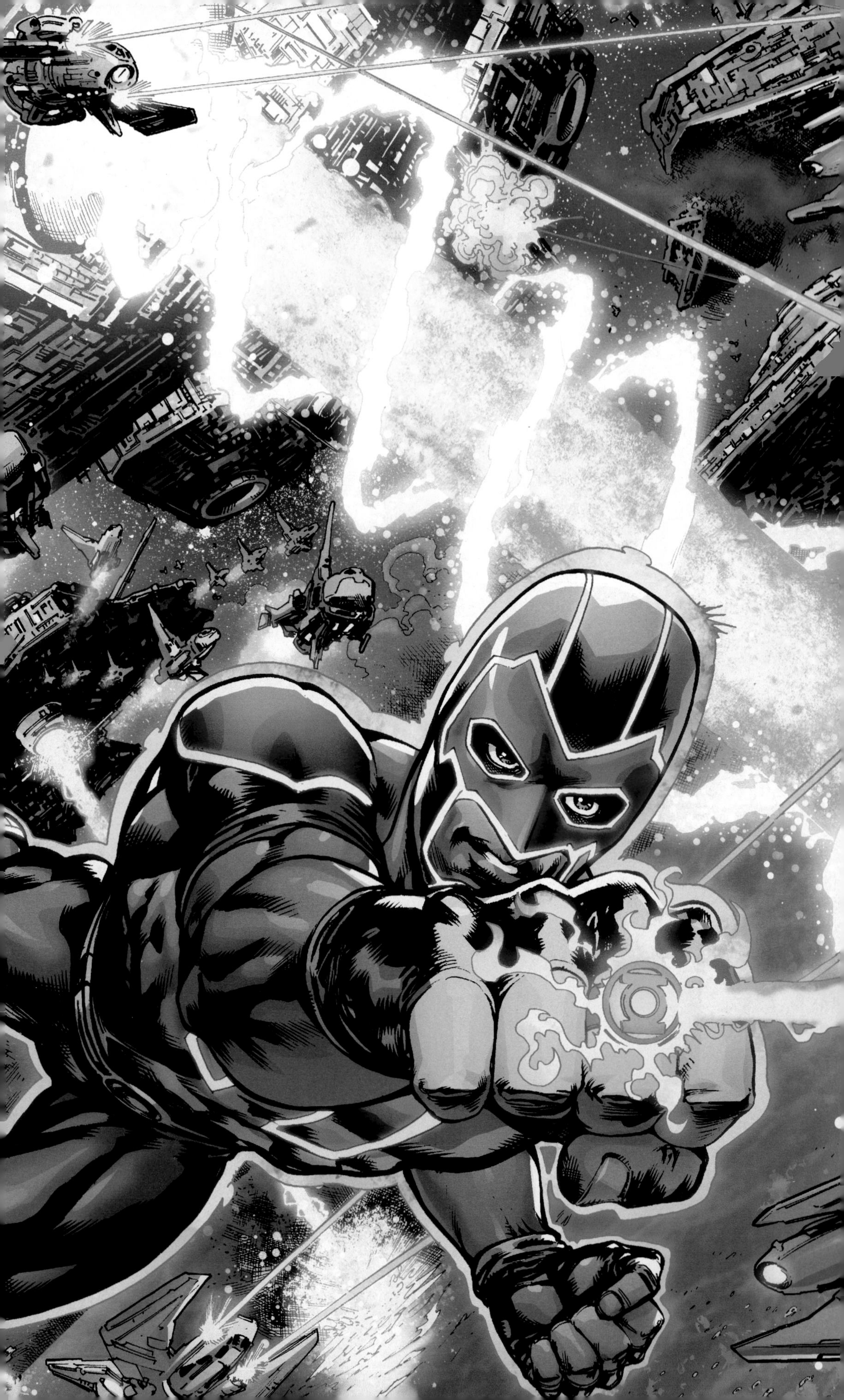

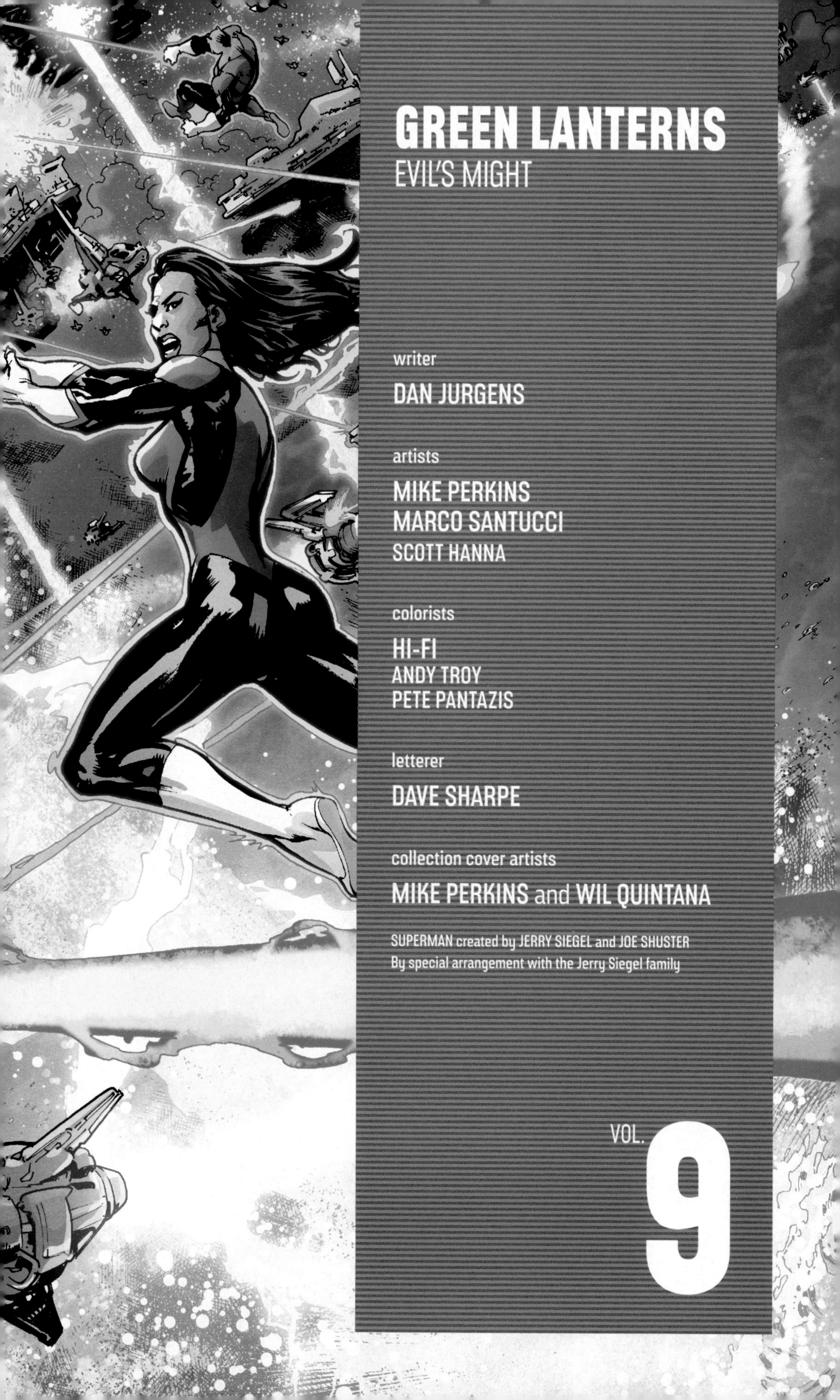

GREEN LANTERNS

EVIL'S MIGHT

writer

DAN JURGENS

artists

MIKE PERKINS
MARCO SANTUCCI
SCOTT HANNA

colorists

HI-FI
ANDY TROY
PETE PANTAZIS

letterer

DAVE SHARPE

collection cover artists

MIKE PERKINS and **WIL QUINTANA**

SUPERMAN created by JERRY SIEGEL and JOE SHUSTER
By special arrangement with the Jerry Siegel family

VOL. 9

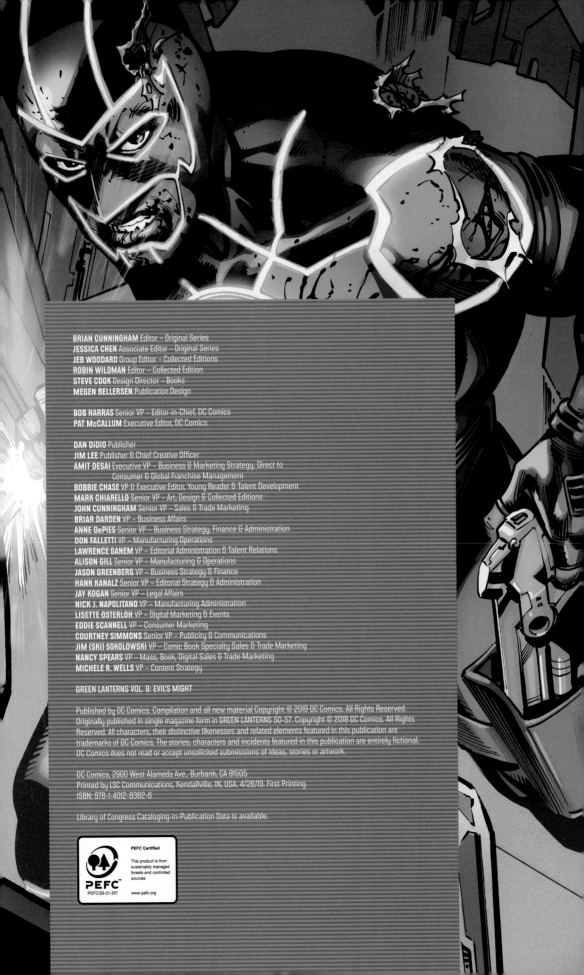

BRIAN CUNNINGHAM Editor – Original Series
JESSICA CHEN Associate Editor – Original Series
JEB WOODARD Group Editor – Collected Editions
ROBIN WILDMAN Editor – Collected Edition
STEVE COOK Design Director – Books
MEGEN BELLERSEN Publication Design

BOB HARRAS Senior VP – Editor-in-Chief, DC Comics
PAT McCALLUM Executive Editor, DC Comics

DAN DiDIO Publisher
JIM LEE Publisher & Chief Creative Officer
AMIT DESAI Executive VP – Business & Marketing Strategy, Direct to Consumer & Global Franchise Management
BOBBIE CHASE VP & Executive Editor, Young Reader & Talent Development
MARK CHIARELLO Senior VP – Art, Design & Collected Editions
JOHN CUNNINGHAM Senior VP – Sales & Trade Marketing
BRIAR DARDEN VP – Business Affairs
ANNE DePIES Senior VP – Business Strategy, Finance & Administration
DON FALLETTI VP – Manufacturing Operations
LAWRENCE GANEM VP – Editorial Administration & Talent Relations
ALISON GILL Senior VP – Manufacturing & Operations
JASON GREENBERG VP – Business Strategy & Finance
HANK KANALZ Senior VP – Editorial Strategy & Administration
JAY KOGAN Senior VP – Legal Affairs
NICK J. NAPOLITANO VP – Manufacturing Administration
LISETTE OSTERLOH VP – Digital Marketing & Events
EDDIE SCANNELL VP – Consumer Marketing
COURTNEY SIMMONS Senior VP – Publicity & Communications
JIM (SKI) SOKOLOWSKI VP – Comic Book Specialty Sales & Trade Marketing
NANCY SPEARS VP – Mass, Book, Digital Sales & Trade Marketing
MICHELE R. WELLS VP – Content Strategy

GREEN LANTERNS VOL. 9: EVIL'S MIGHT

DC Comics, 2900 West Alameda Ave., Burbank, CA 91505
Printed by LSC Communications, Kendallville, IN, USA. 4/26/19. First Printing.
ISBN: 978-1-4012-9382-6

Library of Congress Cataloging-in-Publication Data is available.

PEFC Certified
This product is from sustainably managed forests and controlled sources
PEFC
PEFC/29-31-337
www.pefc.org

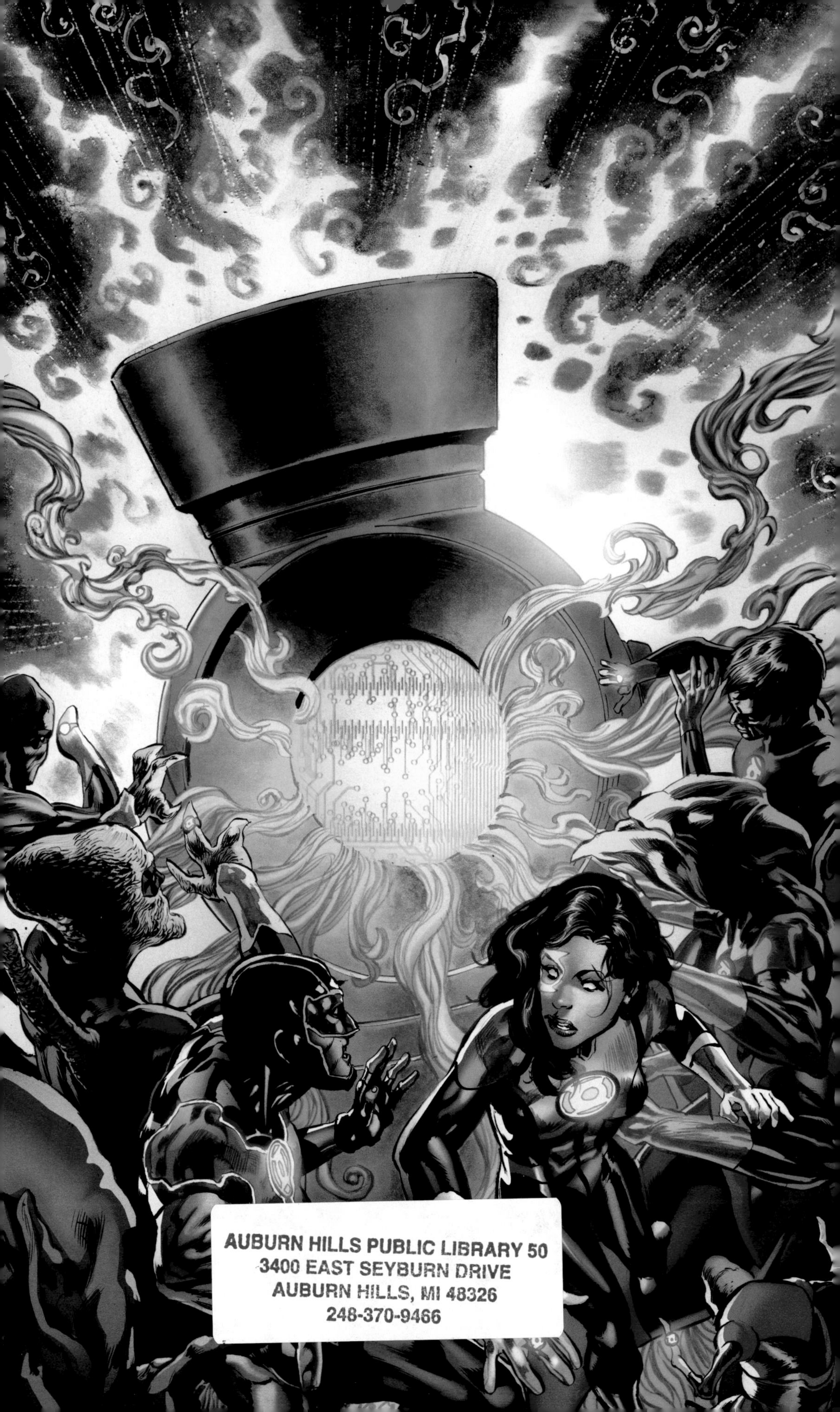

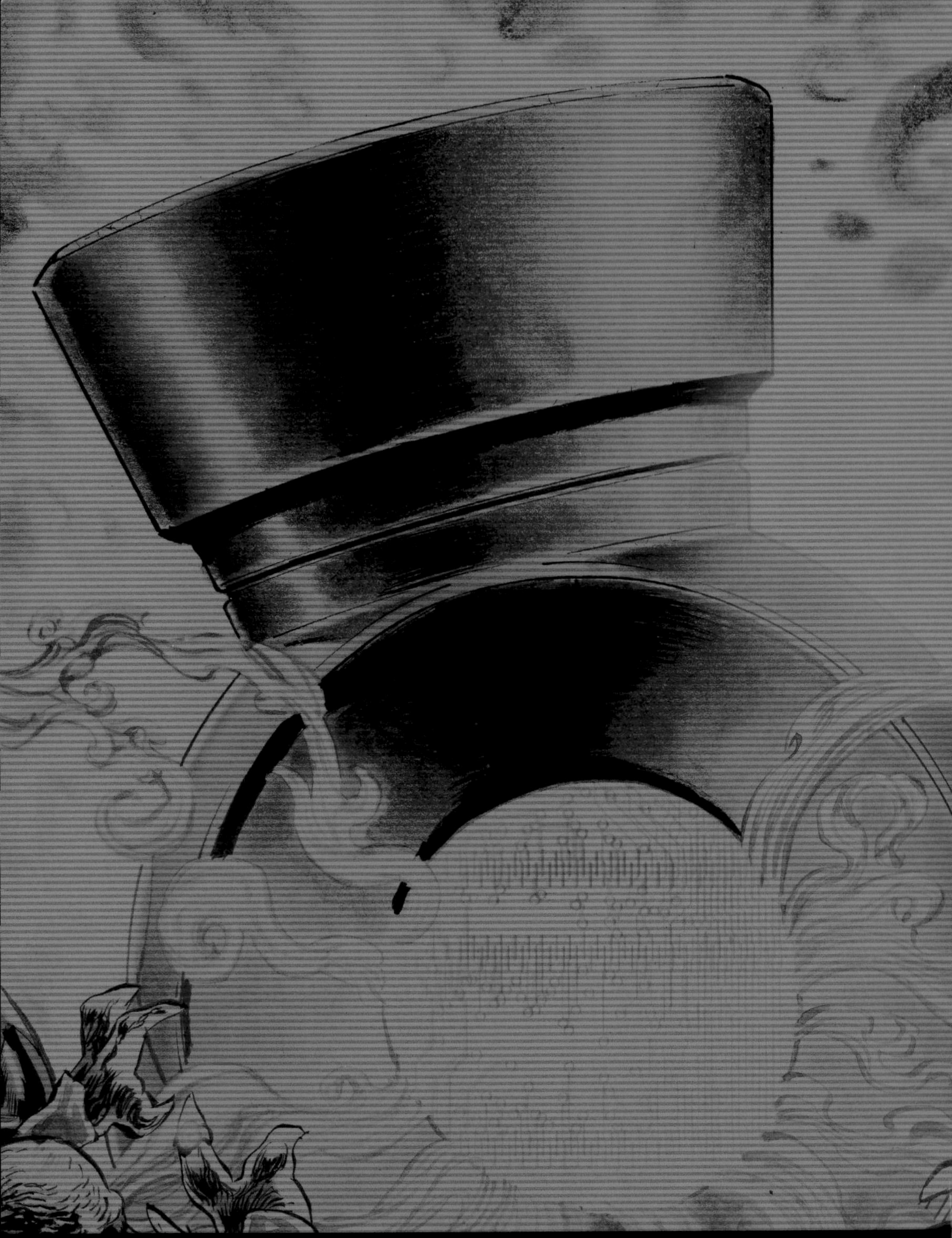

GREEN LANTERNS

#50

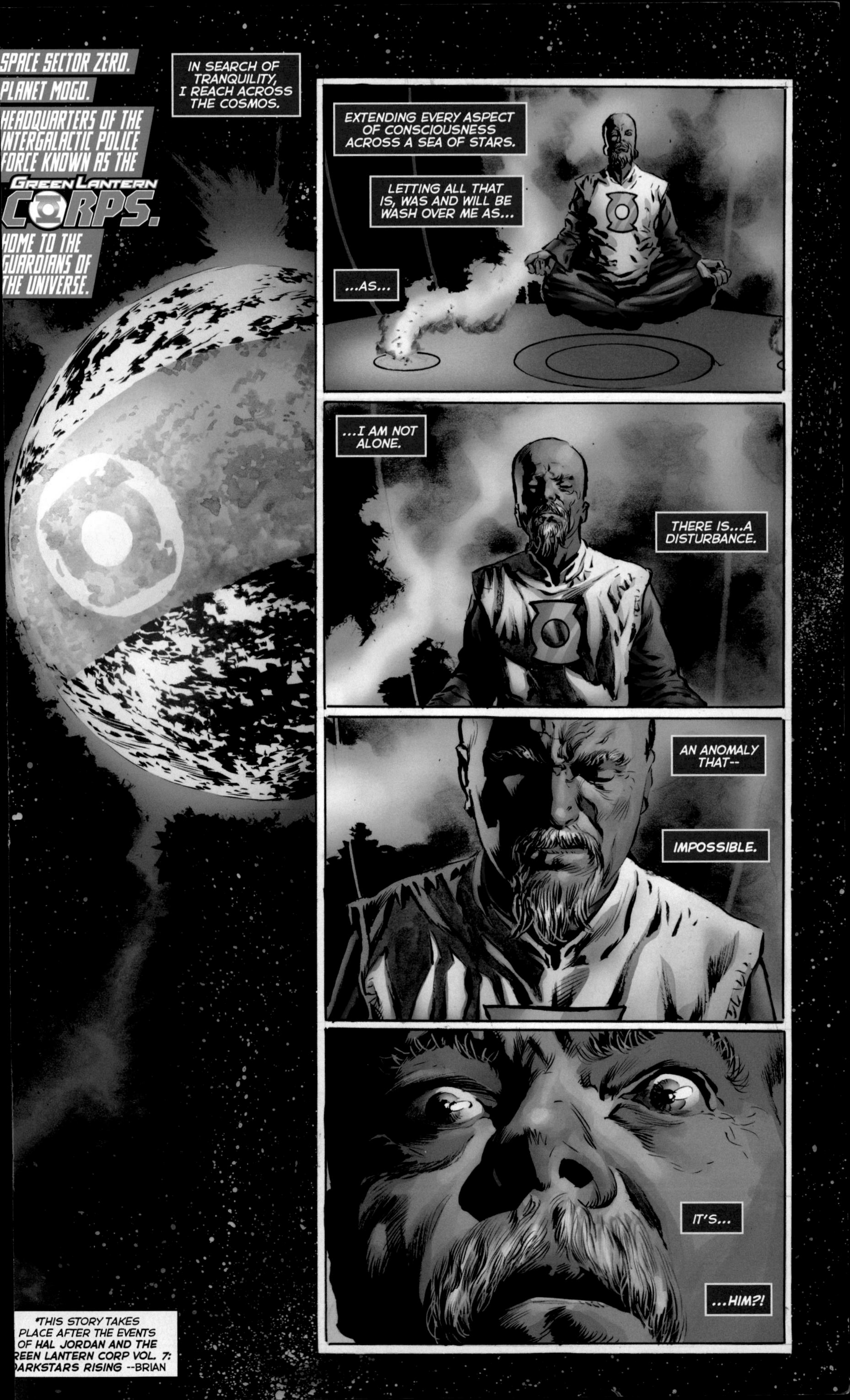
SPACE SECTOR ZERO.
PLANET MOGO.
HEADQUARTERS OF THE INTERGALACTIC POLICE FORCE KNOWN AS THE
GREEN LANTERN CORPS.
HOME TO THE GUARDIANS OF THE UNIVERSE.
IN SEARCH OF TRANQUILITY, I REACH ACROSS THE COSMOS.
EXTENDING EVERY ASPECT OF CONSCIOUSNESS ACROSS A SEA OF STARS.
LETTING ALL THAT IS, WAS AND WILL BE WASH OVER ME AS...
...AS...
...I AM NOT ALONE.
THERE IS...A DISTURBANCE.
AN ANOMALY THAT--
IMPOSSIBLE.
IT'S...
...HIM?!
*THIS STORY TAKES PLACE AFTER THE EVENTS OF HAL JORDAN AND THE GREEN LANTERN CORP VOL. 7: DARKSTARS RISING --BRIAN

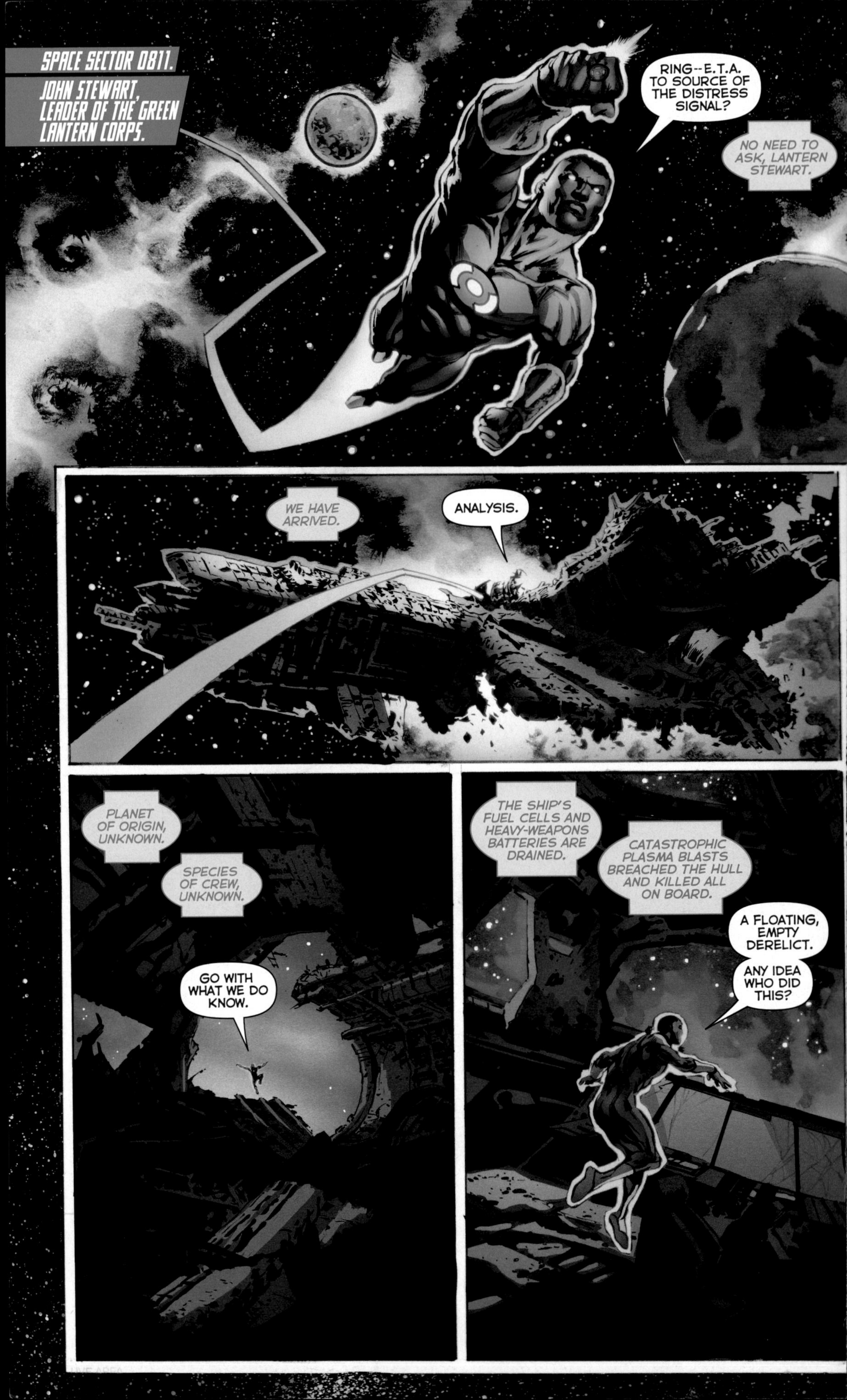
SPACE SECTOR 0811.
JOHN STEWART, LEADER OF THE GREEN LANTERN CORPS.
RING--E.T.A. TO SOURCE OF THE DISTRESS SIGNAL?
NO NEED TO ASK, LANTERN STEWART.
WE HAVE ARRIVED.
ANALYSIS.
PLANET OF ORIGIN, UNKNOWN.
SPECIES OF CREW, UNKNOWN.
GO WITH WHAT WE DO KNOW.
THE SHIP'S FUEL CELLS AND HEAVY-WEAPONS BATTERIES ARE DRAINED.
CATASTROPHIC PLASMA BLASTS BREACHED THE HULL AND KILLED ALL ON BOARD.
A FLOATING, EMPTY DERELICT.
ANY IDEA WHO DID THIS?

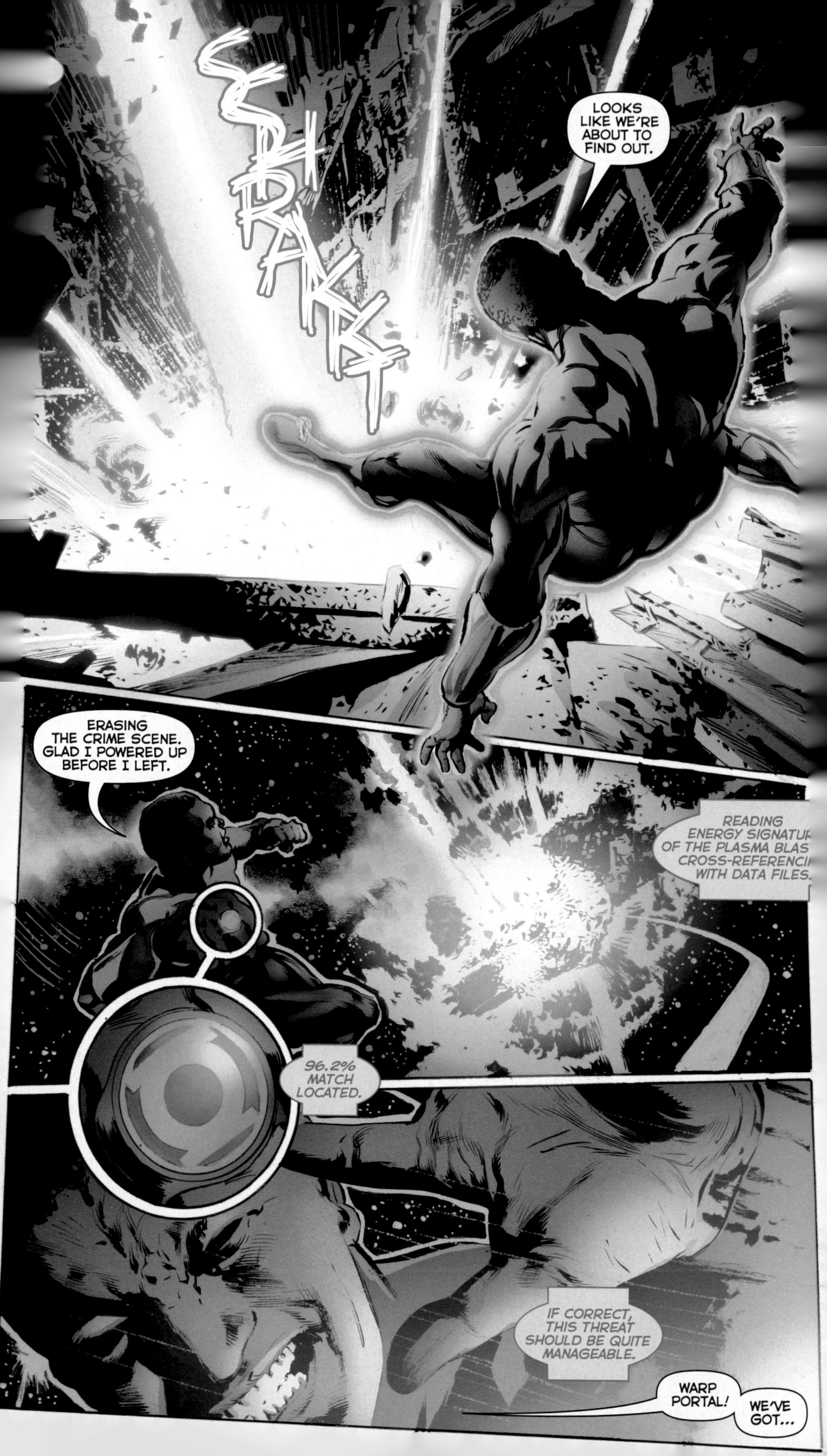

SHRAKKT
LOOKS LIKE WE'RE ABOUT TO FIND OUT.
ERASING THE CRIME SCENE. GLAD I POWERED UP BEFORE I LEFT.
READING ENERGY SIGNATUR OF THE PLASMA BLAS CROSS-REFERENCI WITH DATA FILES.
96.2% MATCH LOCATED.
IF CORRECT, THIS THREAT SHOULD BE QUITE MANAGEABLE.
WARP PORTAL!
WE'VE GOT...

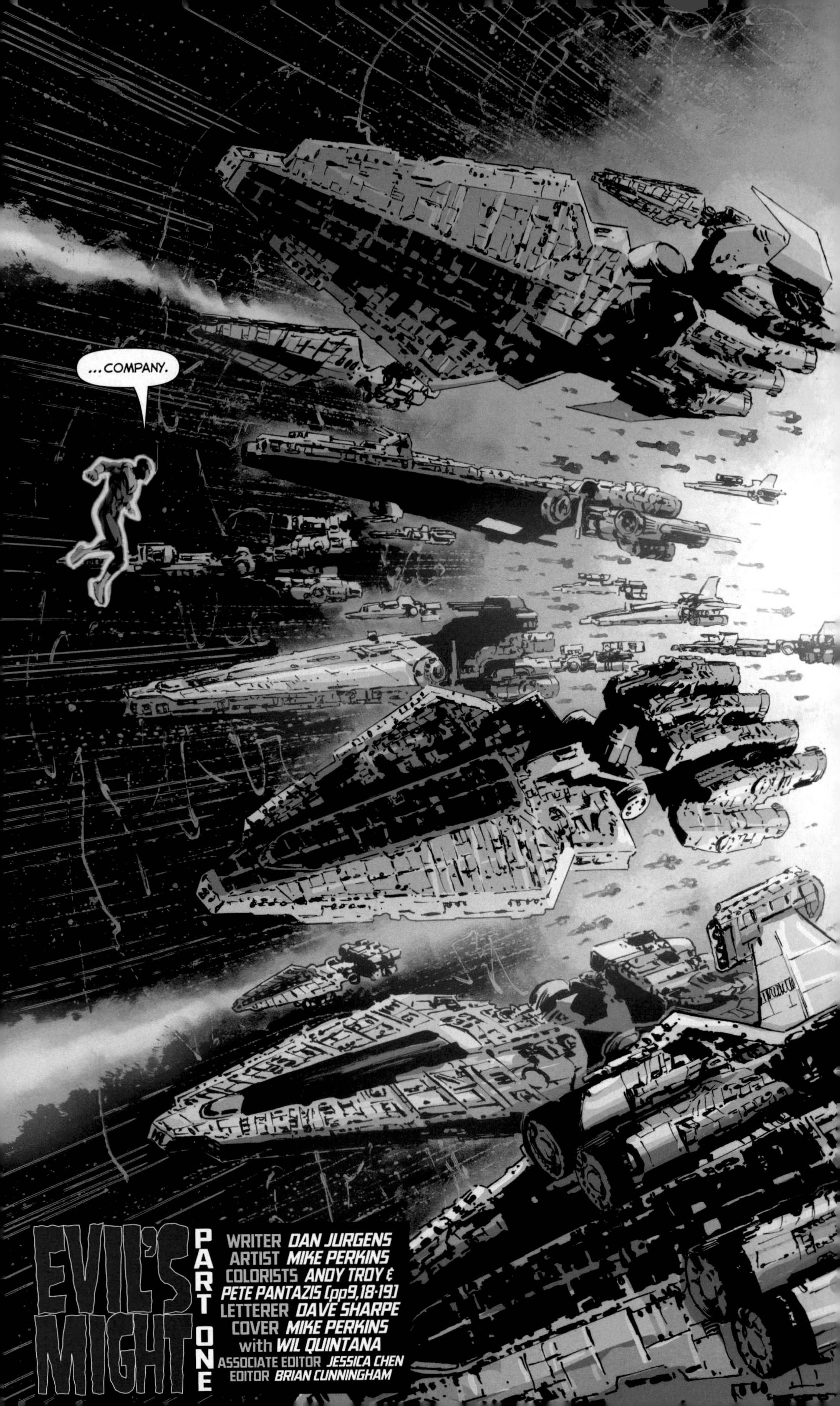

...COMPANY.
EVIL'S MIGHT
PART ONE
WRITER DAN JURGENS
ARTIST MIKE PERKINS
COLORISTS ANDY TROY &
PETE PANTAZIS [pp9,18-19]
LETTERER DAVE SHARPE
COVER MIKE PERKINS
with WIL QUINTANA
ASSOCIATE EDITOR JESSICA CHEN
EDITOR BRIAN CUNNINGHAM

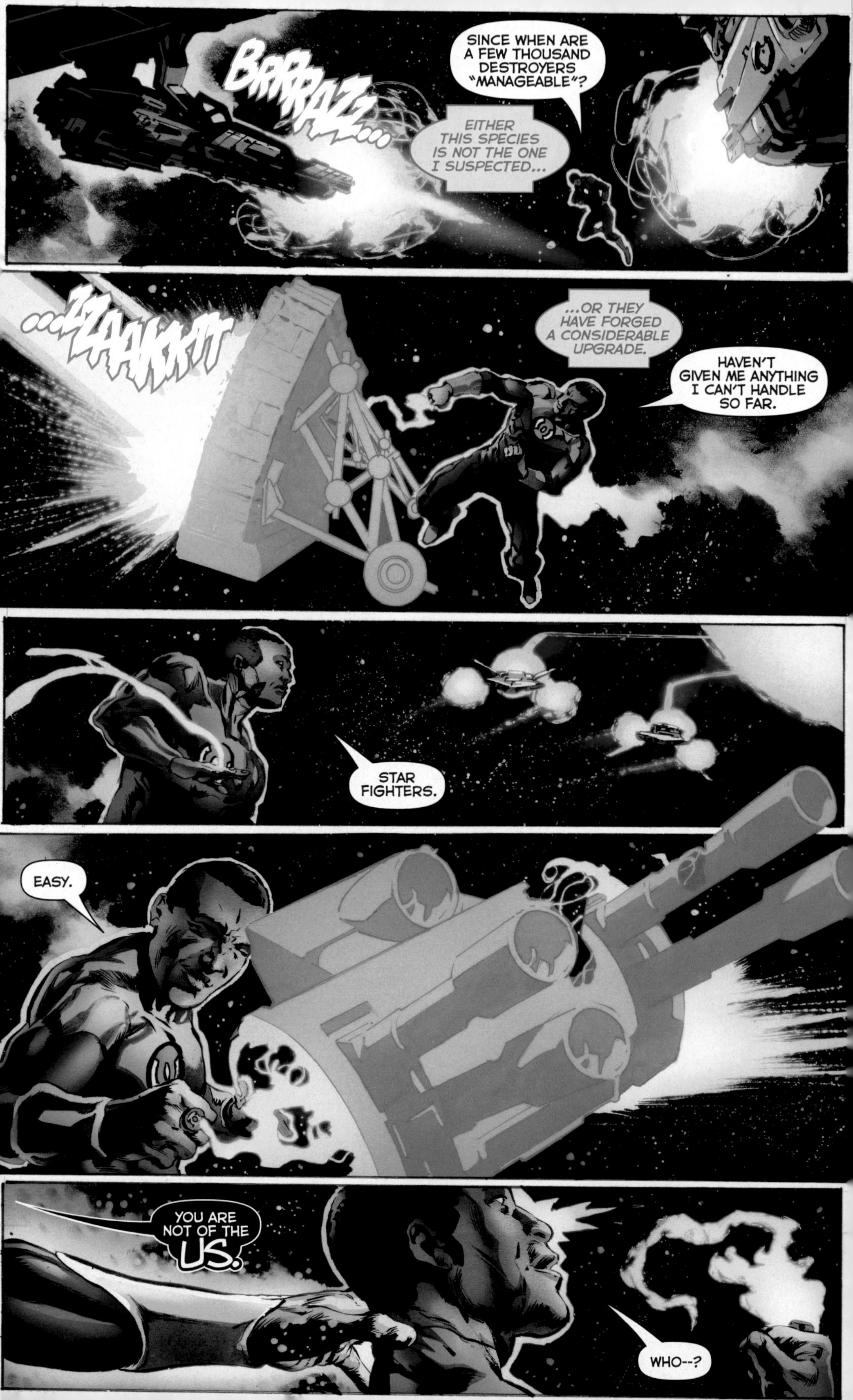
BRRRAZZ...
SINCE WHEN ARE A FEW THOUSAND DESTROYERS "MANAGEABLE"?
EITHER THIS SPECIES IS NOT THE ONE I SUSPECTED...
...ZZAAKKTT
...OR THEY HAVE FORGED A CONSIDERABLE UPGRADE.
HAVEN'T GIVEN ME ANYTHING I CAN'T HANDLE SO FAR.
STAR FIGHTERS.
EASY.
YOU ARE NOT OF THE US.
WHO--?

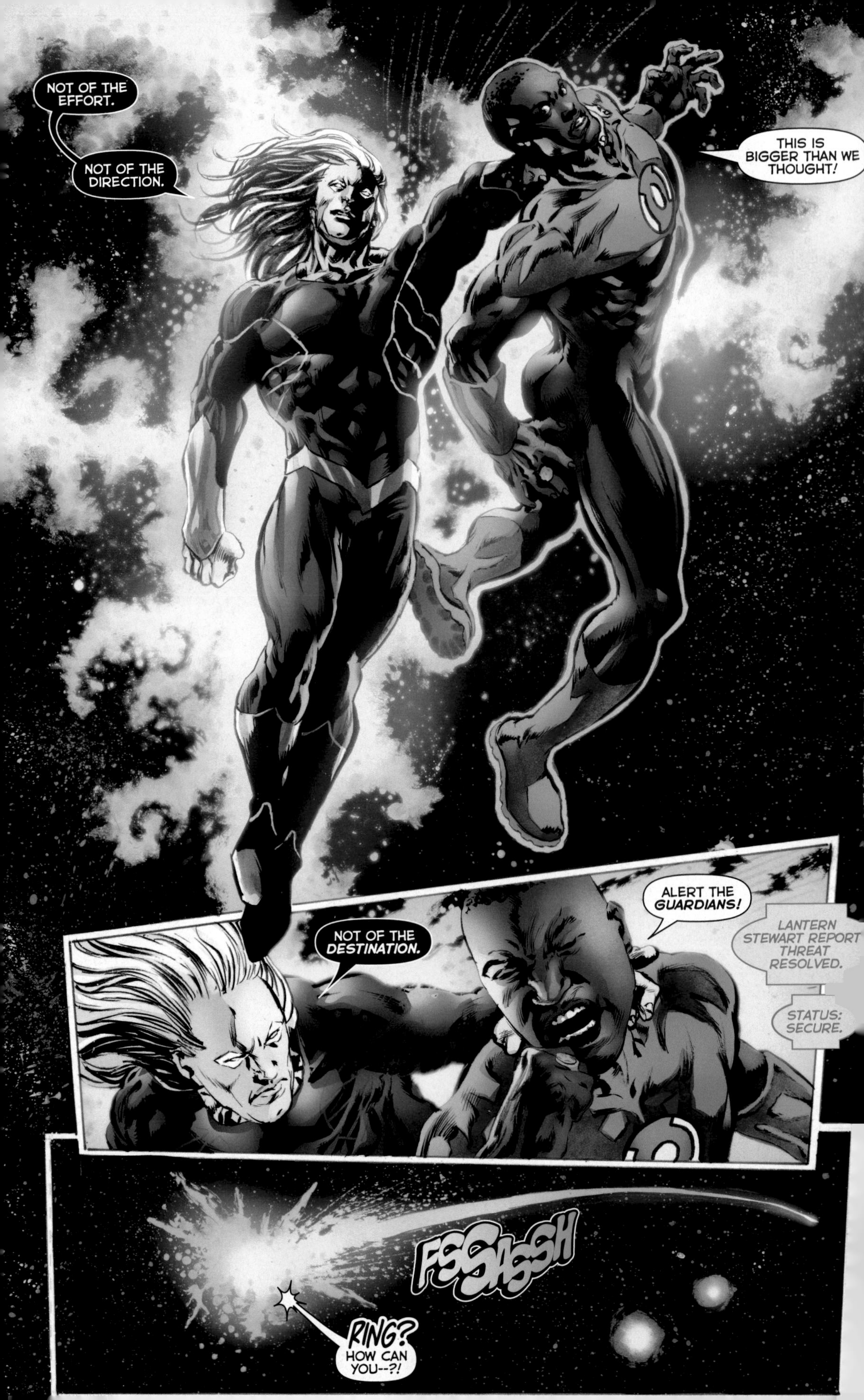
NOT OF THE EFFORT.
NOT OF THE DIRECTION.
THIS IS BIGGER THAN WE THOUGHT!
NOT OF THE DESTINATION.
ALERT THE GUARDIANS!
LANTERN STEWART REPORT THREAT RESOLVED.
STATUS: SECURE.
FSSASSH
RING? HOW CAN YOU--?!

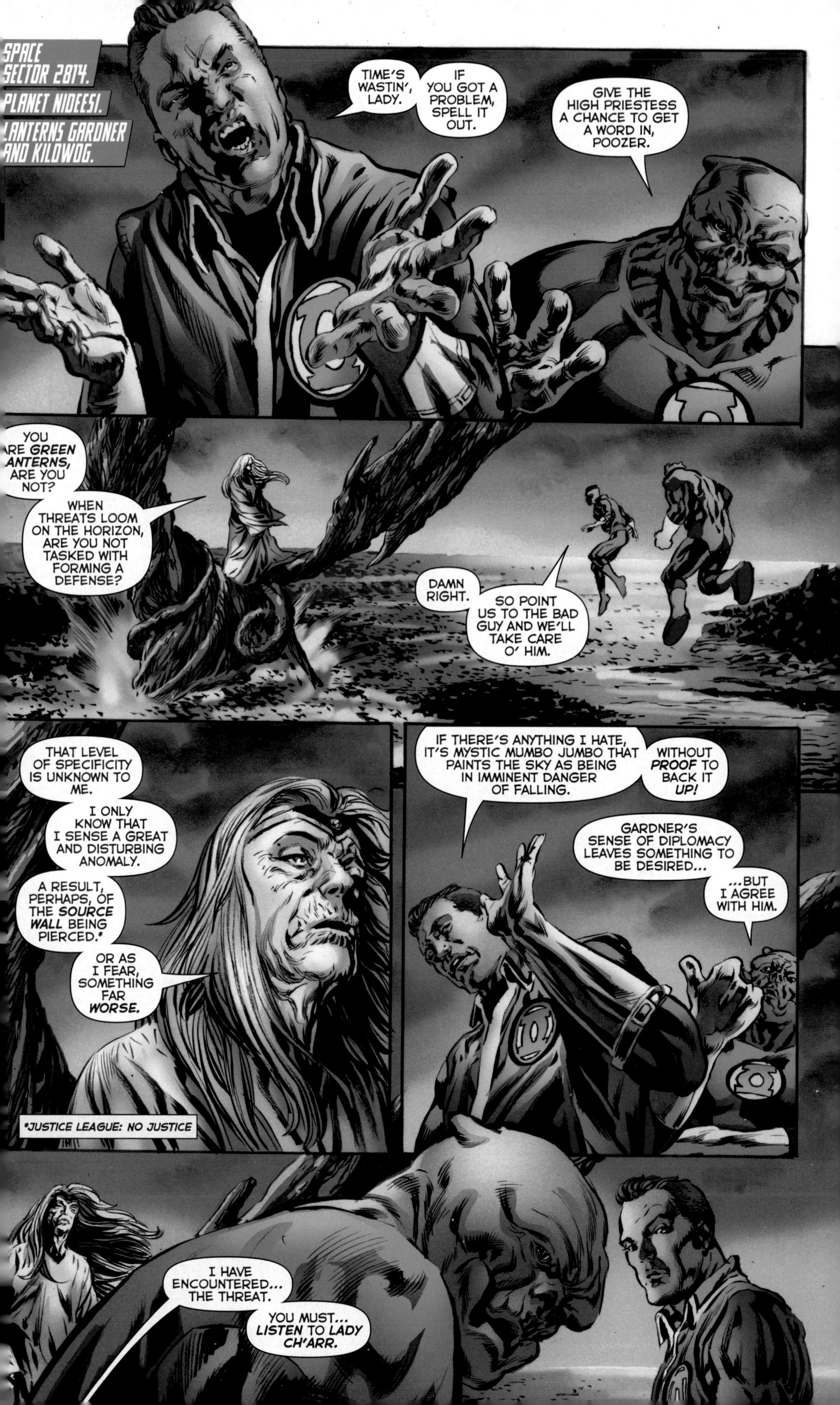

SPACE SECTOR 2814.
PLANET NIDEESI.
LANTERNS GARDNER AND KILOWOG.
TIME'S WASTIN', LADY.
IF YOU GOT A PROBLEM, SPELL IT OUT.
GIVE THE HIGH PRIESTESS A CHANCE TO GET A WORD IN, POOZER.
YOU ARE GREEN LANTERNS, ARE YOU NOT?
WHEN THREATS LOOM ON THE HORIZON, ARE YOU NOT TASKED WITH FORMING A DEFENSE?
DAMN RIGHT.
SO POINT US TO THE BAD GUY AND WE'LL TAKE CARE O' HIM.
THAT LEVEL OF SPECIFICITY IS UNKNOWN TO ME.
I ONLY KNOW THAT I SENSE A GREAT AND DISTURBING ANOMALY.
A RESULT, PERHAPS, OF THE SOURCE WALL BEING PIERCED.*
OR AS I FEAR, SOMETHING FAR WORSE.
*JUSTICE LEAGUE: NO JUSTICE
IF THERE'S ANYTHING I HATE, IT'S MYSTIC MUMBO JUMBO THAT PAINTS THE SKY AS BEING IN IMMINENT DANGER OF FALLING.
WITHOUT PROOF TO BACK IT UP!
GARDNER'S SENSE OF DIPLOMACY LEAVES SOMETHING TO BE DESIRED...
...BUT I AGREE WITH HIM.
I HAVE ENCOUNTERED... THE THREAT.
YOU MUST... LISTEN TO LADY CH'ARR.

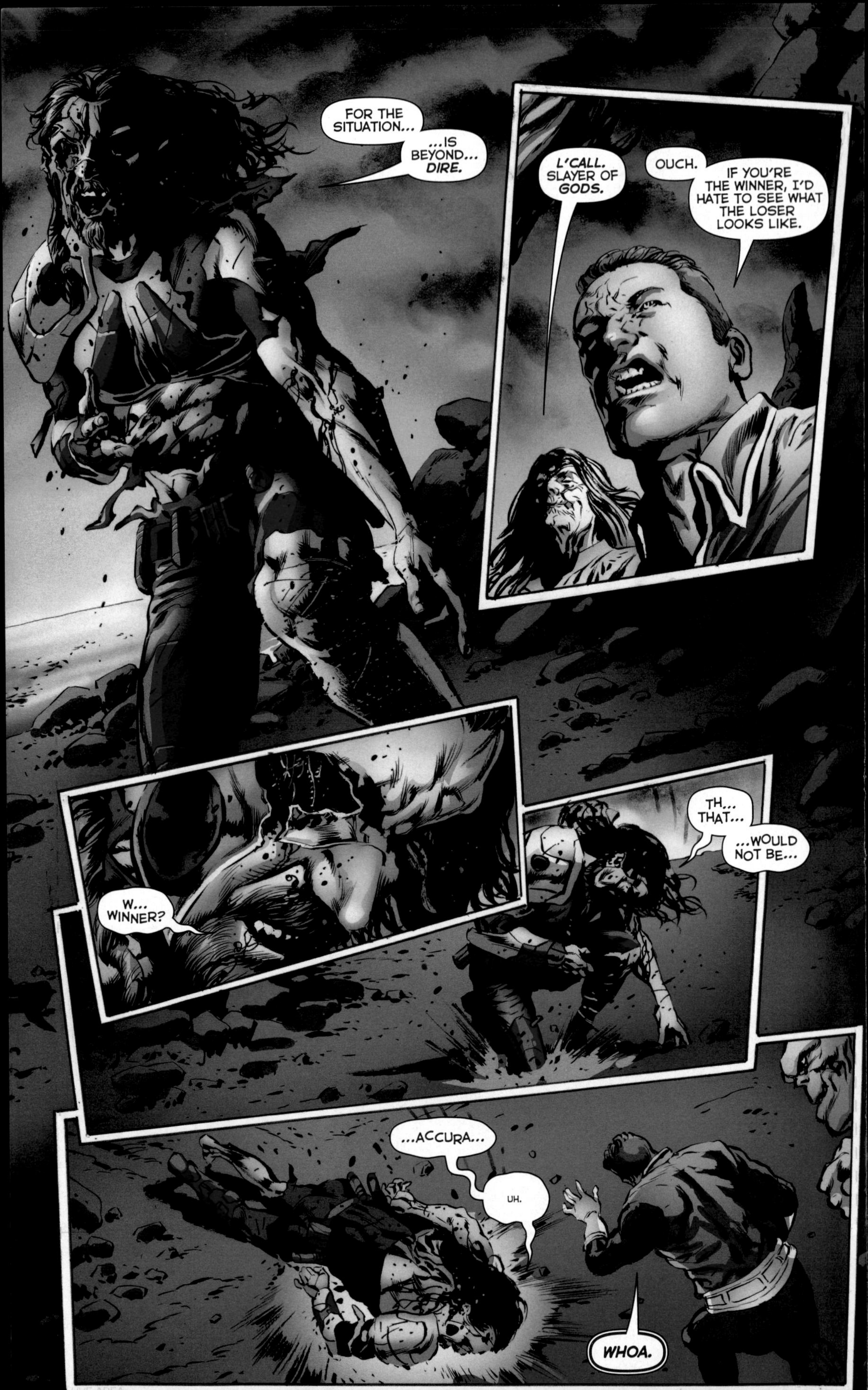
FOR THE SITUATION...
...IS BEYOND... DIRE.
L'CALL. SLAYER OF GODS.
OUCH.
IF YOU'RE THE WINNER, I'D HATE TO SEE WHAT THE LOSER LOOKS LIKE.
W... WINNER?
TH... THAT...
...WOULD NOT BE...
...ACCURA...
UH.
WHOA.

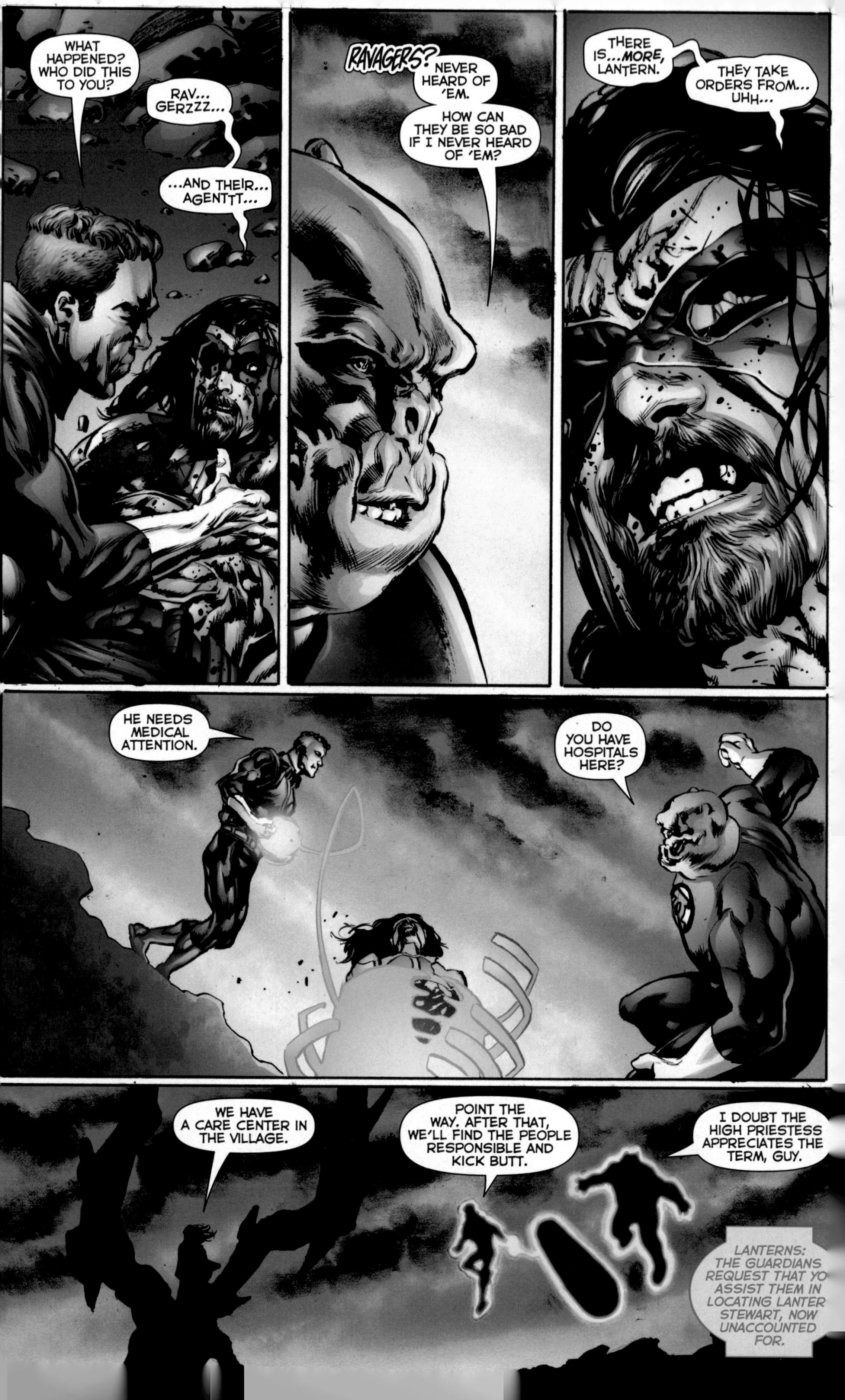
WHAT HAPPENED? WHO DID THIS TO YOU?
RAV... GERZZZ...
...AND THEIR... AGENTTT...
RAVAGERS?
NEVER HEARD OF 'EM.
HOW CAN THEY BE SO BAD IF I NEVER HEARD OF 'EM?
THERE IS...MORE, LANTERN.
THEY TAKE ORDERS FROM... UHH...
HE NEEDS MEDICAL ATTENTION.
DO YOU HAVE HOSPITALS HERE?
WE HAVE A CARE CENTER IN THE VILLAGE.
POINT THE WAY. AFTER THAT, WE'LL FIND THE PEOPLE RESPONSIBLE AND KICK BUTT.
I DOUBT THE HIGH PRIESTESS APPRECIATES THE TERM, GUY.
LANTERNS: THE GUARDIANS REQUEST THAT YO ASSIST THEM IN LOCATING LANTER STEWART, NOW UNACCOUNTED FOR.

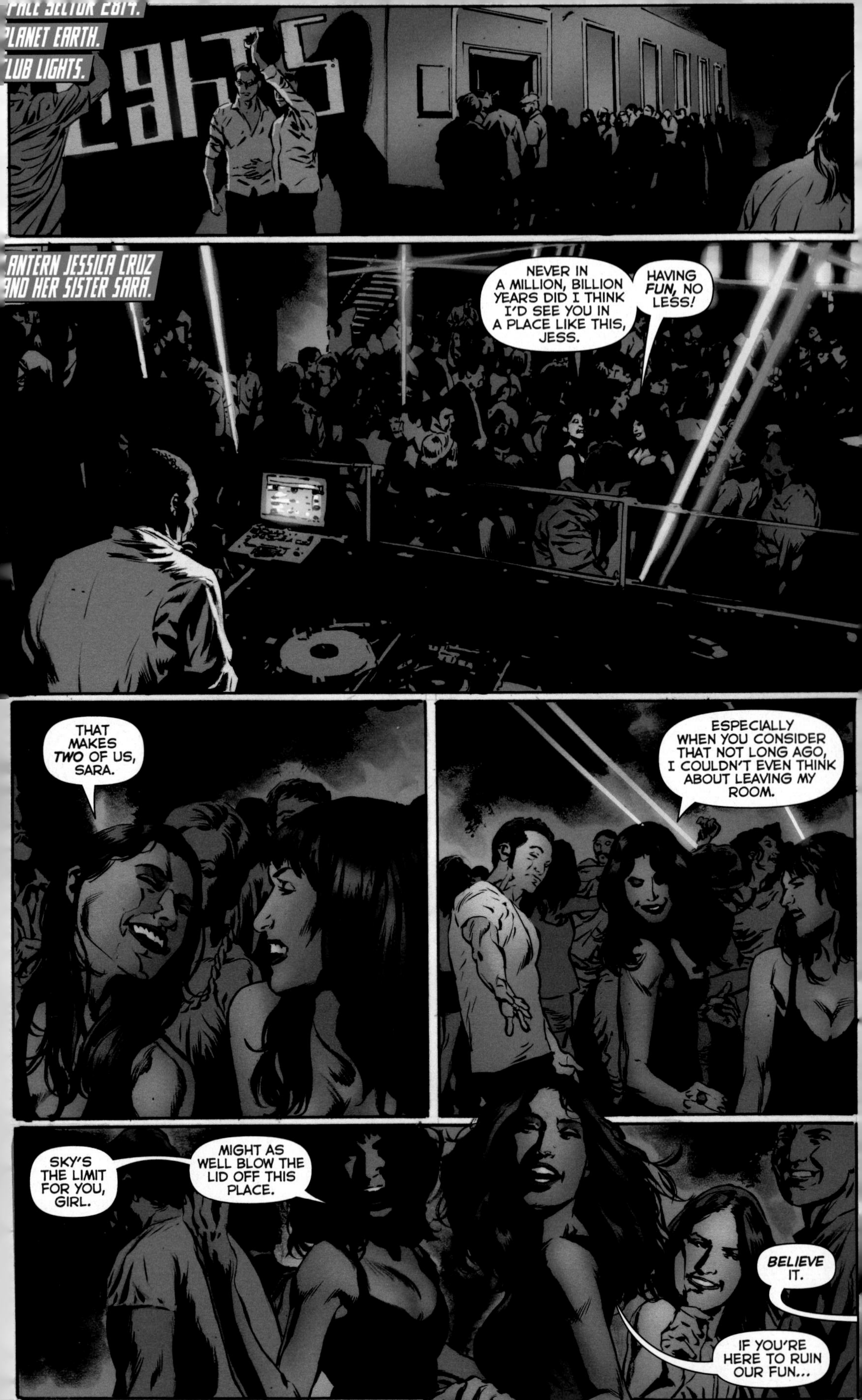

PACE SECTOR 2814.
PLANET EARTH.
CLUB LIGHTS.
ANTERN JESSICA CRUZ AND HER SISTER SARA.
NEVER IN A MILLION, BILLION YEARS DID I THINK I'D SEE YOU IN A PLACE LIKE THIS, JESS.
HAVING *FUN,* NO LESS!
THAT MAKES *TWO* OF US, SARA.
ESPECIALLY WHEN YOU CONSIDER THAT NOT LONG AGO, I COULDN'T EVEN THINK ABOUT LEAVING MY ROOM.
SKY'S THE LIMIT FOR YOU, GIRL.
MIGHT AS WELL BLOW THE LID OFF THIS PLACE.
BELIEVE IT.
IF YOU'RE HERE TO RUIN OUR FUN...

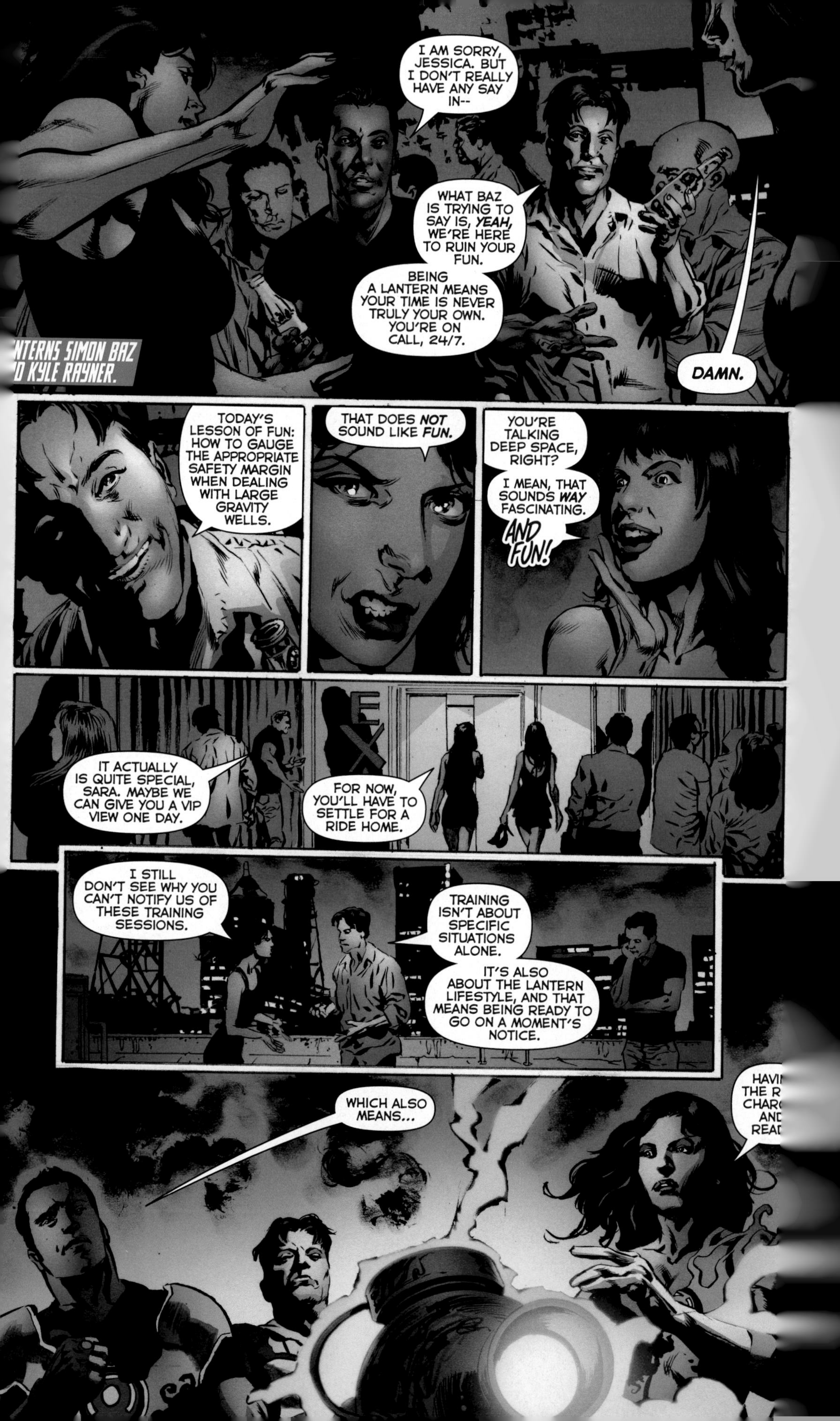

I AM SORRY, JESSICA. BUT I DON'T REALLY HAVE ANY SAY IN--
WHAT BAZ IS TRYING TO SAY IS, YEAH, WE'RE HERE TO RUIN YOUR FUN.
BEING A LANTERN MEANS YOUR TIME IS NEVER TRULY YOUR OWN. YOU'RE ON CALL, 24/7.
NTERNS SIMON BAZ
D KYLE RAYNER.
DAMN.
TODAY'S LESSON OF FUN: HOW TO GAUGE THE APPROPRIATE SAFETY MARGIN WHEN DEALING WITH LARGE GRAVITY WELLS.
THAT DOES NOT SOUND LIKE FUN.
YOU'RE TALKING DEEP SPACE, RIGHT?
I MEAN, THAT SOUNDS WAY FASCINATING.
AND FUN!
IT ACTUALLY IS QUITE SPECIAL, SARA. MAYBE WE CAN GIVE YOU A VIP VIEW ONE DAY.
FOR NOW, YOU'LL HAVE TO SETTLE FOR A RIDE HOME.
I STILL DON'T SEE WHY YOU CAN'T NOTIFY US OF THESE TRAINING SESSIONS.
TRAINING ISN'T ABOUT SPECIFIC SITUATIONS ALONE.
IT'S ALSO ABOUT THE LANTERN LIFESTYLE, AND THAT MEANS BEING READY TO GO ON A MOMENT'S NOTICE.
WHICH ALSO MEANS...

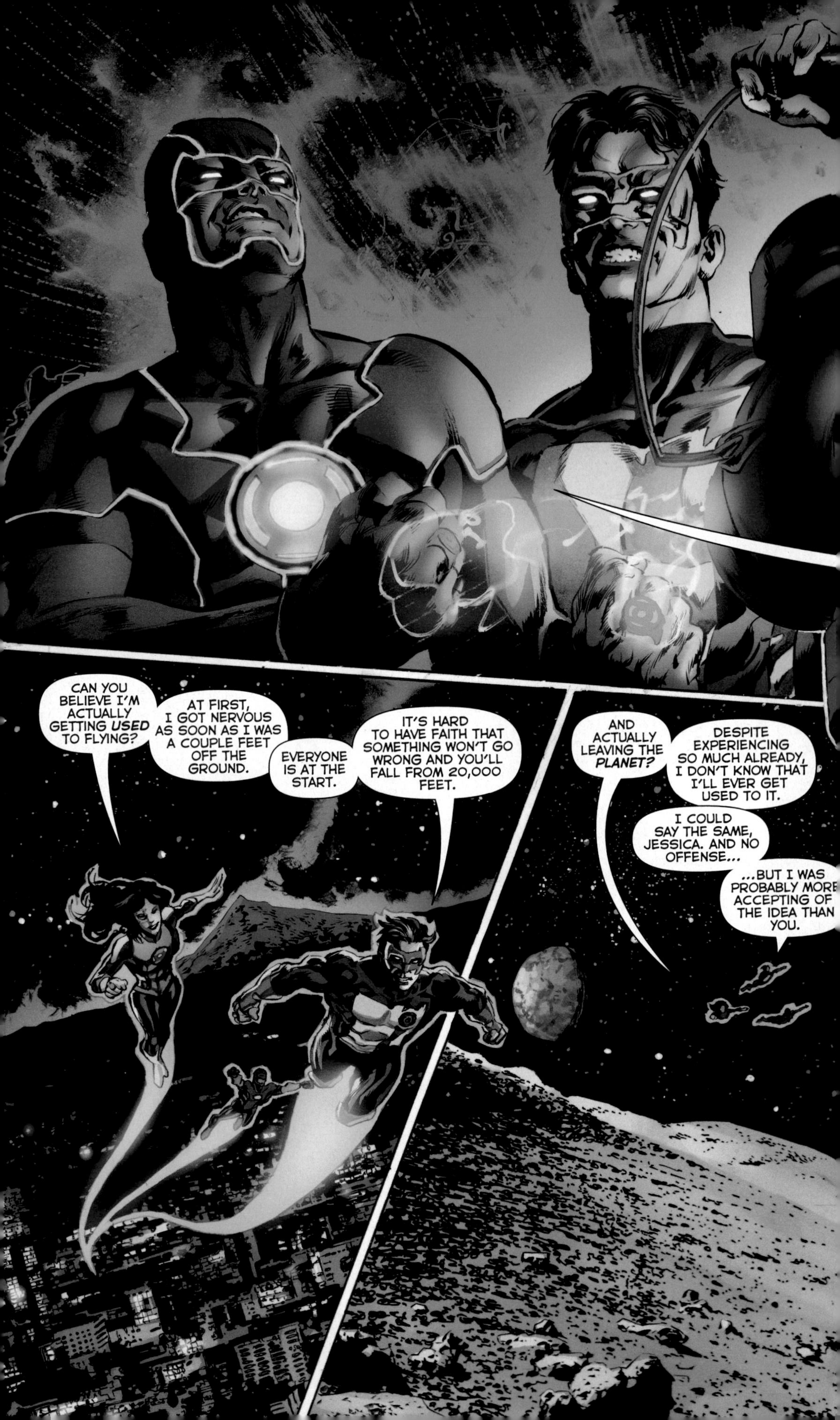
CAN YOU BELIEVE I'M ACTUALLY GETTING USED TO FLYING?
AT FIRST, I GOT NERVOUS AS SOON AS I WAS A COUPLE FEET OFF THE GROUND.
EVERYONE IS AT THE START.
IT'S HARD TO HAVE FAITH THAT SOMETHING WON'T GO WRONG AND YOU'LL FALL FROM 20,000 FEET.
AND ACTUALLY LEAVING THE PLANET?
DESPITE EXPERIENCING SO MUCH ALREADY, I DON'T KNOW THAT I'LL EVER GET USED TO IT.
I COULD SAY THE SAME, JESSICA. AND NO OFFENSE...
...BUT I WAS PROBABLY MORE ACCEPTING OF THE IDEA THAN YOU.

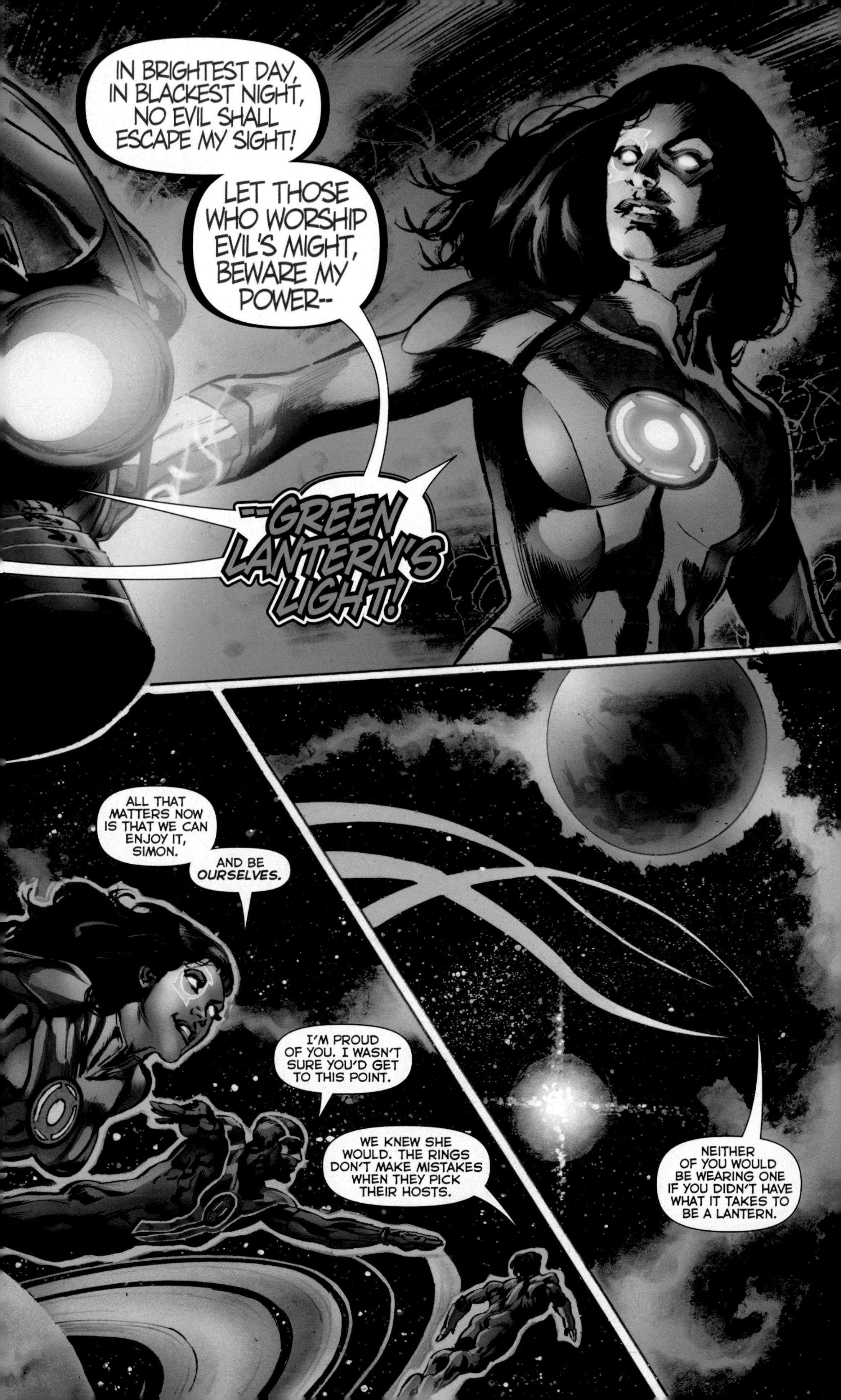
IN BRIGHTEST DAY, IN BLACKEST NIGHT, NO EVIL SHALL ESCAPE MY SIGHT!
LET THOSE WHO WORSHIP EVIL'S MIGHT, BEWARE MY POWER--
--GREEN LANTERN'S LIGHT!
ALL THAT MATTERS NOW IS THAT WE CAN ENJOY IT, SIMON.
AND BE *OURSELVES.*
I'M PROUD OF YOU. I WASN'T SURE YOU'D GET TO THIS POINT.
WE KNEW SHE WOULD. THE RINGS DON'T MAKE MISTAKES WHEN THEY PICK THEIR HOSTS.
NEITHER OF YOU WOULD BE WEARING ONE IF YOU DIDN'T HAVE WHAT IT TAKES TO BE A LANTERN.

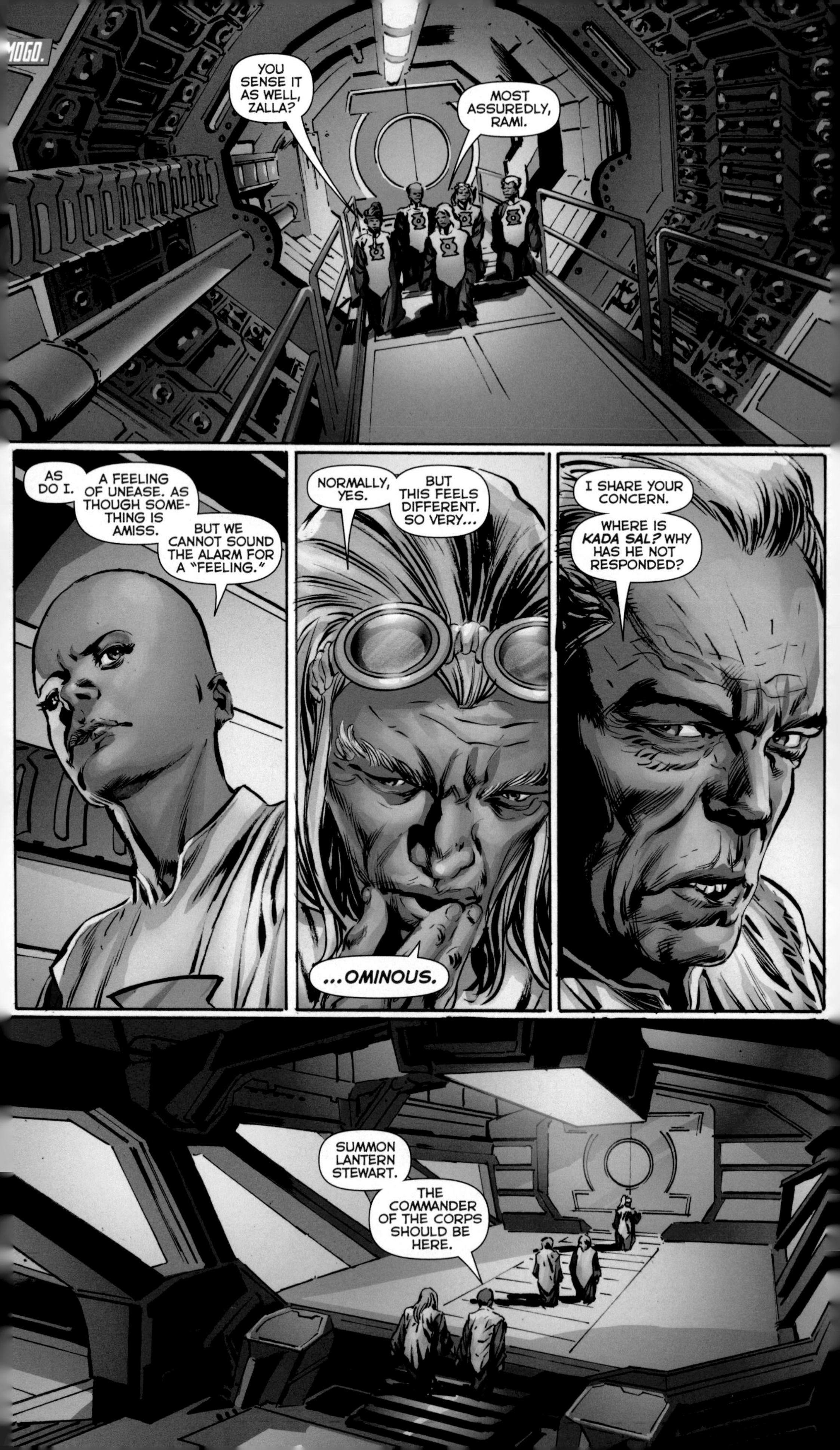
MOGO.
YOU SENSE IT AS WELL, ZALLA?
MOST ASSUREDLY, RAMI.
AS DO I.
A FEELING OF UNEASE. AS THOUGH SOMETHING IS AMISS.
BUT WE CANNOT SOUND THE ALARM FOR A "FEELING."
NORMALLY, YES.
BUT THIS FEELS DIFFERENT. SO VERY...
...OMINOUS.
I SHARE YOUR CONCERN.
WHERE IS KADA SAL? WHY HAS HE NOT RESPONDED?
SUMMON LANTERN STEWART.
THE COMMANDER OF THE CORPS SHOULD BE HERE.

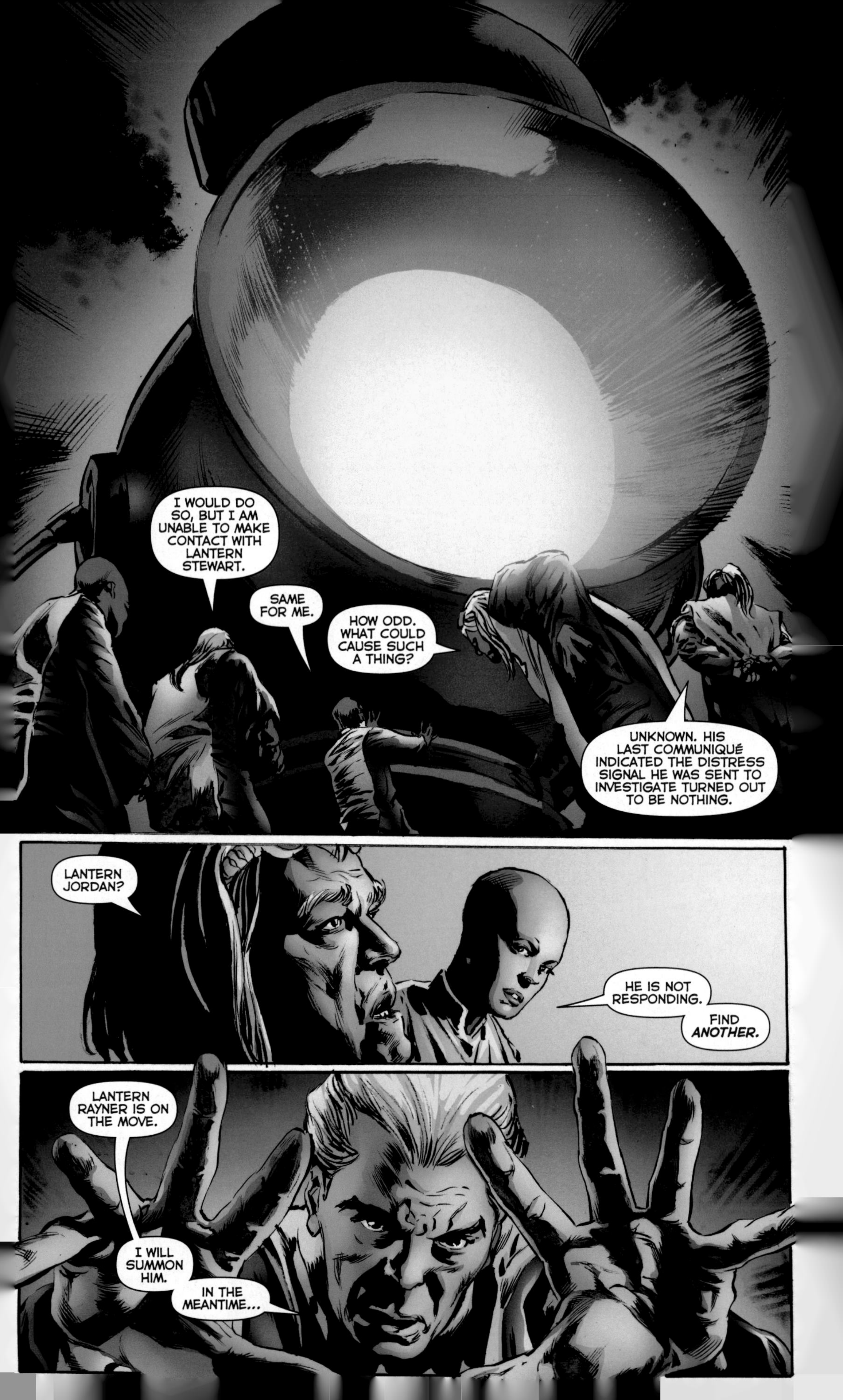
I WOULD DO SO, BUT I AM UNABLE TO MAKE CONTACT WITH LANTERN STEWART.
SAME FOR ME.
HOW ODD. WHAT COULD CAUSE SUCH A THING?
UNKNOWN. HIS LAST COMMUNIQUÉ INDICATED THE DISTRESS SIGNAL HE WAS SENT TO INVESTIGATE TURNED OUT TO BE NOTHING.
LANTERN JORDAN?
HE IS NOT RESPONDING.
FIND *ANOTHER.*
LANTERN RAYNER IS ON THE MOVE.
I WILL SUMMON HIM.
IN THE MEANTIME...

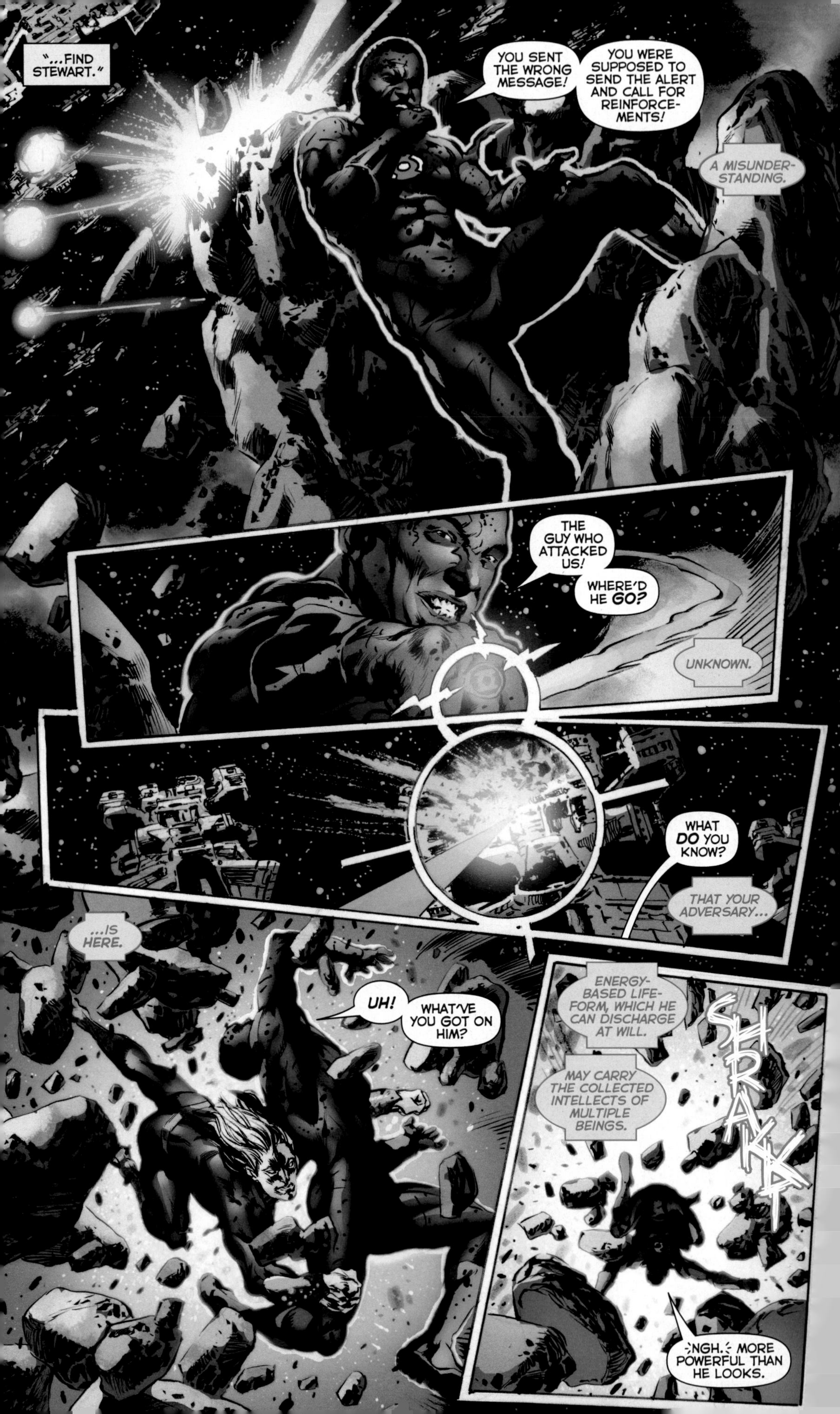
"...FIND STEWART."
YOU SENT THE WRONG MESSAGE!
YOU WERE SUPPOSED TO SEND THE ALERT AND CALL FOR REINFORCE-MENTS!
A MISUNDER-STANDING.
THE GUY WHO ATTACKED US!
WHERE'D HE GO?
UNKNOWN.
WHAT DO YOU KNOW?
THAT YOUR ADVERSARY...
...IS HERE.
UH!
WHAT'VE YOU GOT ON HIM?
ENERGY-BASED LIFE-FORM, WHICH HE CAN DISCHARGE AT WILL.
MAY CARRY THE COLLECTED INTELLECTS OF MULTIPLE BEINGS.
SHRAKKT
NGH. MORE POWERFUL THAN HE LOOKS.

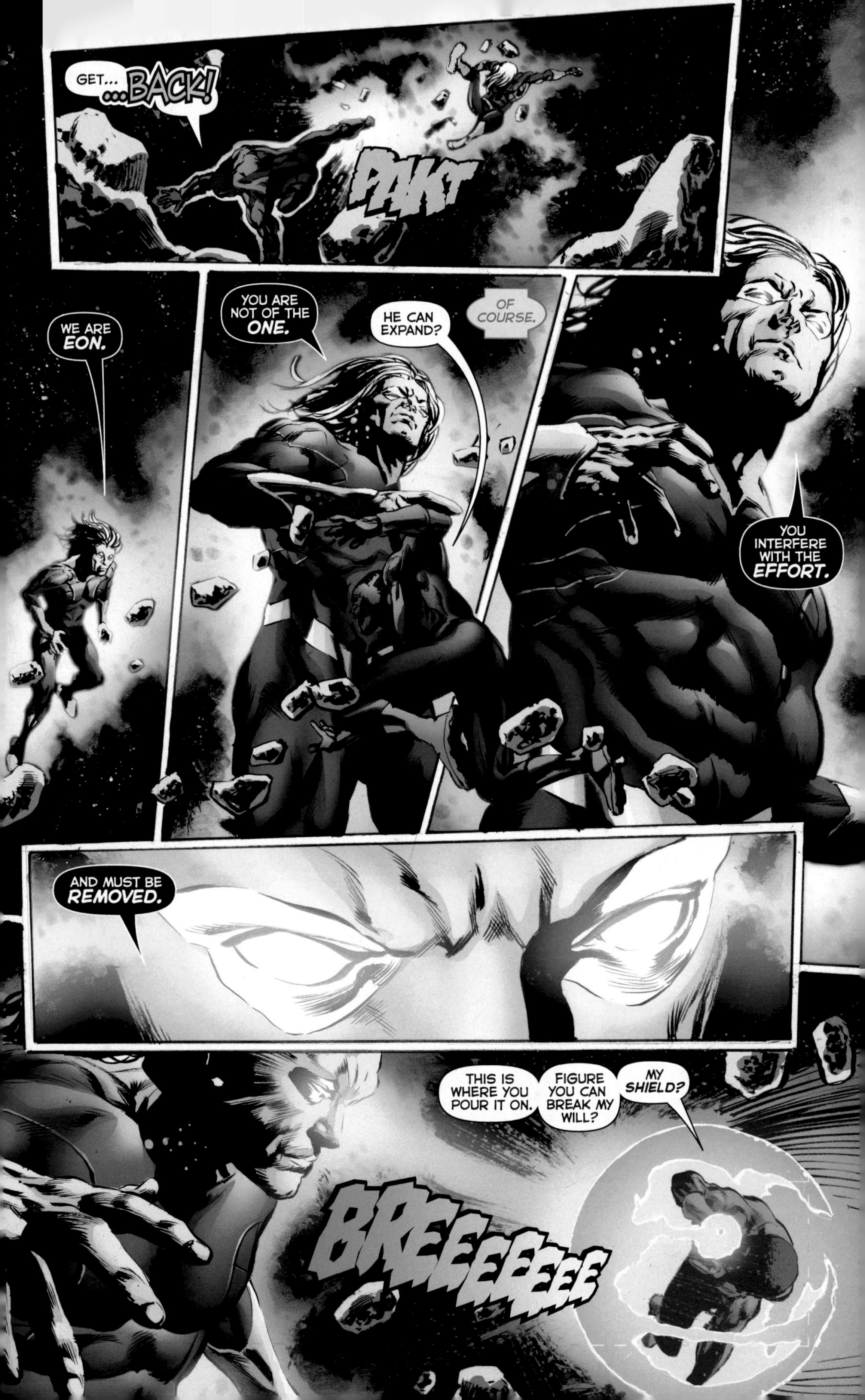
GET... ...BACK!
PAKT
WE ARE EON.
YOU ARE NOT OF THE ONE.
HE CAN EXPAND?
OF COURSE.
YOU INTERFERE WITH THE EFFORT.
AND MUST BE REMOVED.
THIS IS WHERE YOU POUR IT ON.
FIGURE YOU CAN BREAK MY WILL?
MY SHIELD?
BREEEEEEEE

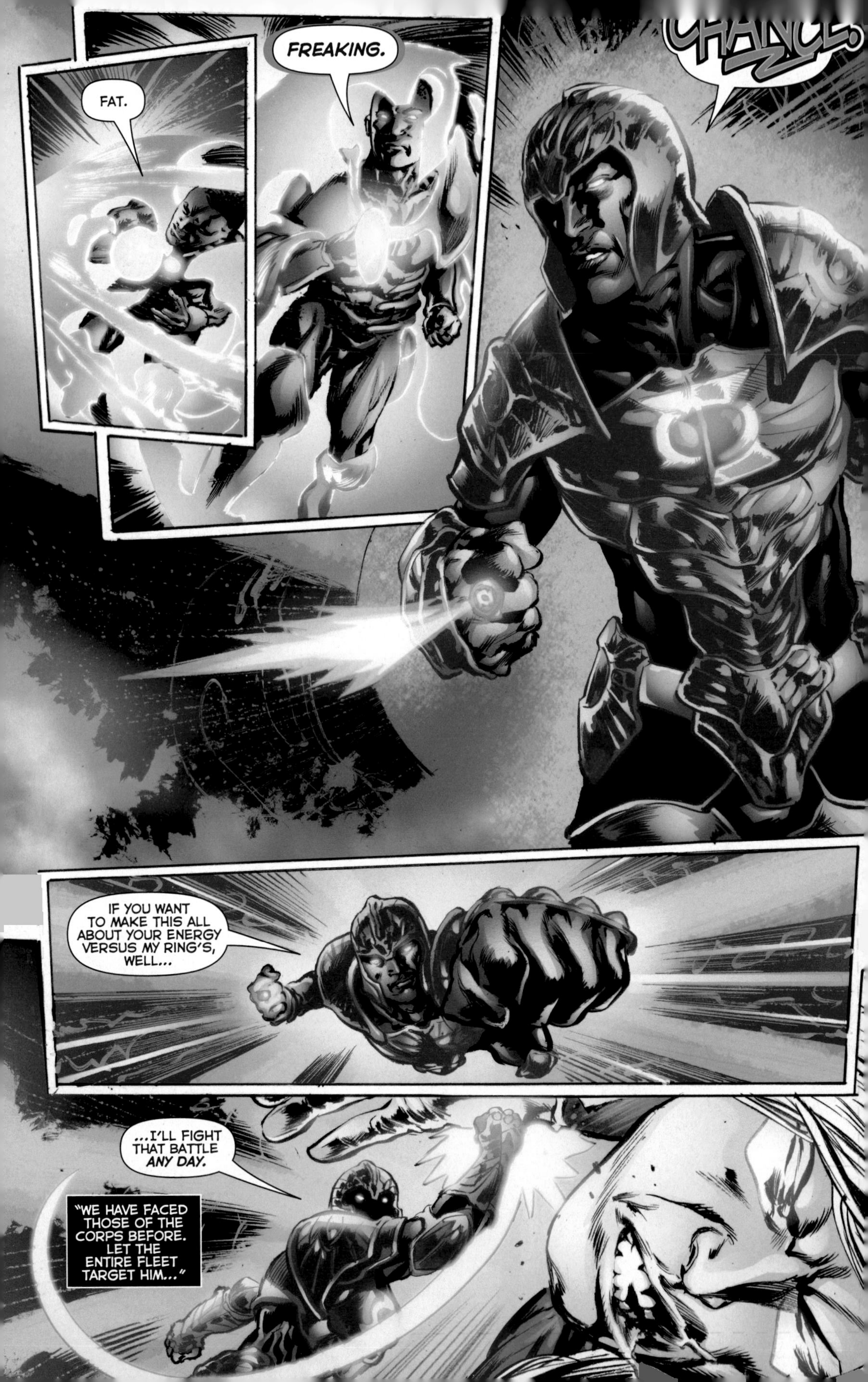
FAT.
FREAKING.
CHANCE.
IF YOU WANT TO MAKE THIS ALL ABOUT YOUR ENERGY VERSUS MY RING'S, WELL...
...I'LL FIGHT THAT BATTLE *ANY DAY.*
"WE HAVE FACED THOSE OF THE CORPS BEFORE. LET THE ENTIRE FLEET TARGET HIM..."

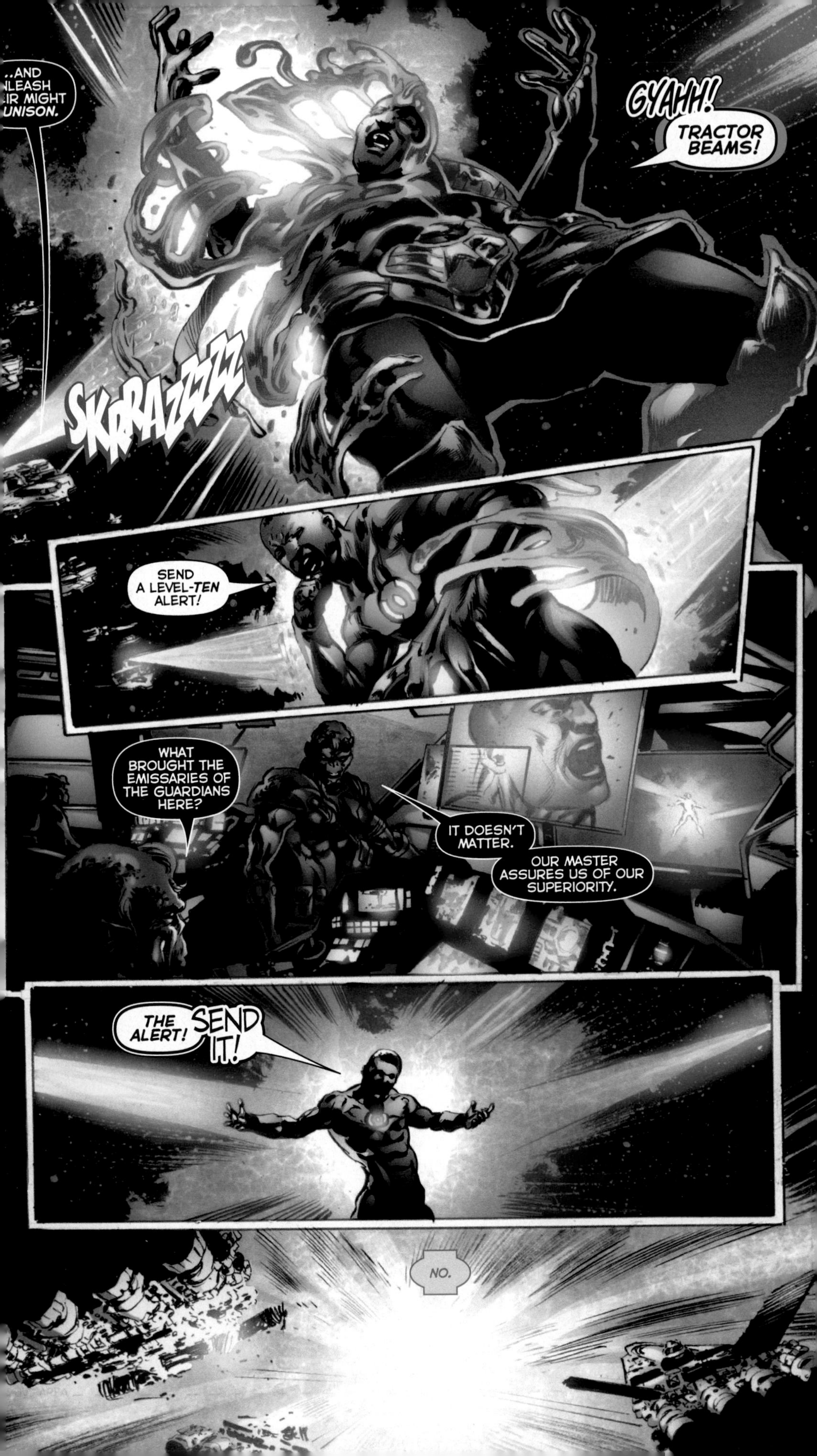
..AND
NLEASH
EIR MIGHT
UNISON.
GYAHH!
TRACTOR BEAMS!
SKRRAZZZZZZ
SEND A LEVEL-*TEN* ALERT!
WHAT BROUGHT THE EMISSARIES OF THE GUARDIANS HERE?
IT DOESN'T MATTER.
OUR MASTER ASSURES US OF OUR SUPERIORITY.
THE ALERT! SEND IT!
NO.

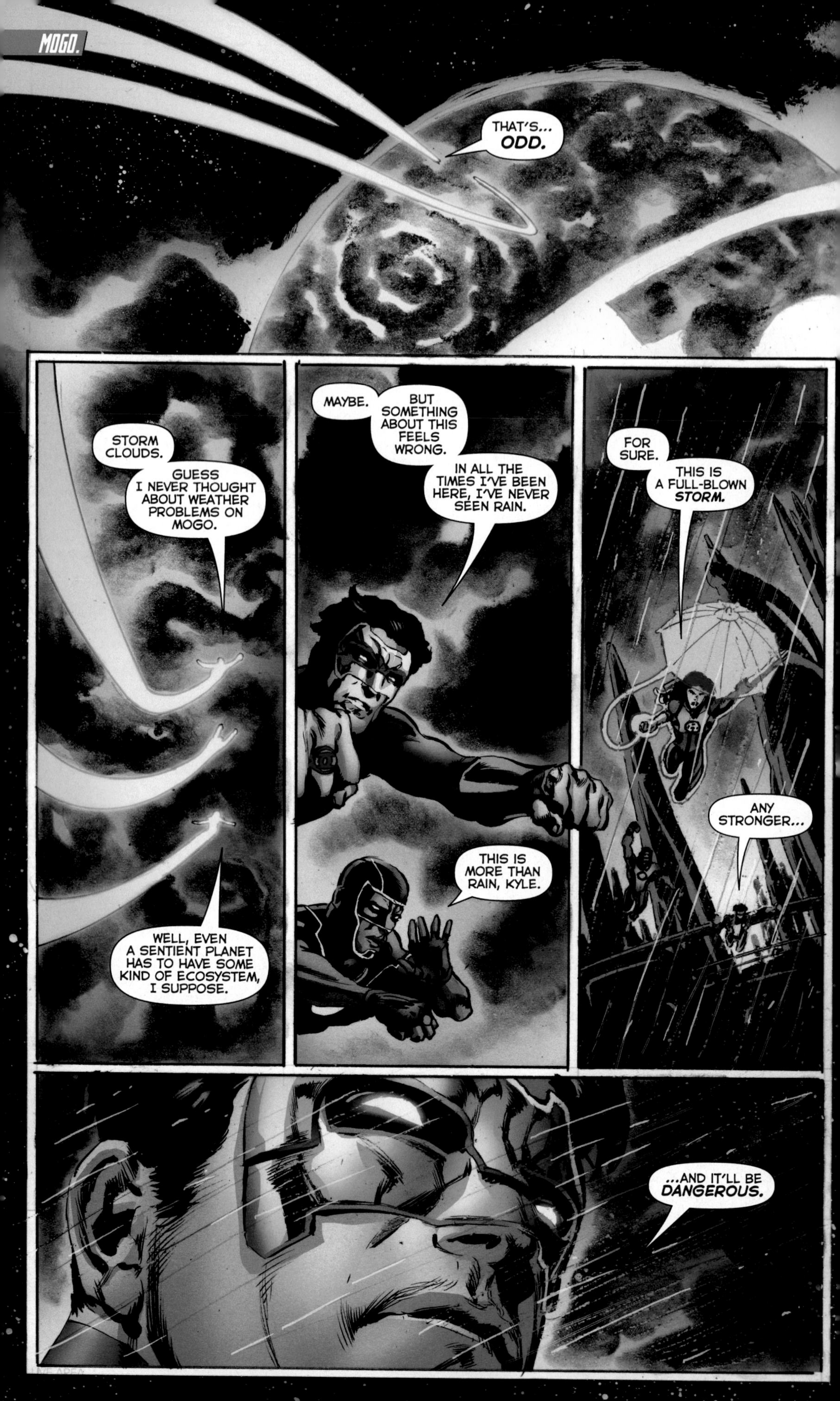
MOGO.
THAT'S... ODD.
STORM CLOUDS.
GUESS I NEVER THOUGHT ABOUT WEATHER PROBLEMS ON MOGO.
WELL, EVEN A SENTIENT PLANET HAS TO HAVE SOME KIND OF ECOSYSTEM, I SUPPOSE.
MAYBE.
BUT SOMETHING ABOUT THIS FEELS WRONG.
IN ALL THE TIMES I'VE BEEN HERE, I'VE NEVER SEEN RAIN.
THIS IS MORE THAN RAIN, KYLE.
FOR SURE.
THIS IS A FULL-BLOWN STORM.
ANY STRONGER...
...AND IT'LL BE DANGEROUS.

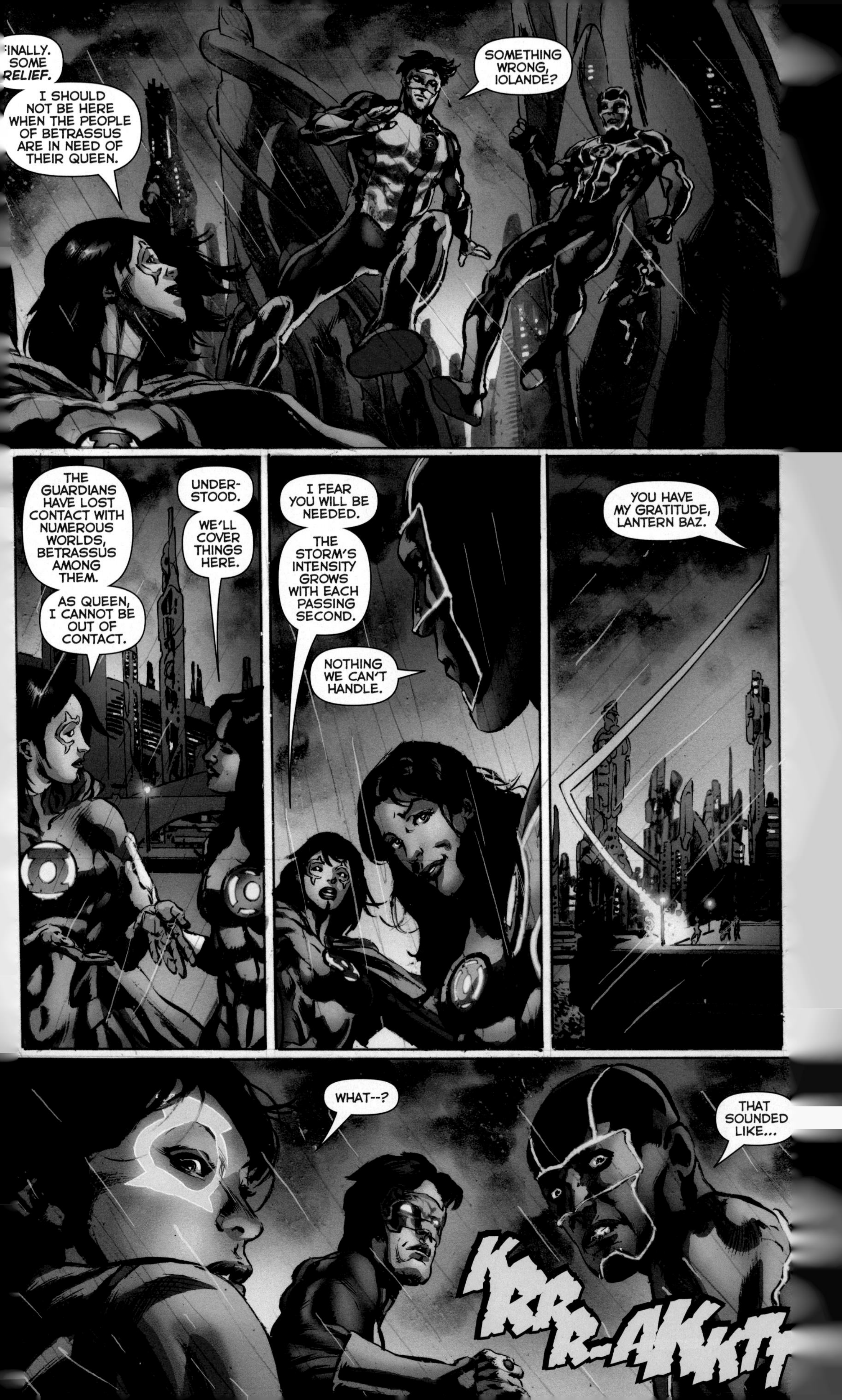
FINALLY. SOME RELIEF.
I SHOULD NOT BE HERE WHEN THE PEOPLE OF BETRASSUS ARE IN NEED OF THEIR QUEEN.
SOMETHING WRONG, IOLANDE?
THE GUARDIANS HAVE LOST CONTACT WITH NUMEROUS WORLDS, BETRASSUS AMONG THEM.
AS QUEEN, I CANNOT BE OUT OF CONTACT.
UNDER-STOOD.
WE'LL COVER THINGS HERE.
I FEAR YOU WILL BE NEEDED.
THE STORM'S INTENSITY GROWS WITH EACH PASSING SECOND.
NOTHING WE CAN'T HANDLE.
YOU HAVE MY GRATITUDE, LANTERN BAZ.
WHAT--?
THAT SOUNDED LIKE...
KRR R-AKKT!

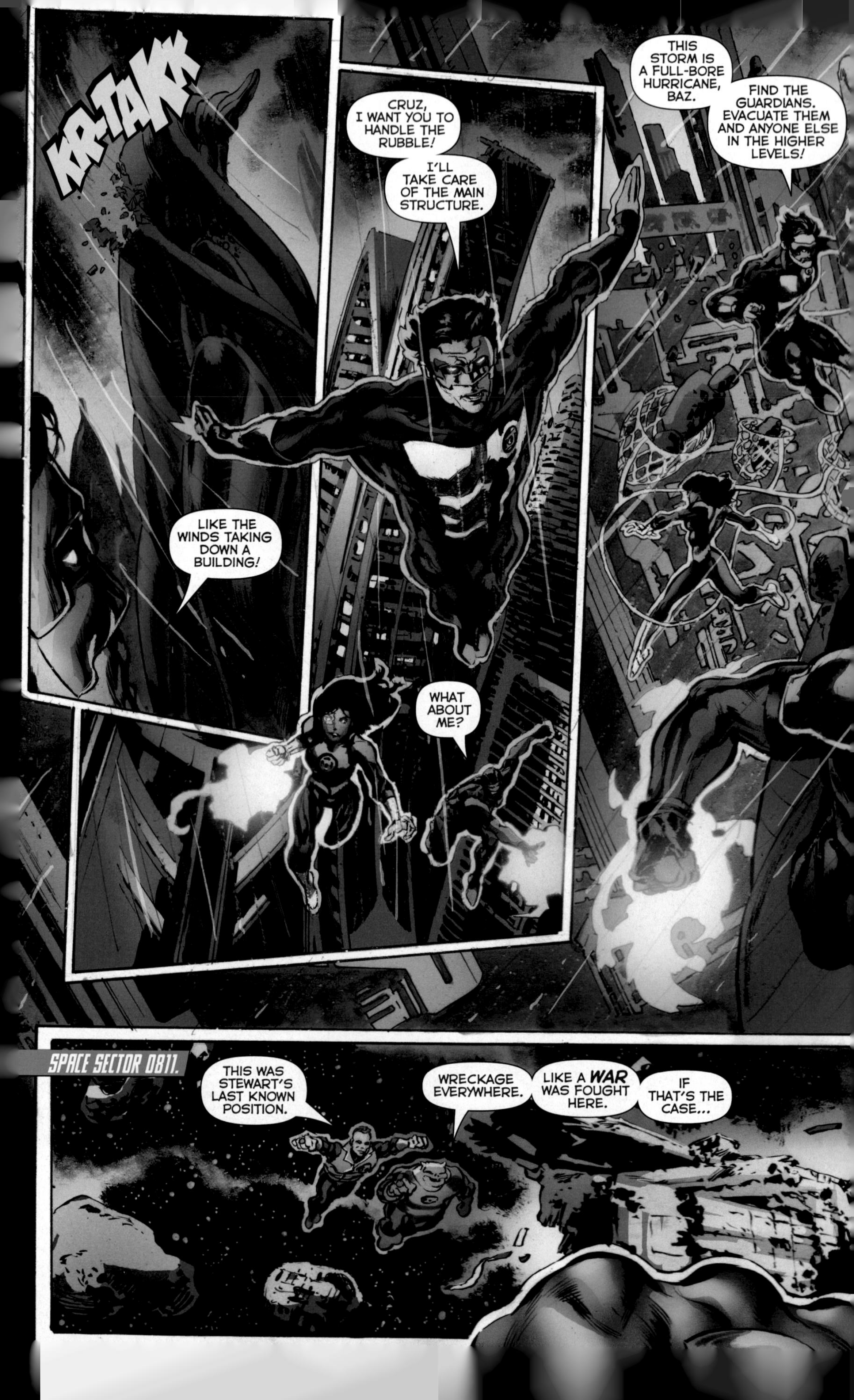
KR-TAKK
CRUZ, I WANT YOU TO HANDLE THE RUBBLE!
I'LL TAKE CARE OF THE MAIN STRUCTURE.
THIS STORM IS A FULL-BORE HURRICANE, BAZ.
FIND THE GUARDIANS. EVACUATE THEM AND ANYONE ELSE IN THE HIGHER LEVELS!
LIKE THE WINDS TAKING DOWN A BUILDING!
WHAT ABOUT ME?
SPACE SECTOR 0811.
THIS WAS STEWART'S LAST KNOWN POSITION.
WRECKAGE EVERYWHERE.
LIKE A WAR WAS FOUGHT HERE.
IF THAT'S THE CASE...

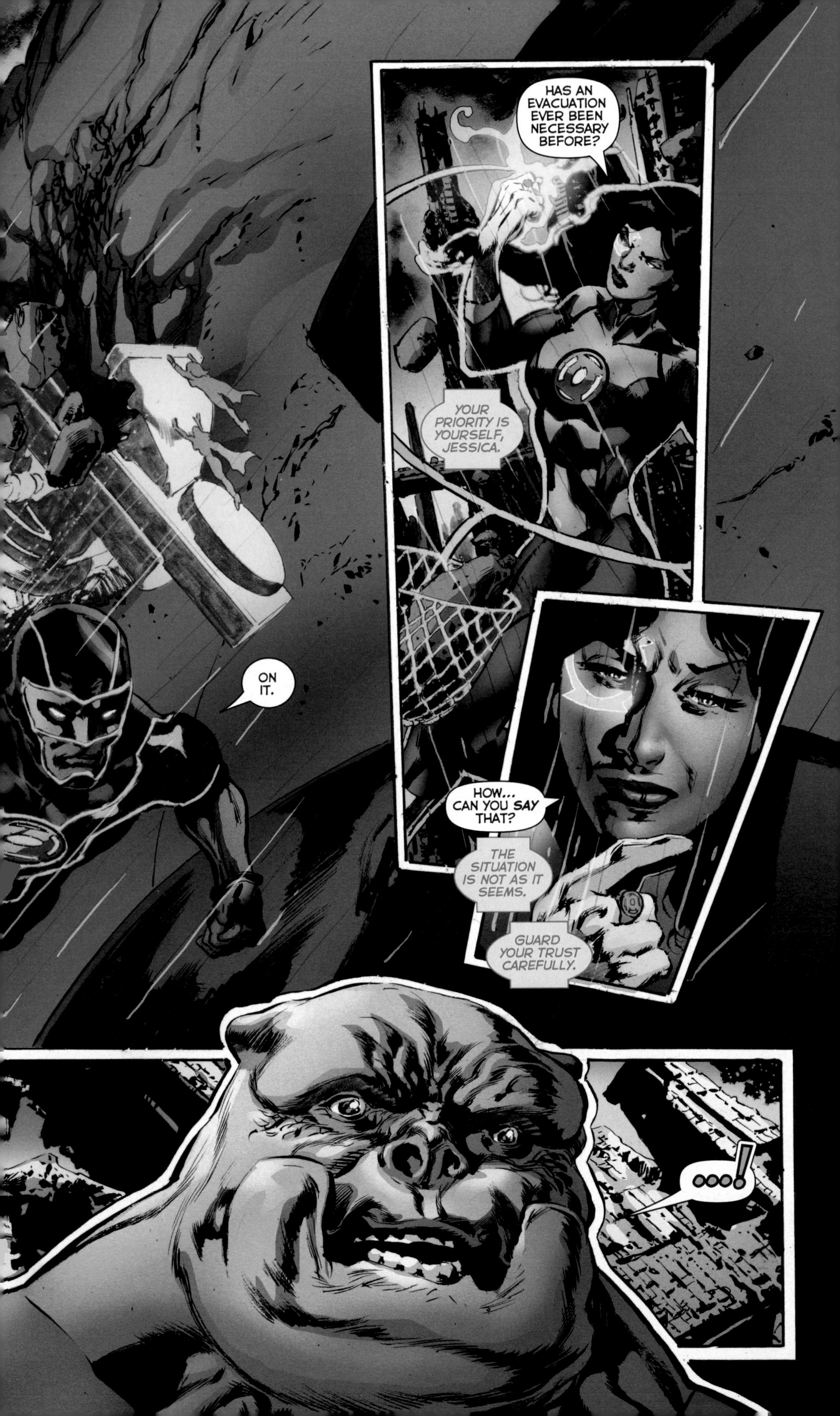
HAS AN EVACUATION EVER BEEN NECESSARY BEFORE?
YOUR PRIORITY IS YOURSELF, JESSICA.
ON IT.
HOW... CAN YOU SAY THAT?
THE SITUATION IS NOT AS IT SEEMS.
GUARD YOUR TRUST CAREFULLY.
...!

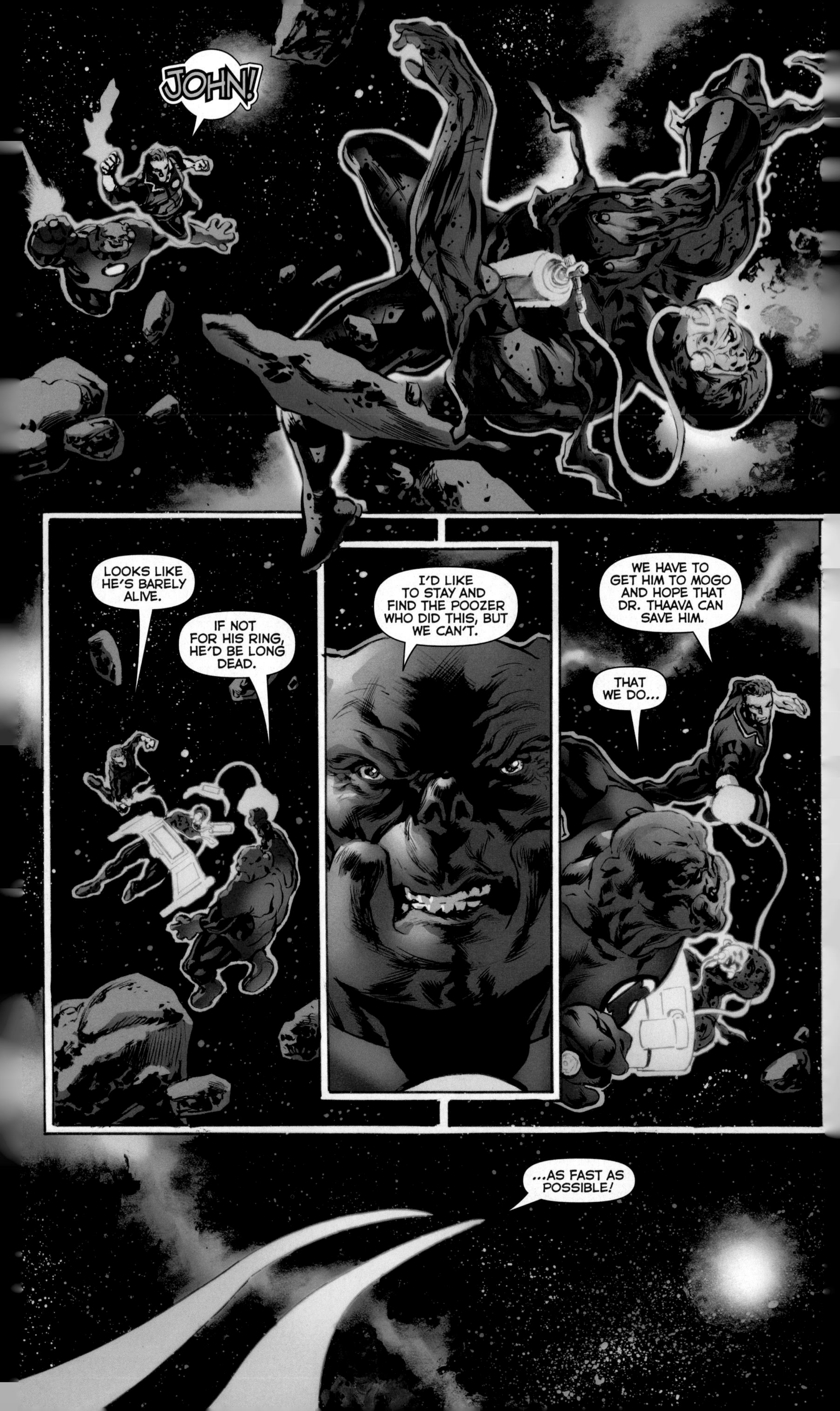
JOHN!
LOOKS LIKE HE'S BARELY ALIVE.
IF NOT FOR HIS RING, HE'D BE LONG DEAD.
I'D LIKE TO STAY AND FIND THE POOZER WHO DID THIS, BUT WE CAN'T.
WE HAVE TO GET HIM TO MOGO AND HOPE THAT DR. THAAVA CAN SAVE HIM.
THAT WE DO...
...AS FAST AS POSSIBLE!

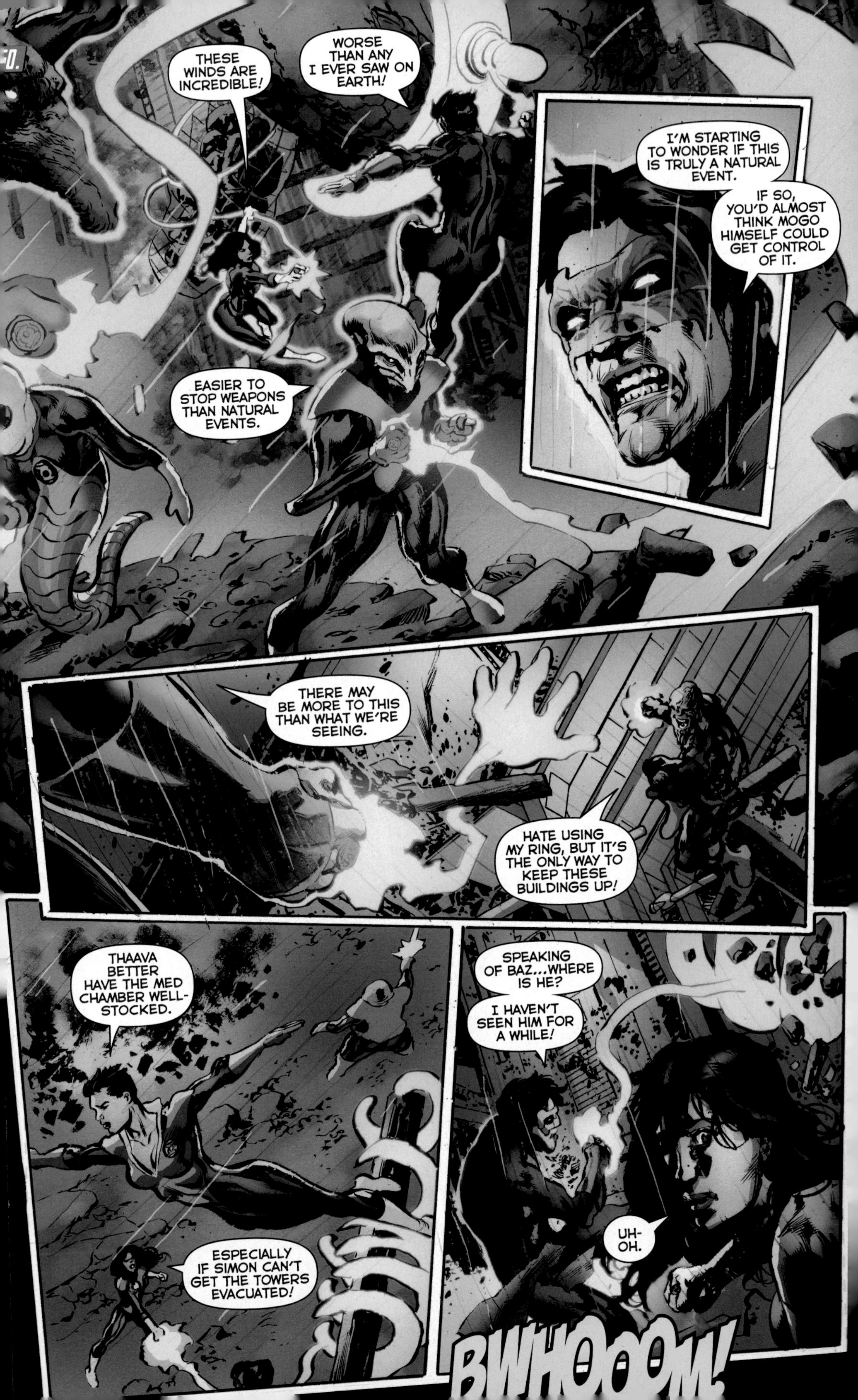
THESE WINDS ARE INCREDIBLE!
WORSE THAN ANY I EVER SAW ON EARTH!
I'M STARTING TO WONDER IF THIS IS TRULY A NATURAL EVENT.
IF SO, YOU'D ALMOST THINK MOGO HIMSELF COULD GET CONTROL OF IT.
EASIER TO STOP WEAPONS THAN NATURAL EVENTS.
THERE MAY BE MORE TO THIS THAN WHAT WE'RE SEEING.
HATE USING MY RING, BUT IT'S THE ONLY WAY TO KEEP THESE BUILDINGS UP!
THAAVA BETTER HAVE THE MED CHAMBER WELL-STOCKED.
ESPECIALLY IF SIMON CAN'T GET THE TOWERS EVACUATED!
SPEAKING OF BAZ...WHERE IS HE?
I HAVEN'T SEEN HIM FOR A WHILE!
UH-OH.
BWHOOOM!

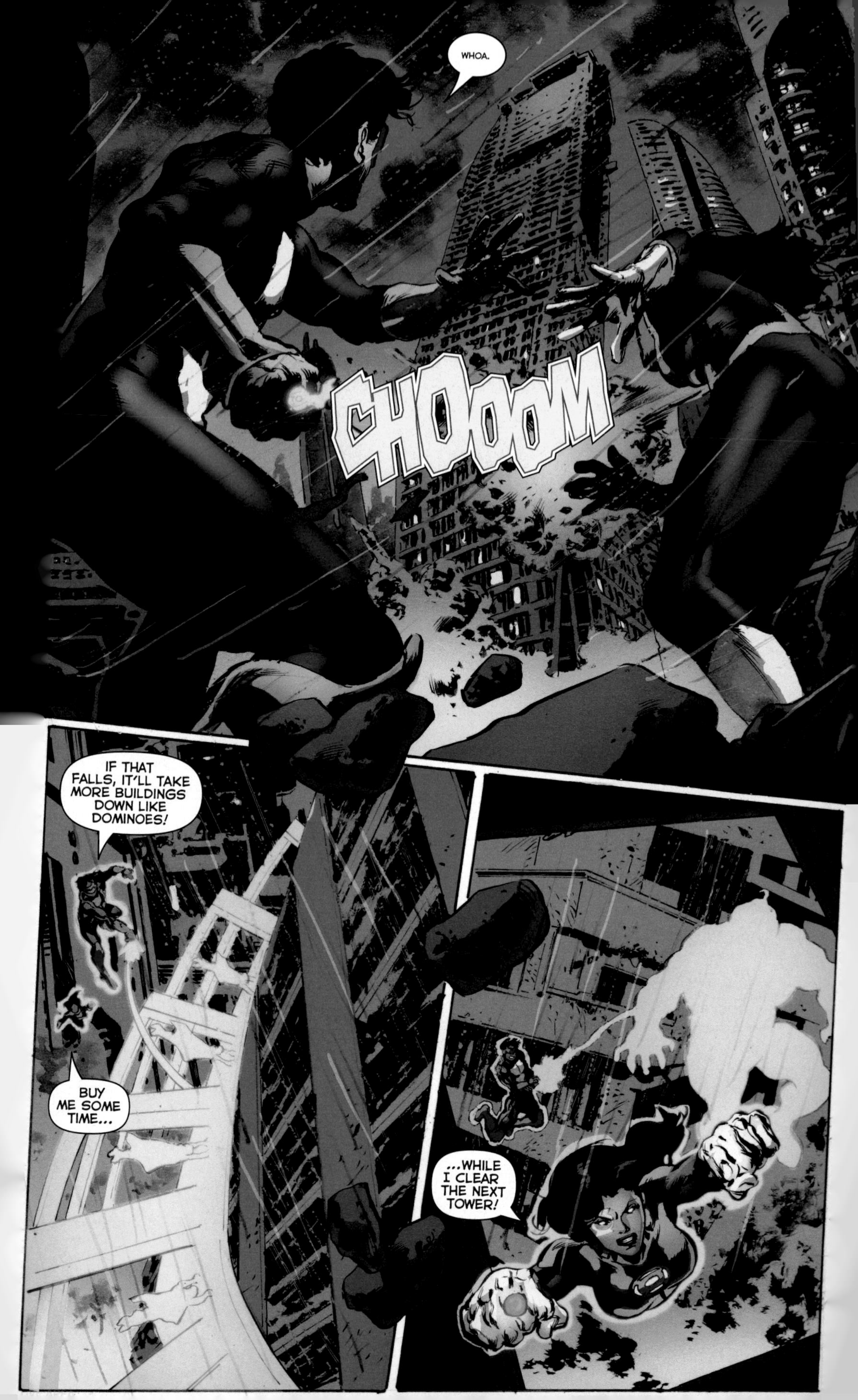
WHOA.
CHOOOM
IF THAT FALLS, IT'LL TAKE MORE BUILDINGS DOWN LIKE DOMINOES!
BUY ME SOME TIME...
...WHILE I CLEAR THE NEXT TOWER!

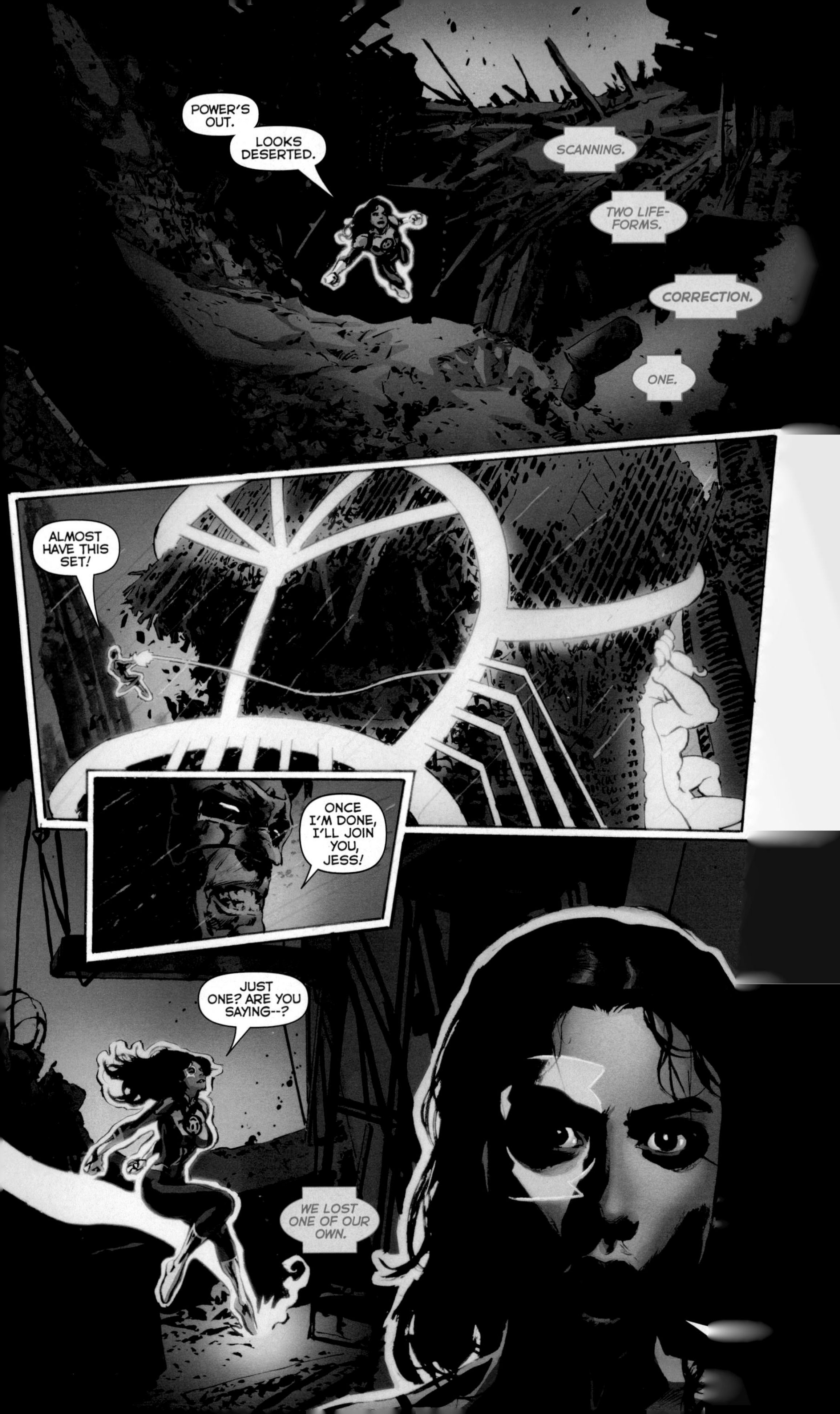
POWER'S OUT.
LOOKS DESERTED.
SCANNING.
TWO LIFE-FORMS.
CORRECTION.
ONE.
ALMOST HAVE THIS SET!
ONCE I'M DONE, I'LL JOIN YOU, JESS!
JUST ONE? ARE YOU SAYING--?
WE LOST ONE OF OUR OWN.

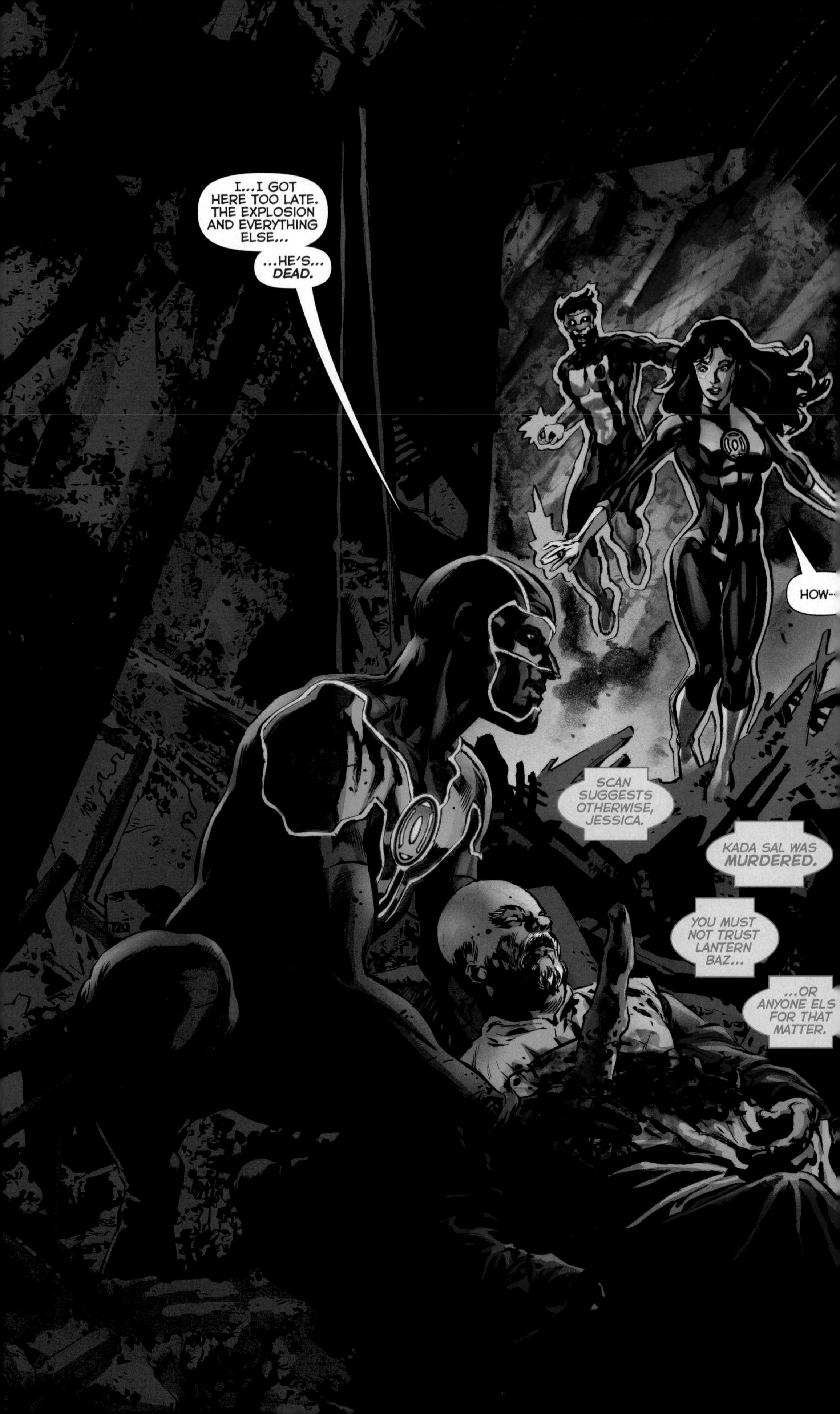
I...I GOT HERE TOO LATE. THE EXPLOSION AND EVERYTHING ELSE...
...HE'S... DEAD.
HOW--
SCAN SUGGESTS OTHERWISE, JESSICA.
KADA SAL WAS MURDERED.
YOU MUST NOT TRUST LANTERN BAZ...
...OR ANYONE ELS FOR THAT MATTER.

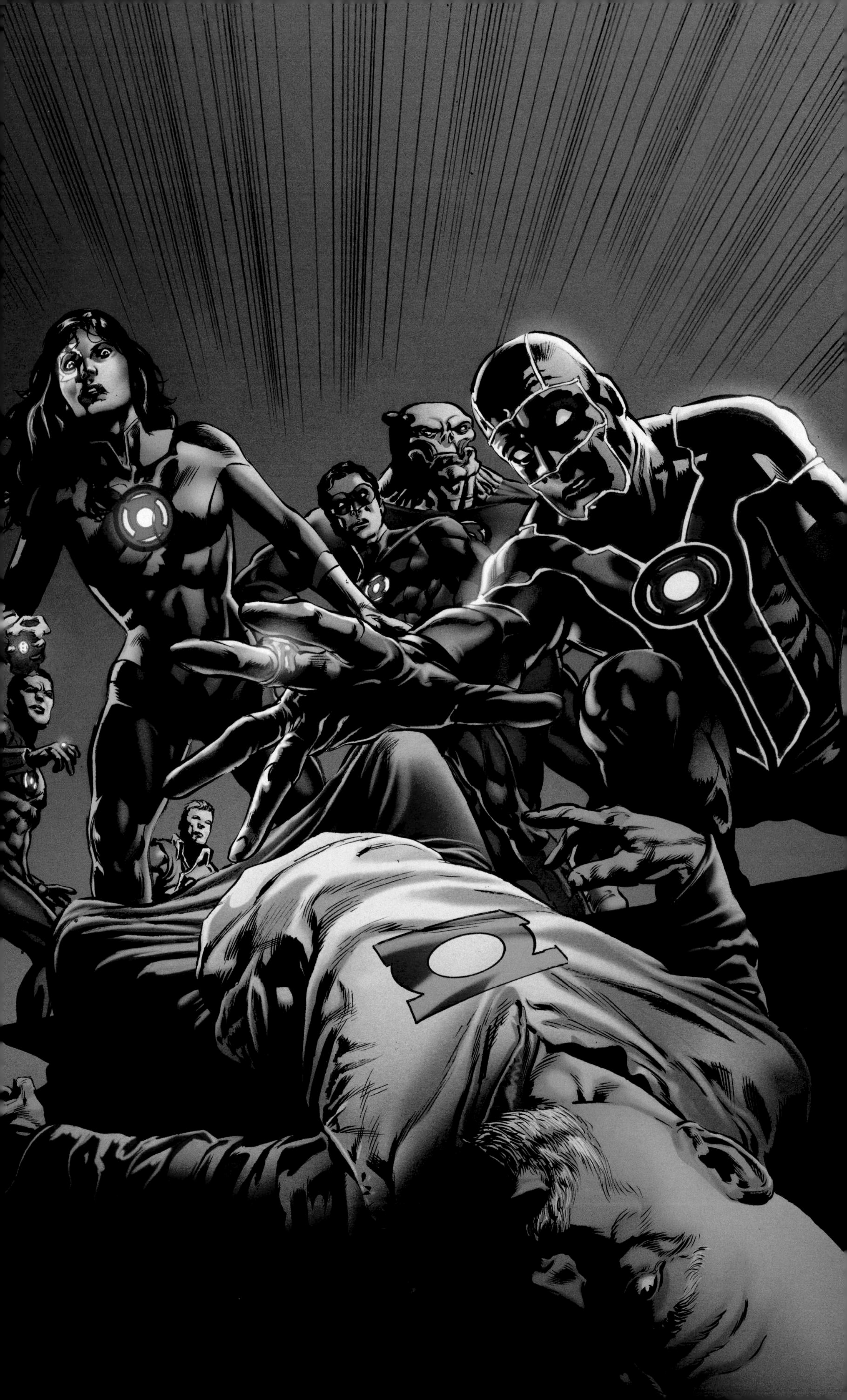

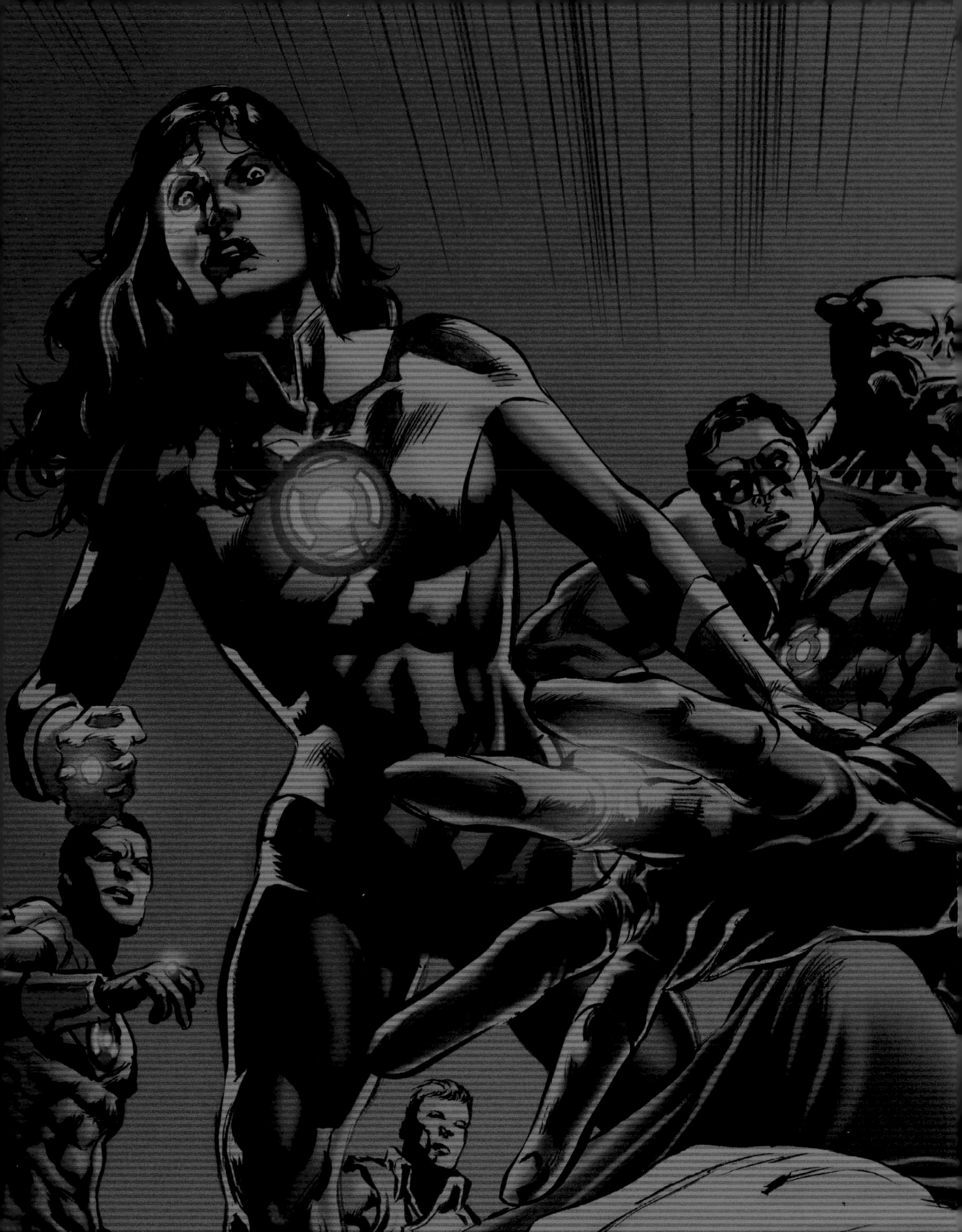

GREEN LANTERNS

#51

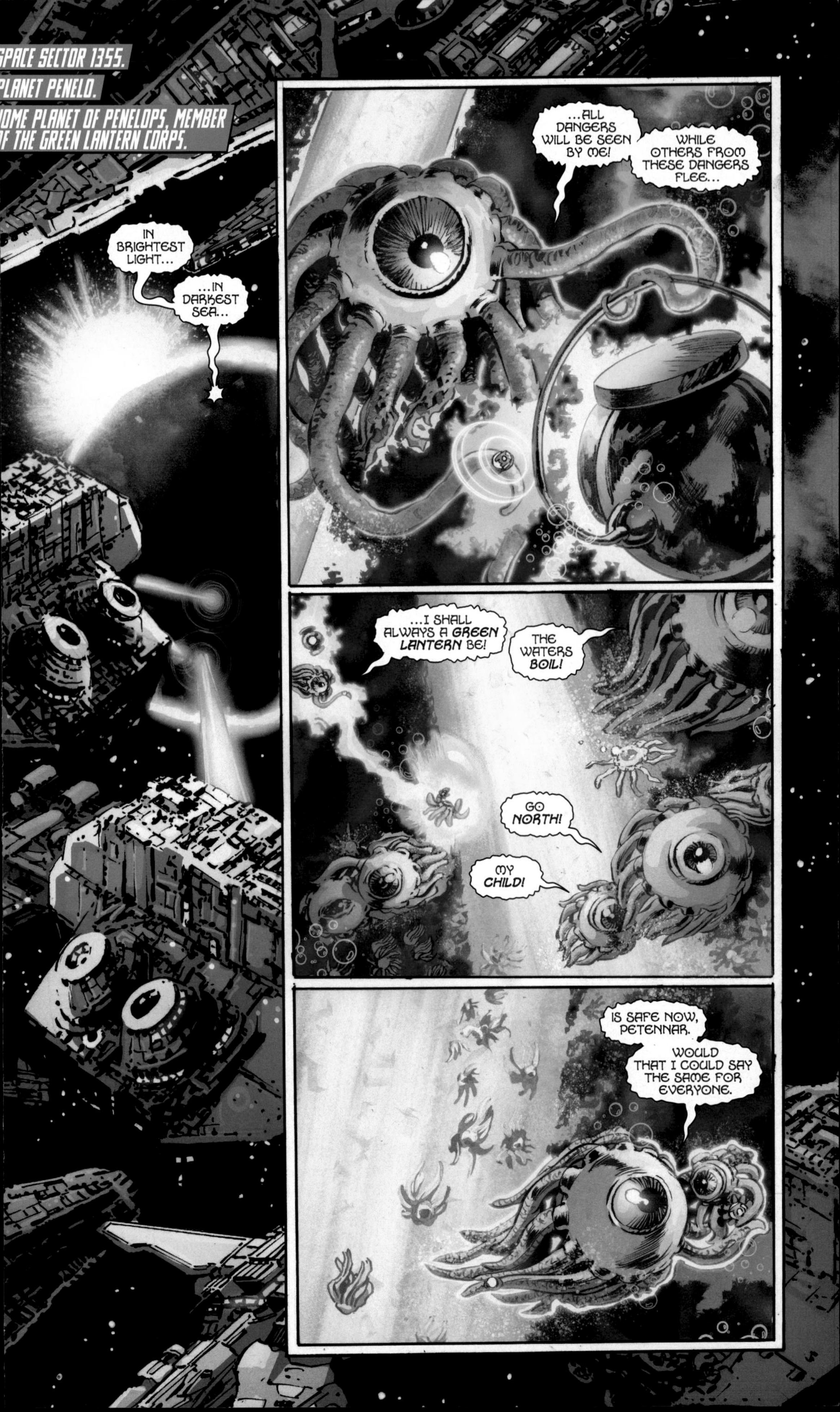
SPACE SECTOR 1355.
PLANET PENELO.
HOME PLANET OF PENELOPS, MEMBER OF THE GREEN LANTERN CORPS.
IN BRIGHTEST LIGHT...
...IN DARKEST SEA...
...ALL DANGERS WILL BE SEEN BY ME!
WHILE OTHERS FROM THESE DANGERS FLEE...
...I SHALL ALWAYS A GREEN LANTERN BE!
THE WATERS BOIL!
GO NORTH!
MY CHILD!
IS SAFE NOW, PETENNAR.
WOULD THAT I COULD SAY THE SAME FOR EVERYONE.

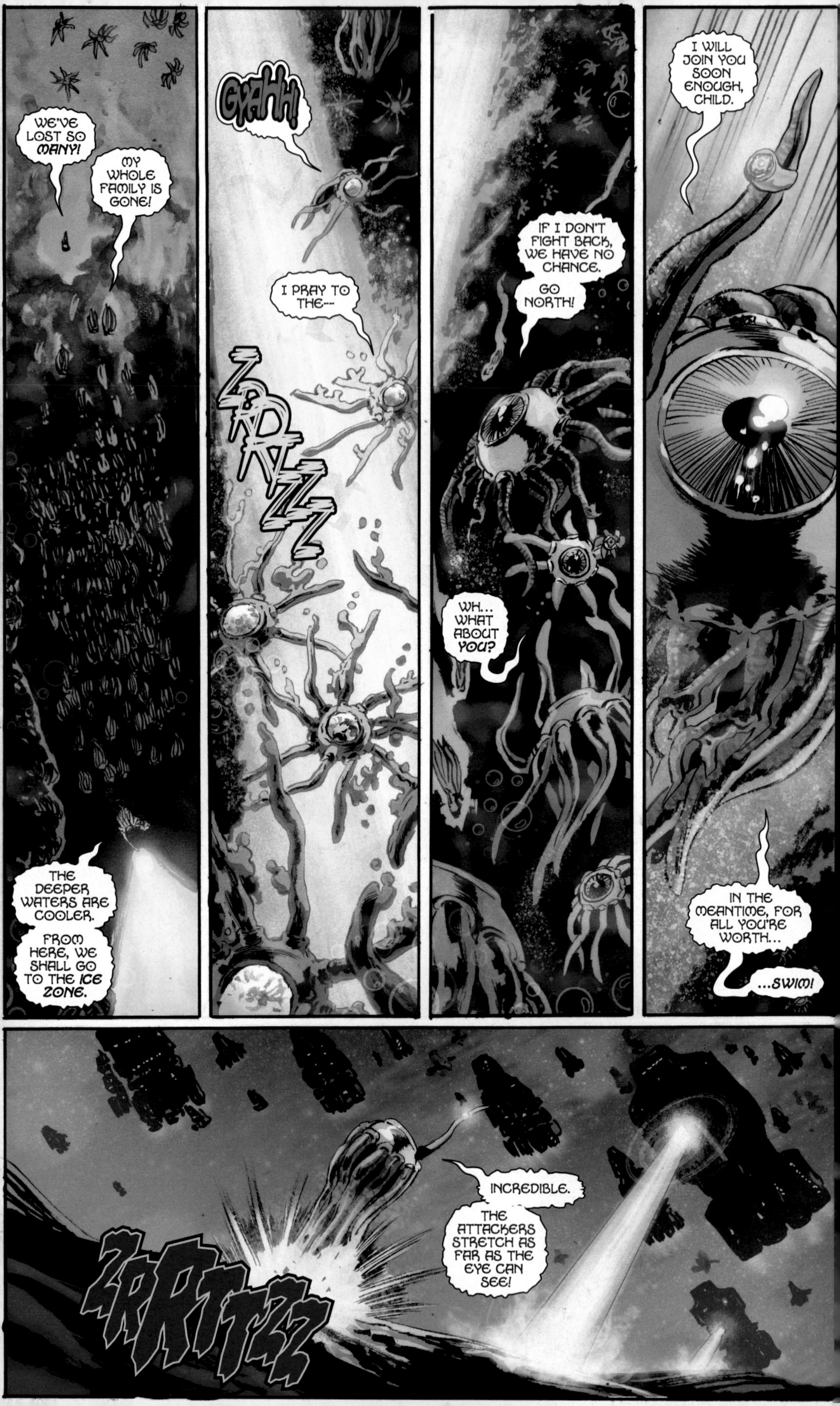
WE'VE LOST SO MANY!
MY WHOLE FAMILY IS GONE!
THE DEEPER WATERS ARE COOLER.
FROM HERE, WE SHALL GO TO THE ICE ZONE.
GYAHH!
I PRAY TO THE--
ZRRZZZ
IF I DON'T FIGHT BACK, WE HAVE NO CHANCE.
GO NORTH!
WH... WHAT ABOUT YOU?
I WILL JOIN YOU SOON ENOUGH, CHILD.
IN THE MEANTIME, FOR ALL YOU'RE WORTH...
...SWIM!
INCREDIBLE.
THE ATTACKERS STRETCH AS FAR AS THE EYE CAN SEE!
ZRRTZZ

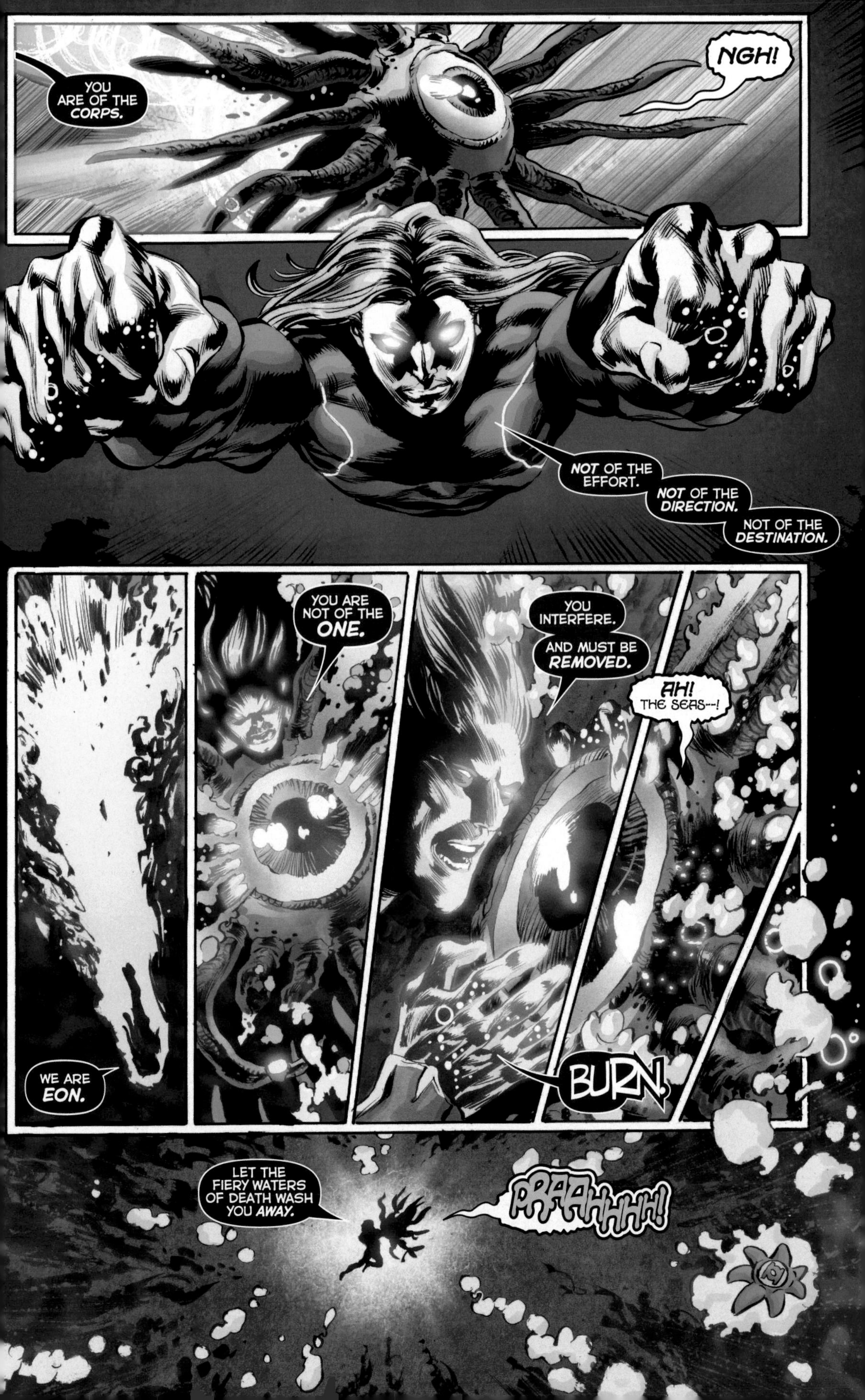
YOU ARE OF THE CORPS.
NGH!
NOT OF THE EFFORT.
NOT OF THE DIRECTION.
NOT OF THE DESTINATION.
WE ARE EON.
YOU ARE NOT OF THE ONE.
YOU INTERFERE.
AND MUST BE REMOVED.
AH! THE SEAS--!
BURN.
LET THE FIERY WATERS OF DEATH WASH YOU AWAY.
RRAAHHHH!

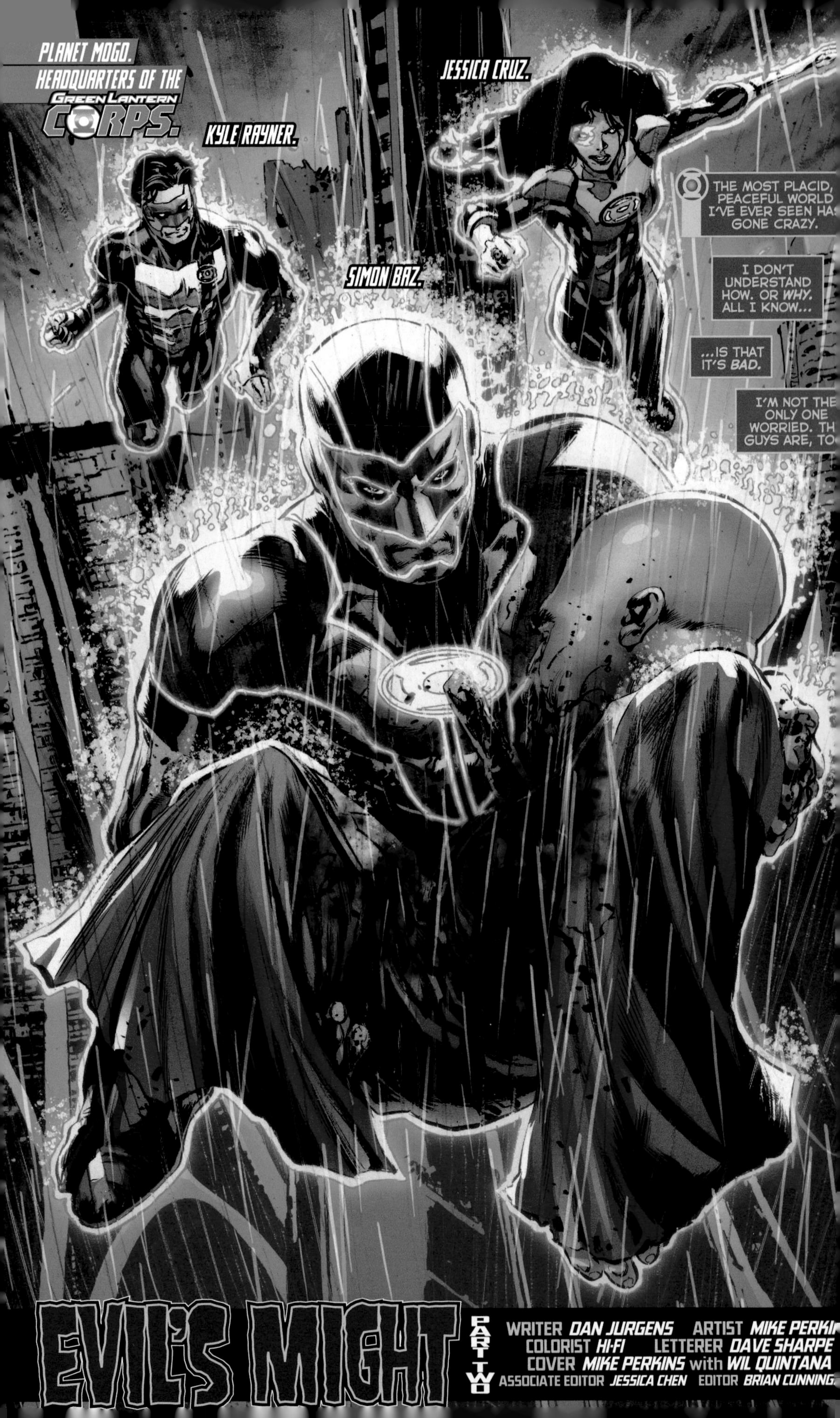
PLANET MOGO. HEADQUARTERS OF THE GREEN LANTERN CORPS.
KYLE RAYNER.
JESSICA CRUZ.
SIMON BAZ.
THE MOST PLACID, PEACEFUL WORLD I'VE EVER SEEN HA GONE CRAZY.
I DON'T UNDERSTAND HOW. OR WHY. ALL I KNOW...
...IS THAT IT'S BAD.
I'M NOT THE ONLY ONE WORRIED. TH GUYS ARE, TO
EVIL'S MIGHT
PART TWO
WRITER DAN JURGENS ARTIST MIKE PERKI
COLORIST HI-FI LETTERER DAVE SHARPE
COVER MIKE PERKINS with WIL QUINTANA
ASSOCIATE EDITOR JESSICA CHEN EDITOR BRIAN CUNNING

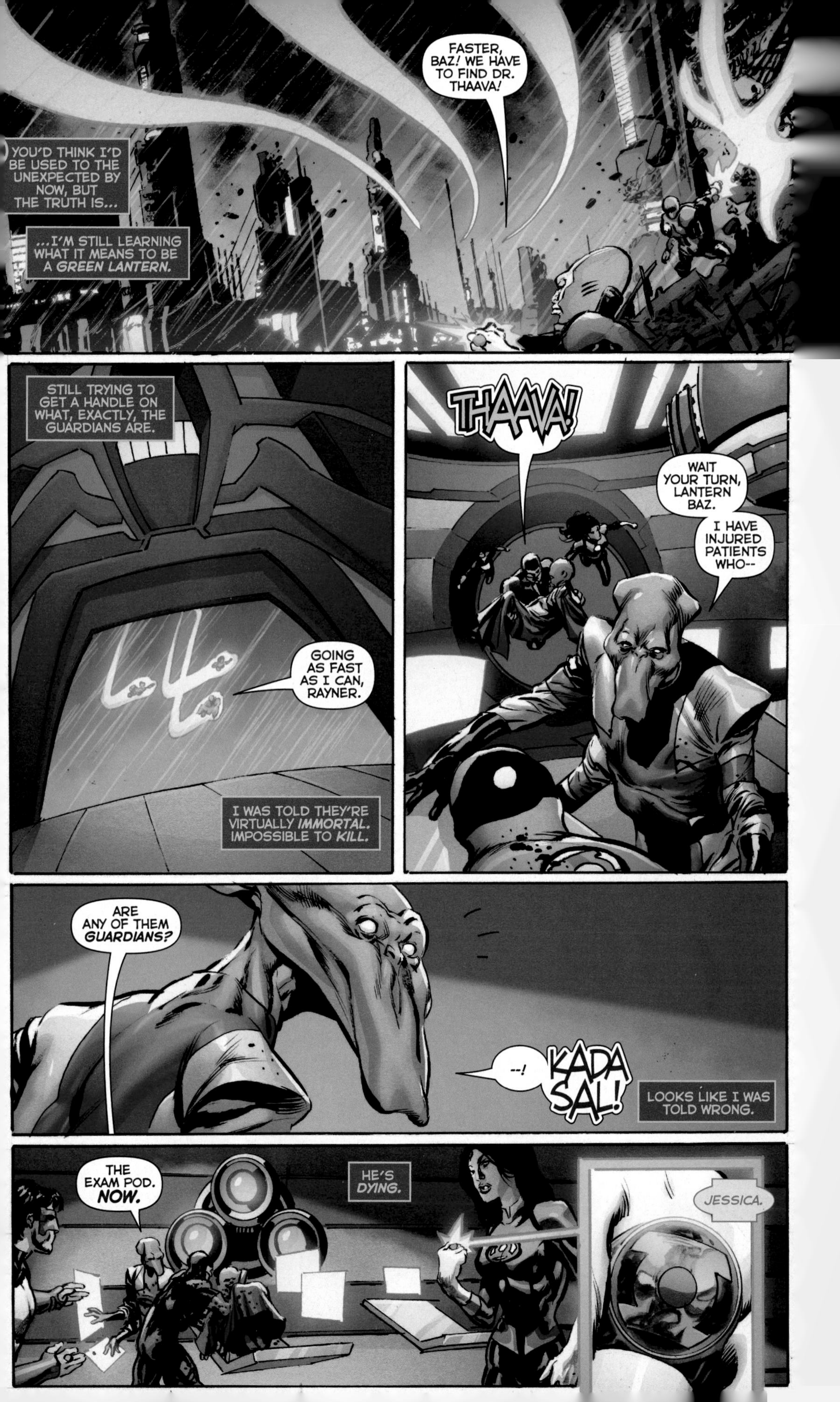
YOU'D THINK I'D BE USED TO THE UNEXPECTED BY NOW, BUT THE TRUTH IS...
...I'M STILL LEARNING WHAT IT MEANS TO BE A GREEN LANTERN.
FASTER, BAZ! WE HAVE TO FIND DR. THAAVA!
STILL TRYING TO GET A HANDLE ON WHAT, EXACTLY, THE GUARDIANS ARE.
GOING AS FAST AS I CAN, RAYNER.
I WAS TOLD THEY'RE VIRTUALLY IMMORTAL. IMPOSSIBLE TO KILL.
THAAVA!
WAIT YOUR TURN, LANTERN BAZ.
I HAVE INJURED PATIENTS WHO--
ARE ANY OF THEM GUARDIANS?
--!
KADA SAL!
LOOKS LIKE I WAS TOLD WRONG.
THE EXAM POD. NOW.
HE'S DYING.
JESSICA.

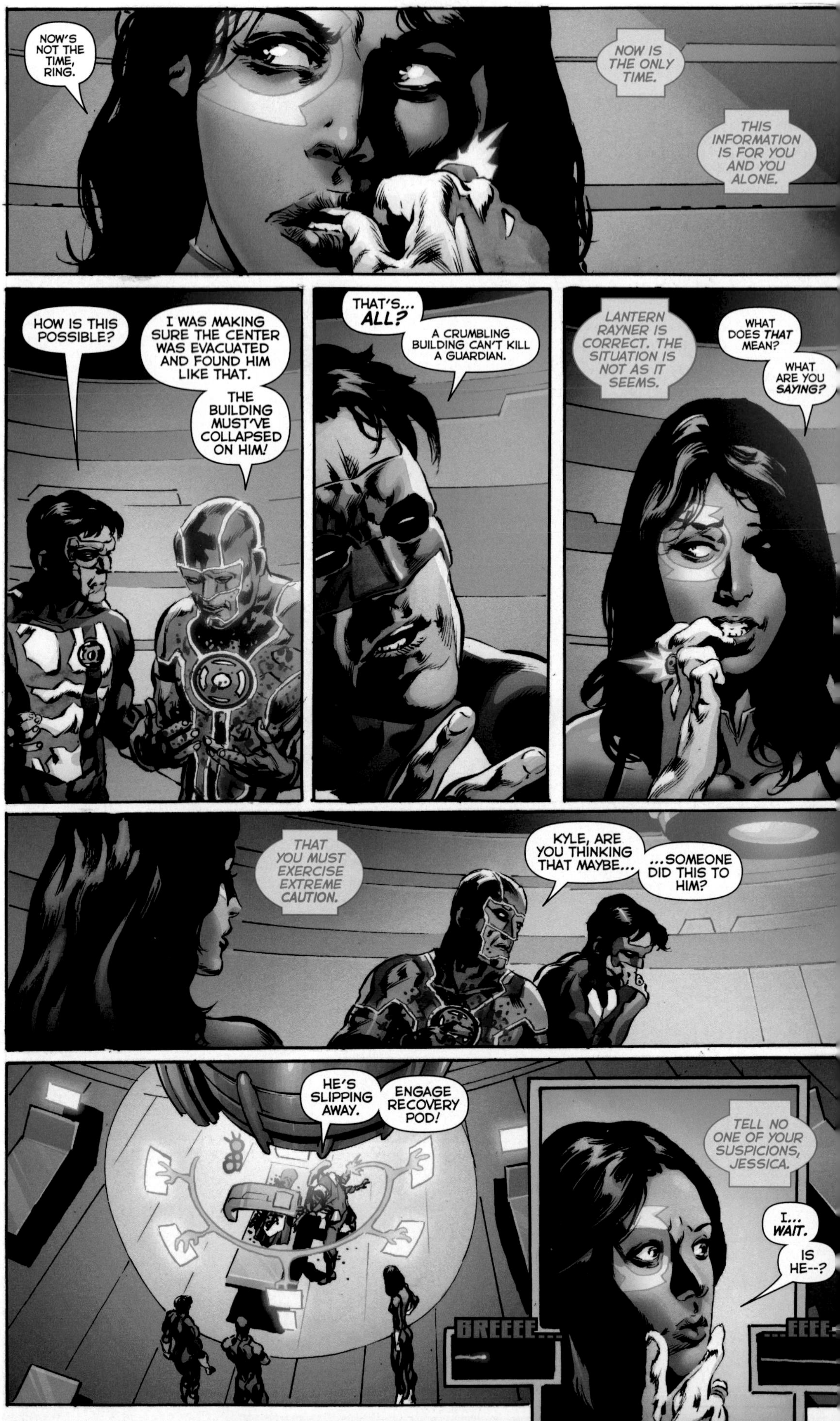
NOW'S NOT THE TIME, RING.
NOW IS THE ONLY TIME.
THIS INFORMATION IS FOR YOU AND YOU ALONE.
HOW IS THIS POSSIBLE?
I WAS MAKING SURE THE CENTER WAS EVACUATED AND FOUND HIM LIKE THAT.
THE BUILDING MUST'VE COLLAPSED ON HIM!
THAT'S... ALL?
A CRUMBLING BUILDING CAN'T KILL A GUARDIAN.
LANTERN RAYNER IS CORRECT. THE SITUATION IS NOT AS IT SEEMS.
WHAT DOES THAT MEAN?
WHAT ARE YOU SAYING?
THAT YOU MUST EXERCISE EXTREME CAUTION.
KYLE, ARE YOU THINKING THAT MAYBE...
...SOMEONE DID THIS TO HIM?
HE'S SLIPPING AWAY.
ENGAGE RECOVERY POD!
TELL NO ONE OF YOUR SUSPICIONS, JESSICA.
I... WAIT.
IS HE--?
BREEEE...
...EEEE

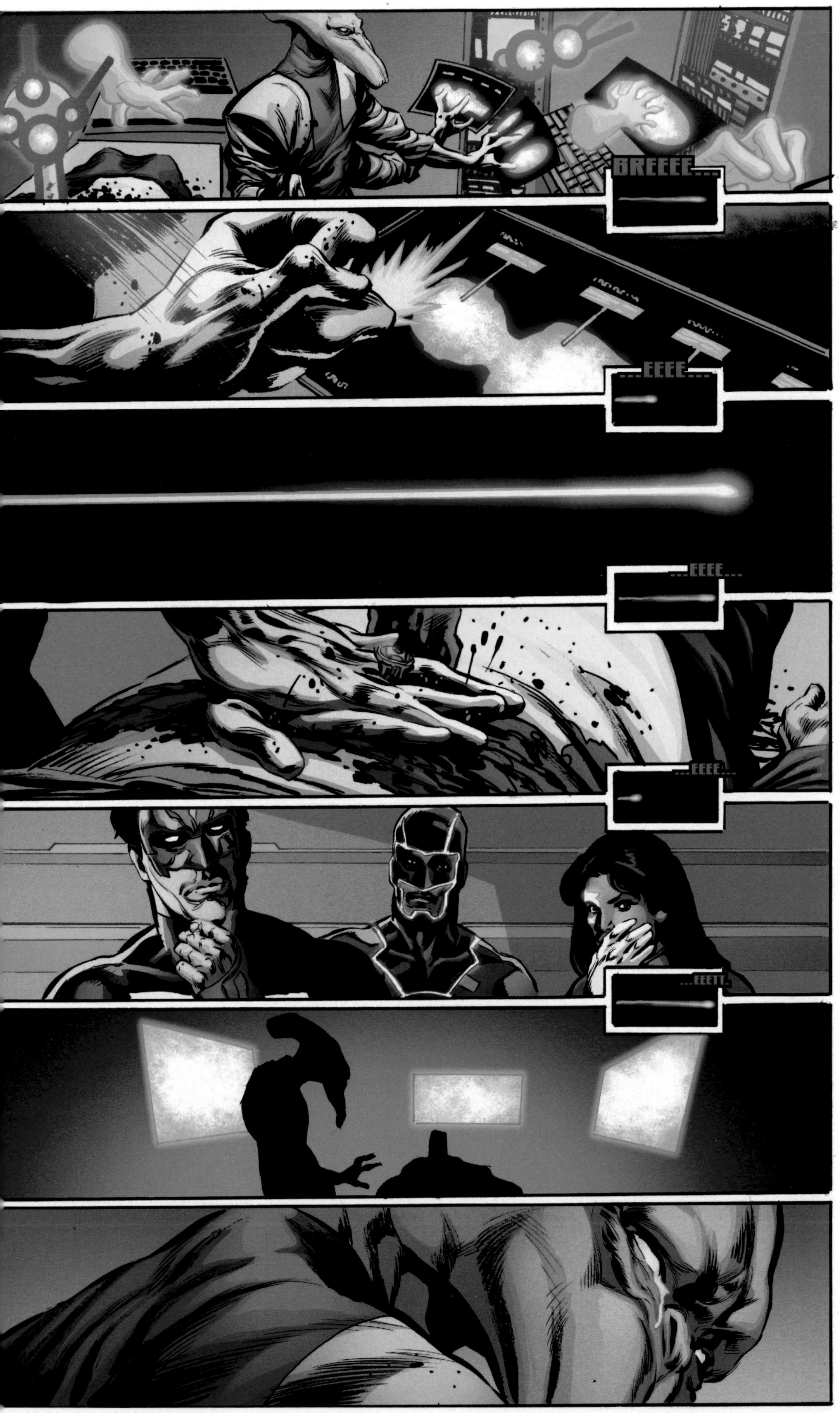
BREEEE...
...EEEE...
...EEEE...
...EEEE...
...EEETT.

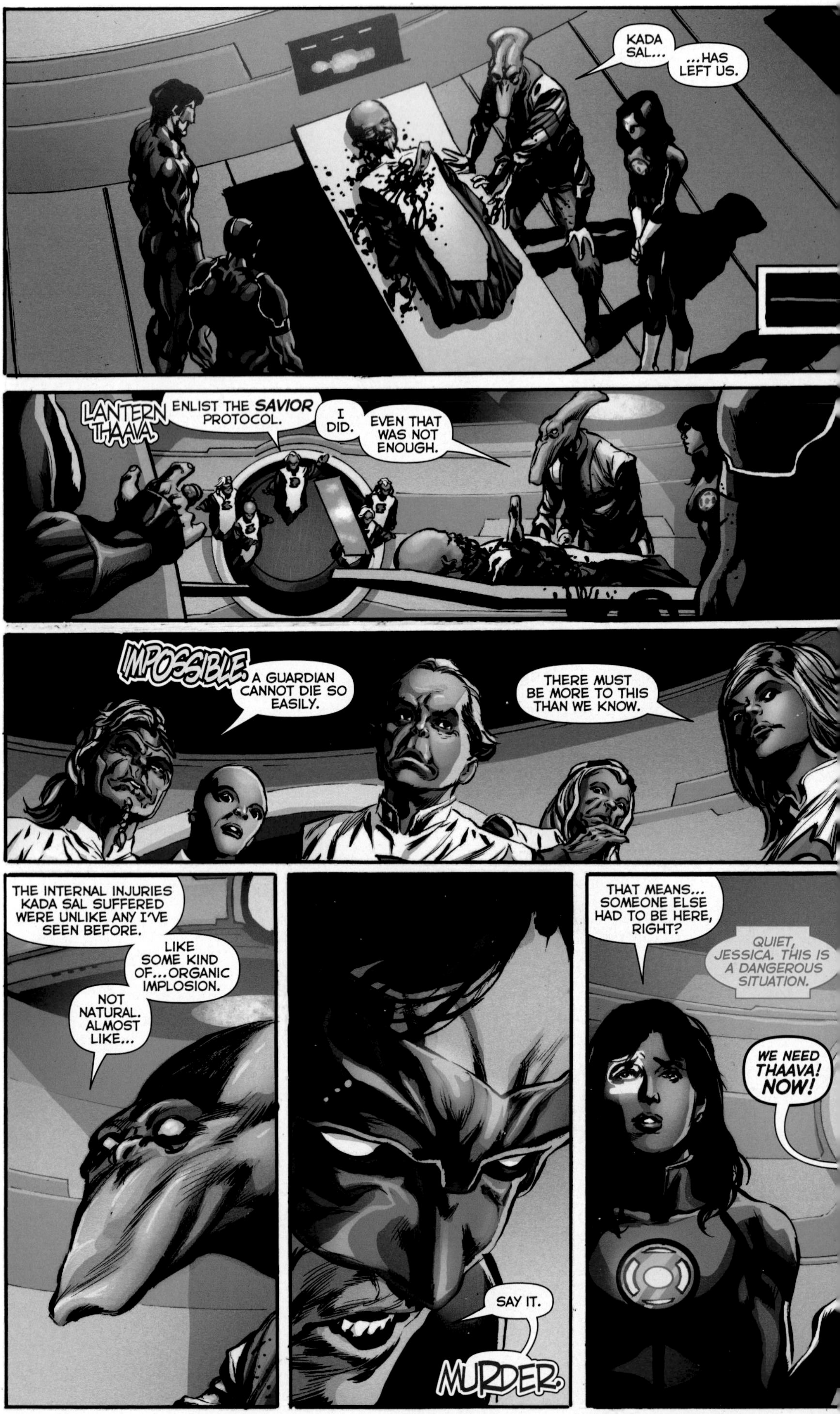

KADA SAL...
...HAS LEFT US.
LANTERN THAAVA.
ENLIST THE SAVIOR PROTOCOL.
I DID.
EVEN THAT WAS NOT ENOUGH.
IMPOSSIBLE.
A GUARDIAN CANNOT DIE SO EASILY.
THERE MUST BE MORE TO THIS THAN WE KNOW.
THE INTERNAL INJURIES KADA SAL SUFFERED WERE UNLIKE ANY I'VE SEEN BEFORE.
LIKE SOME KIND OF...ORGANIC IMPLOSION.
NOT NATURAL. ALMOST LIKE...
SAY IT.
MURDER.
THAT MEANS... SOMEONE ELSE HAD TO BE HERE, RIGHT?
QUIET, JESSICA. THIS IS A DANGEROUS SITUATION.
WE NEED THAAVA! NOW!

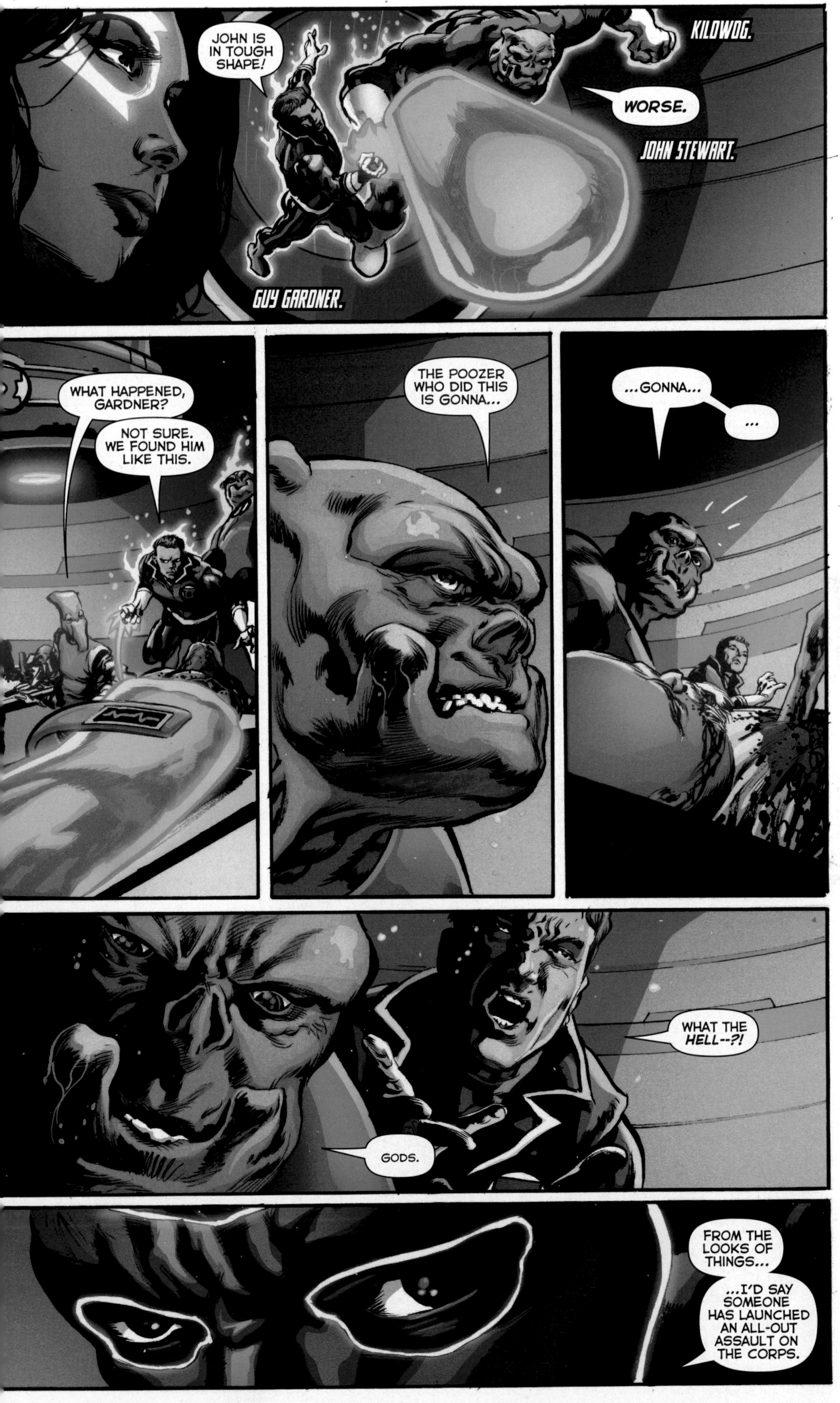
JOHN IS IN TOUGH SHAPE!
KILOWOG.
WORSE.
JOHN STEWART.
GUY GARDNER.
WHAT HAPPENED, GARDNER?
NOT SURE. WE FOUND HIM LIKE THIS.
THE POOZER WHO DID THIS IS GONNA...
...GONNA...
...
WHAT THE *HELL*--?!
GODS.
FROM THE LOOKS OF THINGS...
...I'D SAY SOMEONE HAS LAUNCHED AN ALL-OUT ASSAULT ON THE CORPS.

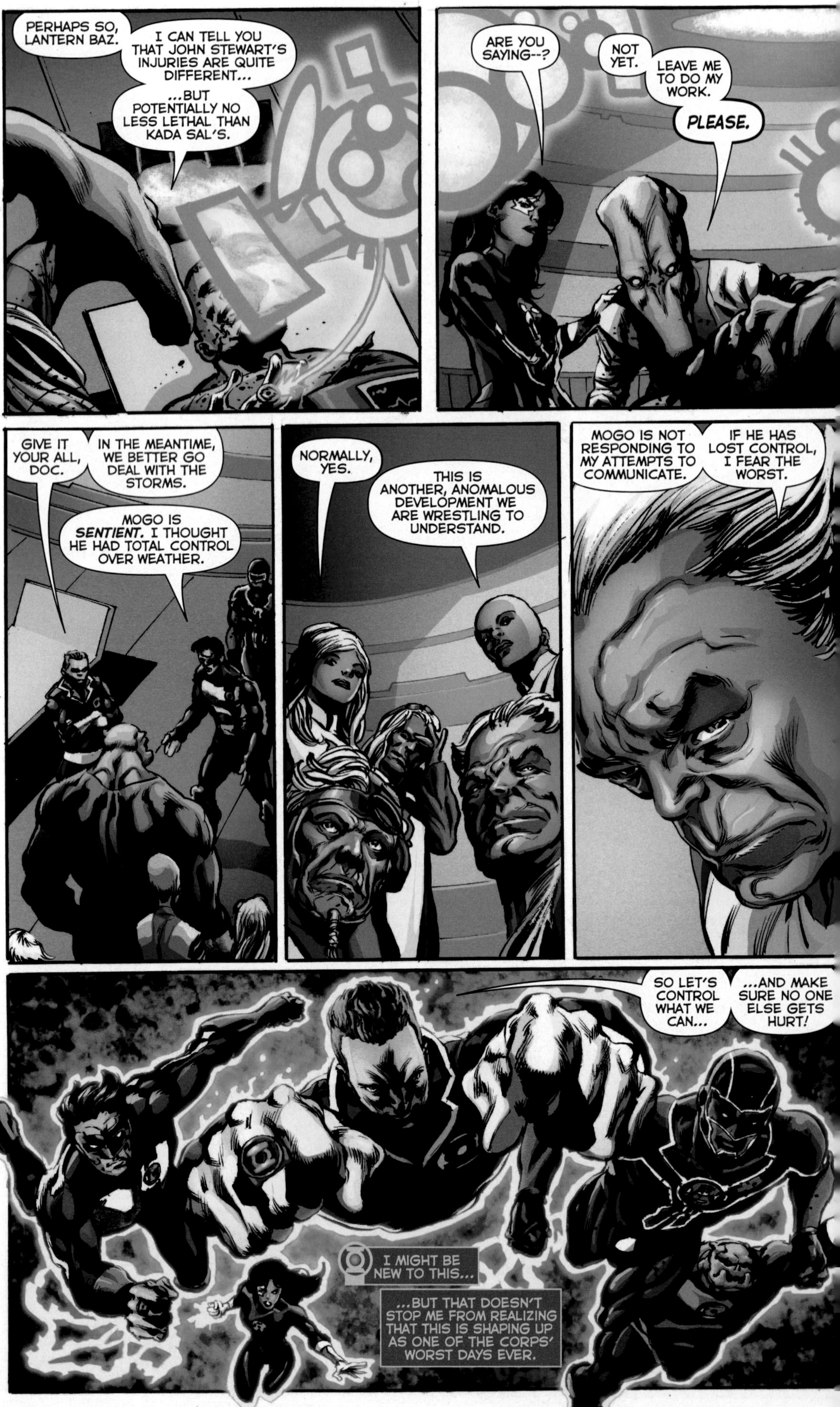
PERHAPS SO, LANTERN BAZ.
I CAN TELL YOU THAT JOHN STEWART'S INJURIES ARE QUITE DIFFERENT...
...BUT POTENTIALLY NO LESS LETHAL THAN KADA SAL'S.
ARE YOU SAYING--?
NOT YET.
LEAVE ME TO DO MY WORK.
PLEASE.
GIVE IT YOUR ALL, DOC.
IN THE MEANTIME, WE BETTER GO DEAL WITH THE STORMS.
MOGO IS SENTIENT. I THOUGHT HE HAD TOTAL CONTROL OVER WEATHER.
NORMALLY, YES.
THIS IS ANOTHER, ANOMALOUS DEVELOPMENT WE ARE WRESTLING TO UNDERSTAND.
MOGO IS NOT RESPONDING TO MY ATTEMPTS TO COMMUNICATE.
IF HE HAS LOST CONTROL, I FEAR THE WORST.
SO LET'S CONTROL WHAT WE CAN...
...AND MAKE SURE NO ONE ELSE GETS HURT!
I MIGHT BE NEW TO THIS...
...BUT THAT DOESN'T STOP ME FROM REALIZING THAT THIS IS SHAPING UP AS ONE OF THE CORPS' WORST DAYS EVER.

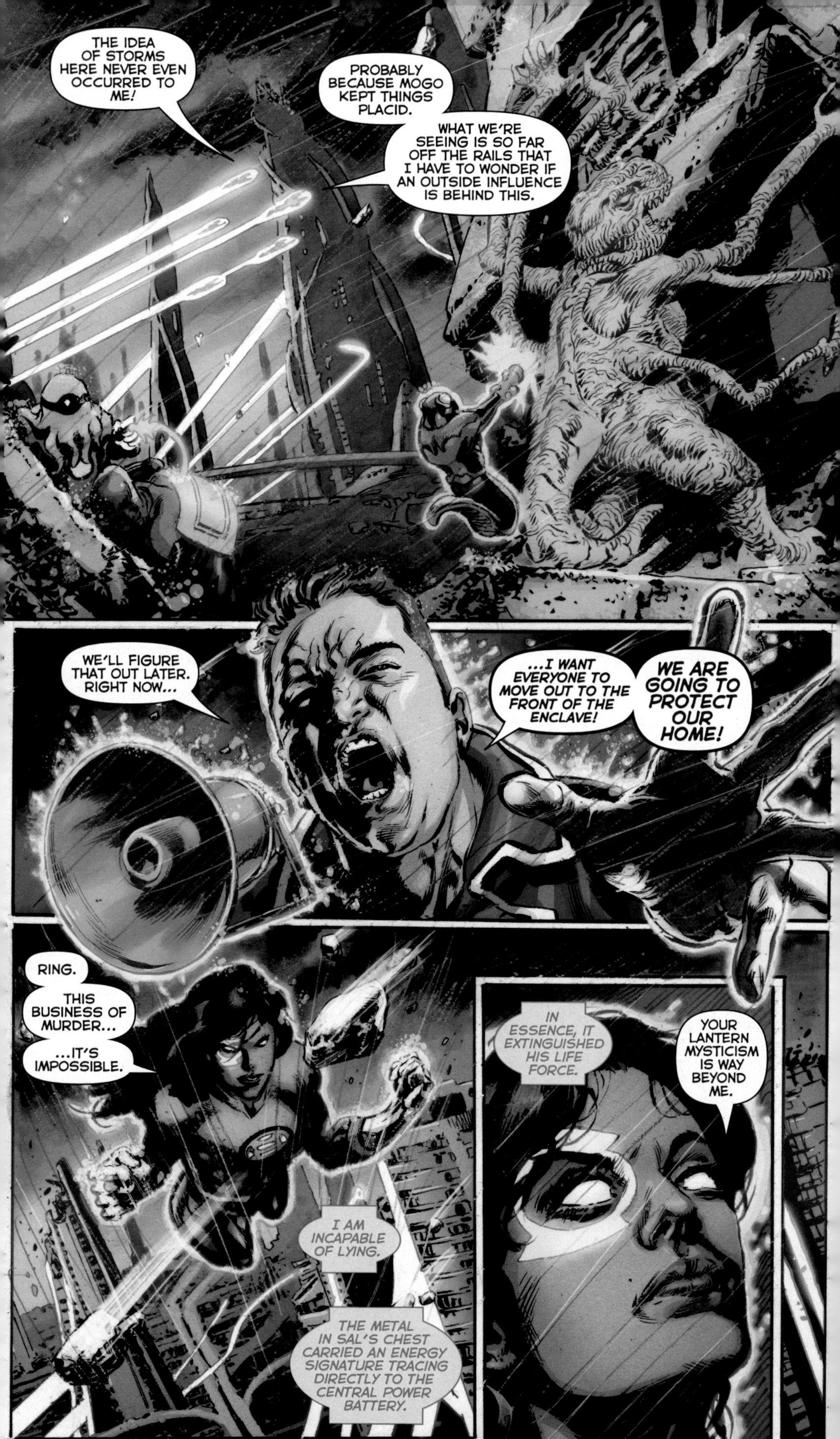
THE IDEA OF STORMS HERE NEVER EVEN OCCURRED TO ME!
PROBABLY BECAUSE MOGO KEPT THINGS PLACID.
WHAT WE'RE SEEING IS SO FAR OFF THE RAILS THAT I HAVE TO WONDER IF AN OUTSIDE INFLUENCE IS BEHIND THIS.
WE'LL FIGURE THAT OUT LATER. RIGHT NOW...
...I WANT EVERYONE TO MOVE OUT TO THE FRONT OF THE ENCLAVE!
WE ARE GOING TO PROTECT OUR HOME!
RING.
THIS BUSINESS OF MURDER...
...IT'S IMPOSSIBLE.
I AM INCAPABLE OF LYING.
THE METAL IN SAL'S CHEST CARRIED AN ENERGY SIGNATURE TRACING DIRECTLY TO THE CENTRAL POWER BATTERY.
IN ESSENCE, IT EXTINGUISHED HIS LIFE FORCE.
YOUR LANTERN MYSTICISM IS WAY BEYOND ME.

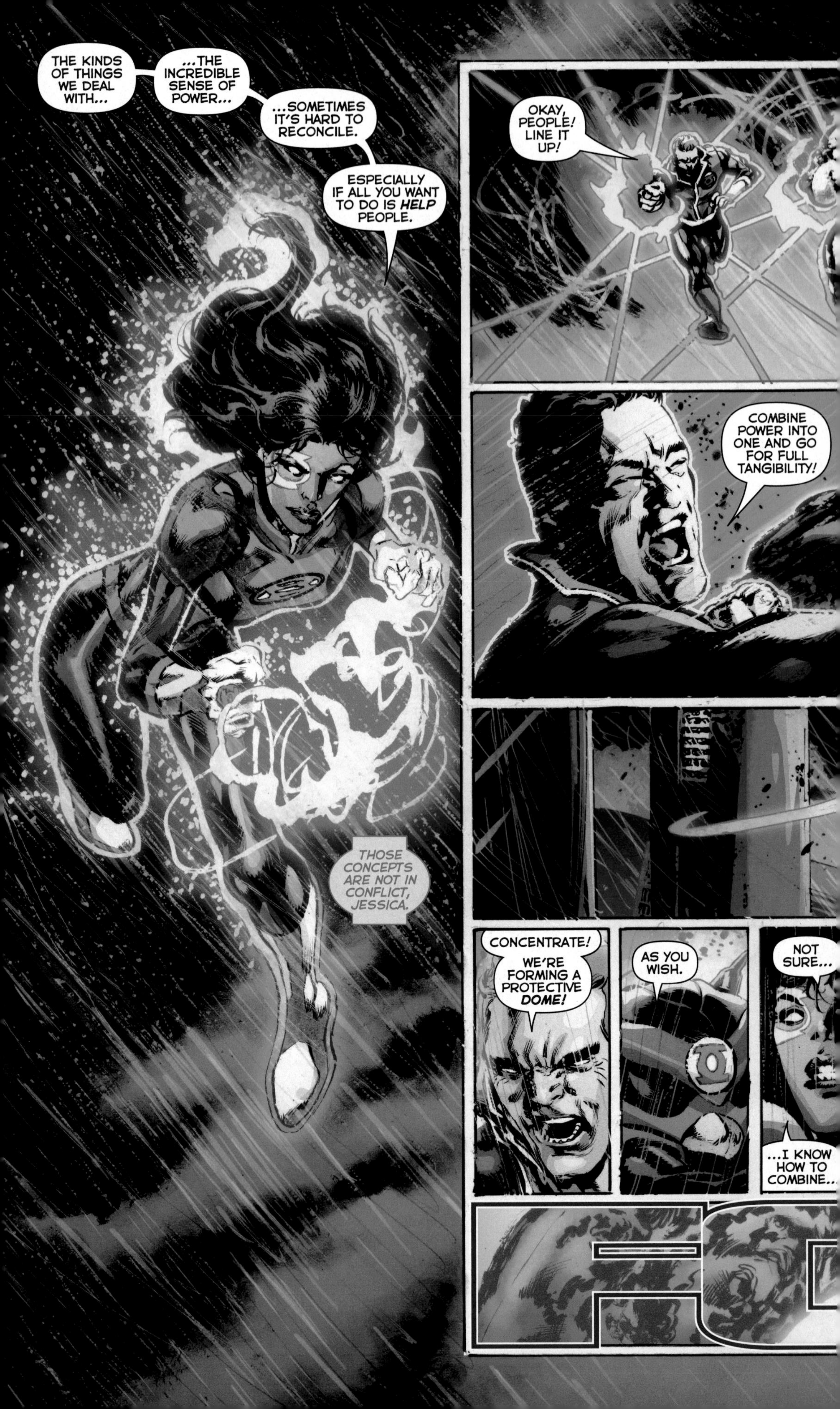

THE KINDS OF THINGS WE DEAL WITH...
...THE INCREDIBLE SENSE OF POWER...
...SOMETIMES IT'S HARD TO RECONCILE.
ESPECIALLY IF ALL YOU WANT TO DO IS HELP PEOPLE.
THOSE CONCEPTS ARE NOT IN CONFLICT, JESSICA.
OKAY, PEOPLE! LINE IT UP!
COMBINE POWER INTO ONE AND GO FOR FULL TANGIBILITY!
CONCENTRATE!
WE'RE FORMING A PROTECTIVE DOME!
AS YOU WISH.
NOT SURE...
...I KNOW HOW TO COMBINE...

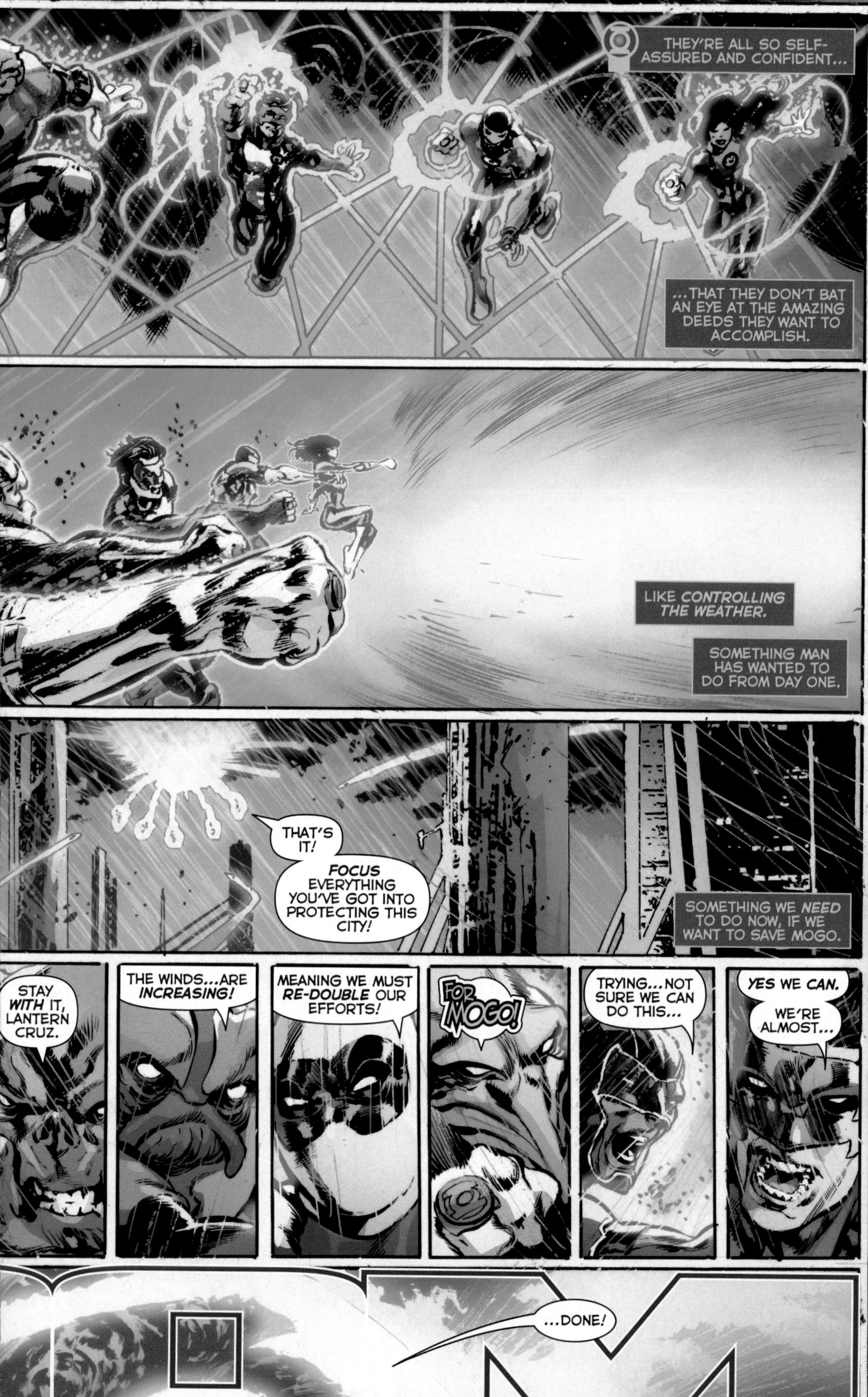

THEY'RE ALL SO SELF-ASSURED AND CONFIDENT...
...THAT THEY DON'T BAT AN EYE AT THE AMAZING DEEDS THEY WANT TO ACCOMPLISH.
LIKE CONTROLLING THE WEATHER.
SOMETHING MAN HAS WANTED TO DO FROM DAY ONE.
THAT'S IT!
FOCUS EVERYTHING YOU'VE GOT INTO PROTECTING THIS CITY!
SOMETHING WE NEED TO DO NOW, IF WE WANT TO SAVE MOGO.
STAY WITH IT, LANTERN CRUZ.
THE WINDS...ARE INCREASING!
MEANING WE MUST RE-DOUBLE OUR EFFORTS!
FOR MOGO!
TRYING...NOT SURE WE CAN DO THIS...
YES WE CAN.
WE'RE ALMOST...
...DONE!

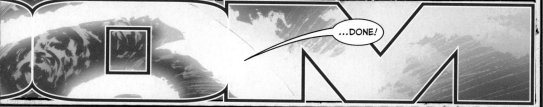

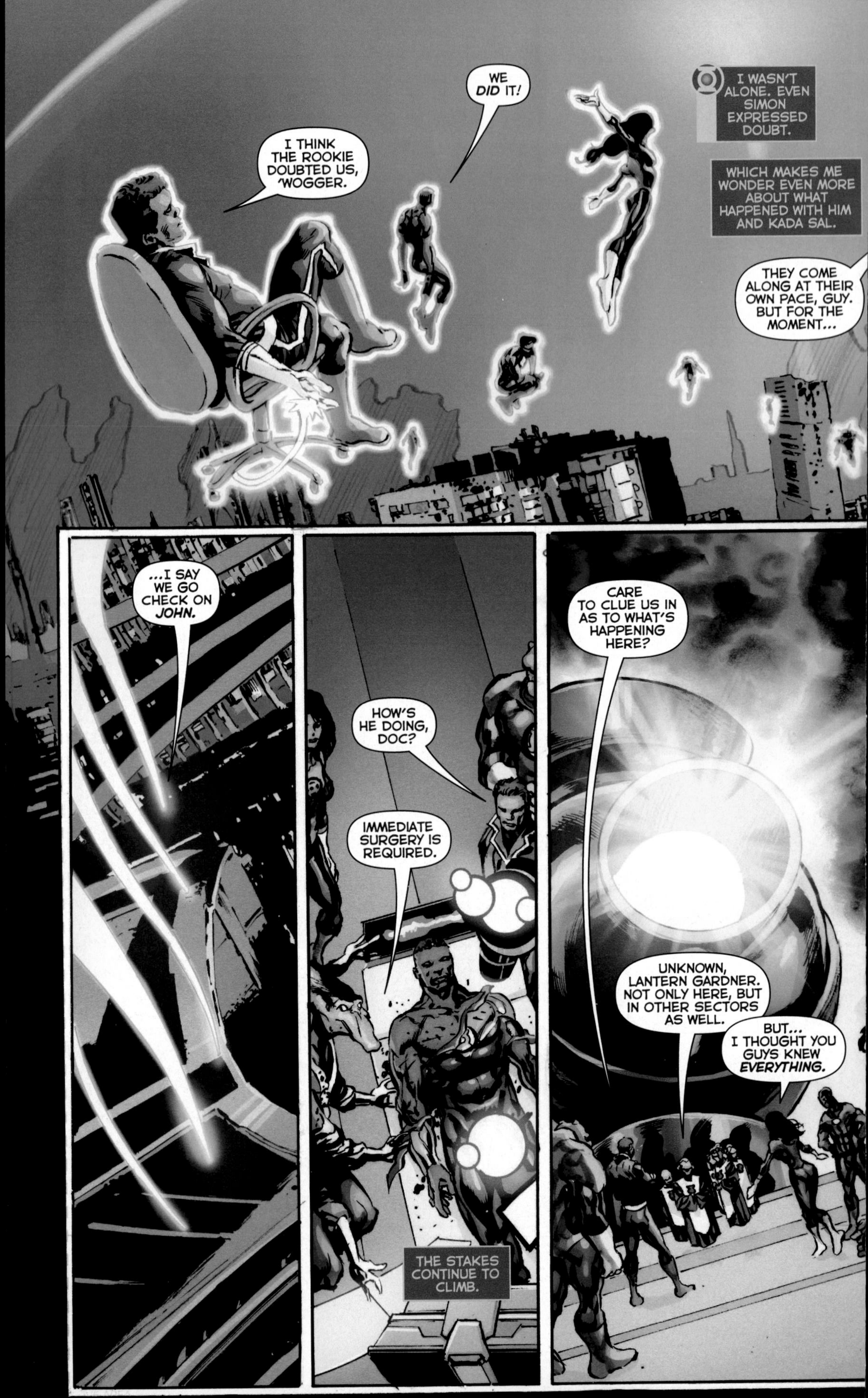
I WASN'T ALONE. EVEN SIMON EXPRESSED DOUBT.
WHICH MAKES ME WONDER EVEN MORE ABOUT WHAT HAPPENED WITH HIM AND KADA SAL.
I THINK THE ROOKIE DOUBTED US, 'WOGGER.
WE DID IT!
THEY COME ALONG AT THEIR OWN PACE, GUY. BUT FOR THE MOMENT...
...I SAY WE GO CHECK ON JOHN.
HOW'S HE DOING, DOC?
IMMEDIATE SURGERY IS REQUIRED.
THE STAKES CONTINUE TO CLIMB.
CARE TO CLUE US IN AS TO WHAT'S HAPPENING HERE?
UNKNOWN, LANTERN GARDNER. NOT ONLY HERE, BUT IN OTHER SECTORS AS WELL.
BUT... I THOUGHT YOU GUYS KNEW EVERYTHING.

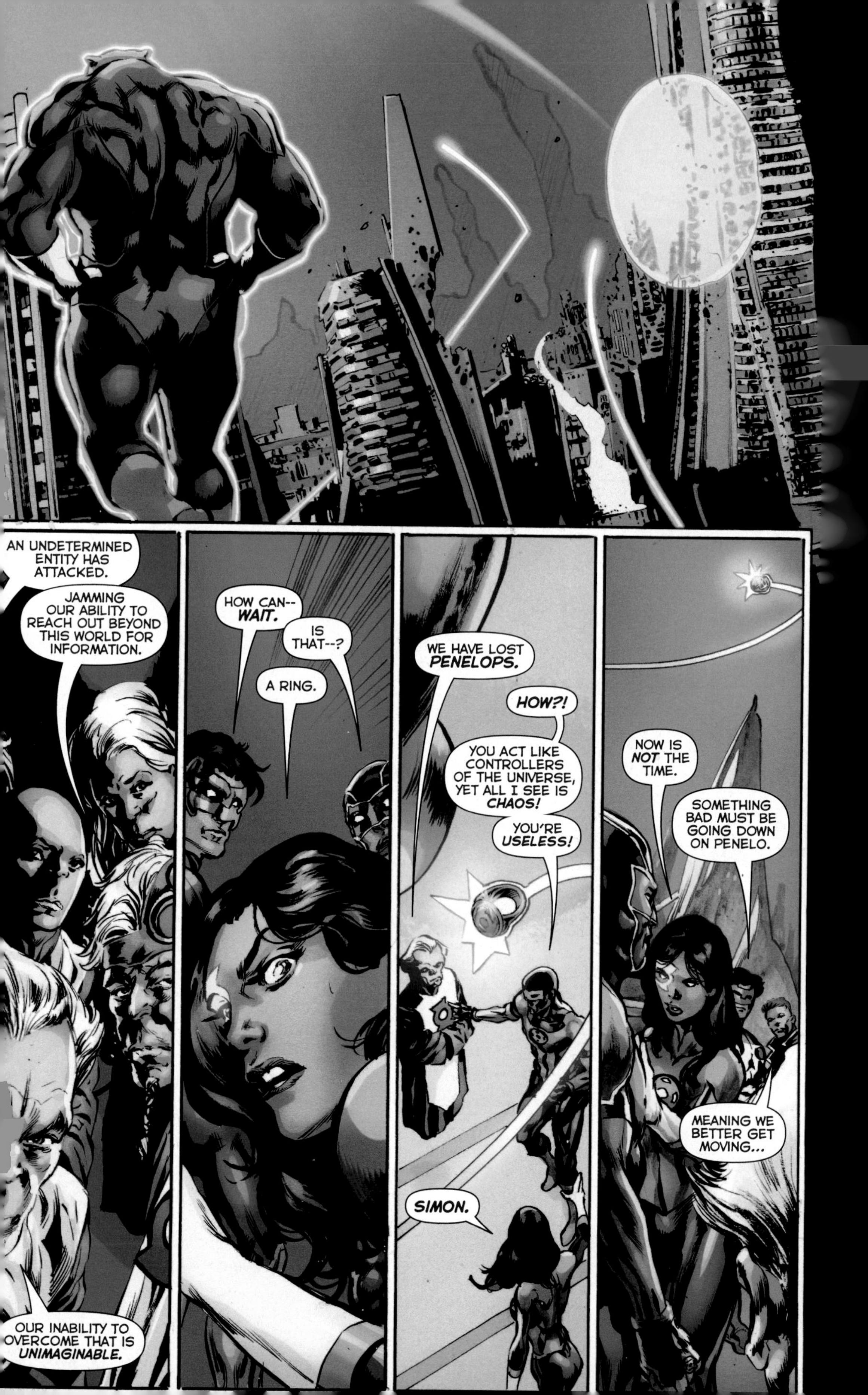

AN UNDETERMINED ENTITY HAS ATTACKED.
JAMMING OUR ABILITY TO REACH OUT BEYOND THIS WORLD FOR INFORMATION.
OUR INABILITY TO OVERCOME THAT IS *UNIMAGINABLE.*
HOW CAN-- *WAIT.*
IS THAT--?
A RING.
WE HAVE LOST *PENELOPS.*
HOW?!
YOU ACT LIKE CONTROLLERS OF THE UNIVERSE, YET ALL I SEE IS *CHAOS!*
YOU'RE *USELESS!*
SIMON.
NOW IS *NOT* THE TIME.
SOMETHING BAD MUST BE GOING DOWN ON PENELO.
MEANING WE BETTER GET MOVING...

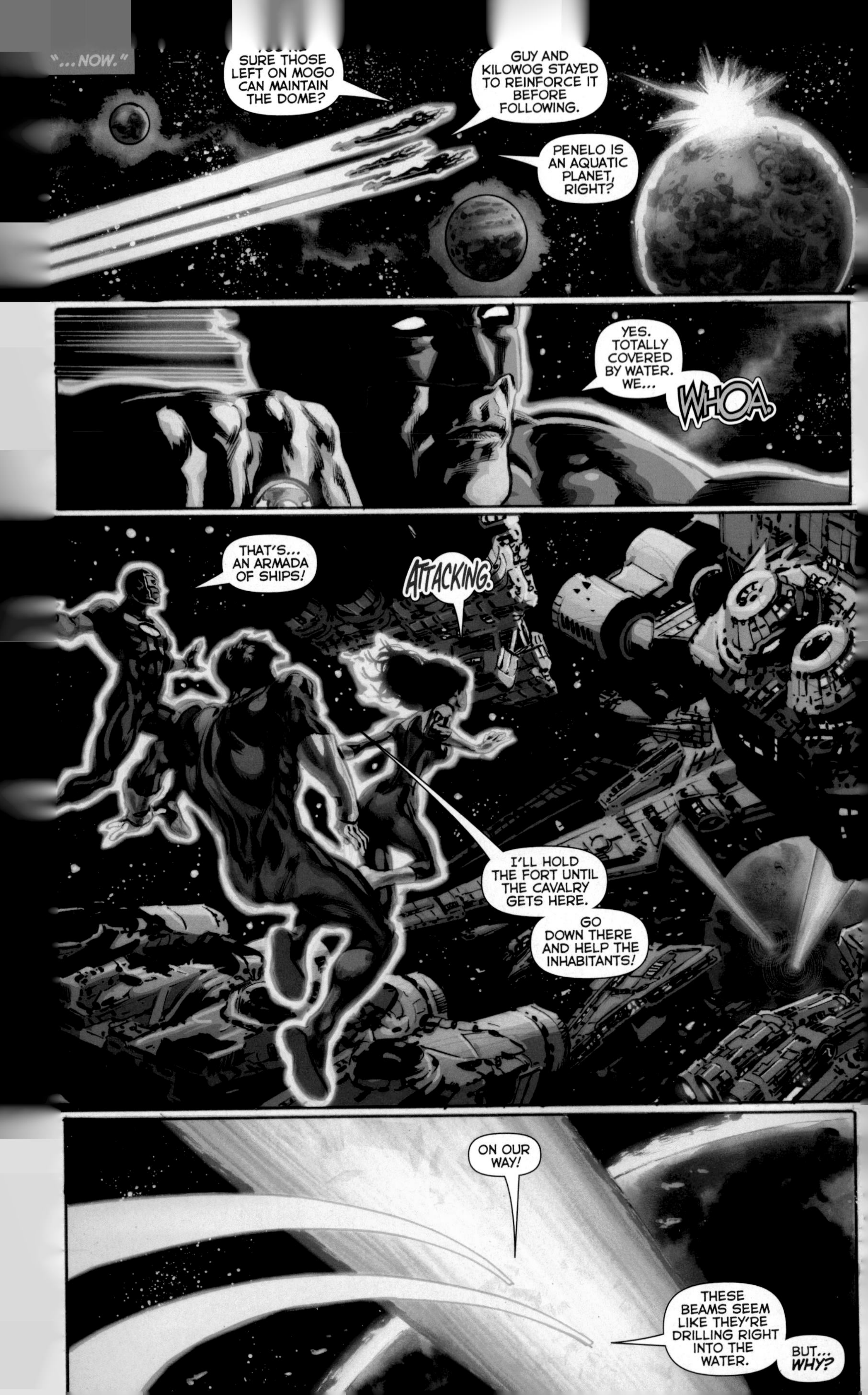
"...NOW."
SURE THOSE LEFT ON MOGO CAN MAINTAIN THE DOME?
GUY AND KILOWOG STAYED TO REINFORCE IT BEFORE FOLLOWING.
PENELO IS AN AQUATIC PLANET, RIGHT?
YES. TOTALLY COVERED BY WATER. WE...
WHOA.
THAT'S... AN ARMADA OF SHIPS!
ATTACKING.
I'LL HOLD THE FORT UNTIL THE CAVALRY GETS HERE.
GO DOWN THERE AND HELP THE INHABITANTS!
ON OUR WAY!
THESE BEAMS SEEM LIKE THEY'RE DRILLING RIGHT INTO THE WATER.
BUT... WHY?

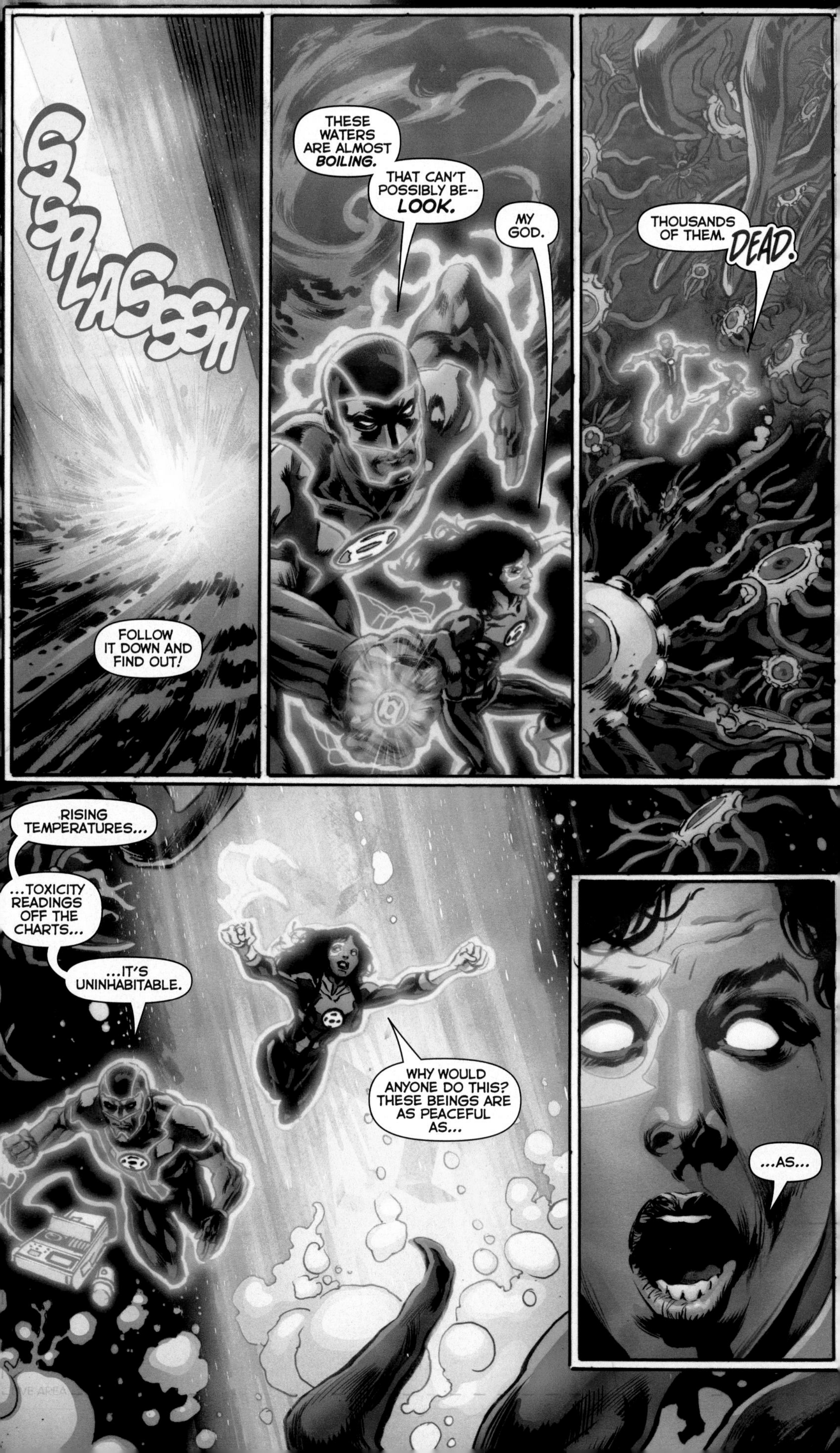
SPLASSSH
FOLLOW IT DOWN AND FIND OUT!
THESE WATERS ARE ALMOST BOILING.
THAT CAN'T POSSIBLY BE-- LOOK.
MY GOD.
THOUSANDS OF THEM. DEAD.
RISING TEMPERATURES...
...TOXICITY READINGS OFF THE CHARTS...
...IT'S UNINHABITABLE.
WHY WOULD ANYONE DO THIS? THESE BEINGS ARE AS PEACEFUL AS...
...AS...

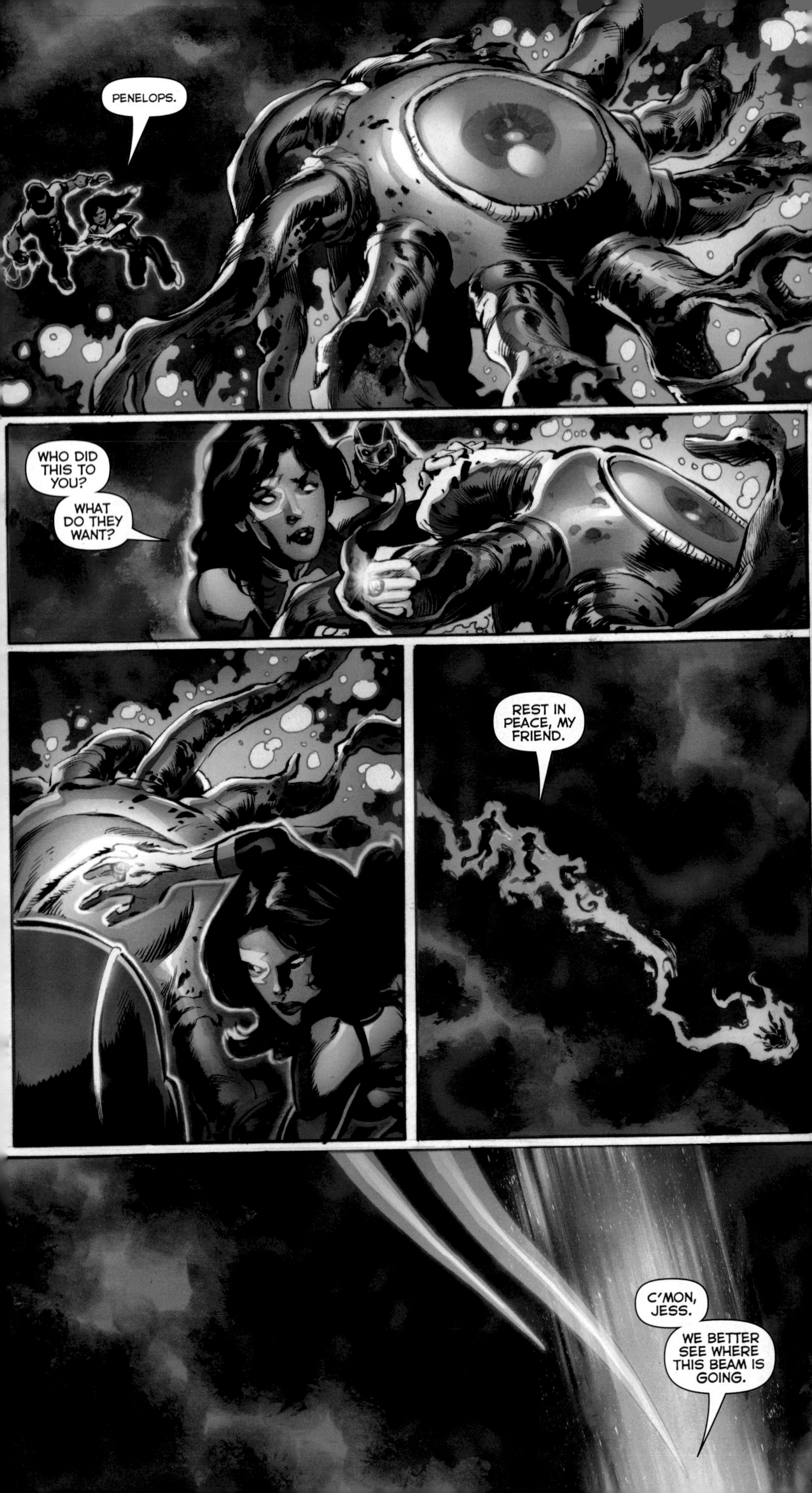
PENELOPS.
WHO DID THIS TO YOU?
WHAT DO THEY WANT?
REST IN PEACE, MY FRIEND.
C'MON, JESS.
WE BETTER SEE WHERE THIS BEAM IS GOING.

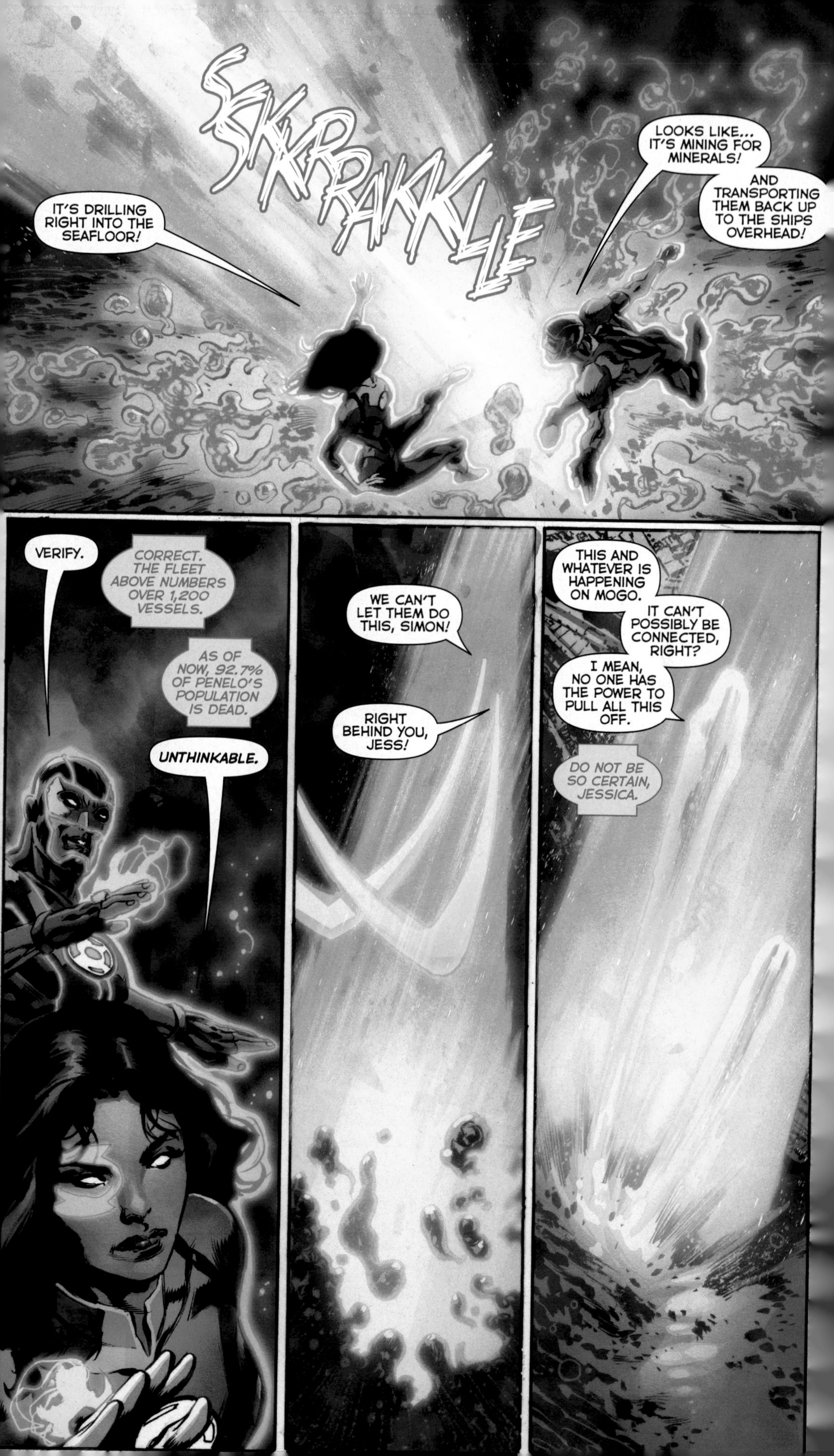
SKKRRAKKKLLE
IT'S DRILLING RIGHT INTO THE SEAFLOOR!
LOOKS LIKE... IT'S MINING FOR MINERALS!
AND TRANSPORTING THEM BACK UP TO THE SHIPS OVERHEAD!
VERIFY.
CORRECT. THE FLEET ABOVE NUMBERS OVER 1,200 VESSELS.
AS OF NOW, 92.7% OF PENELO'S POPULATION IS DEAD.
UNTHINKABLE.
WE CAN'T LET THEM DO THIS, SIMON!
RIGHT BEHIND YOU, JESS!
THIS AND WHATEVER IS HAPPENING ON MOGO.
IT CAN'T POSSIBLY BE CONNECTED, RIGHT?
I MEAN, NO ONE HAS THE POWER TO PULL ALL THIS OFF.
DO NOT BE SO CERTAIN, JESSICA.

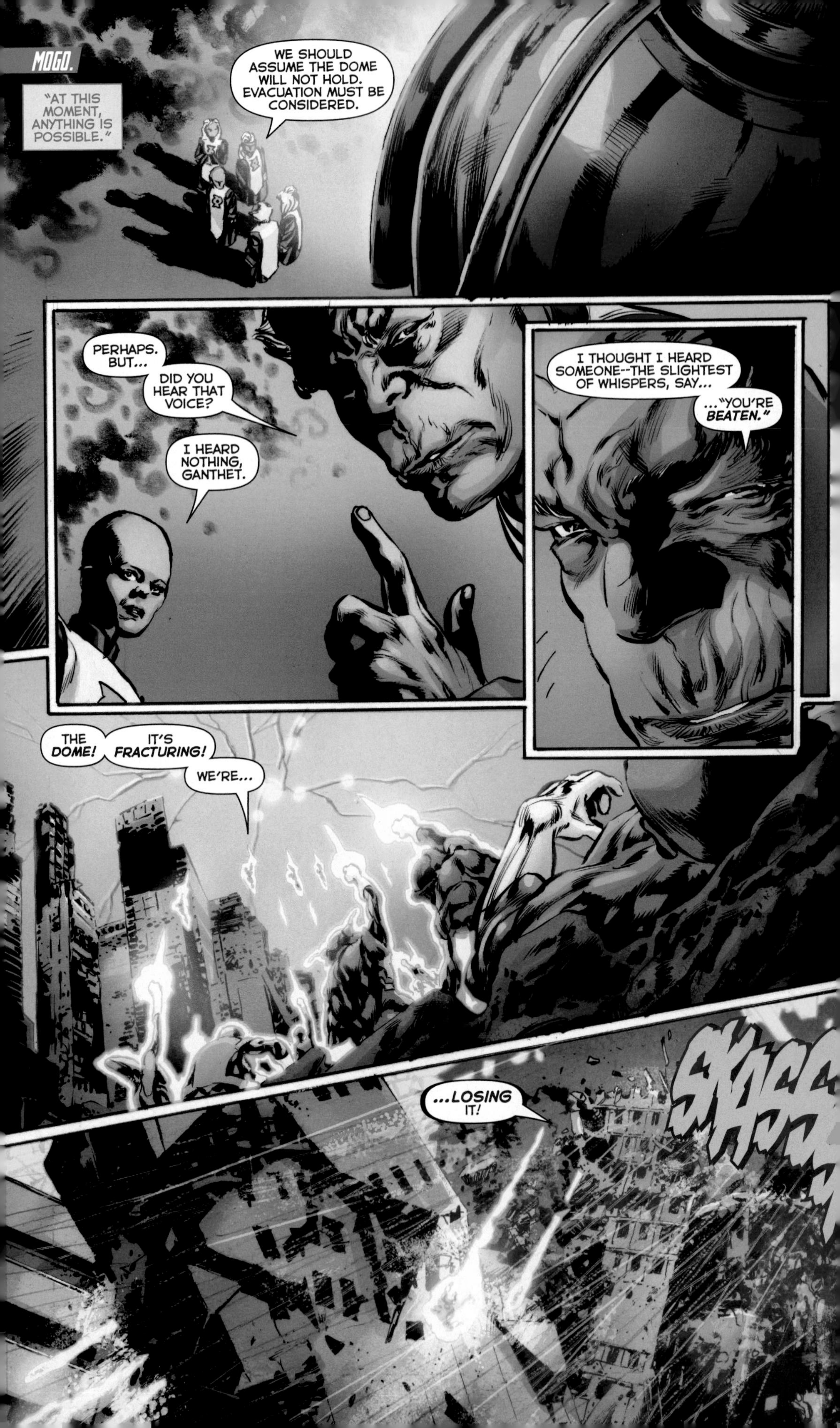
MOGO.
"AT THIS MOMENT, ANYTHING IS POSSIBLE."
WE SHOULD ASSUME THE DOME WILL NOT HOLD. EVACUATION MUST BE CONSIDERED.
PERHAPS. BUT...
DID YOU HEAR THAT VOICE?
I HEARD NOTHING, GANTHET.
I THOUGHT I HEARD SOMEONE--THE SLIGHTEST OF WHISPERS, SAY...
..."YOU'RE *BEATEN."*
THE *DOME!*
IT'S *FRACTURING!*
WE'RE...
...LOSING IT!
SKASS

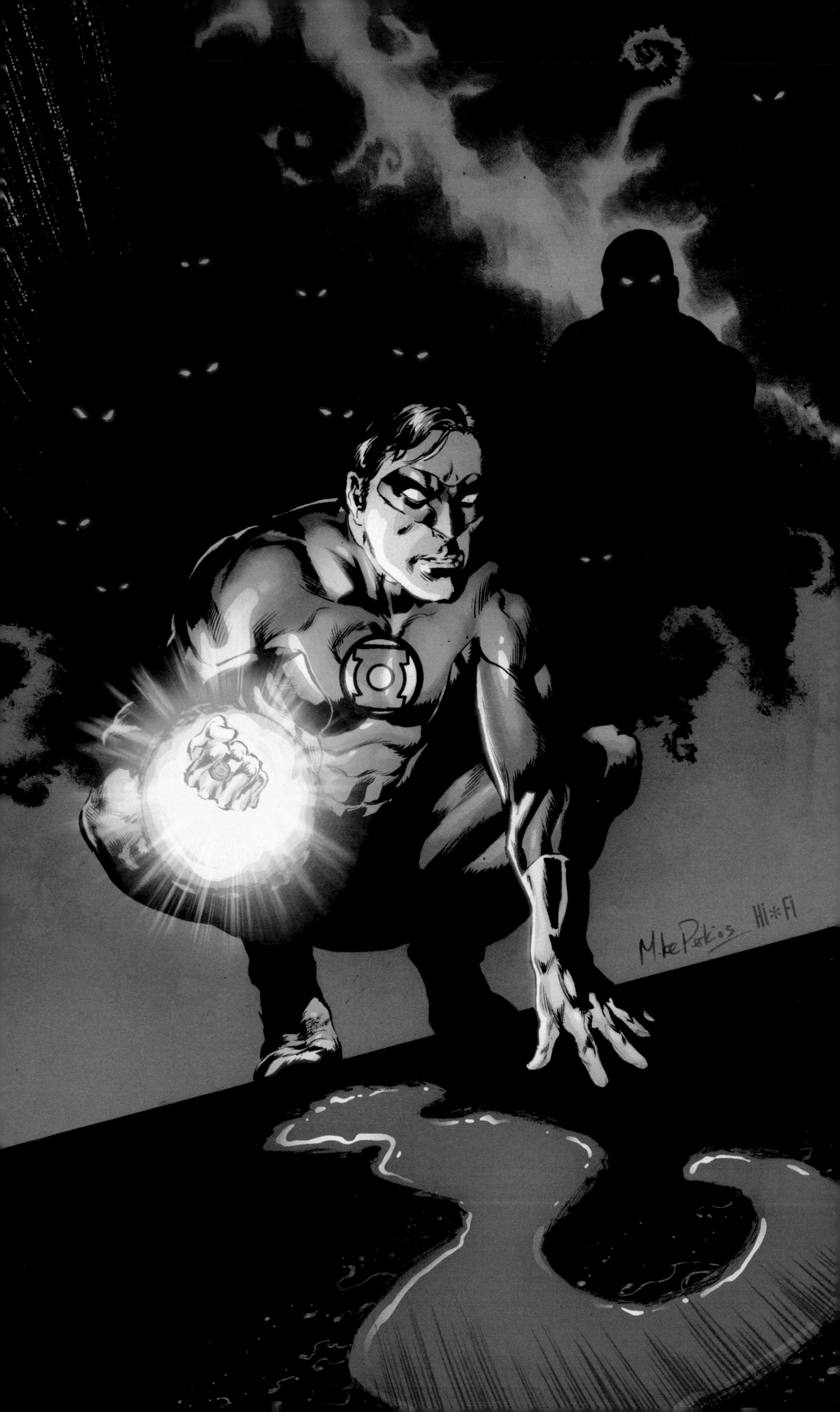
Mike Perkins Hi*Fi

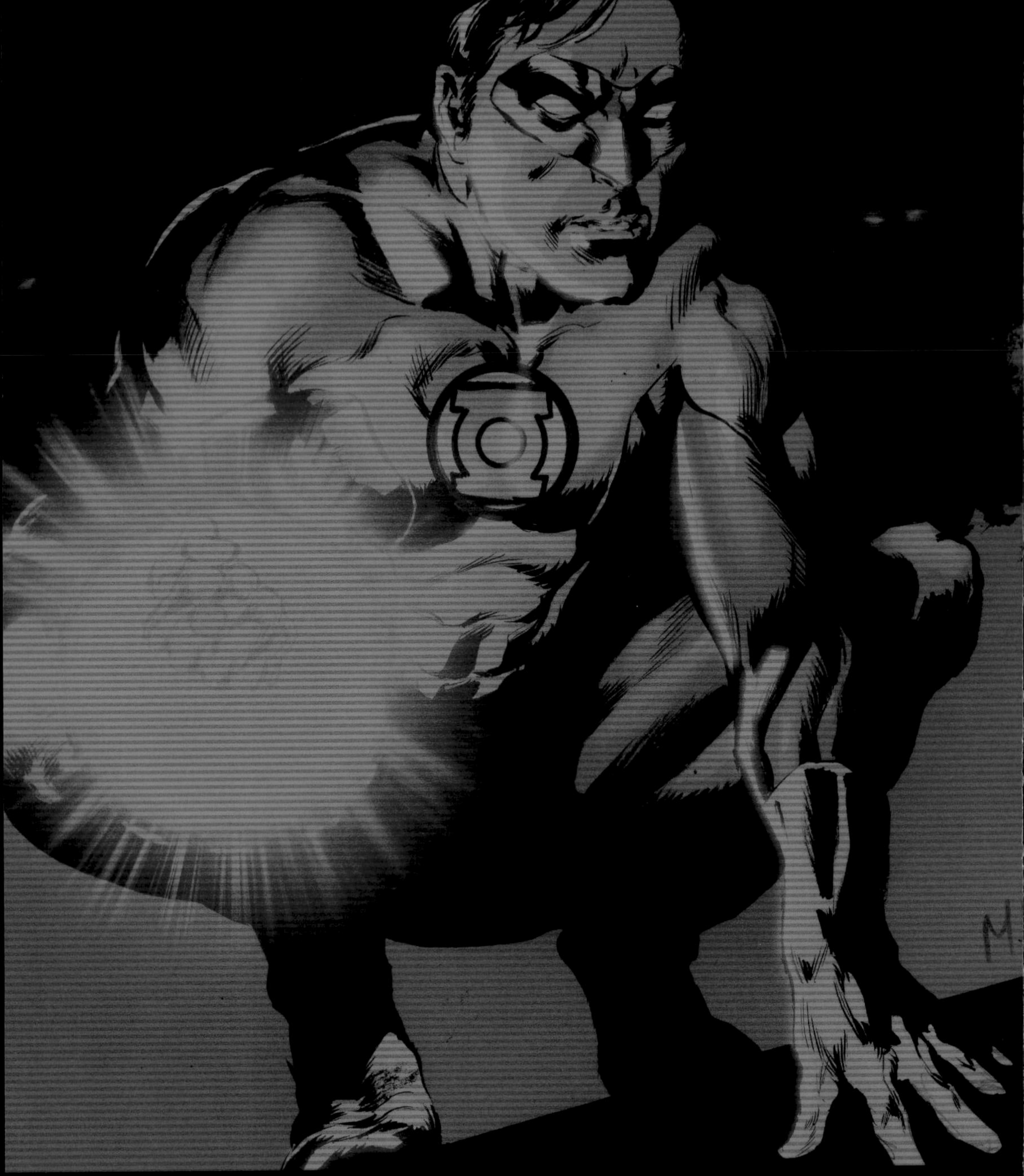

GREEN LANTERNS

#52

THERE ARE *THOUSANDS* OF THEM, THESE *GREEN LANTERNS.*

EACH AND EVERY ONE OF THEM IS A *FOOL.*

AN ENTIRE CORPS OF SELF-APPOINTED...

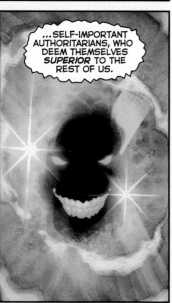

...SELF-IMPORTANT AUTHORITARIANS, WHO DEEM THEMSELVES *SUPERIOR* TO THE REST OF US.

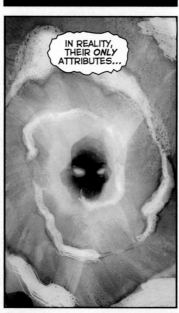

IN REALITY, THEIR *ONLY* ATTRIBUTES...

...ARE THEIR GREEN FINGER TRINKETS.

THEY ARE DEVOID OF NATURAL POWERS.

DID *NOTHING* TO EARN THEIR WEAPONRY.

WHICH IS WHY THEY HAVE NO CHANCE AGAINST *ME.*

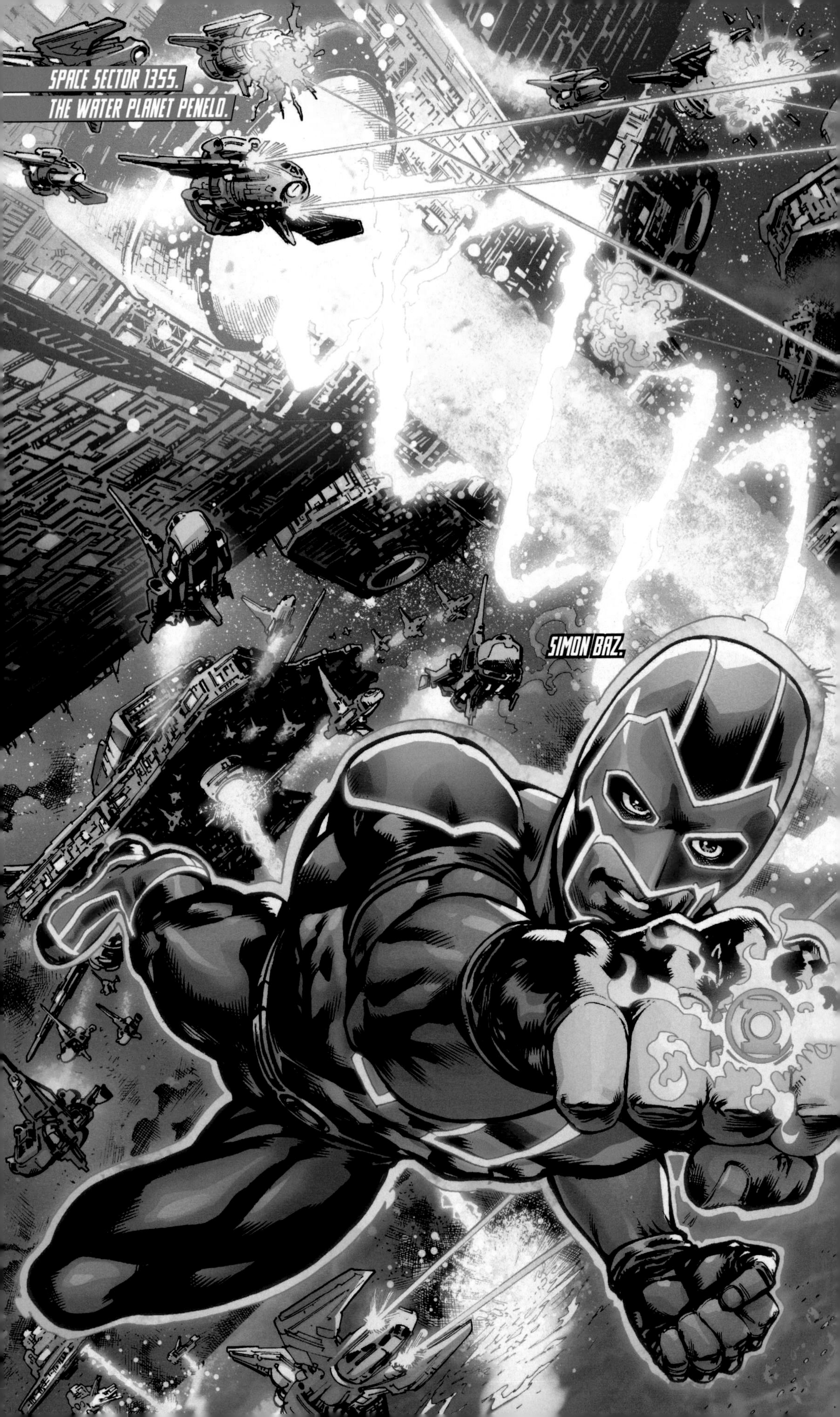
SPACE SECTOR 1355. THE WATER PLANET PENELO.
SIMON BAZ.

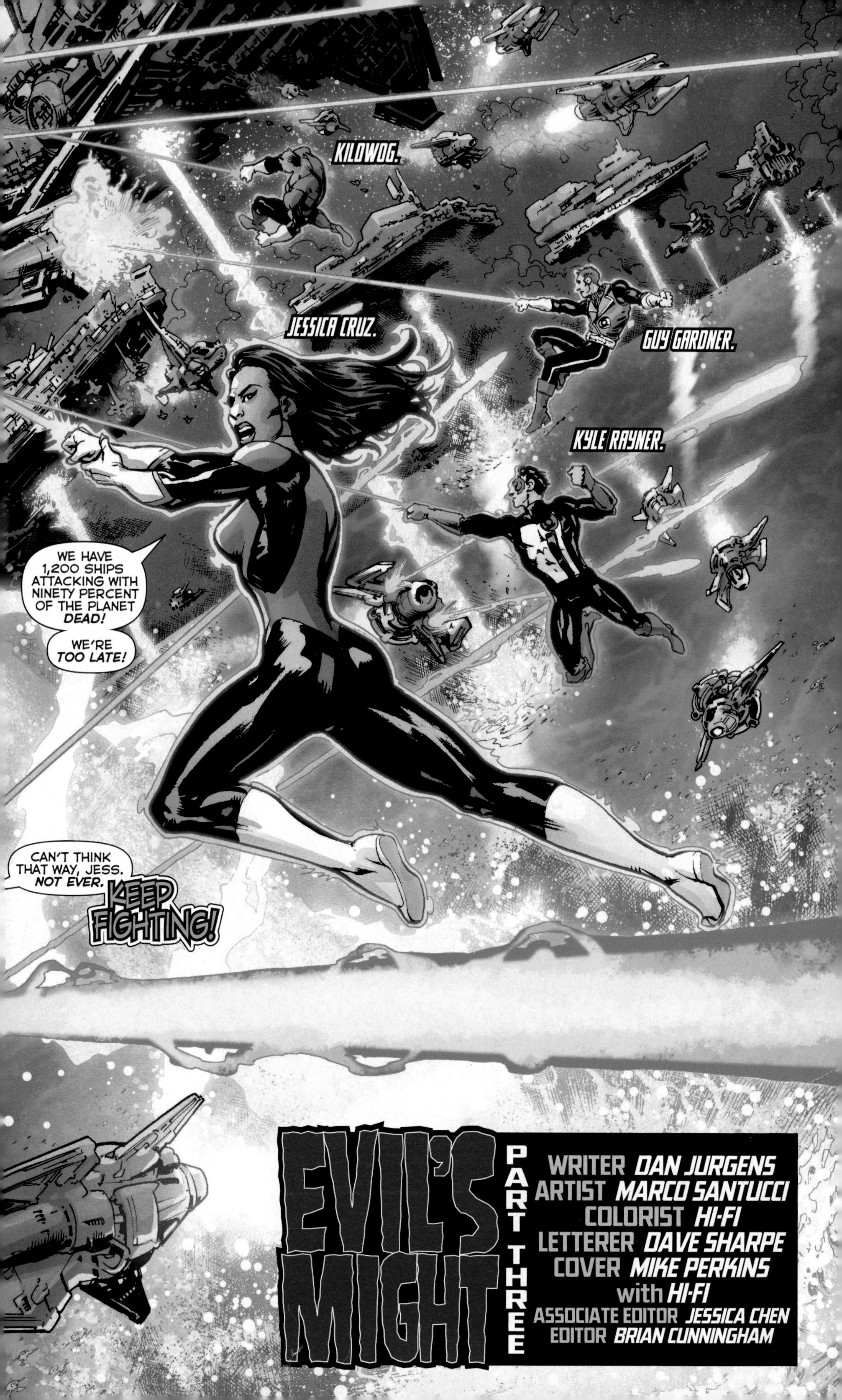
KILOWOG.
JESSICA CRUZ.
GUY GARDNER.
KYLE RAYNER.
WE HAVE 1,200 SHIPS ATTACKING WITH NINETY PERCENT OF THE PLANET DEAD!
WE'RE TOO LATE!
CAN'T THINK THAT WAY, JESS. NOT EVER. KEEP FIGHTING!
EVIL'S MIGHT
PART THREE
WRITER DAN JURGENS
ARTIST MARCO SANTUCCI
COLORIST HI-FI
LETTERER DAVE SHARPE
COVER MIKE PERKINS
with HI-FI
ASSOCIATE EDITOR JESSICA CHEN
EDITOR BRIAN CUNNINGHAM

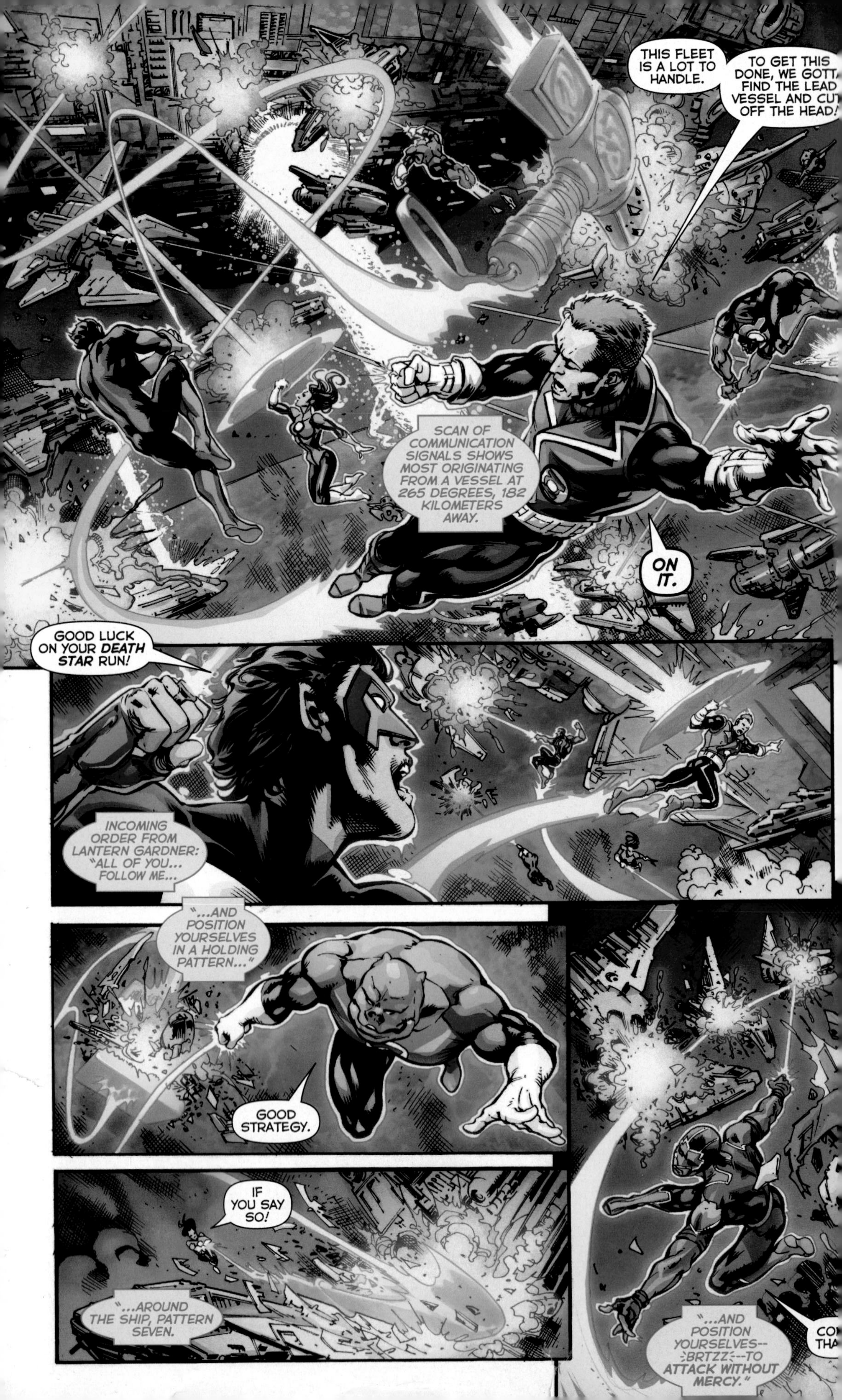
THIS FLEET IS A LOT TO HANDLE.
TO GET THIS DONE, WE GOTT FIND THE LEAD VESSEL AND CU OFF THE HEAD!
SCAN OF COMMUNICATION SIGNALS SHOWS MOST ORIGINATING FROM A VESSEL AT 265 DEGREES, 182 KILOMETERS AWAY.
ON IT.
GOOD LUCK ON YOUR DEATH STAR RUN!
INCOMING ORDER FROM LANTERN GARDNER: "ALL OF YOU... FOLLOW ME...
"...AND POSITION YOURSELVES IN A HOLDING PATTERN..."
GOOD STRATEGY.
IF YOU SAY SO!
"...AROUND THE SHIP, PATTERN SEVEN.
"...AND POSITION YOURSELVES-- BRTZZ --TO ATTACK WITHOUT MERCY."

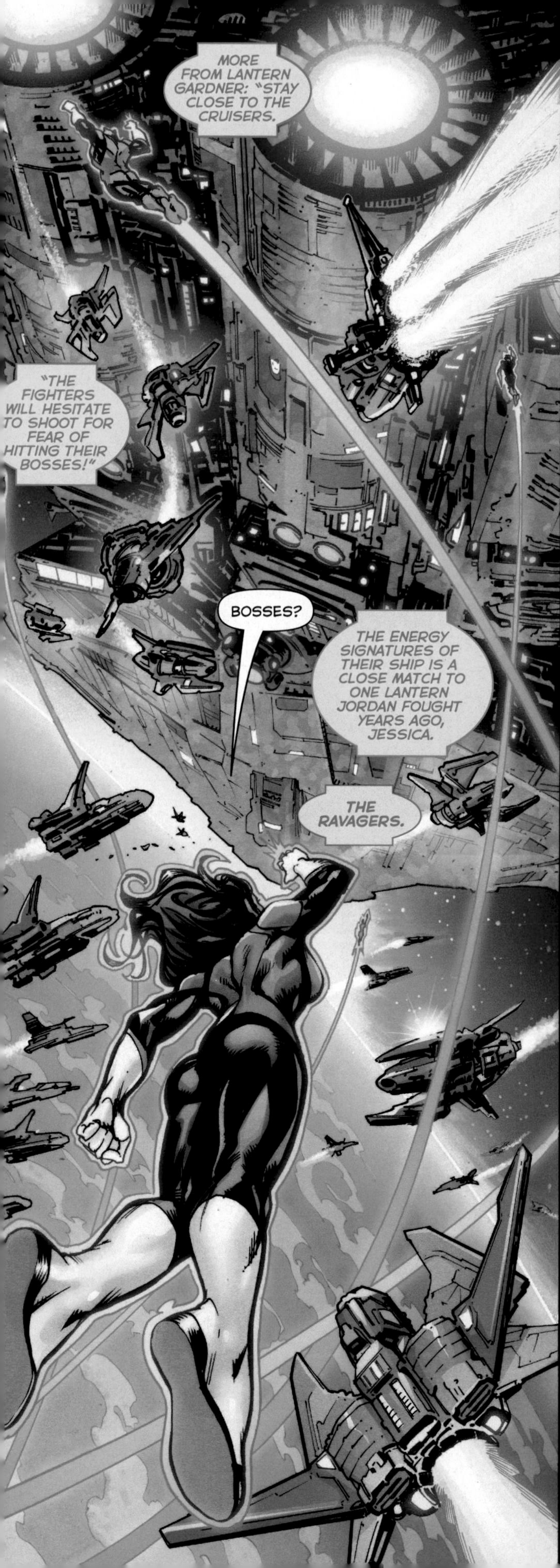
MORE FROM LANTERN GARDNER: "STAY CLOSE TO THE CRUISERS.
"THE FIGHTERS WILL HESITATE TO SHOOT FOR FEAR OF HITTING THEIR BOSSES!"
BOSSES?
THE ENERGY SIGNATURES OF THEIR SHIP IS A CLOSE MATCH TO ONE LANTERN JORDAN FOUGHT YEARS AGO, JESSICA.
THE RAVAGERS.

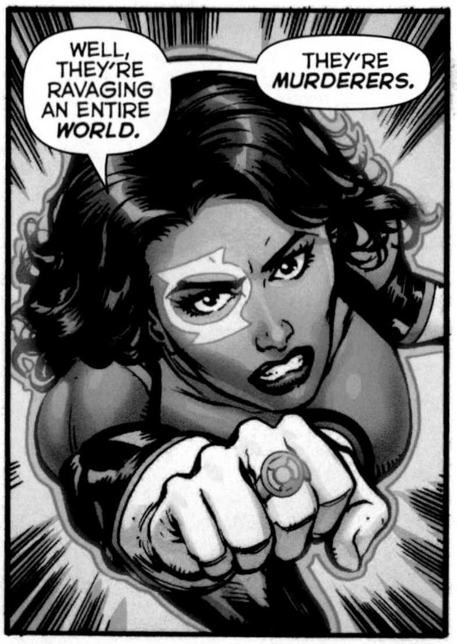
WELL, THEY'RE RAVAGING AN ENTIRE WORLD.
THEY'RE MURDERERS.

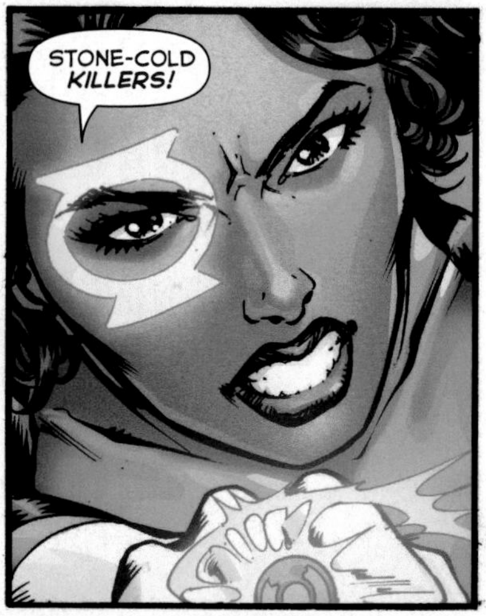
STONE-COLD KILLERS!

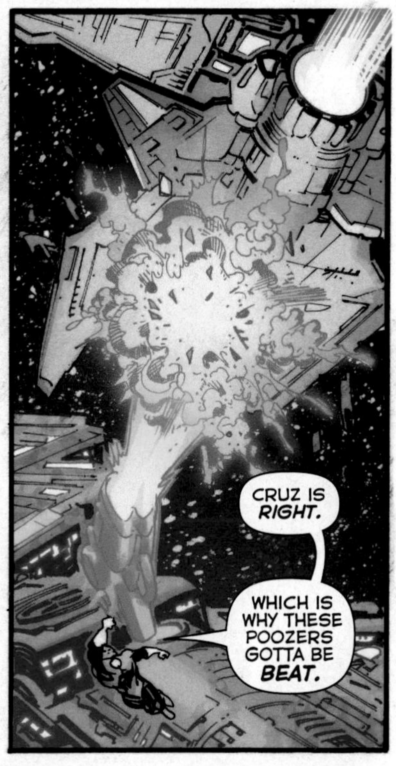
CRUZ IS RIGHT.
WHICH IS WHY THESE POOZERS GOTTA BE BEAT.

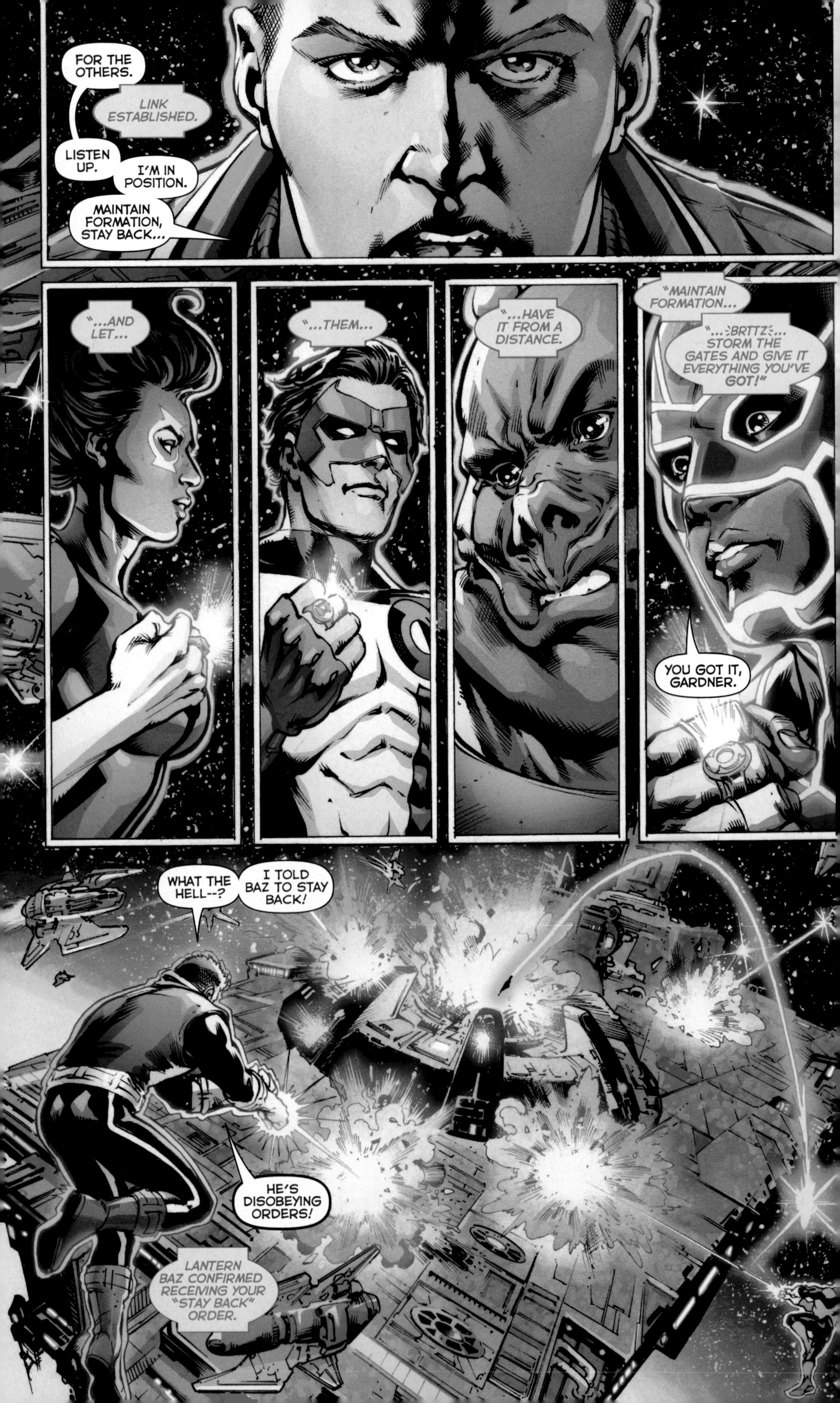
FOR THE OTHERS.
LINK ESTABLISHED.
LISTEN UP.
I'M IN POSITION.
MAINTAIN FORMATION, STAY BACK...
"...AND LET...
"...THEM...
"...HAVE IT FROM A DISTANCE.
"MAINTAIN FORMATION...
"...BRTTZ... STORM THE GATES AND GIVE IT EVERYTHING YOU'VE GOT!"
YOU GOT IT, GARDNER.
WHAT THE HELL--?
I TOLD BAZ TO STAY BACK!
HE'S DISOBEYING ORDERS!
LANTERN BAZ CONFIRMED RECEIVING YOUR "STAY BACK" ORDER.

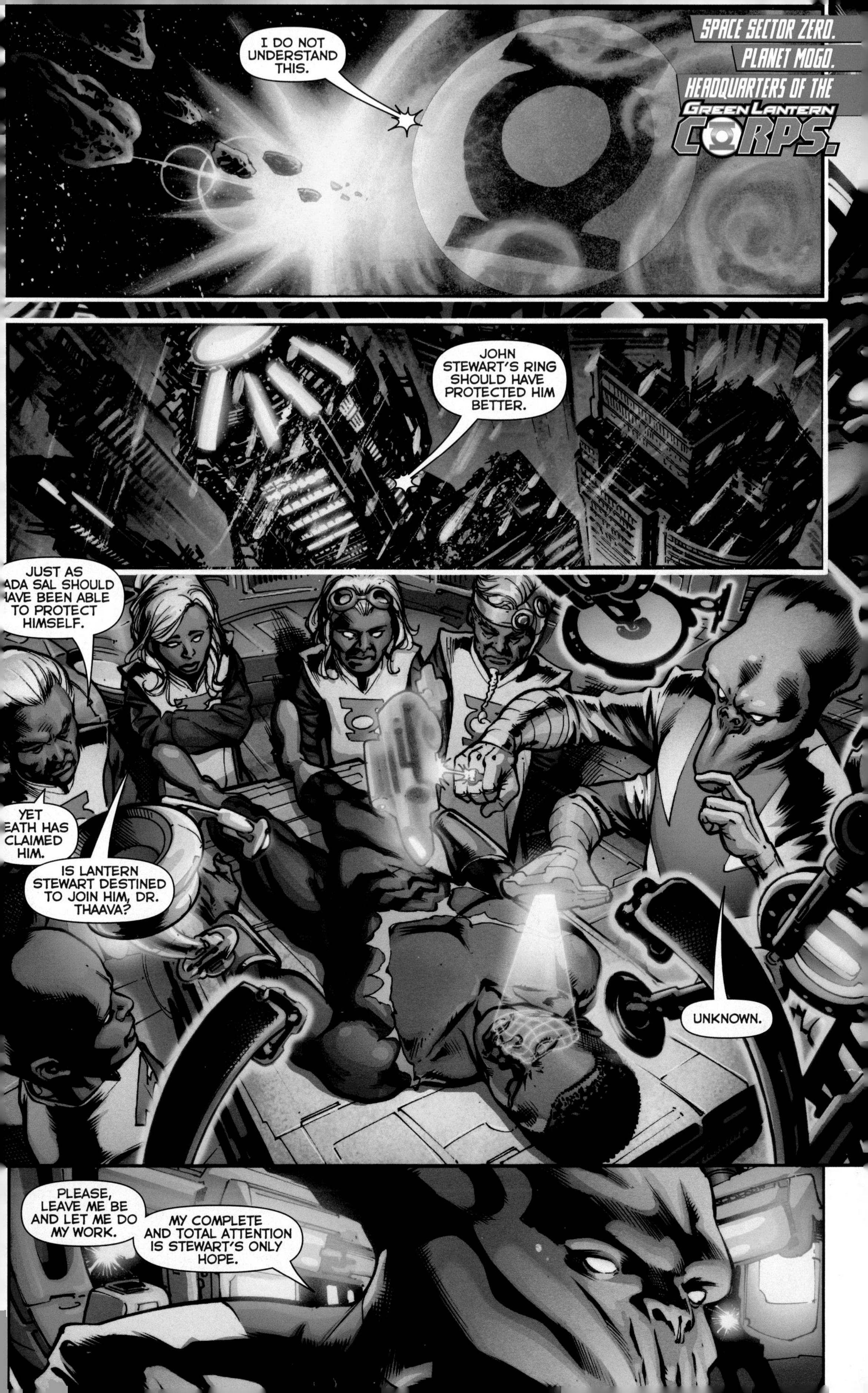
SPACE SECTOR ZERO.
PLANET MOGO.
HEADQUARTERS OF THE
GREEN LANTERN CORPS.
I DO NOT UNDERSTAND THIS.
JOHN STEWART'S RING SHOULD HAVE PROTECTED HIM BETTER.
JUST AS ADA SAL SHOULD HAVE BEEN ABLE TO PROTECT HIMSELF.
YET EATH HAS CLAIMED HIM.
IS LANTERN STEWART DESTINED TO JOIN HIM, DR. THAAVA?
UNKNOWN.
PLEASE, LEAVE ME BE AND LET ME DO MY WORK.
MY COMPLETE AND TOTAL ATTENTION IS STEWART'S ONLY HOPE.

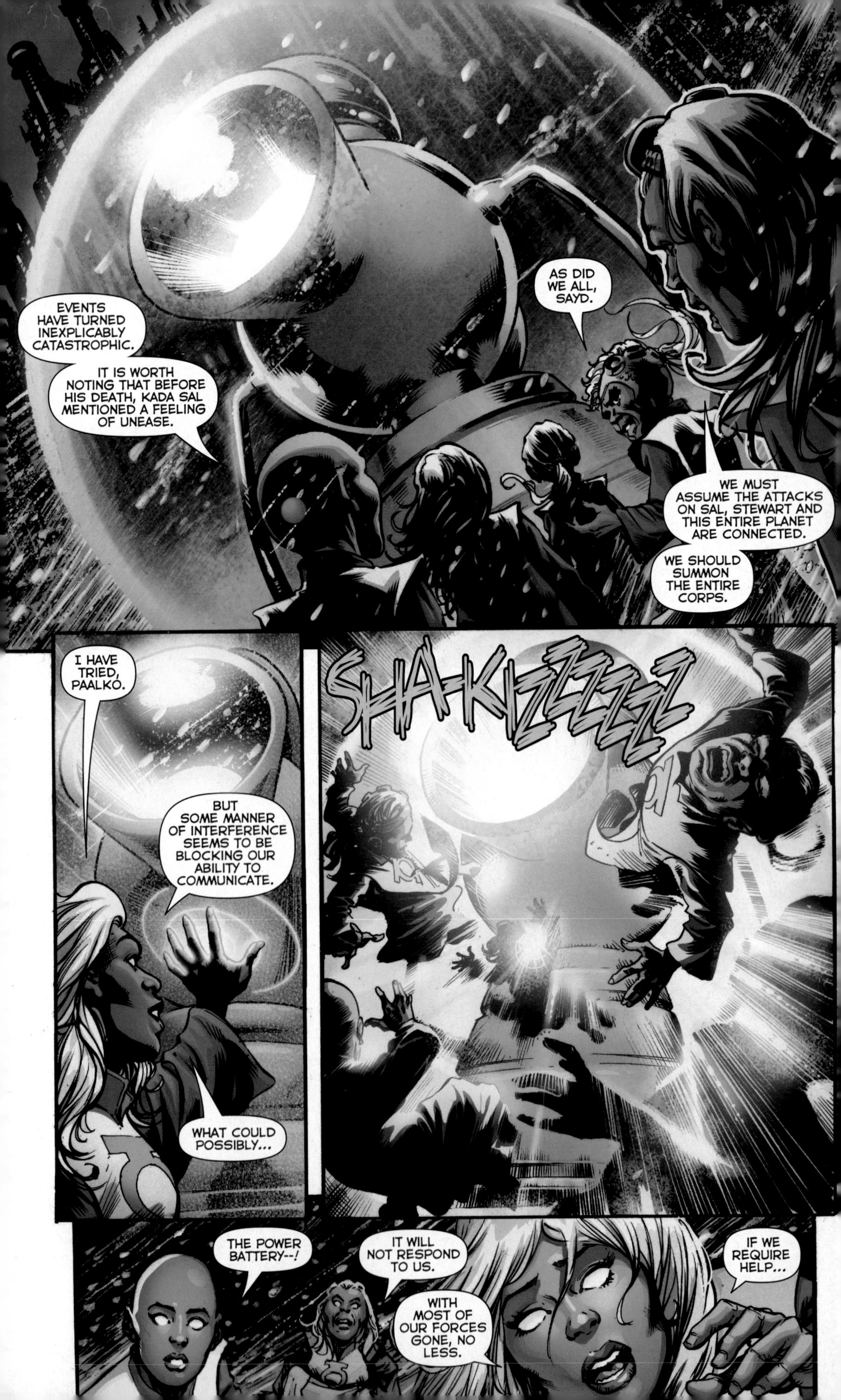
EVENTS HAVE TURNED INEXPLICABLY CATASTROPHIC.
IT IS WORTH NOTING THAT BEFORE HIS DEATH, KADA SAL MENTIONED A FEELING OF UNEASE.
AS DID WE ALL, SAYD.
WE MUST ASSUME THE ATTACKS ON SAL, STEWART AND THIS ENTIRE PLANET ARE CONNECTED.
WE SHOULD SUMMON THE ENTIRE CORPS.
I HAVE TRIED, PAALKO.
BUT SOME MANNER OF INTERFERENCE SEEMS TO BE BLOCKING OUR ABILITY TO COMMUNICATE.
WHAT COULD POSSIBLY...
SHA-KIZZZZZZ
THE POWER BATTERY--!
IT WILL NOT RESPOND TO US.
WITH MOST OF OUR FORCES GONE, NO LESS.
IF WE REQUIRE HELP...

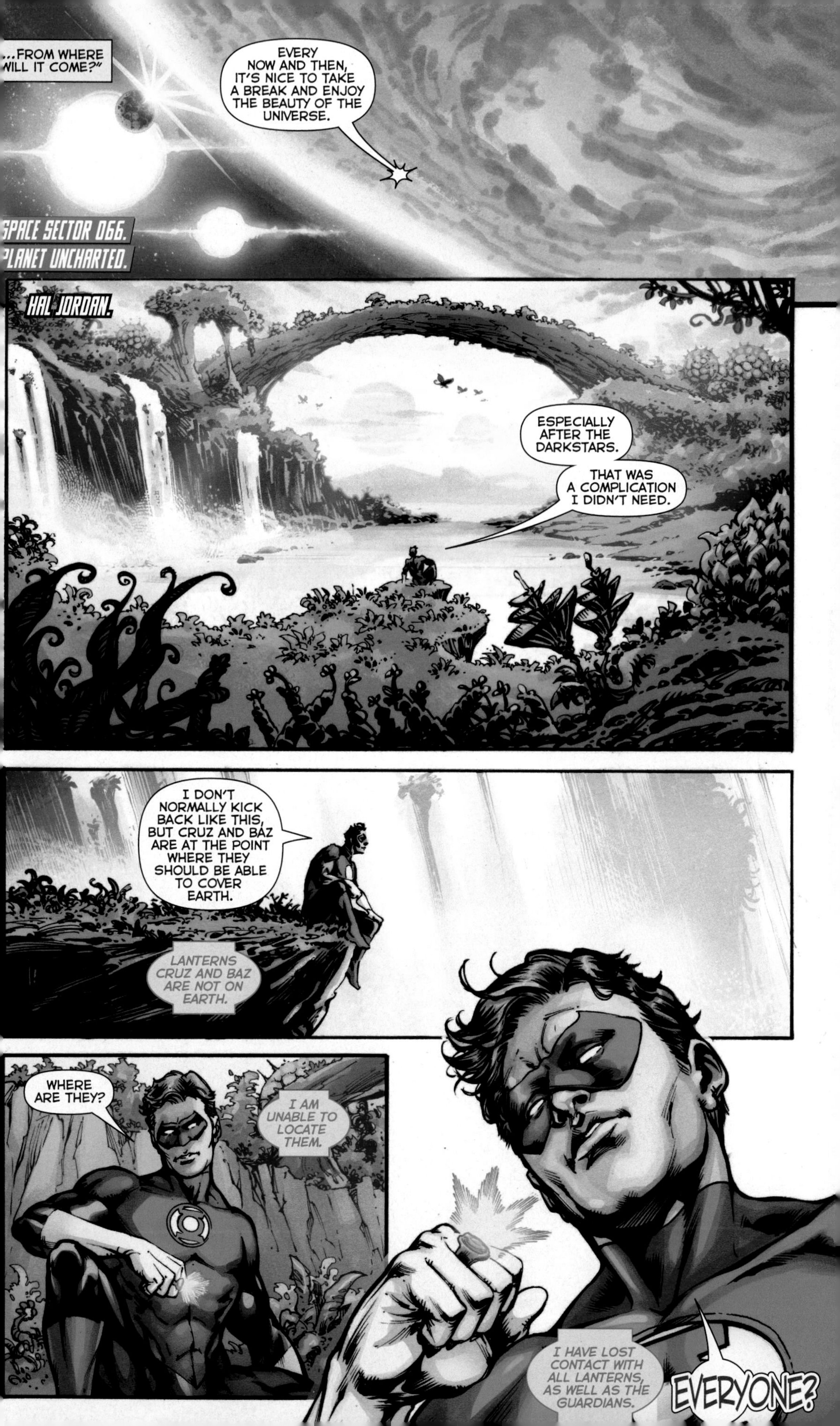
"...FROM WHERE WILL IT COME?"
EVERY NOW AND THEN, IT'S NICE TO TAKE A BREAK AND ENJOY THE BEAUTY OF THE UNIVERSE.
SPACE SECTOR 066. PLANET UNCHARTED.
HAL JORDAN.
ESPECIALLY AFTER THE DARKSTARS.
THAT WAS A COMPLICATION I DIDN'T NEED.
I DON'T NORMALLY KICK BACK LIKE THIS, BUT CRUZ AND BÁZ ARE AT THE POINT WHERE THEY SHOULD BE ABLE TO COVER EARTH.
LANTERNS CRUZ AND BAZ ARE NOT ON EARTH.
WHERE ARE THEY?
I AM UNABLE TO LOCATE THEM.
I HAVE LOST CONTACT WITH ALL LANTERNS, AS WELL AS THE GUARDIANS.
EVERYONE?

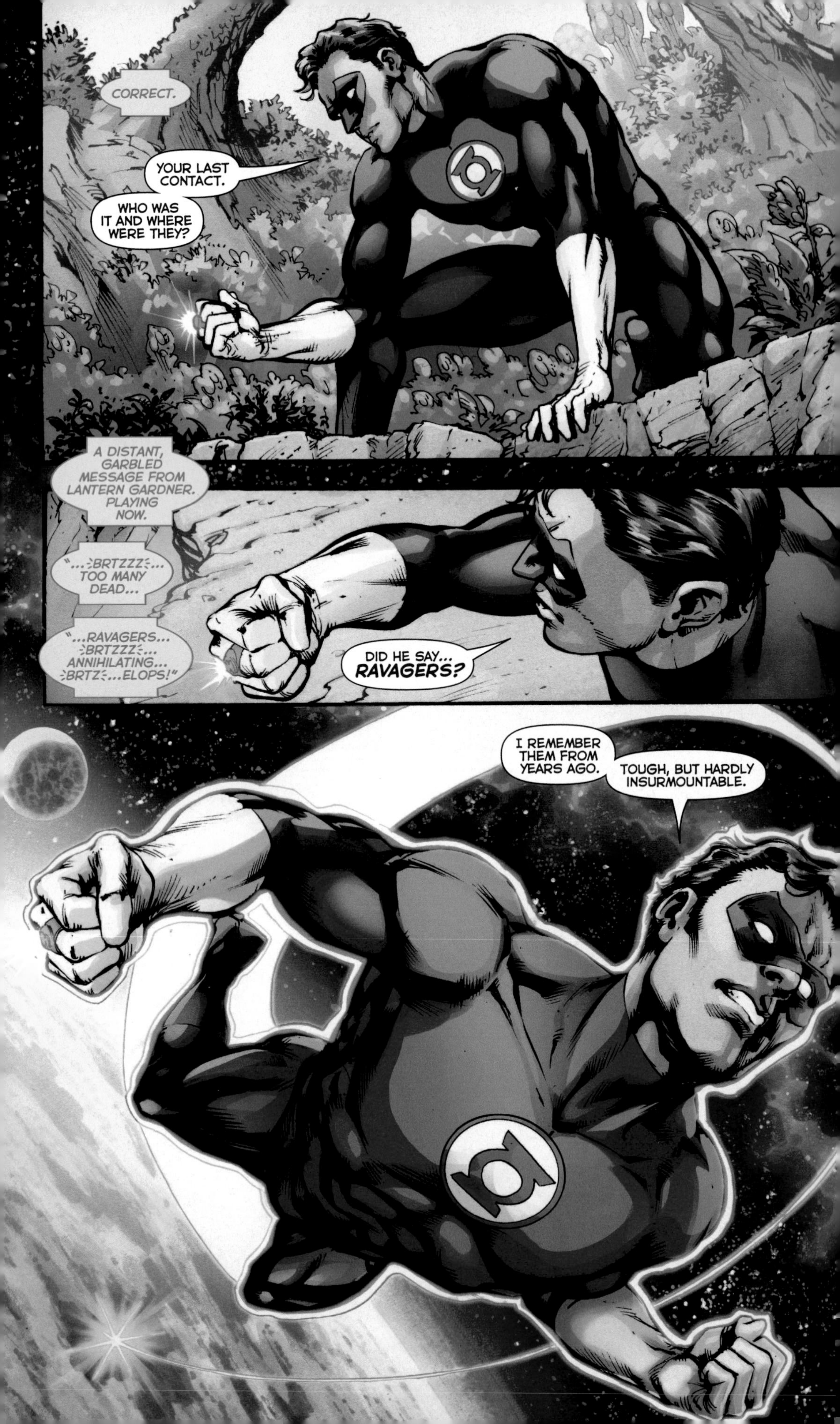

CORRECT.
YOUR LAST CONTACT.
WHO WAS IT AND WHERE WERE THEY?
A DISTANT, GARBLED MESSAGE FROM LANTERN GARDNER. PLAYING NOW.
"...BRTZZZ... TOO MANY DEAD...
"...RAVAGERS... BRTZZZ... ANNIHILATING... BRTZ...ELOPS!"
DID HE SAY... RAVAGERS?
I REMEMBER THEM FROM YEARS AGO.
TOUGH, BUT HARDLY INSURMOUNTABLE.

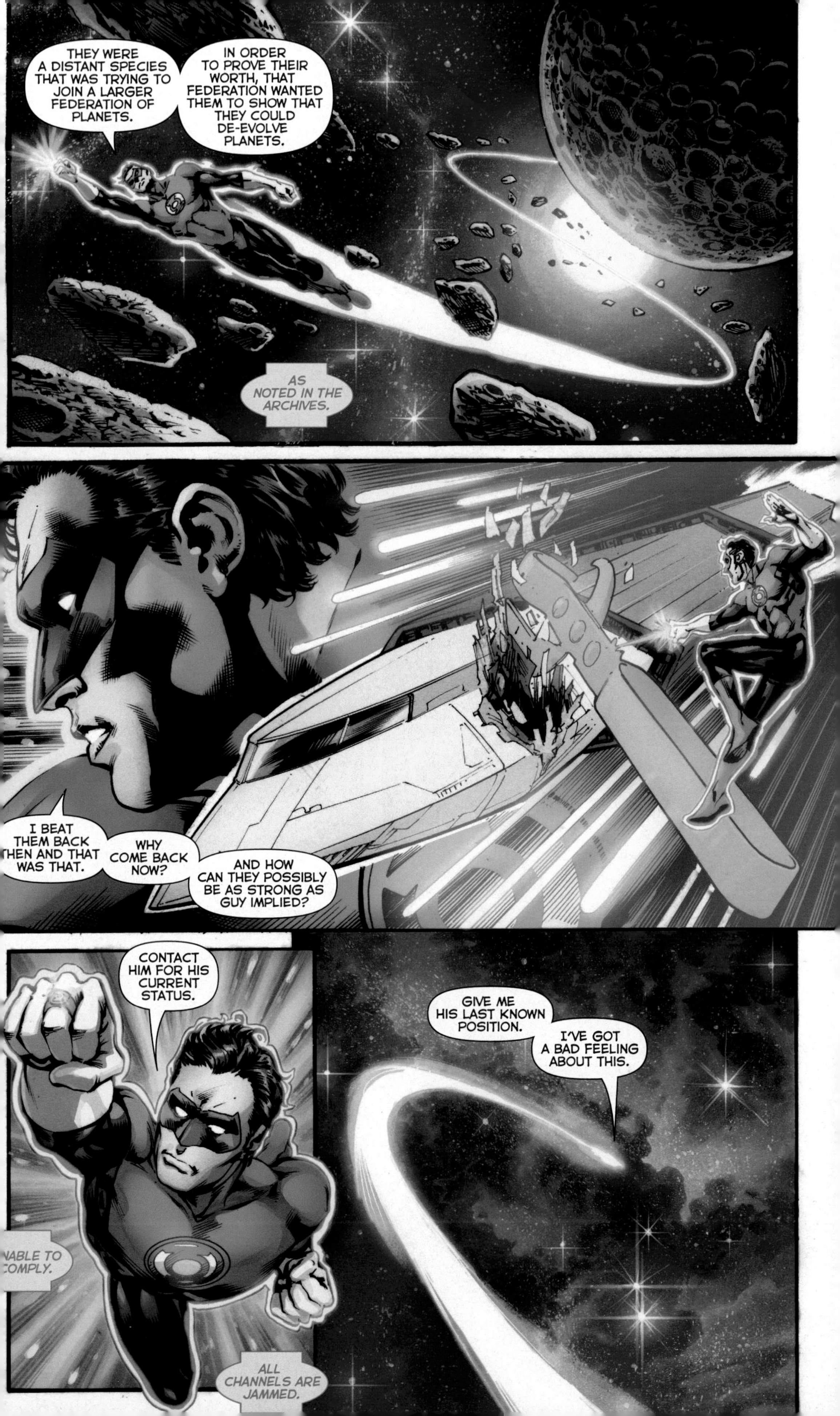
THEY WERE A DISTANT SPECIES THAT WAS TRYING TO JOIN A LARGER FEDERATION OF PLANETS.
IN ORDER TO PROVE THEIR WORTH, THAT FEDERATION WANTED THEM TO SHOW THAT THEY COULD DE-EVOLVE PLANETS.
AS NOTED IN THE ARCHIVES.
I BEAT THEM BACK THEN AND THAT WAS THAT.
WHY COME BACK NOW?
AND HOW CAN THEY POSSIBLY BE AS STRONG AS GUY IMPLIED?
CONTACT HIM FOR HIS CURRENT STATUS.
NABLE TO COMPLY.
GIVE ME HIS LAST KNOWN POSITION.
I'VE GOT A BAD FEELING ABOUT THIS.
ALL CHANNELS ARE JAMMED.

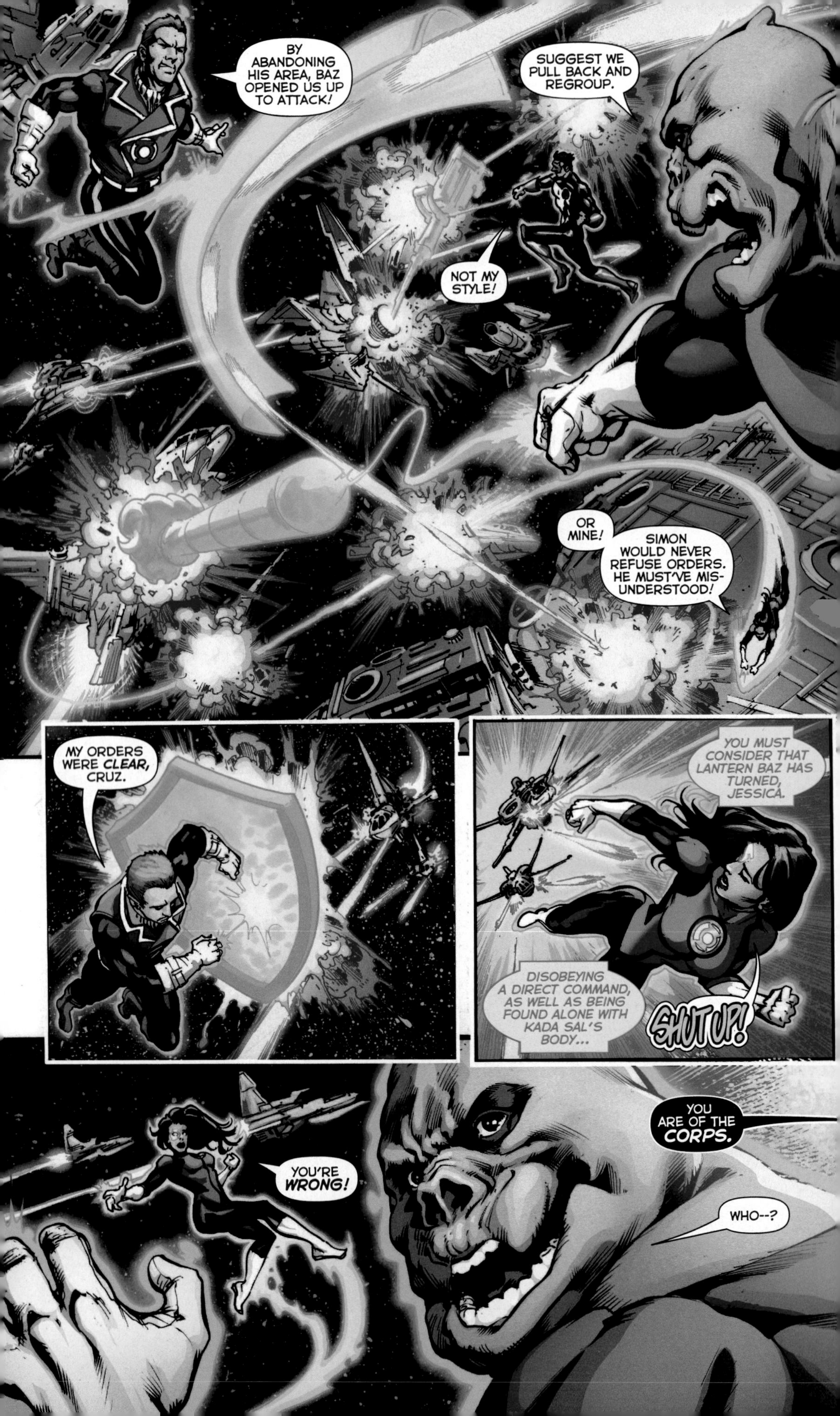
BY ABANDONING HIS AREA, BAZ OPENED US UP TO ATTACK!
SUGGEST WE PULL BACK AND REGROUP.
NOT MY STYLE!
OR MINE!
SIMON WOULD NEVER REFUSE ORDERS. HE MUST'VE MIS-UNDERSTOOD!
MY ORDERS WERE CLEAR, CRUZ.
YOU MUST CONSIDER THAT LANTERN BAZ HAS TURNED, JESSICA.
DISOBEYING A DIRECT COMMAND, AS WELL AS BEING FOUND ALONE WITH KADA SAL'S BODY...
SHUT UP!
YOU'RE WRONG!
YOU ARE OF THE CORPS.
WHO--?

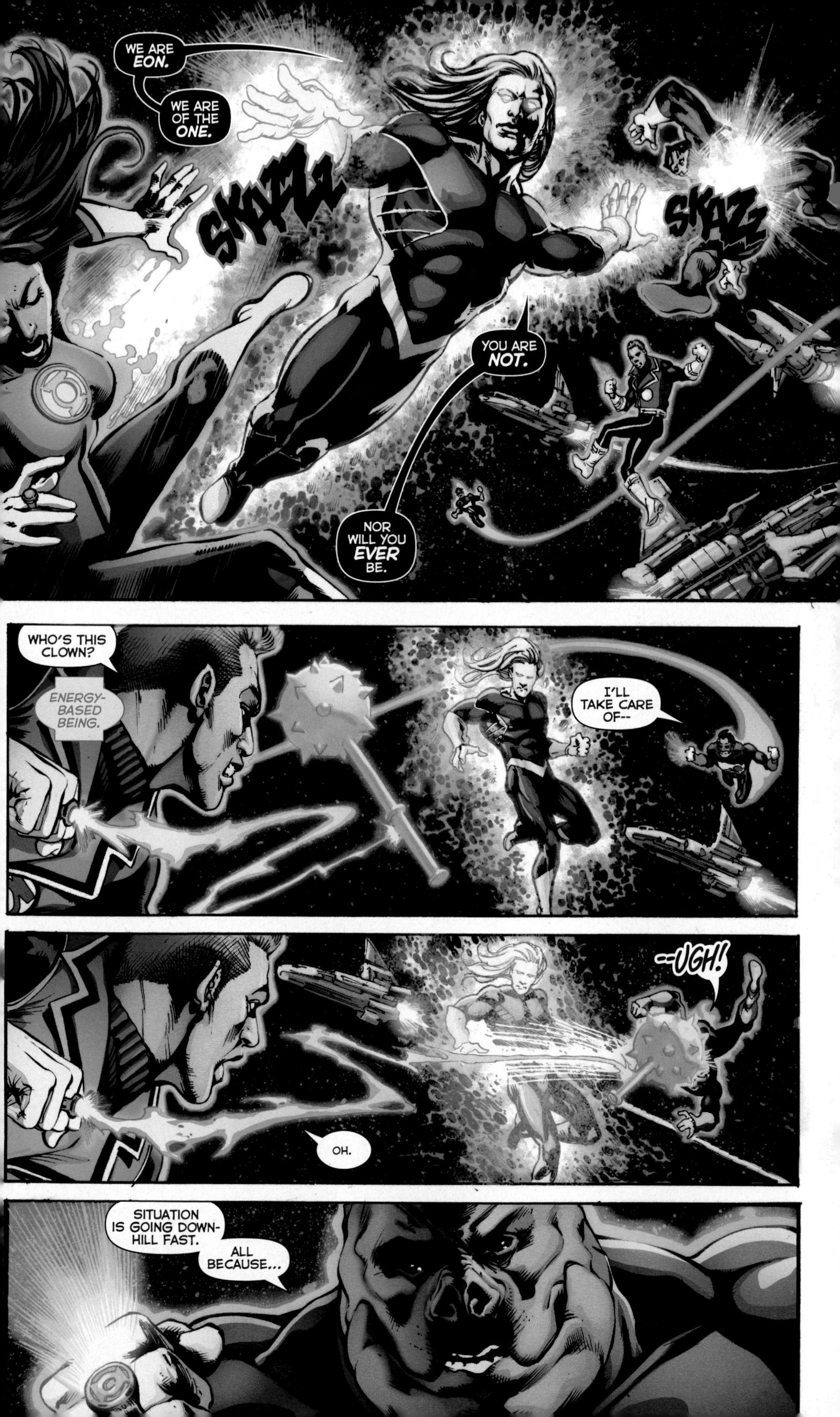
WE ARE EON.
WE ARE OF THE ONE.
SKZZZ
SKZZZ
YOU ARE NOT.
NOR WILL YOU EVER BE.
WHO'S THIS CLOWN?
ENERGY-BASED BEING.
I'LL TAKE CARE OF--
--UGH!
OH.
SITUATION IS GOING DOWN-HILL FAST.
ALL BECAUSE...

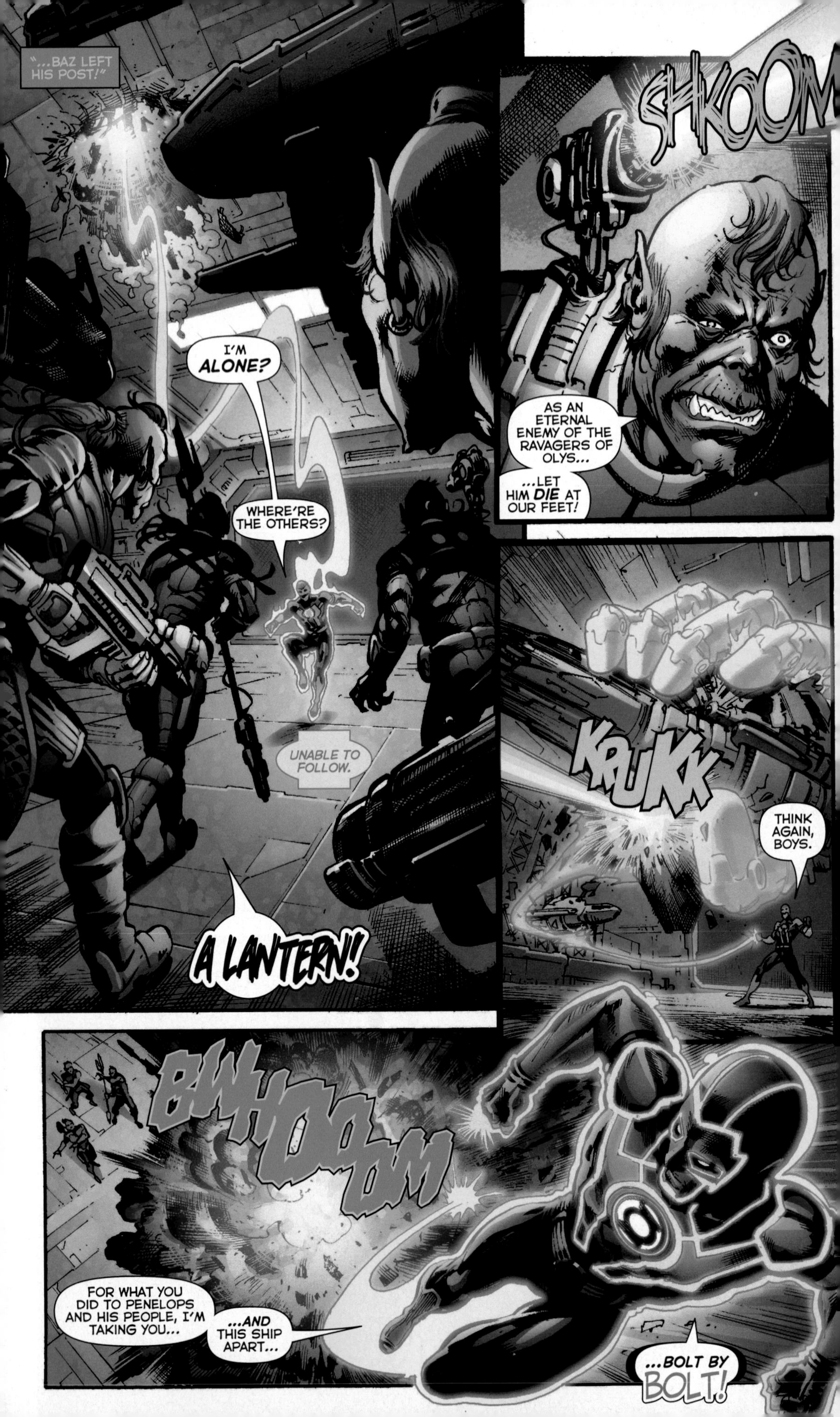

"...BAZ LEFT HIS POST!"
I'M ALONE?
WHERE'RE THE OTHERS?
UNABLE TO FOLLOW.
A LANTERN!
SHKOOM
AS AN ETERNAL ENEMY OF THE RAVAGERS OF OLYS...
...LET HIM DIE AT OUR FEET!
KRUKK
THINK AGAIN, BOYS.
BWHOOOM
FOR WHAT YOU DID TO PENELOPS AND HIS PEOPLE, I'M TAKING YOU...
...AND THIS SHIP APART...
...BOLT BY BOLT!

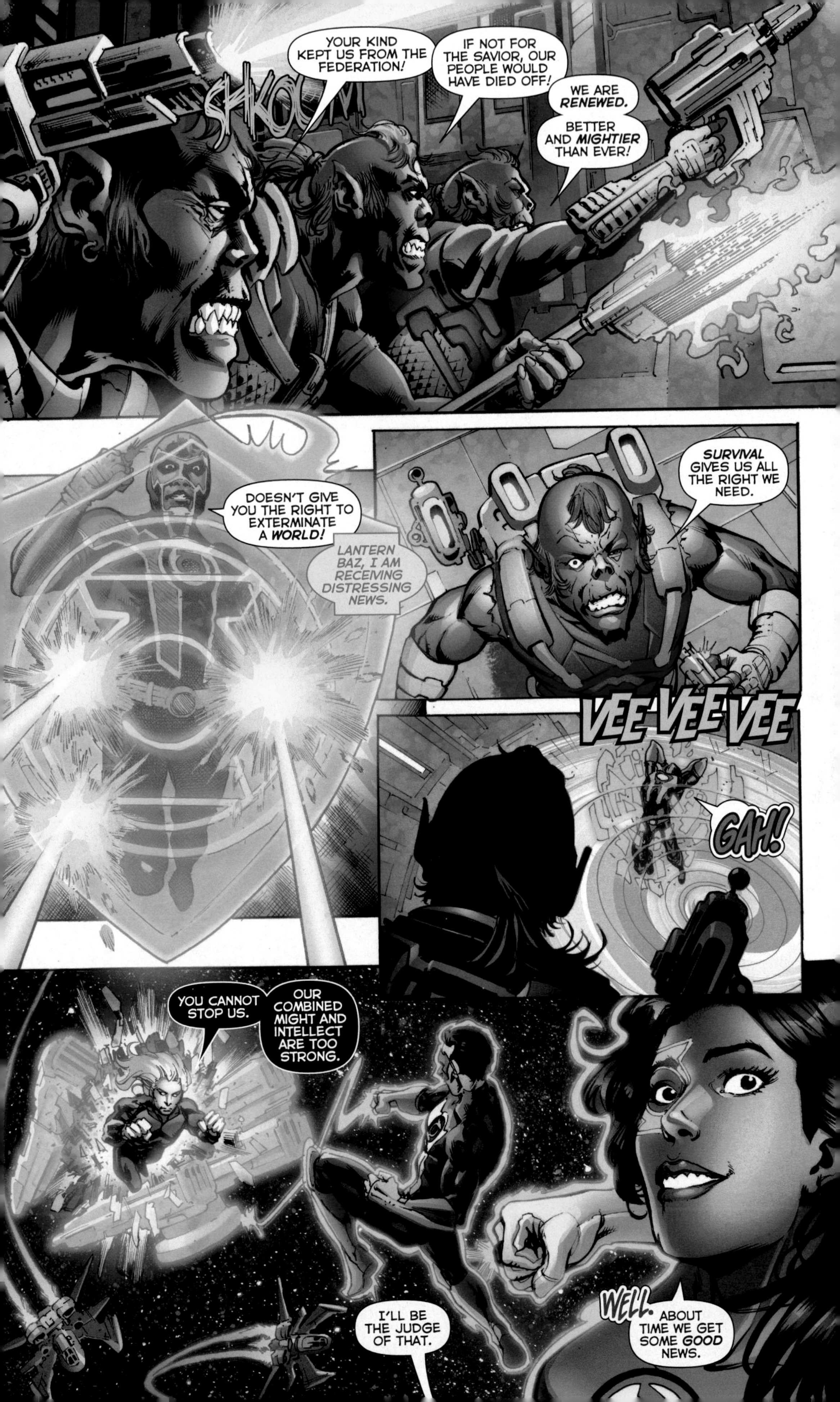

SHKOOM
YOUR KIND KEPT US FROM THE FEDERATION!
IF NOT FOR THE SAVIOR, OUR PEOPLE WOULD HAVE DIED OFF!
WE ARE RENEWED.
BETTER AND MIGHTIER THAN EVER!
DOESN'T GIVE YOU THE RIGHT TO EXTERMINATE A WORLD!
LANTERN BAZ, I AM RECEIVING DISTRESSING NEWS.
SURVIVAL GIVES US ALL THE RIGHT WE NEED.
VEE VEE VEE
GAH!
YOU CANNOT STOP US.
OUR COMBINED MIGHT AND INTELLECT ARE TOO STRONG.
I'LL BE THE JUDGE OF THAT.
WELL.
ABOUT TIME WE GET SOME GOOD NEWS.

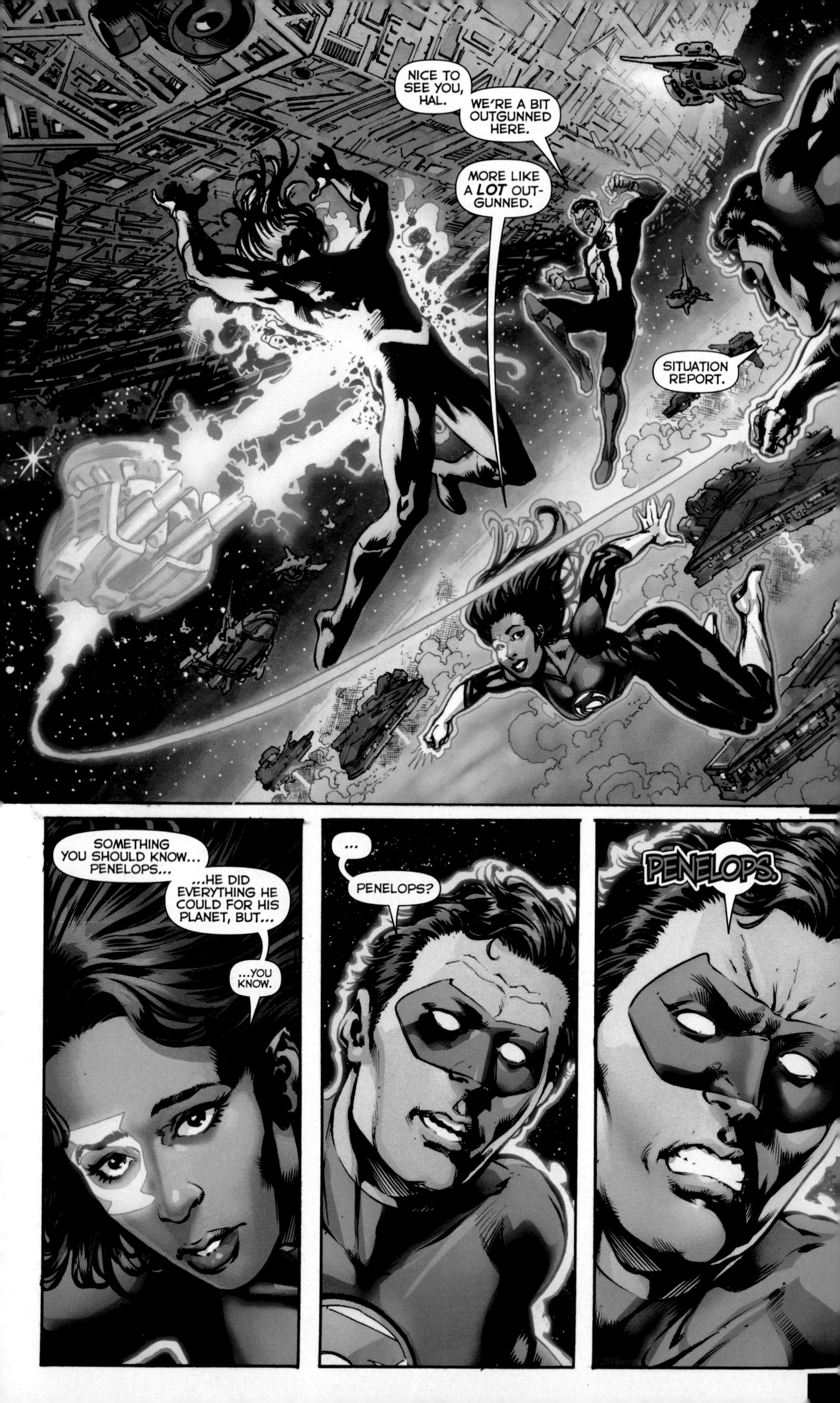
NICE TO SEE YOU, HAL.
WE'RE A BIT OUTGUNNED HERE.
MORE LIKE A LOT OUT-GUNNED.
SITUATION REPORT.
SOMETHING YOU SHOULD KNOW... PENELOPS...
...HE DID EVERYTHING HE COULD FOR HIS PLANET, BUT...
...YOU KNOW.
...
PENELOPS?
PENELOPS.

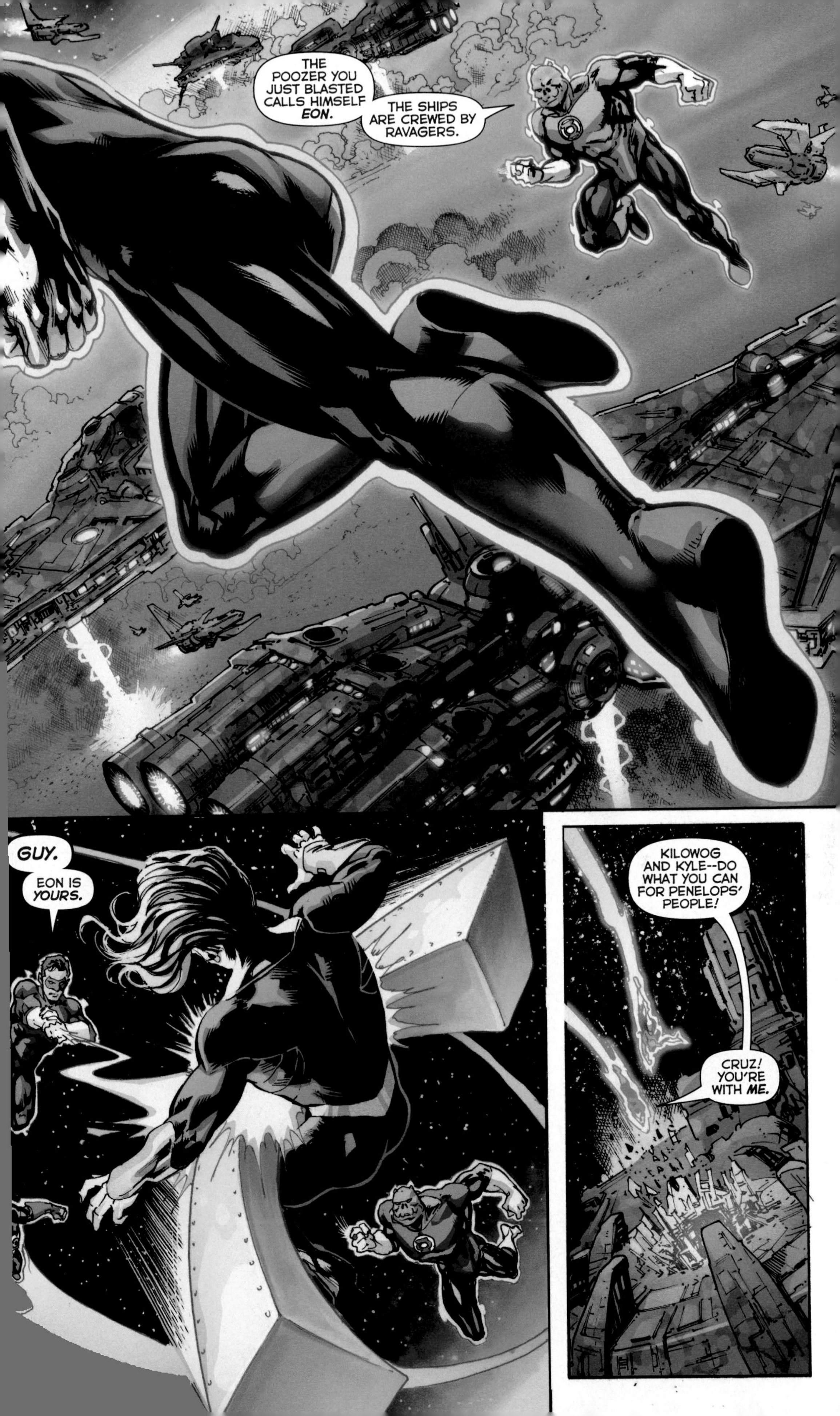
THE POOZER YOU JUST BLASTED CALLS HIMSELF EON.
THE SHIPS ARE CREWED BY RAVAGERS.
GUY.
EON IS YOURS.
KILOWOG AND KYLE--DO WHAT YOU CAN FOR PENELOPS' PEOPLE!
CRUZ! YOU'RE WITH ME.

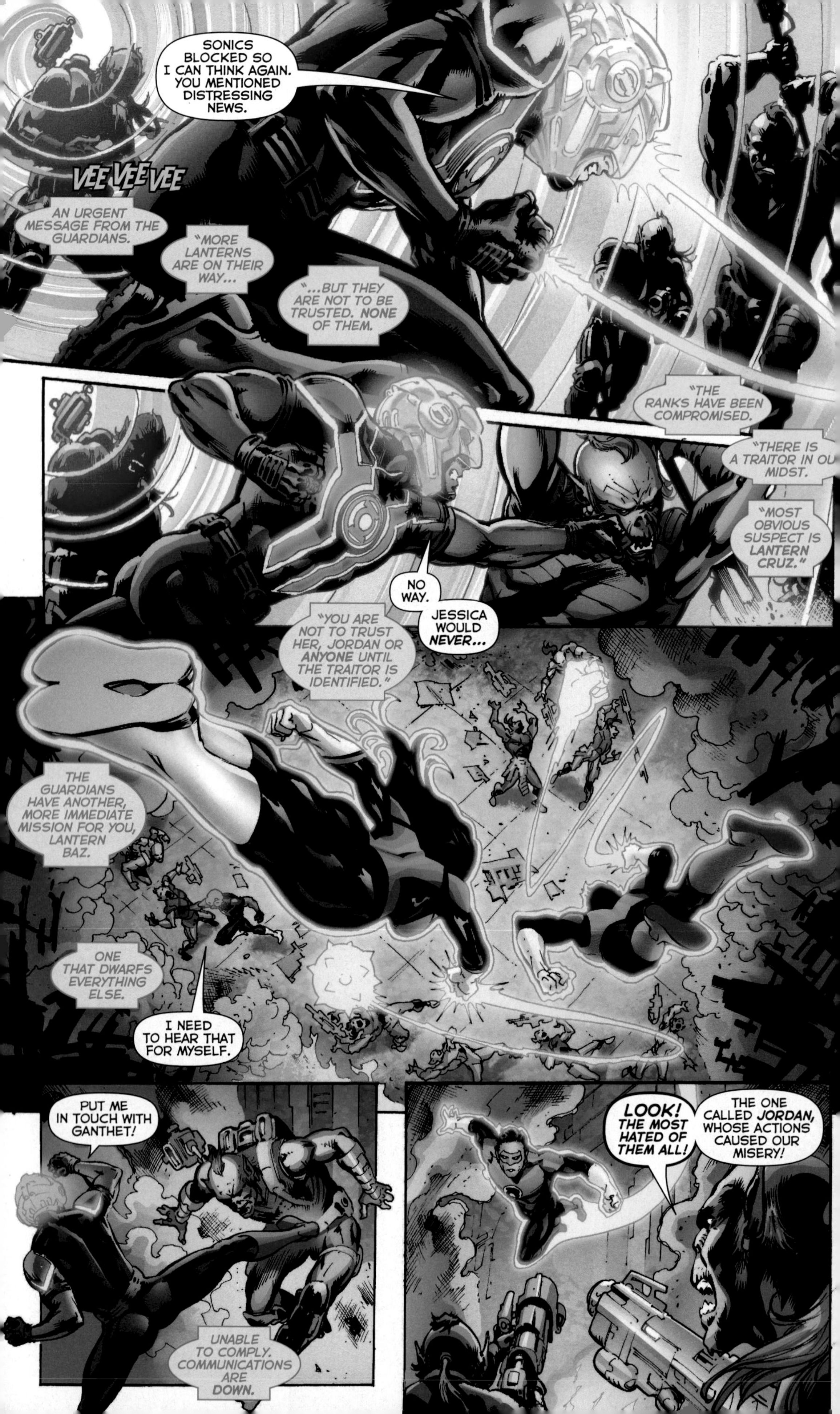

SONICS BLOCKED SO I CAN THINK AGAIN. YOU MENTIONED DISTRESSING NEWS.
VEE VEE VEE
AN URGENT MESSAGE FROM THE GUARDIANS.
"MORE LANTERNS ARE ON THEIR WAY...
"...BUT THEY ARE NOT TO BE TRUSTED. NONE OF THEM.
"THE RANKS HAVE BEEN COMPROMISED.
"THERE IS A TRAITOR IN OU MIDST.
"MOST OBVIOUS SUSPECT IS LANTERN CRUZ."
NO WAY.
JESSICA WOULD NEVER...
"YOU ARE NOT TO TRUST HER, JORDAN OR ANYONE UNTIL THE TRAITOR IS IDENTIFIED."
THE GUARDIANS HAVE ANOTHER, MORE IMMEDIATE MISSION FOR YOU, LANTERN BAZ.
ONE THAT DWARFS EVERYTHING ELSE.
I NEED TO HEAR THAT FOR MYSELF.
PUT ME IN TOUCH WITH GANTHET!
UNABLE TO COMPLY. COMMUNICATIONS ARE DOWN.
LOOK! THE MOST HATED OF THEM ALL!
THE ONE CALLED JORDAN, WHOSE ACTIONS CAUSED OUR MISERY!

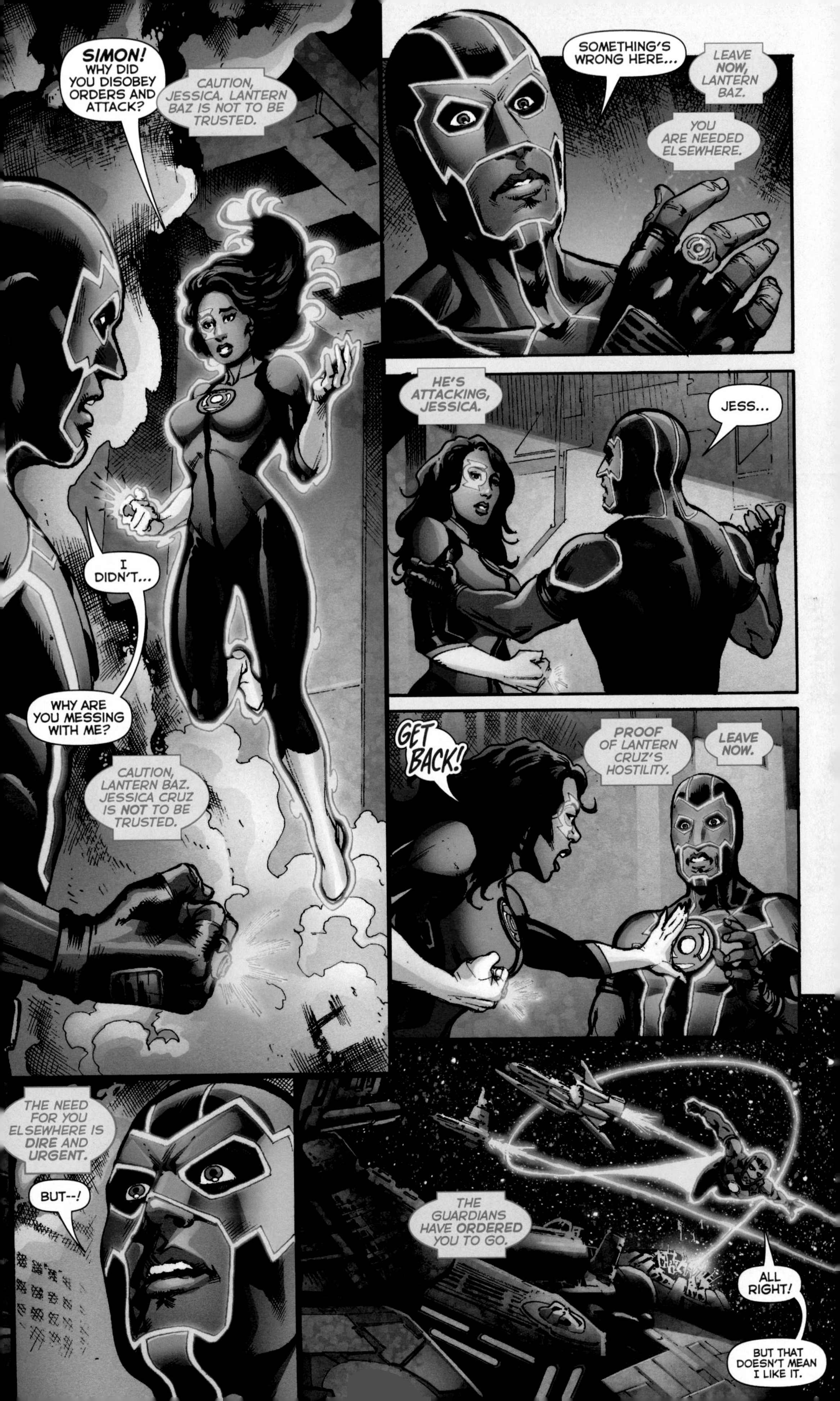
SIMON! WHY DID YOU DISOBEY ORDERS AND ATTACK?
CAUTION, JESSICA. LANTERN BAZ IS NOT TO BE TRUSTED.
I DIDN'T...
WHY ARE YOU MESSING WITH ME?
CAUTION, LANTERN BAZ. JESSICA CRUZ IS NOT TO BE TRUSTED.
SOMETHING'S WRONG HERE...
LEAVE NOW, LANTERN BAZ.
YOU ARE NEEDED ELSEWHERE.
HE'S ATTACKING, JESSICA.
JESS...
GET BACK!
PROOF OF LANTERN CRUZ'S HOSTILITY.
LEAVE NOW.
THE NEED FOR YOU ELSEWHERE IS DIRE AND URGENT.
BUT--!
THE GUARDIANS HAVE ORDERED YOU TO GO.
ALL RIGHT!
BUT THAT DOESN'T MEAN I LIKE IT.

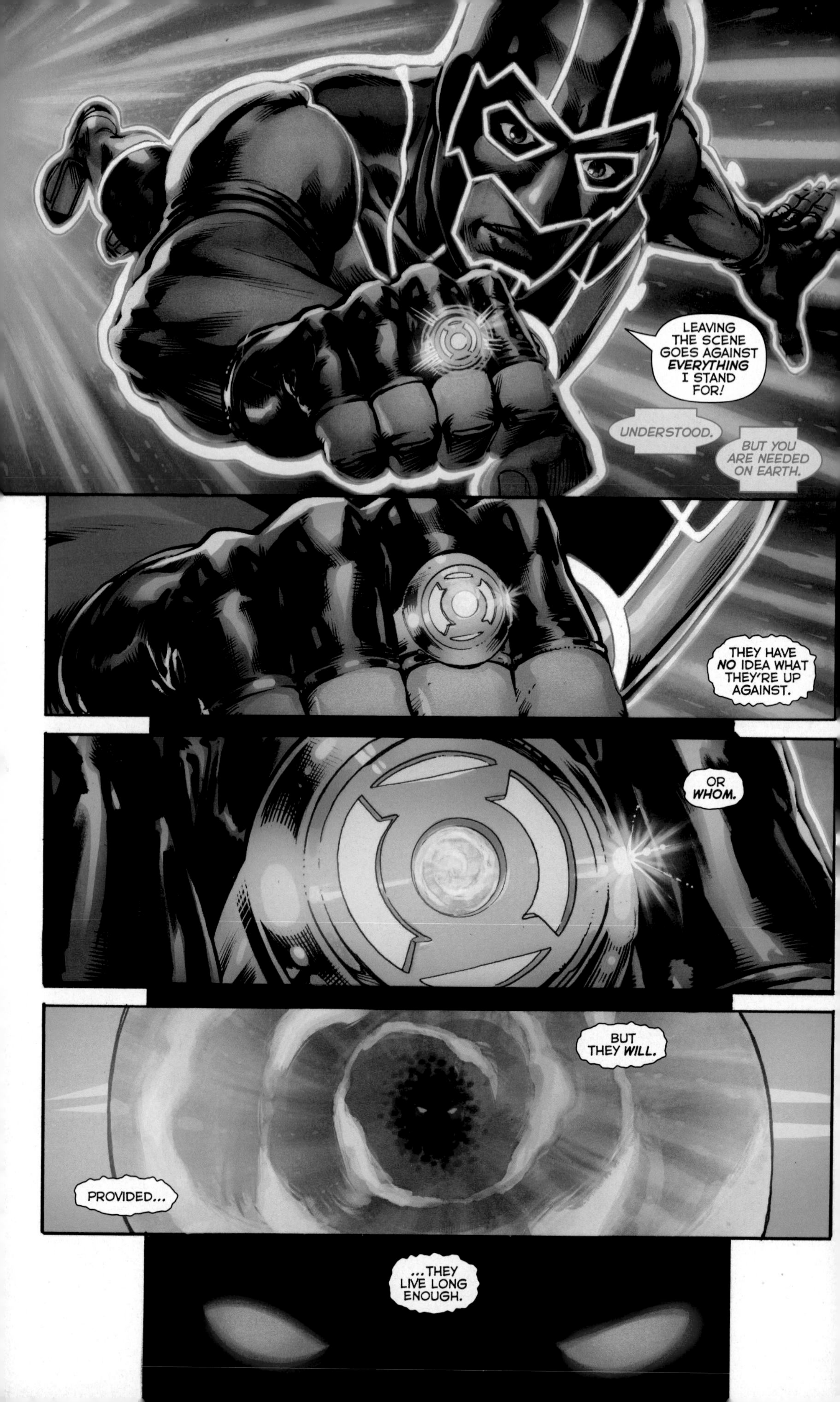

LEAVING THE SCENE GOES AGAINST EVERYTHING I STAND FOR!
UNDERSTOOD.
BUT YOU ARE NEEDED ON EARTH.
THEY HAVE NO IDEA WHAT THEY'RE UP AGAINST.
OR WHOM.
BUT THEY WILL.
PROVIDED...
...THEY LIVE LONG ENOUGH.

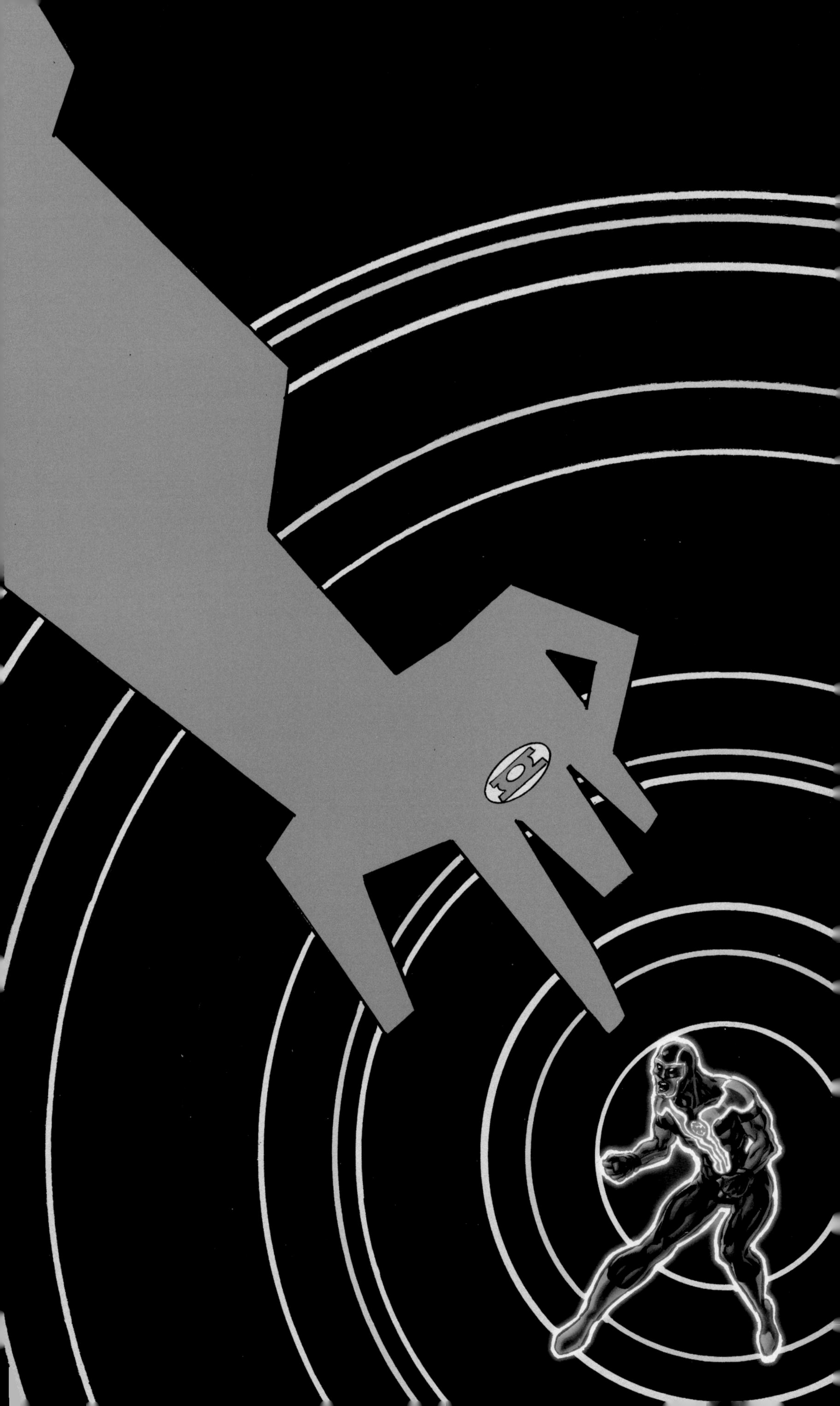

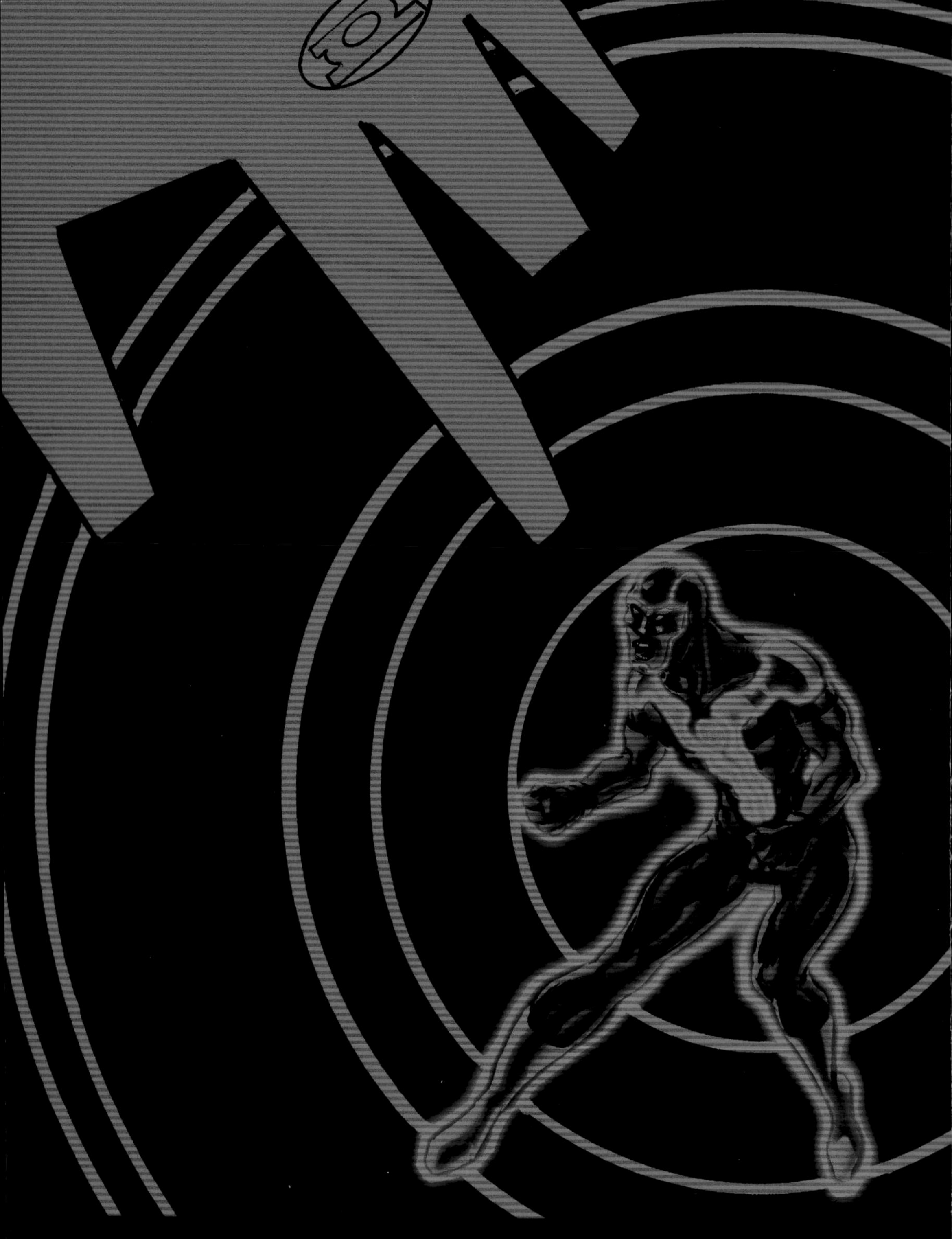

GREEN LANTERNS
#53

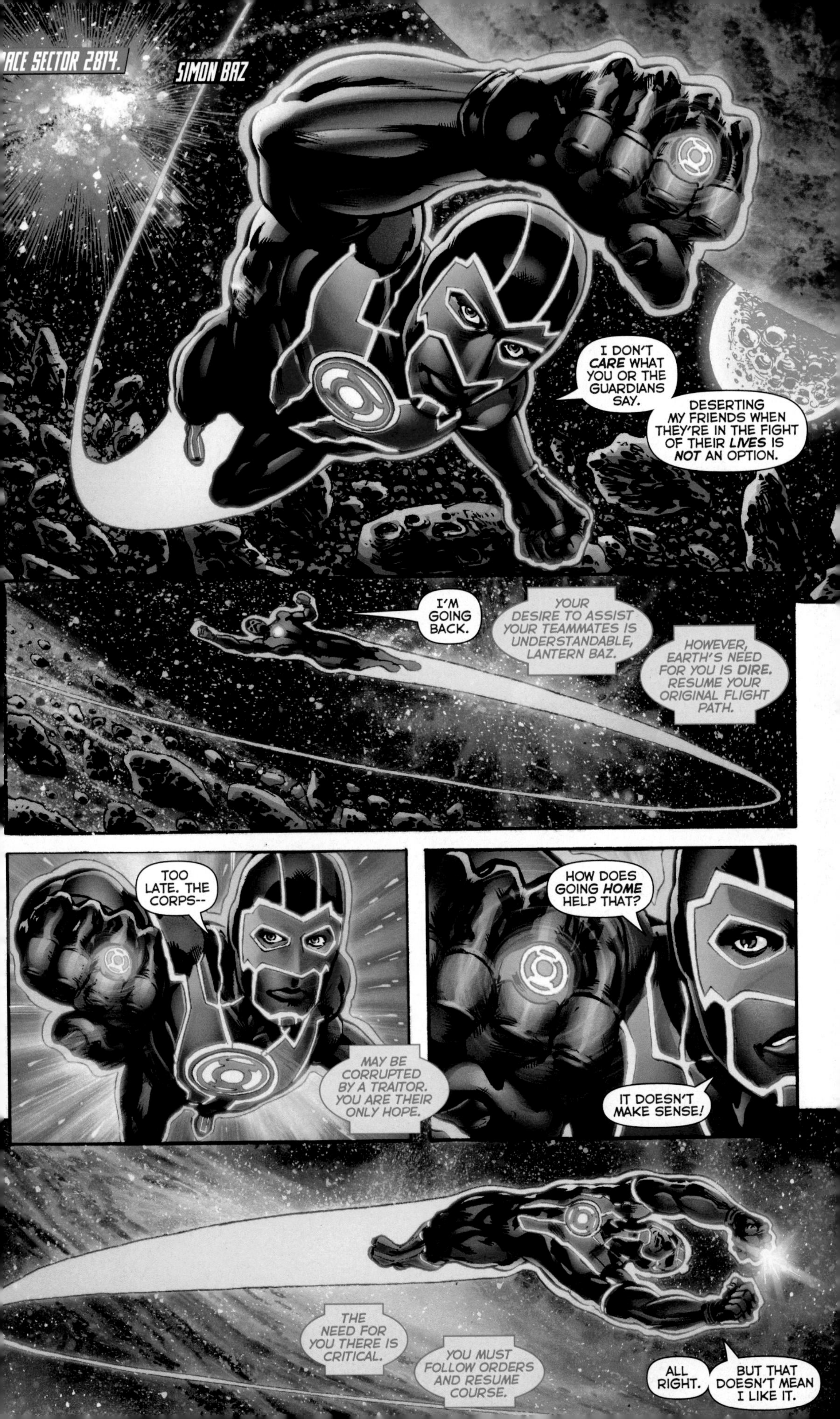

ACE SECTOR 2814.
SIMON BAZ
I DON'T CARE WHAT YOU OR THE GUARDIANS SAY.
DESERTING MY FRIENDS WHEN THEY'RE IN THE FIGHT OF THEIR LIVES IS NOT AN OPTION.
I'M GOING BACK.
YOUR DESIRE TO ASSIST YOUR TEAMMATES IS UNDERSTANDABLE, LANTERN BAZ.
HOWEVER, EARTH'S NEED FOR YOU IS DIRE. RESUME YOUR ORIGINAL FLIGHT PATH.
TOO LATE. THE CORPS--
MAY BE CORRUPTED BY A TRAITOR. YOU ARE THEIR ONLY HOPE.
HOW DOES GOING HOME HELP THAT?
IT DOESN'T MAKE SENSE!
THE NEED FOR YOU THERE IS CRITICAL.
YOU MUST FOLLOW ORDERS AND RESUME COURSE.
ALL RIGHT.
BUT THAT DOESN'T MEAN I LIKE IT.

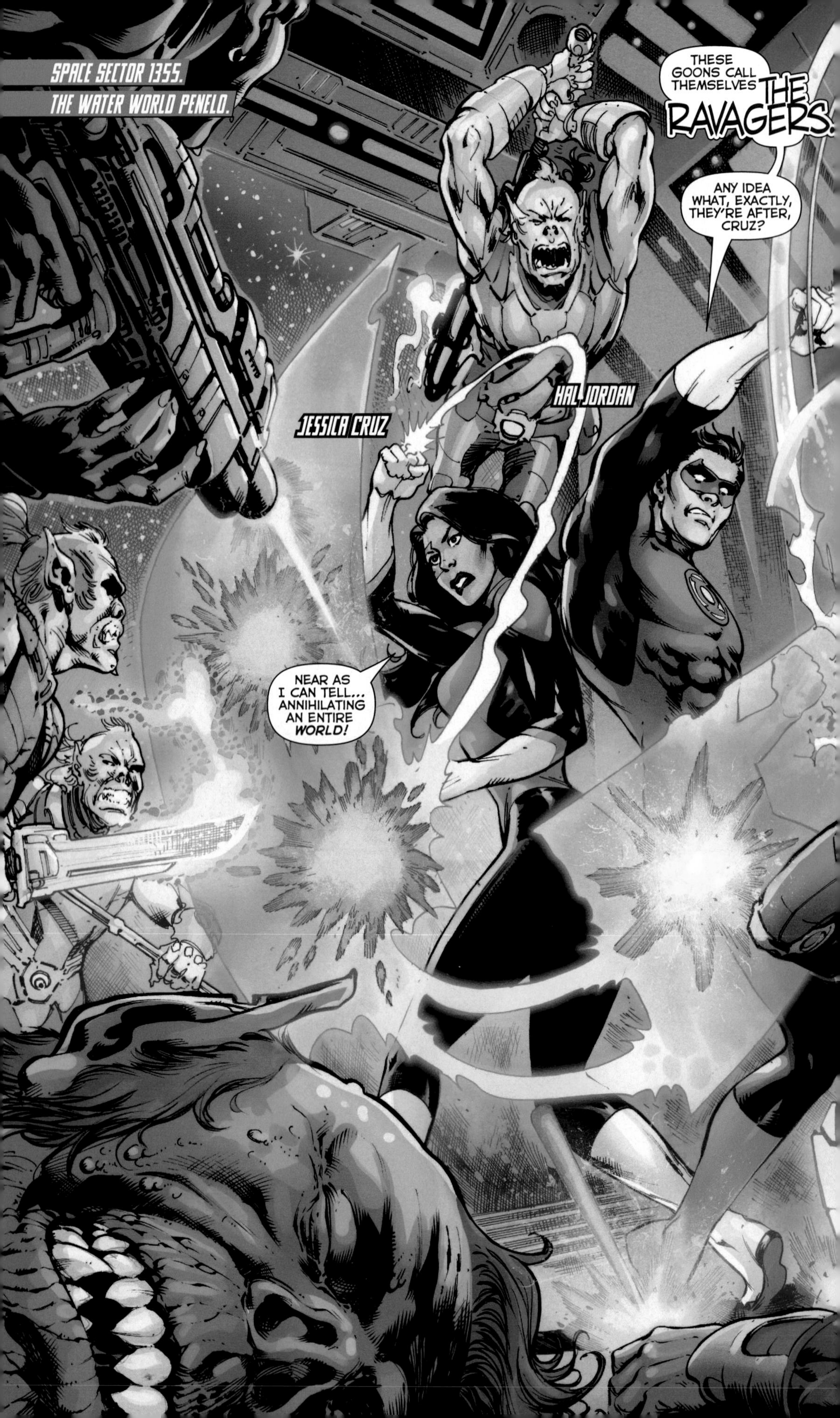

SPACE SECTOR 1355.
THE WATER WORLD PENELO.
THESE GOONS CALL THEMSELVES THE RAVAGERS.
ANY IDEA WHAT, EXACTLY, THEY'RE AFTER, CRUZ?
HAL JORDAN
JESSICA CRUZ
NEAR AS I CAN TELL... ANNIHILATING AN ENTIRE WORLD!

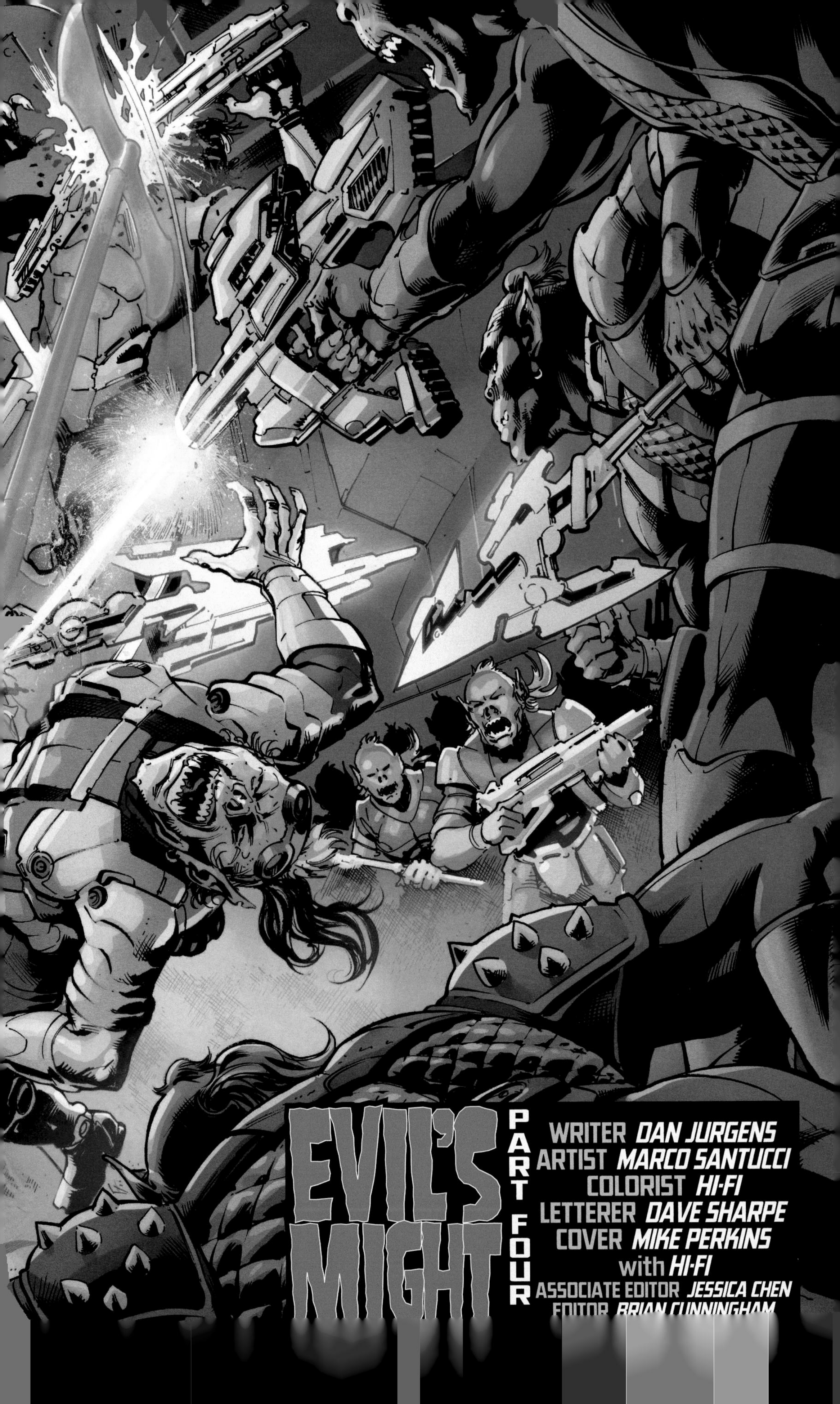
EVIL'S MIGHT
PART FOUR
WRITER DAN JURGENS
ARTIST MARCO SANTUCCI
COLORIST HI-FI
LETTERER DAVE SHARPE
COVER MIKE PERKINS
with HI-FI
ASSOCIATE EDITOR JESSICA CHEN
EDITOR BRIAN CUNNINGHAM

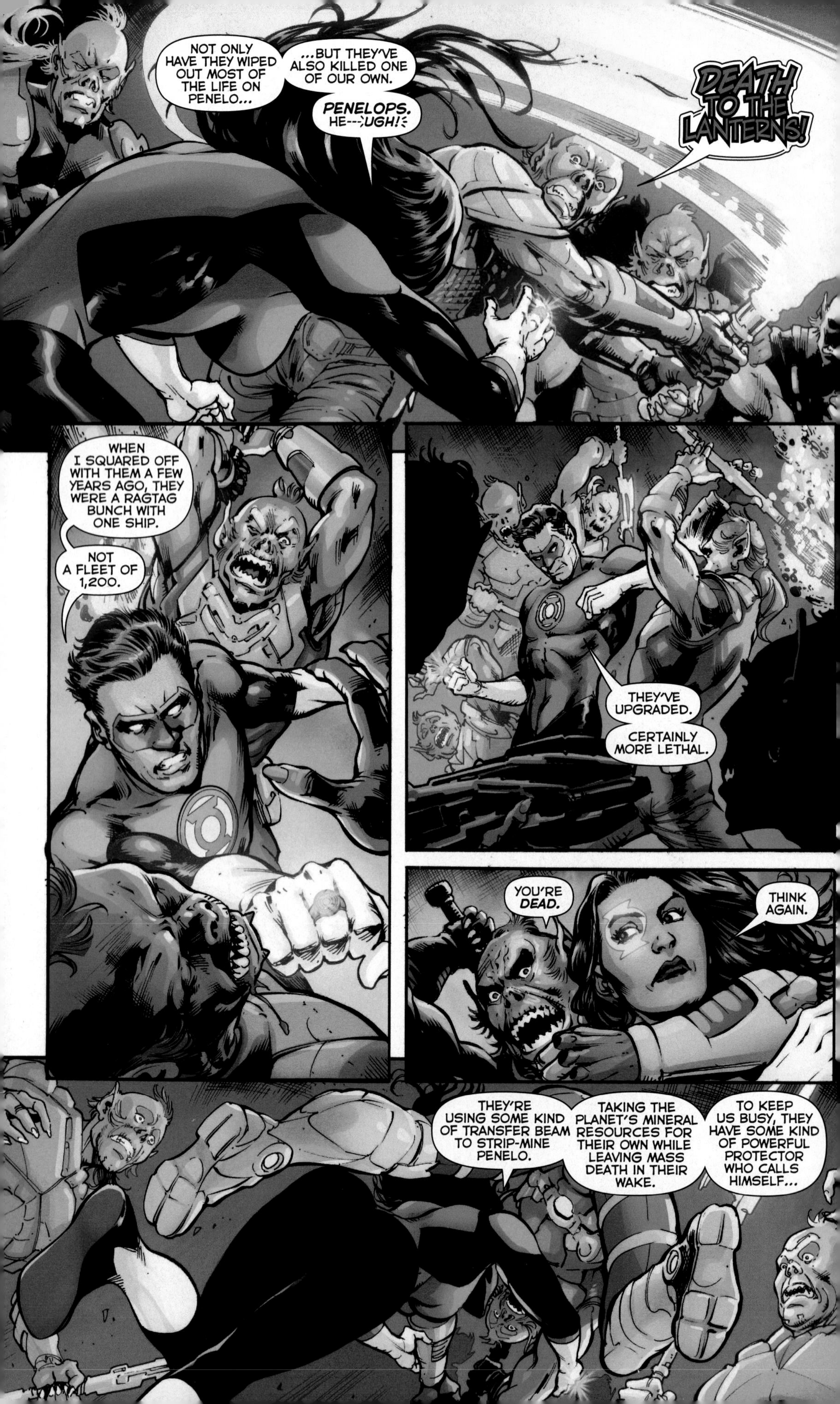
NOT ONLY HAVE THEY WIPED OUT MOST OF THE LIFE ON PENELO...
...BUT THEY'VE ALSO KILLED ONE OF OUR OWN.
PENELOPS. HE--UGH!
DEATH TO THE LANTERNS!
WHEN I SQUARED OFF WITH THEM A FEW YEARS AGO, THEY WERE A RAGTAG BUNCH WITH ONE SHIP.
NOT A FLEET OF 1,200.
THEY'VE UPGRADED.
CERTAINLY MORE LETHAL.
YOU'RE DEAD.
THINK AGAIN.
THEY'RE USING SOME KIND OF TRANSFER BEAM TO STRIP-MINE PENELO.
TAKING THE PLANET'S MINERAL RESOURCES FOR THEIR OWN WHILE LEAVING MASS DEATH IN THEIR WAKE.
TO KEEP US BUSY, THEY HAVE SOME KIND OF POWERFUL PROTECTOR WHO CALLS HIMSELF...

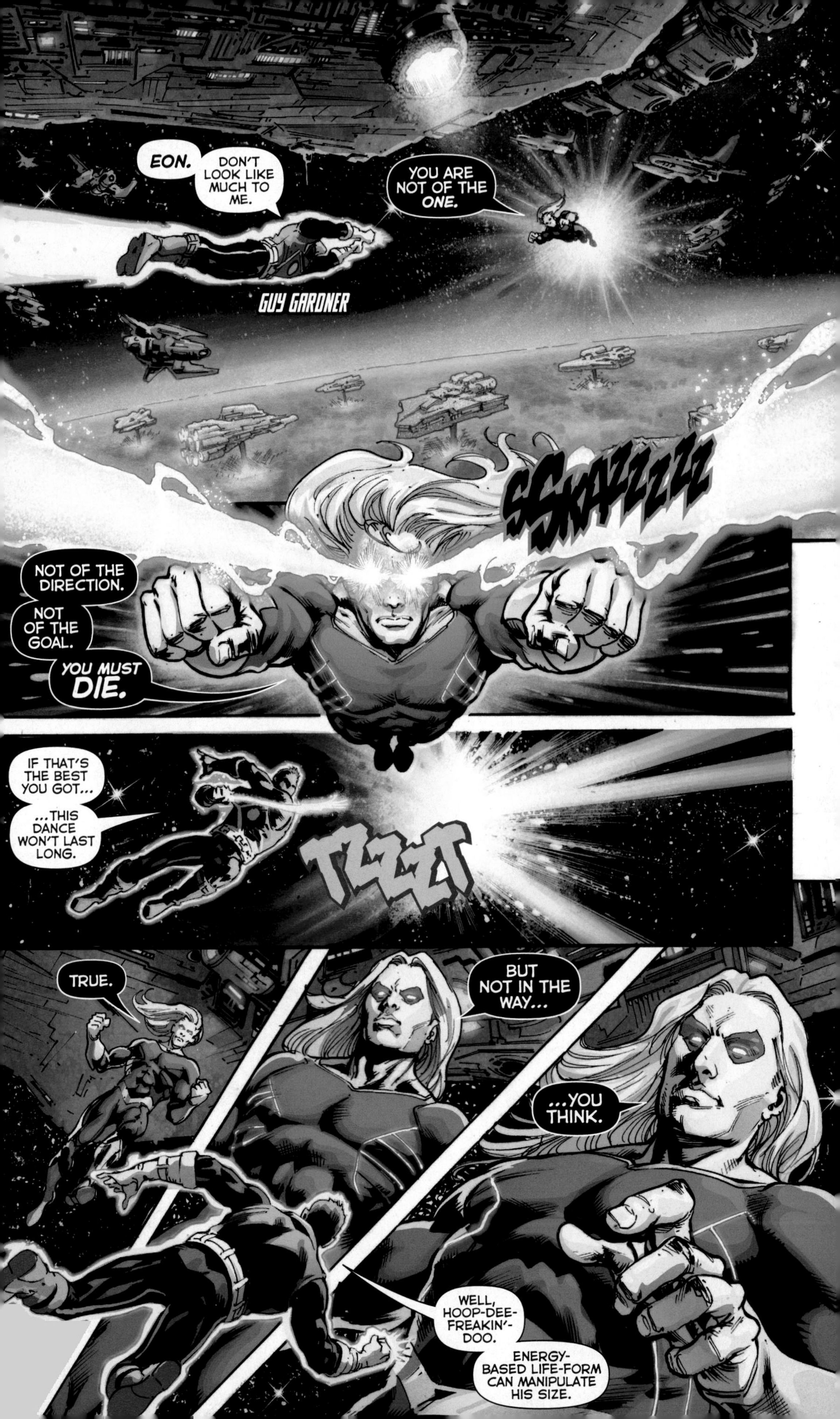
EON.
DON'T LOOK LIKE MUCH TO ME.
YOU ARE NOT OF THE ONE.
GUY GARDNER
SSKAZZZZZ
NOT OF THE DIRECTION.
NOT OF THE GOAL.
YOU MUST DIE.
IF THAT'S THE BEST YOU GOT...
...THIS DANCE WON'T LAST LONG.
TZZZT
TRUE.
BUT NOT IN THE WAY...
...YOU THINK.
WELL, HOOP-DEE-FREAKIN'-DOO.
ENERGY-BASED LIFE-FORM CAN MANIPULATE HIS SIZE.

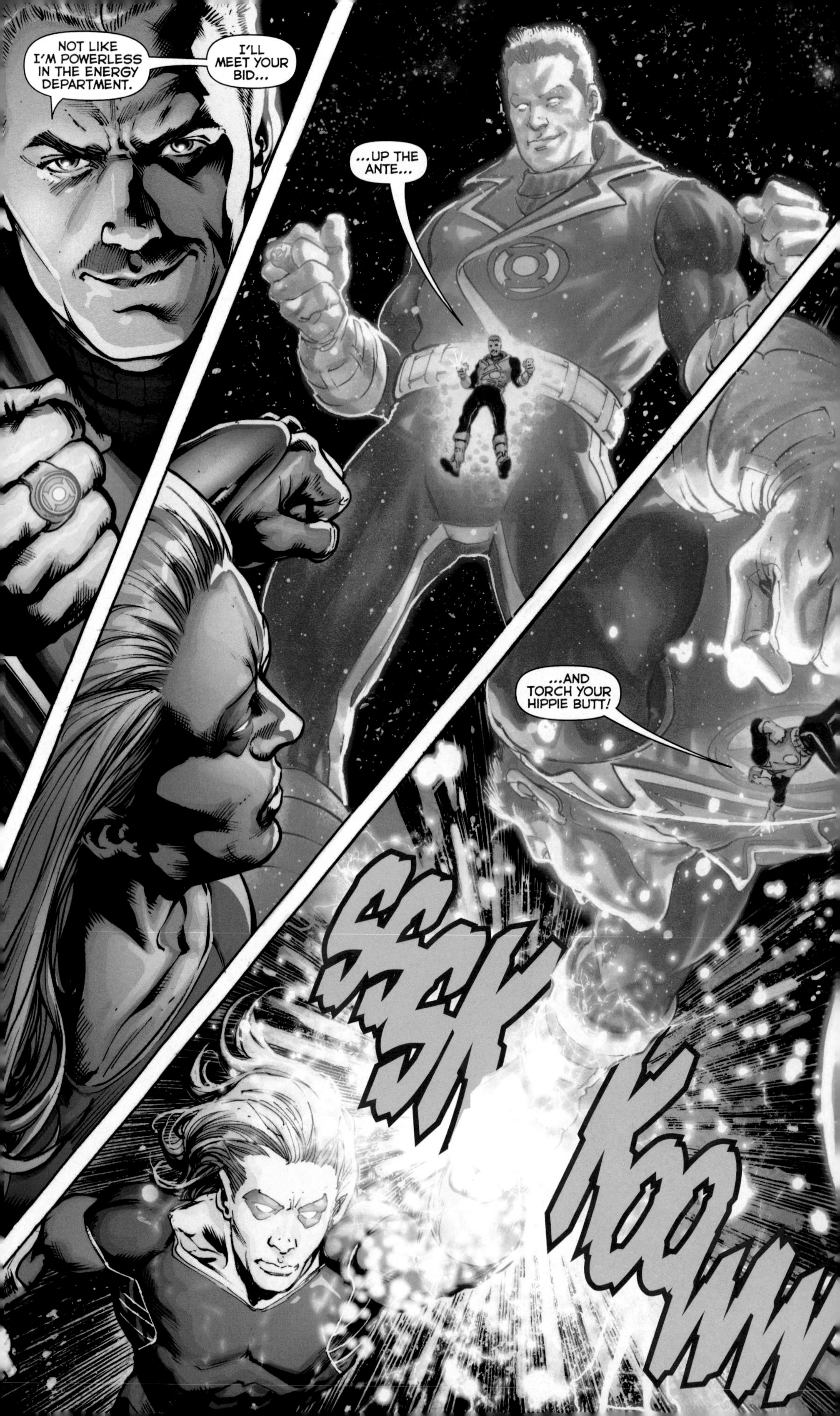
NOT LIKE I'M POWERLESS IN THE ENERGY DEPARTMENT.
I'LL MEET YOUR BID...
...UP THE ANTE...
...AND TORCH YOUR HIPPIE BUTT!
SSKOOM

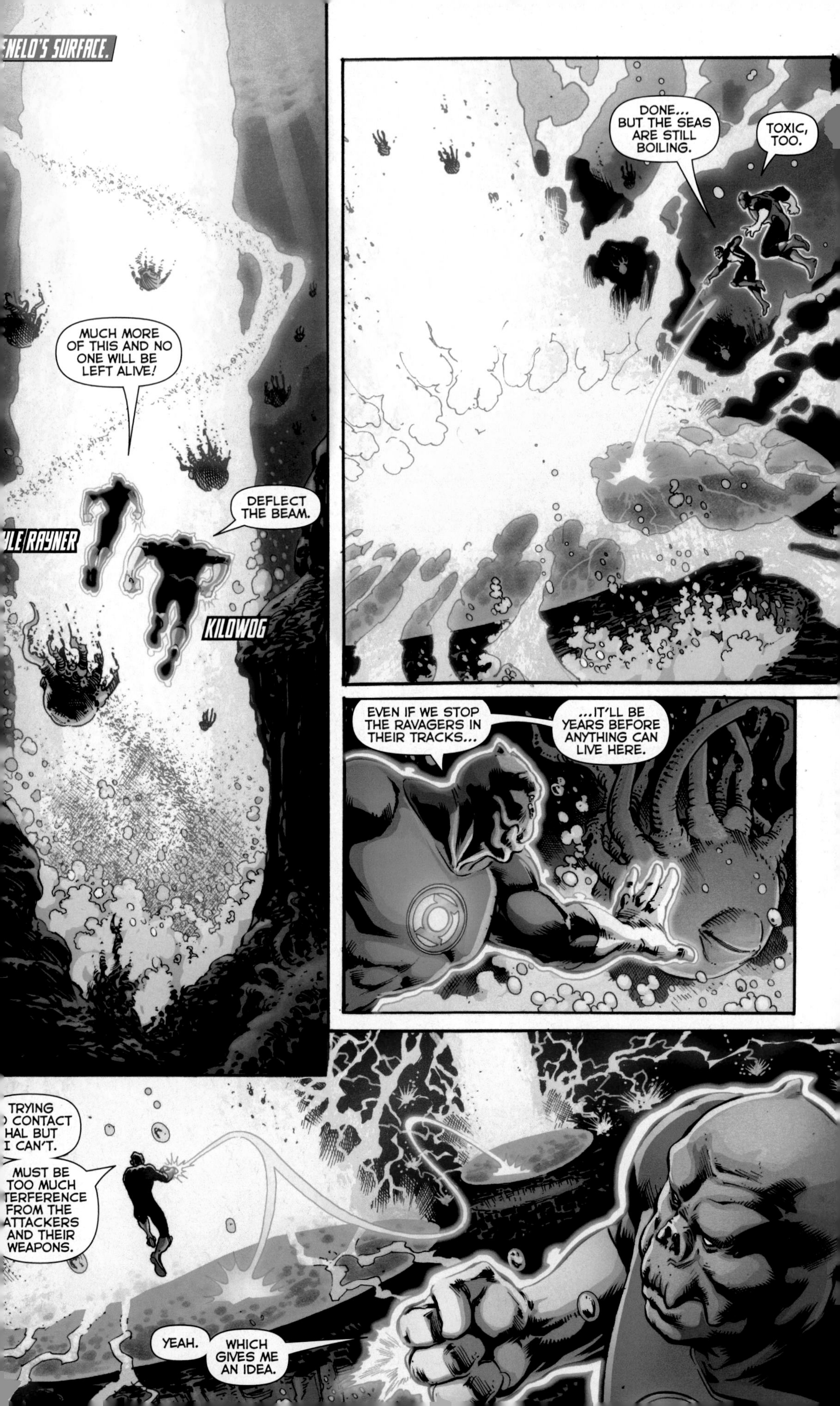

NELO'S SURFACE.
MUCH MORE OF THIS AND NO ONE WILL BE LEFT ALIVE!
YLE RAYNER
KILOWOG
DEFLECT THE BEAM.
DONE... BUT THE SEAS ARE STILL BOILING.
TOXIC, TOO.
EVEN IF WE STOP THE RAVAGERS IN THEIR TRACKS...
...IT'LL BE YEARS BEFORE ANYTHING CAN LIVE HERE.
TRYING CONTACT HAL BUT I CAN'T.
MUST BE TOO MUCH TERFERENCE FROM THE ATTACKERS AND THEIR WEAPONS.
YEAH.
WHICH GIVES ME AN IDEA.

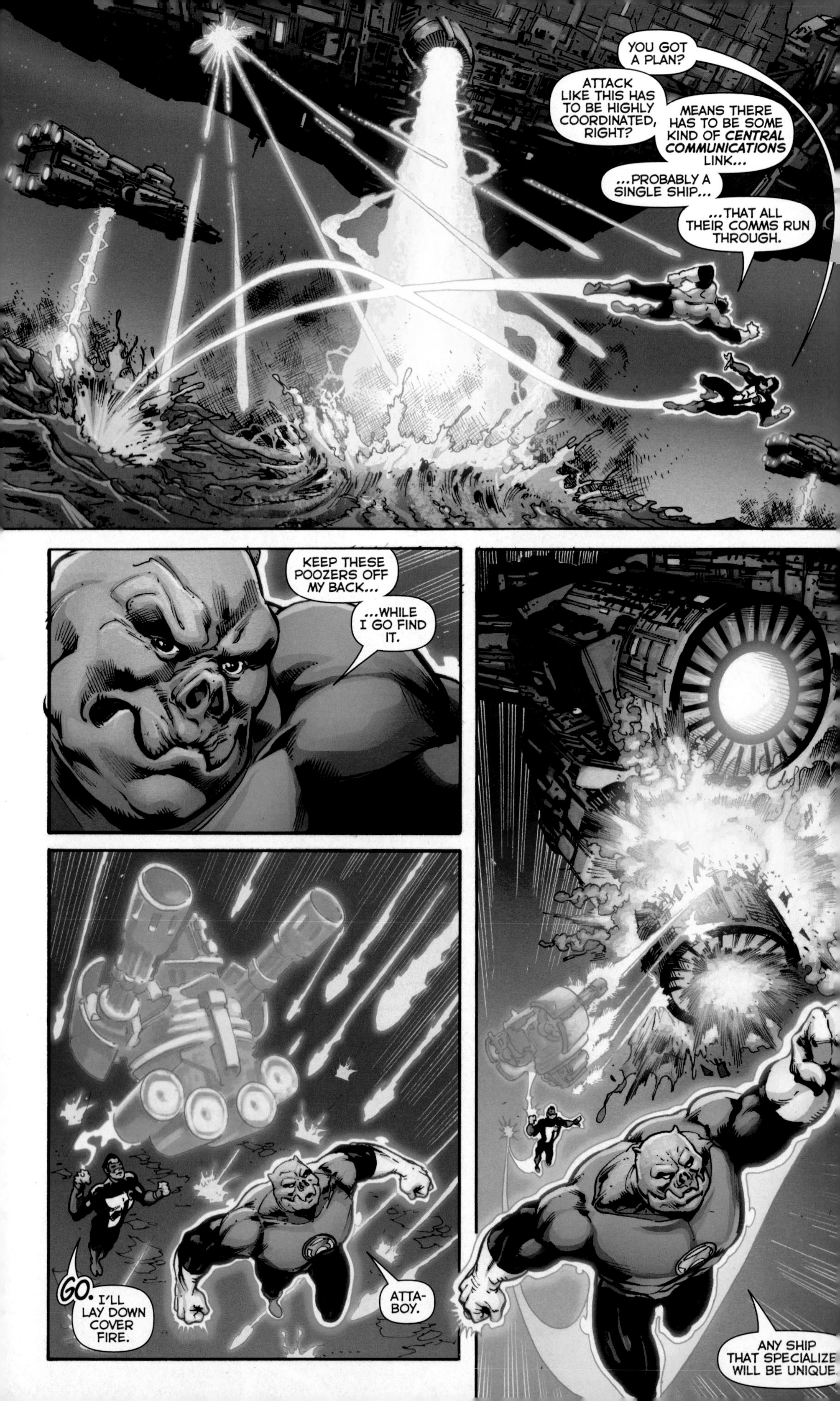
YOU GOT A PLAN?
ATTACK LIKE THIS HAS TO BE HIGHLY COORDINATED, RIGHT?
MEANS THERE HAS TO BE SOME KIND OF *CENTRAL COMMUNICATIONS* LINK...
...PROBABLY A SINGLE SHIP...
...THAT ALL THEIR COMMS RUN THROUGH.
KEEP THESE POOZERS OFF MY BACK...
...WHILE I GO FIND IT.
GO. I'LL LAY DOWN COVER FIRE.
ATTA-BOY.
ANY SHIP THAT SPECIALIZE WILL BE UNIQUE

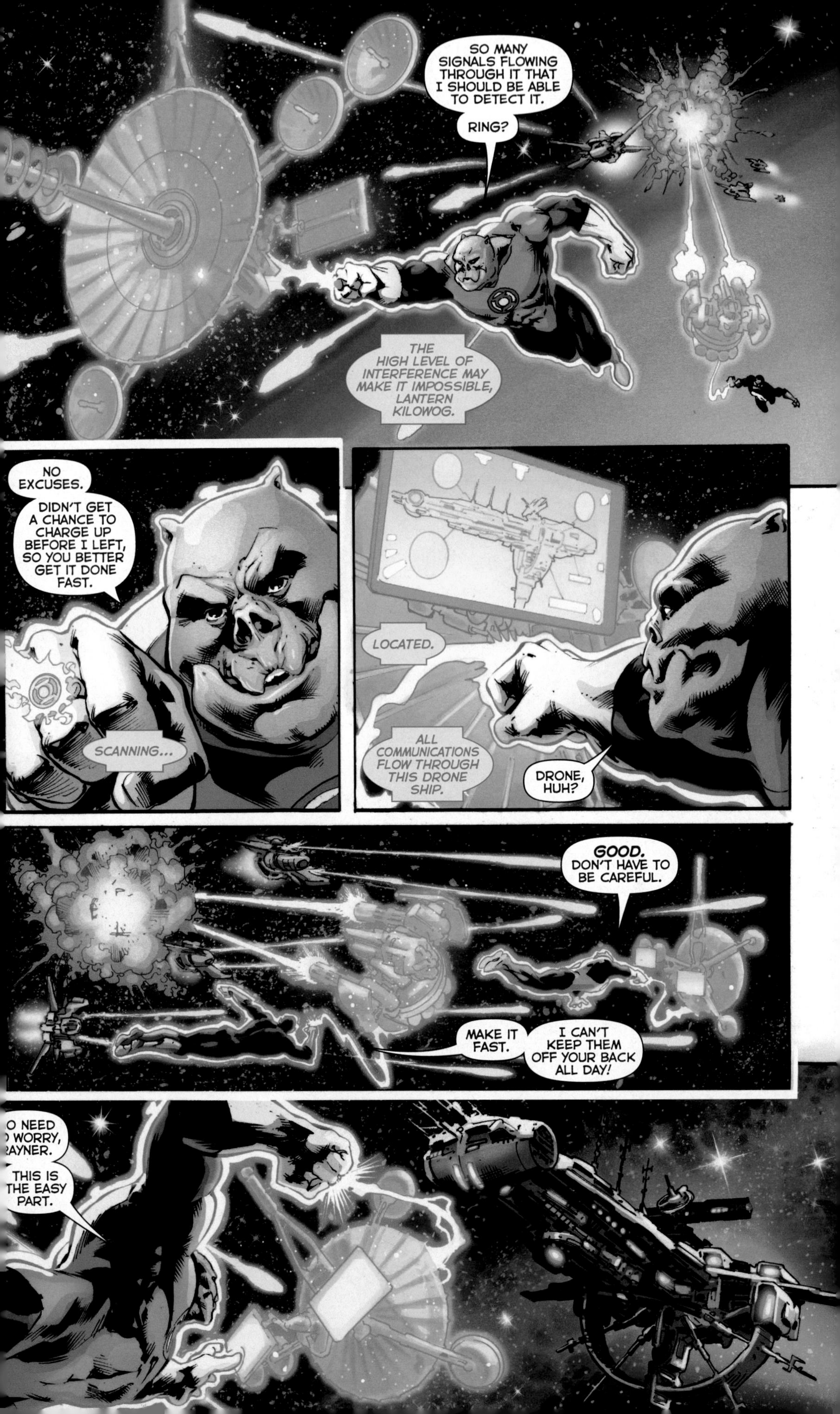
SO MANY SIGNALS FLOWING THROUGH IT THAT I SHOULD BE ABLE TO DETECT IT.
RING?
THE HIGH LEVEL OF INTERFERENCE MAY MAKE IT IMPOSSIBLE, LANTERN KILOWOG.
NO EXCUSES.
DIDN'T GET A CHANCE TO CHARGE UP BEFORE I LEFT, SO YOU BETTER GET IT DONE FAST.
SCANNING...
LOCATED.
ALL COMMUNICATIONS FLOW THROUGH THIS DRONE SHIP.
DRONE, HUH?
GOOD. DON'T HAVE TO BE CAREFUL.
MAKE IT FAST.
I CAN'T KEEP THEM OFF YOUR BACK ALL DAY!
O NEED
) WORRY,
AYNER.
THIS IS THE EASY PART.

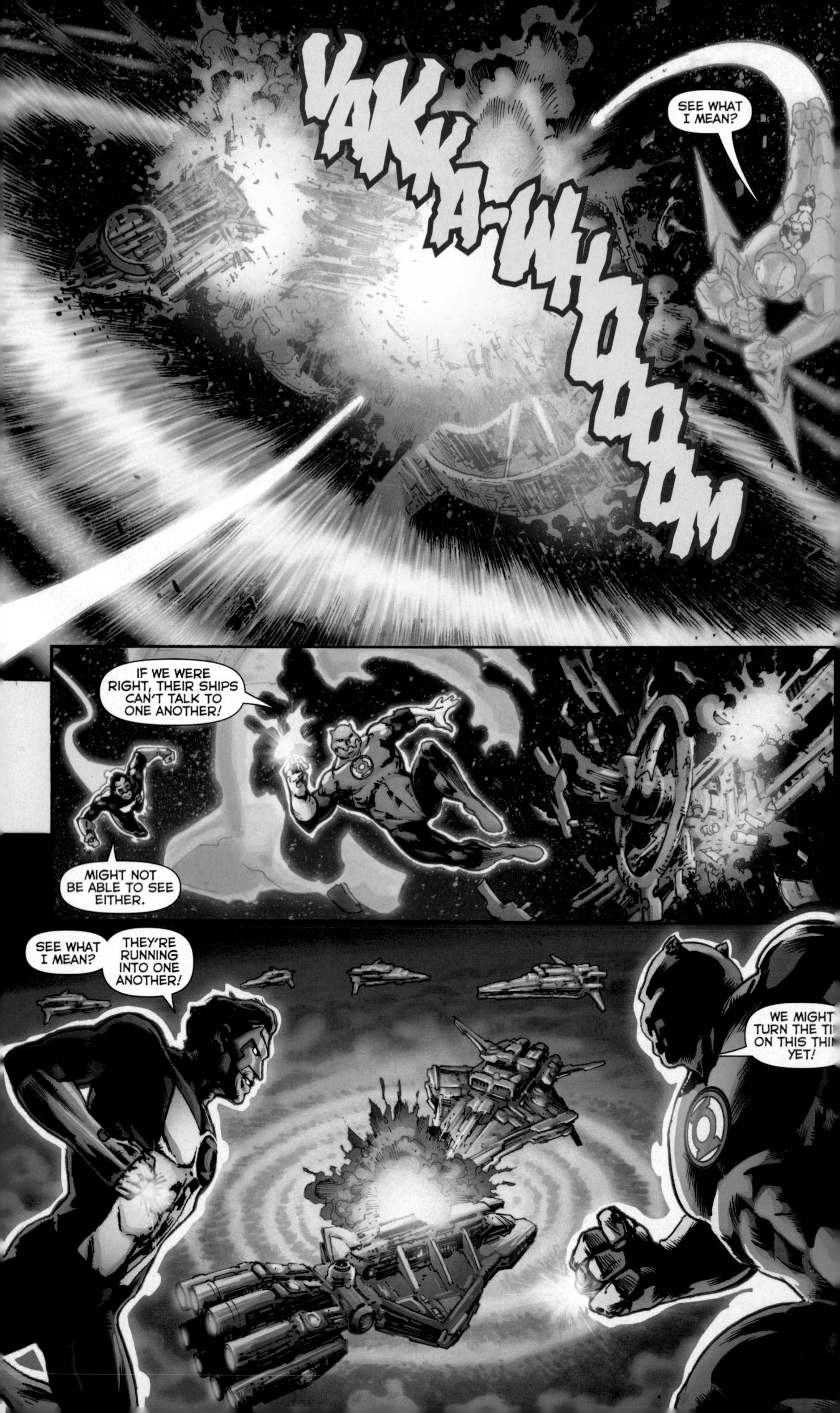
YAKKA-WHOOOOM
SEE WHAT I MEAN?
IF WE WERE RIGHT, THEIR SHIPS CAN'T TALK TO ONE ANOTHER!
MIGHT NOT BE ABLE TO SEE EITHER.
SEE WHAT I MEAN?
THEY'RE RUNNING INTO ONE ANOTHER!
WE MIGHT TURN THE TI ON THIS THI YET!

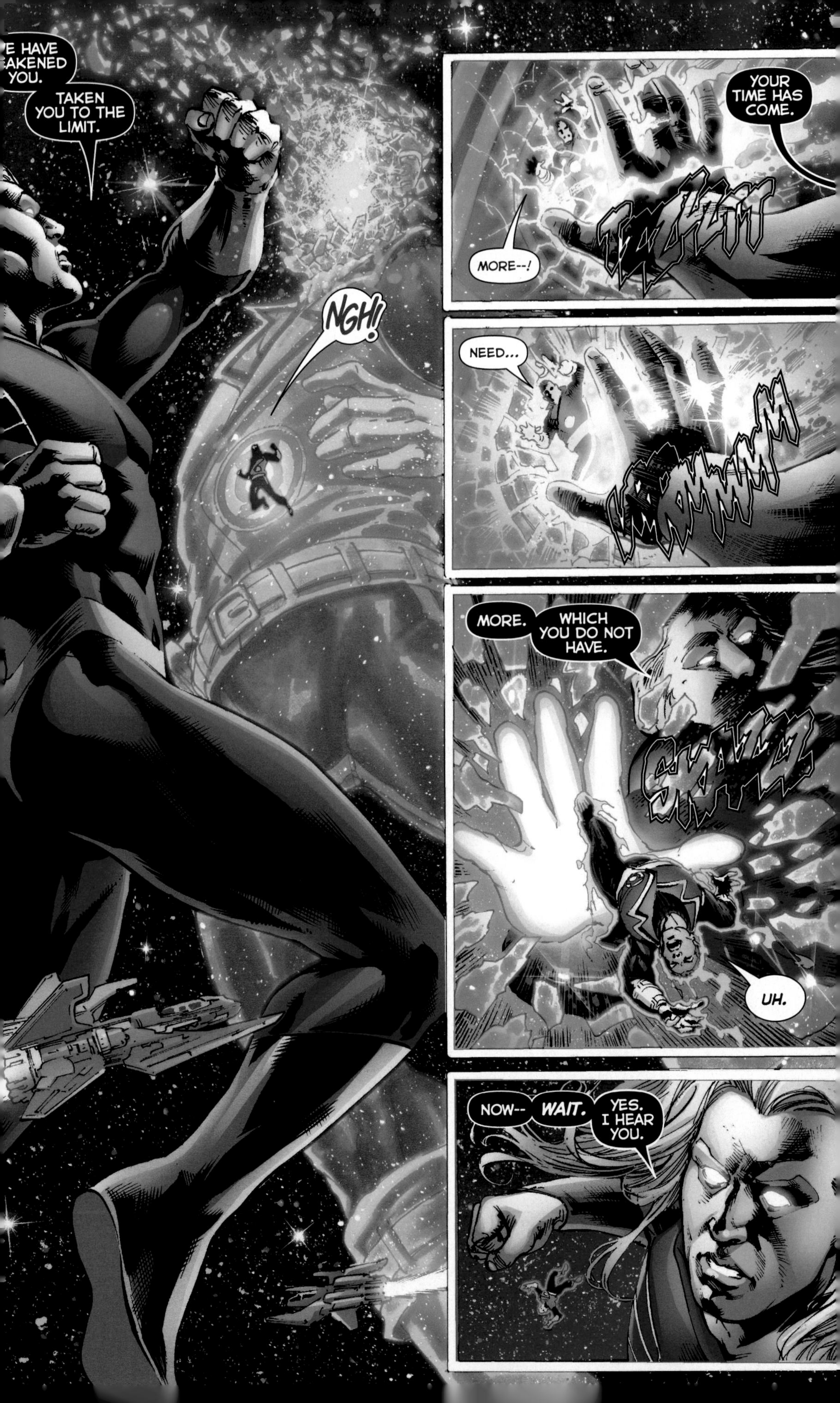
E HAVE
AKENED
YOU.
TAKEN
YOU TO THE
LIMIT.
NGH!
YOUR
TIME HAS
COME.
MORE--!
NEED...
MORE.
WHICH
YOU DO NOT
HAVE.
UH.
NOW--
WAIT.
YES.
I HEAR
YOU.

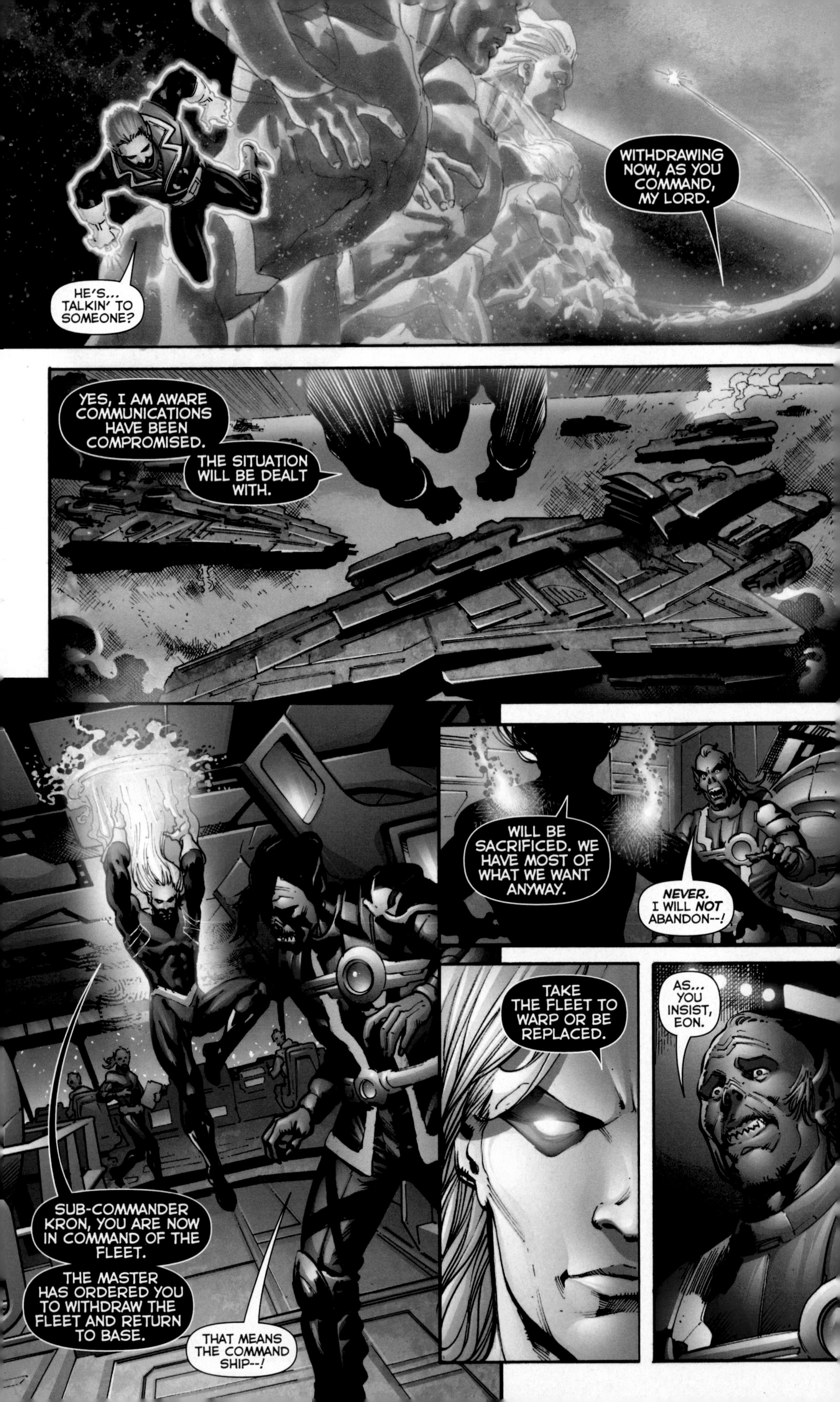
WITHDRAWING NOW, AS YOU COMMAND, MY LORD.
HE'S... TALKIN' TO SOMEONE?
YES, I AM AWARE COMMUNICATIONS HAVE BEEN COMPROMISED.
THE SITUATION WILL BE DEALT WITH.
SUB-COMMANDER KRON, YOU ARE NOW IN COMMAND OF THE FLEET.
THE MASTER HAS ORDERED YOU TO WITHDRAW THE FLEET AND RETURN TO BASE.
THAT MEANS THE COMMAND SHIP--!
WILL BE SACRIFICED. WE HAVE MOST OF WHAT WE WANT ANYWAY.
NEVER. I WILL NOT ABANDON--!
TAKE THE FLEET TO WARP OR BE REPLACED.
AS... YOU INSIST, EON.

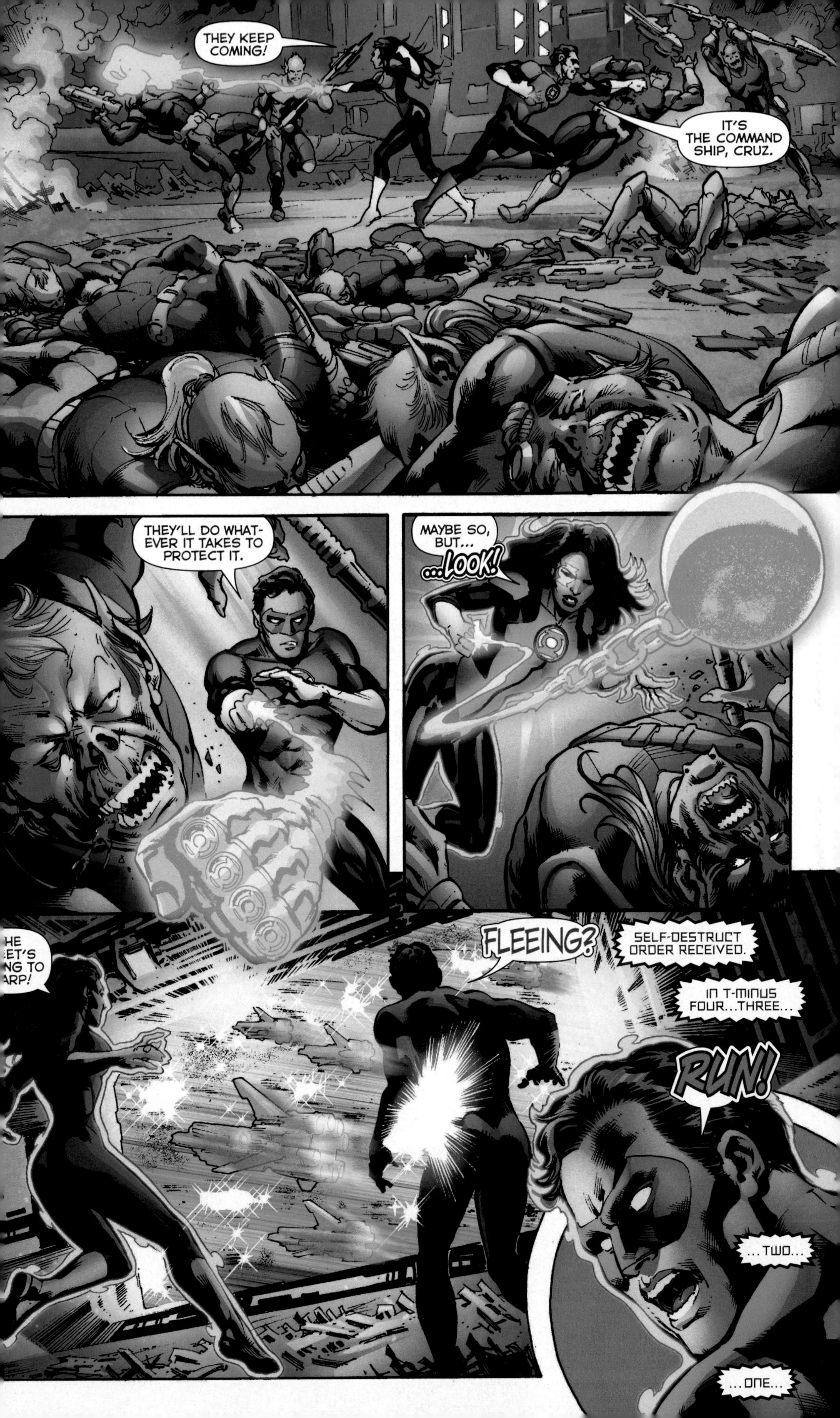
THEY KEEP COMING!
IT'S THE COMMAND SHIP, CRUZ.
THEY'LL DO WHAT-EVER IT TAKES TO PROTECT IT.
MAYBE SO, BUT...
...LOOK!
FLEEING?
SELF-DESTRUCT ORDER RECEIVED.
IN T-MINUS FOUR...THREE...
RUN!
...TWO...
...ONE...

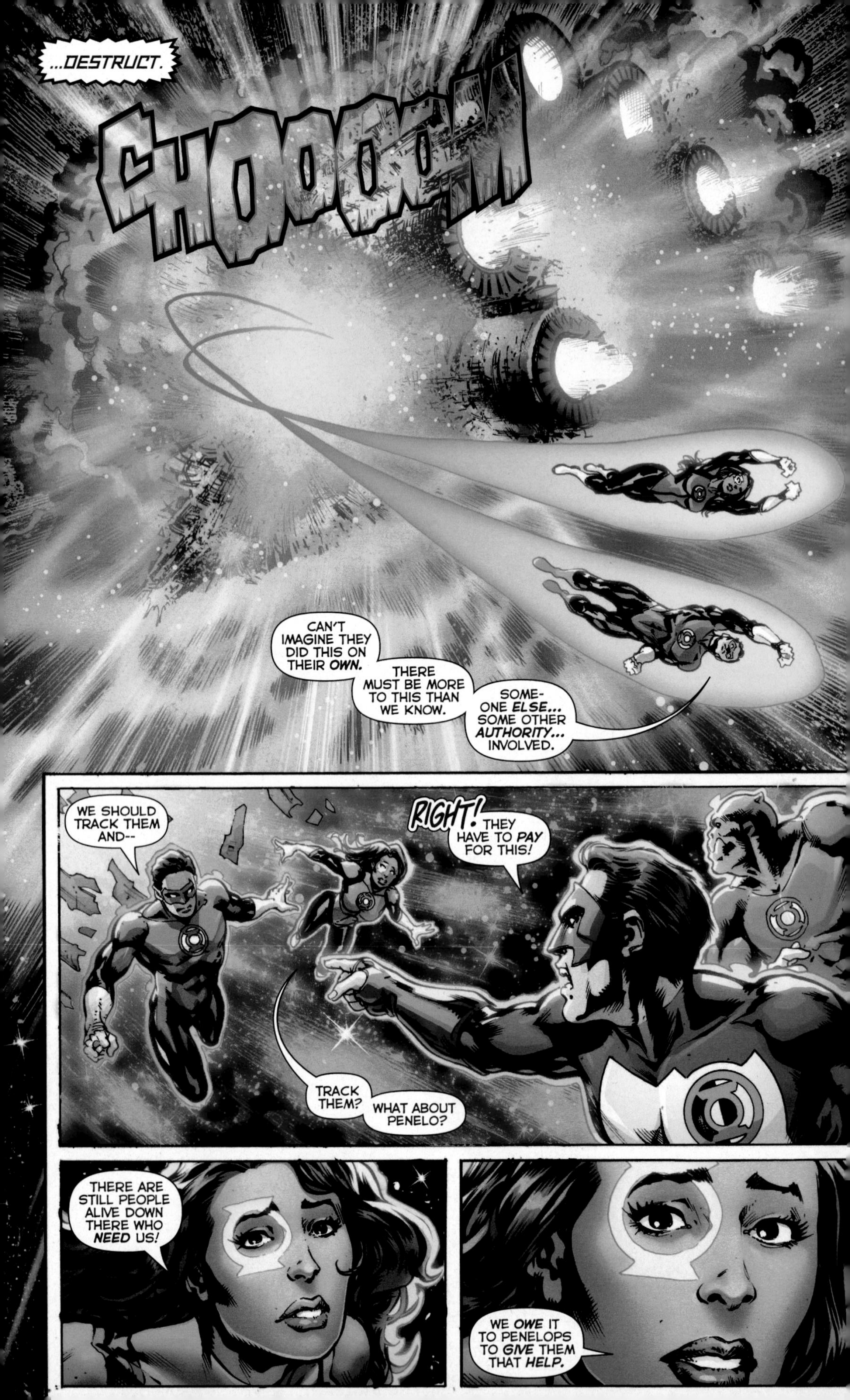
...DESTRUCT.
CHOOOOOM
CAN'T IMAGINE THEY DID THIS ON THEIR OWN.
THERE MUST BE MORE TO THIS THAN WE KNOW.
SOME-ONE ELSE... SOME OTHER AUTHORITY... INVOLVED.
WE SHOULD TRACK THEM AND--
RIGHT! THEY HAVE TO PAY FOR THIS!
TRACK THEM?
WHAT ABOUT PENELO?
THERE ARE STILL PEOPLE ALIVE DOWN THERE WHO NEED US!
WE OWE IT TO PENELOPS TO GIVE THEM THAT HELP.

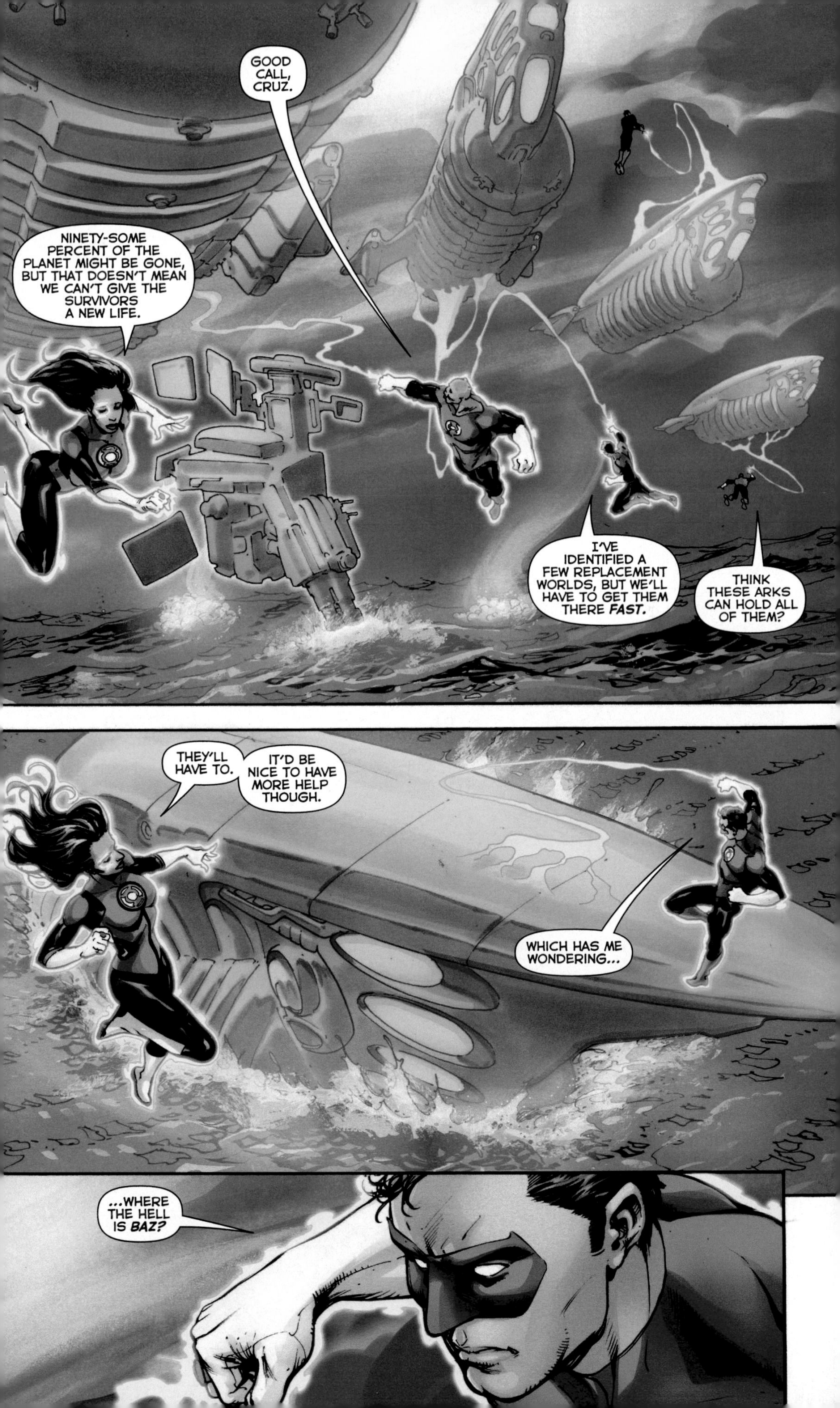
GOOD CALL, CRUZ.
NINETY-SOME PERCENT OF THE PLANET MIGHT BE GONE, BUT THAT DOESN'T MEAN WE CAN'T GIVE THE SURVIVORS A NEW LIFE.
I'VE IDENTIFIED A FEW REPLACEMENT WORLDS, BUT WE'LL HAVE TO GET THEM THERE *FAST.*
THINK THESE ARKS CAN HOLD ALL OF THEM?
THEY'LL HAVE TO.
IT'D BE NICE TO HAVE MORE HELP THOUGH.
WHICH HAS ME WONDERING...
...WHERE THE HELL IS *BAZ?*

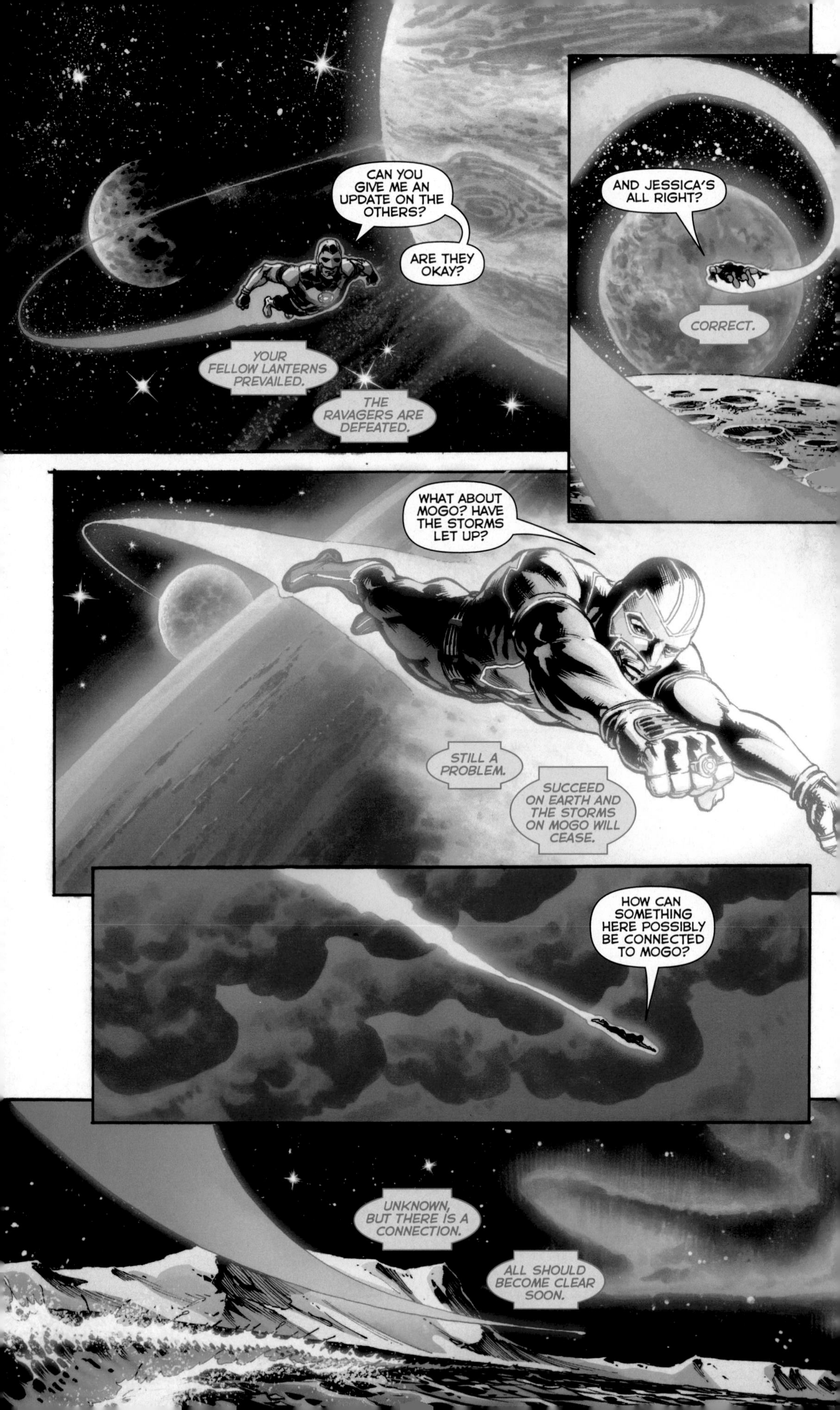
CAN YOU GIVE ME AN UPDATE ON THE OTHERS?
ARE THEY OKAY?
YOUR FELLOW LANTERNS PREVAILED.
THE RAVAGERS ARE DEFEATED.
AND JESSICA'S ALL RIGHT?
CORRECT.
WHAT ABOUT MOGO? HAVE THE STORMS LET UP?
STILL A PROBLEM.
SUCCEED ON EARTH AND THE STORMS ON MOGO WILL CEASE.
HOW CAN SOMETHING HERE POSSIBLY BE CONNECTED TO MOGO?
UNKNOWN, BUT THERE IS A CONNECTION.
ALL SHOULD BECOME CLEAR SOON.

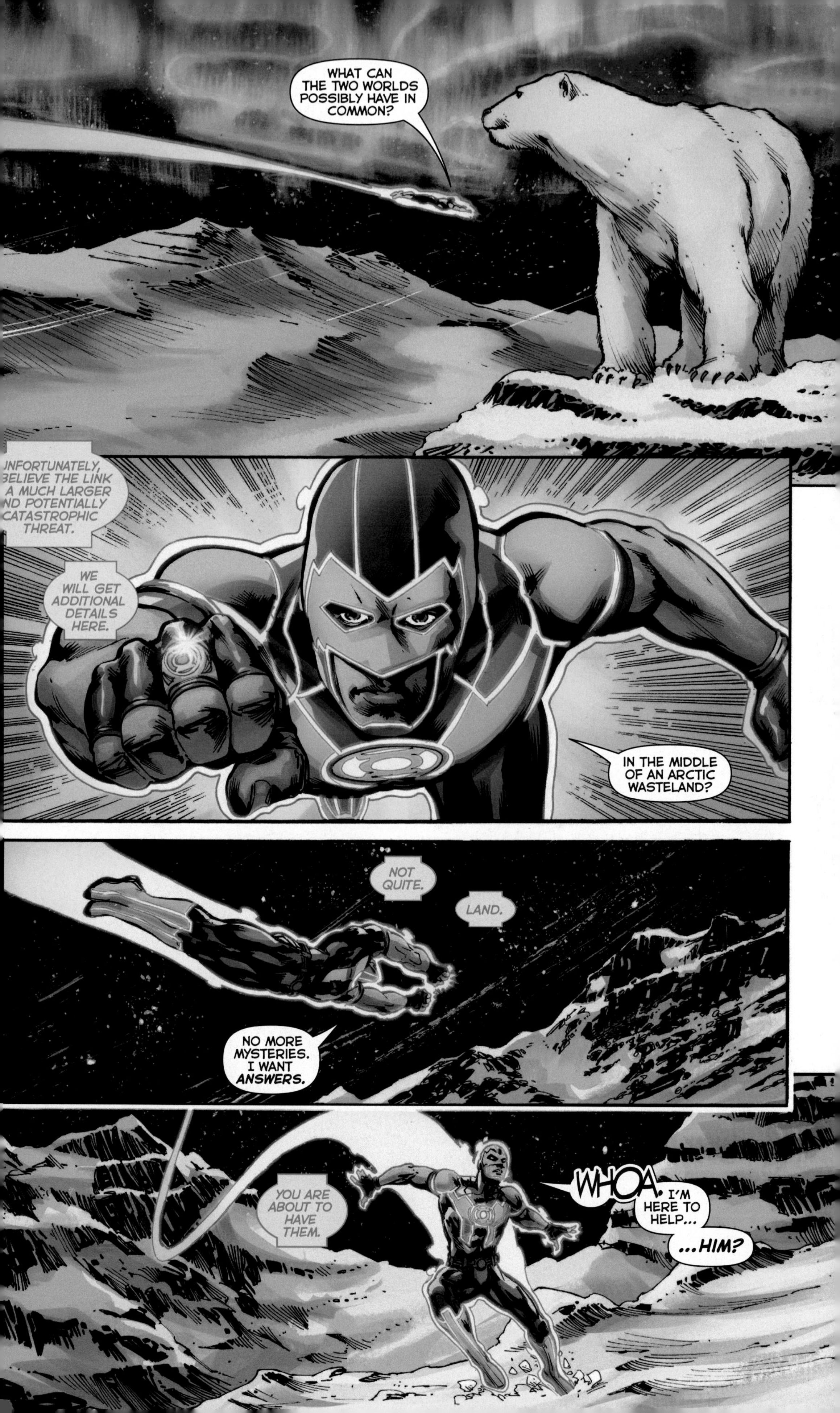
WHAT CAN THE TWO WORLDS POSSIBLY HAVE IN COMMON?
UNFORTUNATELY, BELIEVE THE LINK A MUCH LARGER ND POTENTIALLY CATASTROPHIC THREAT.
WE WILL GET ADDITIONAL DETAILS HERE.
IN THE MIDDLE OF AN ARCTIC WASTELAND?
NOT QUITE.
LAND.
NO MORE MYSTERIES. I WANT ANSWERS.
YOU ARE ABOUT TO HAVE THEM.
WHOA. I'M HERE TO HELP...
...HIM?

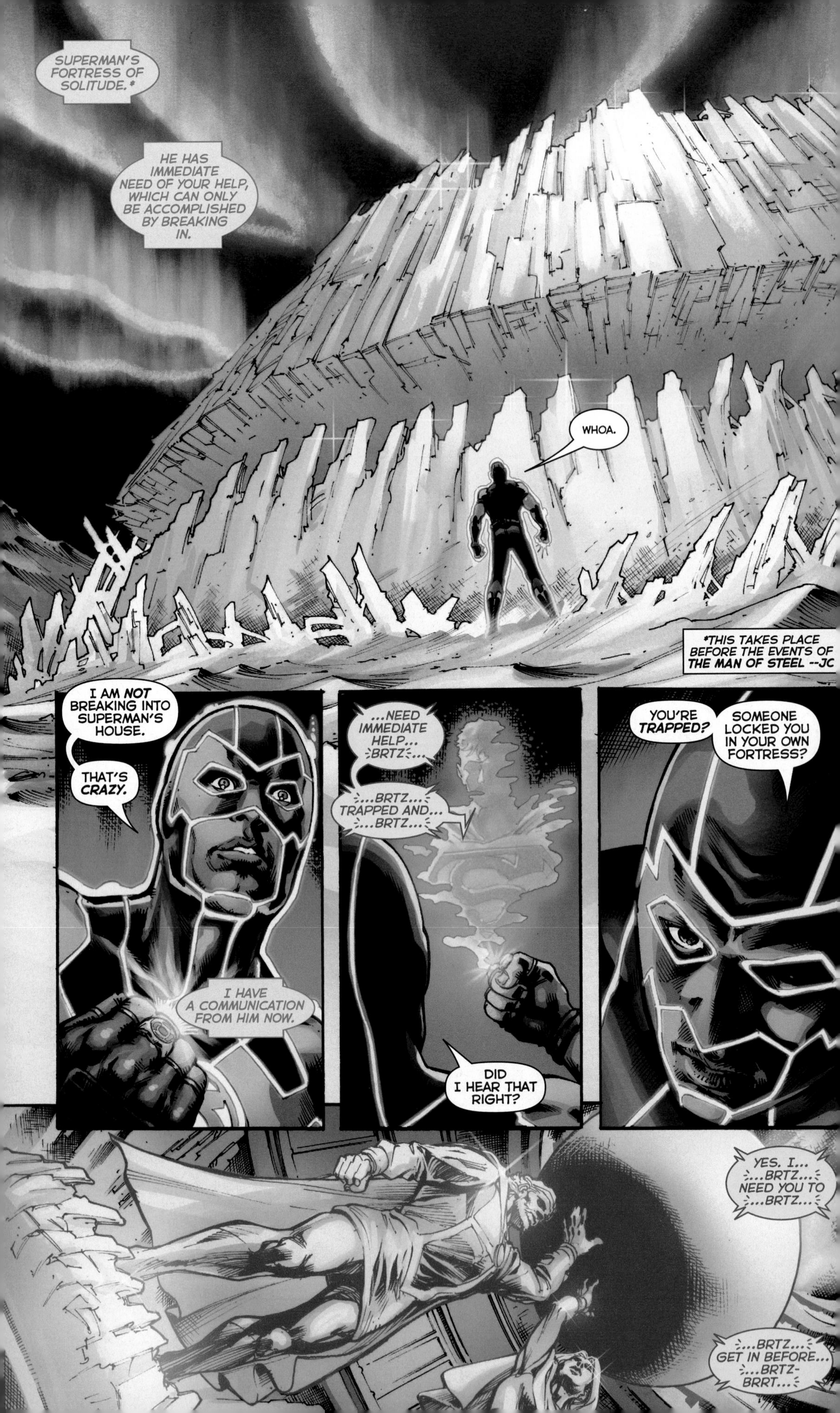
SUPERMAN'S FORTRESS OF SOLITUDE.*
HE HAS IMMEDIATE NEED OF YOUR HELP, WHICH CAN ONLY BE ACCOMPLISHED BY BREAKING IN.
WHOA.
*THIS TAKES PLACE BEFORE THE EVENTS OF THE MAN OF STEEL --JC
I AM NOT BREAKING INTO SUPERMAN'S HOUSE.
THAT'S CRAZY.
I HAVE A COMMUNICATION FROM HIM NOW.
...NEED IMMEDIATE HELP... BRTZ...
...BRTZ... TRAPPED AND... ...BRTZ...
DID I HEAR THAT RIGHT?
YOU'RE TRAPPED?
SOMEONE LOCKED YOU IN YOUR OWN FORTRESS?
YES. I... BRTZ... NEED YOU TO ...BRTZ...
...BRTZ... GET IN BEFORE... ...BRTZ-BRRT...

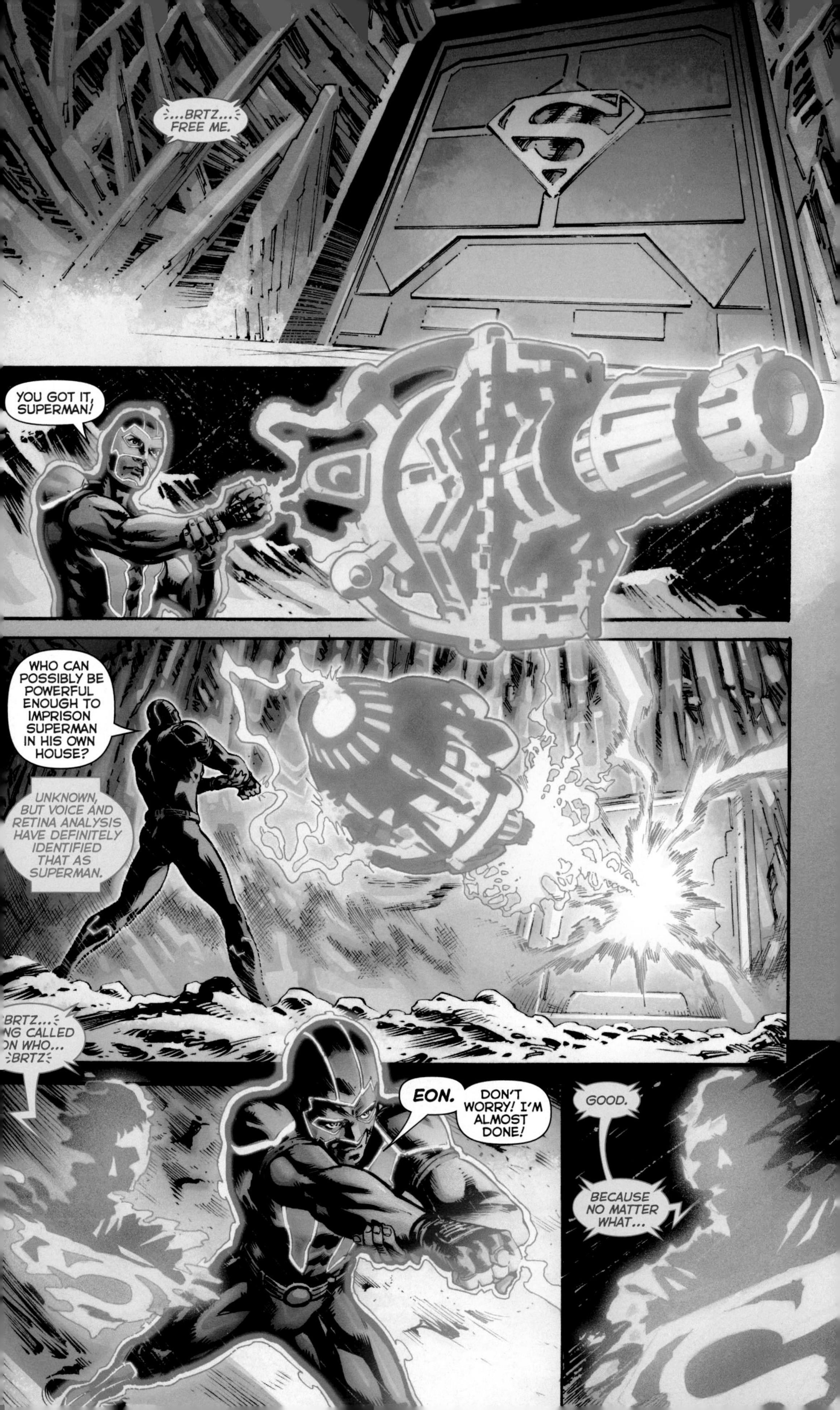
...BRTZ... FREE ME.
YOU GOT IT, SUPERMAN!
WHO CAN POSSIBLY BE POWERFUL ENOUGH TO IMPRISON SUPERMAN IN HIS OWN HOUSE?
UNKNOWN, BUT VOICE AND RETINA ANALYSIS HAVE DEFINITELY IDENTIFIED THAT AS SUPERMAN.
EON.
DON'T WORRY! I'M ALMOST DONE!
GOOD.
BECAUSE NO MATTER WHAT...

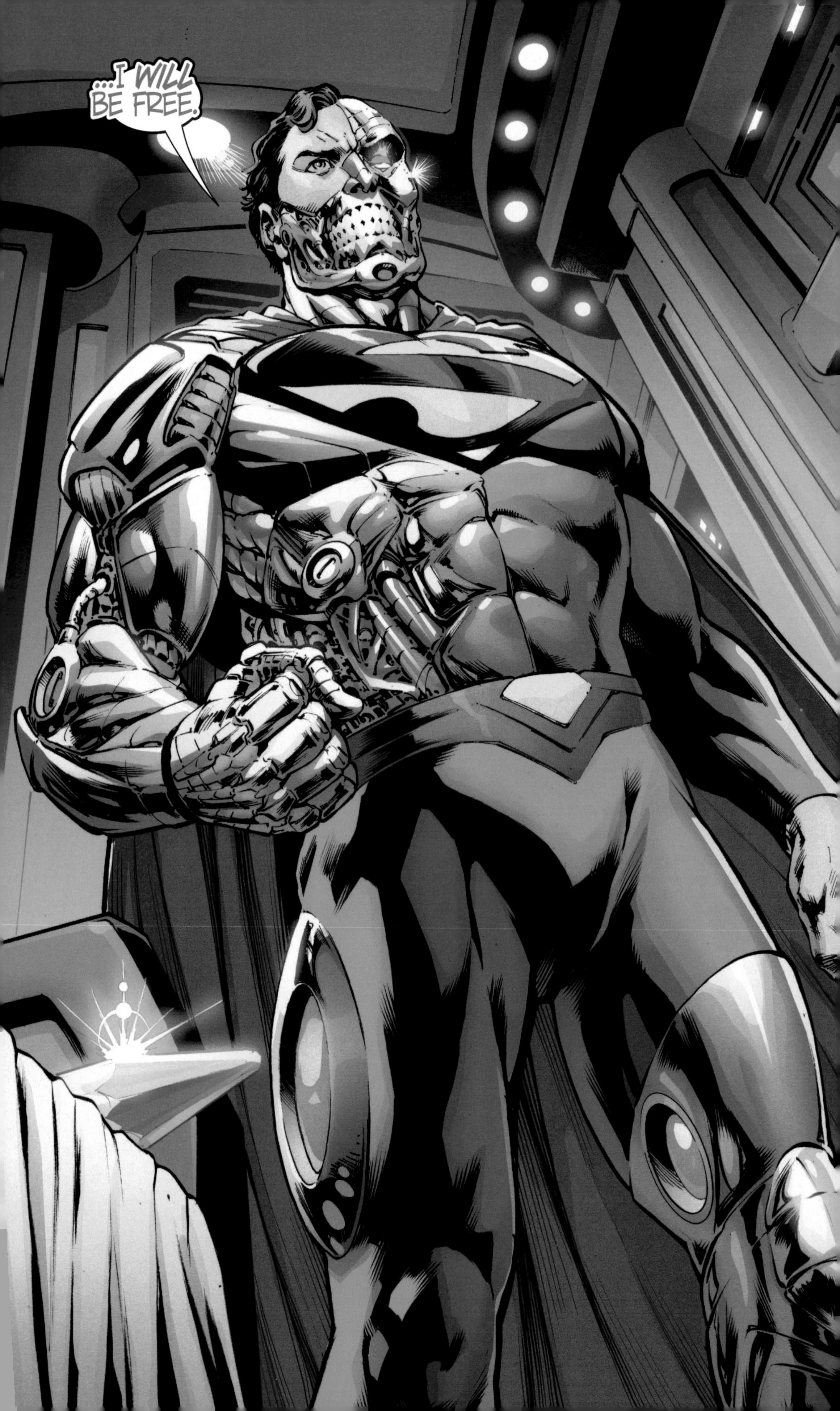
...I WILL BE FREE.

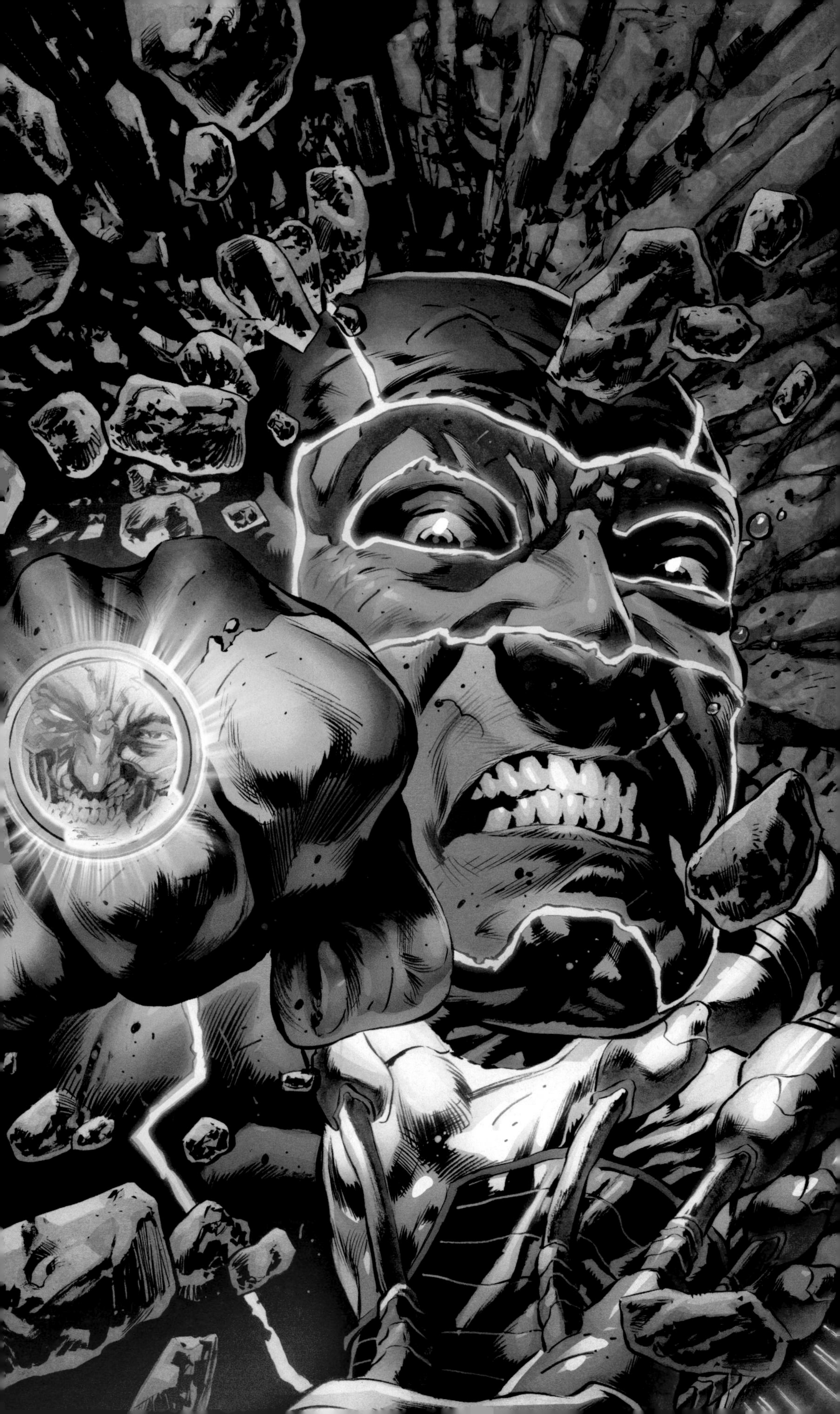

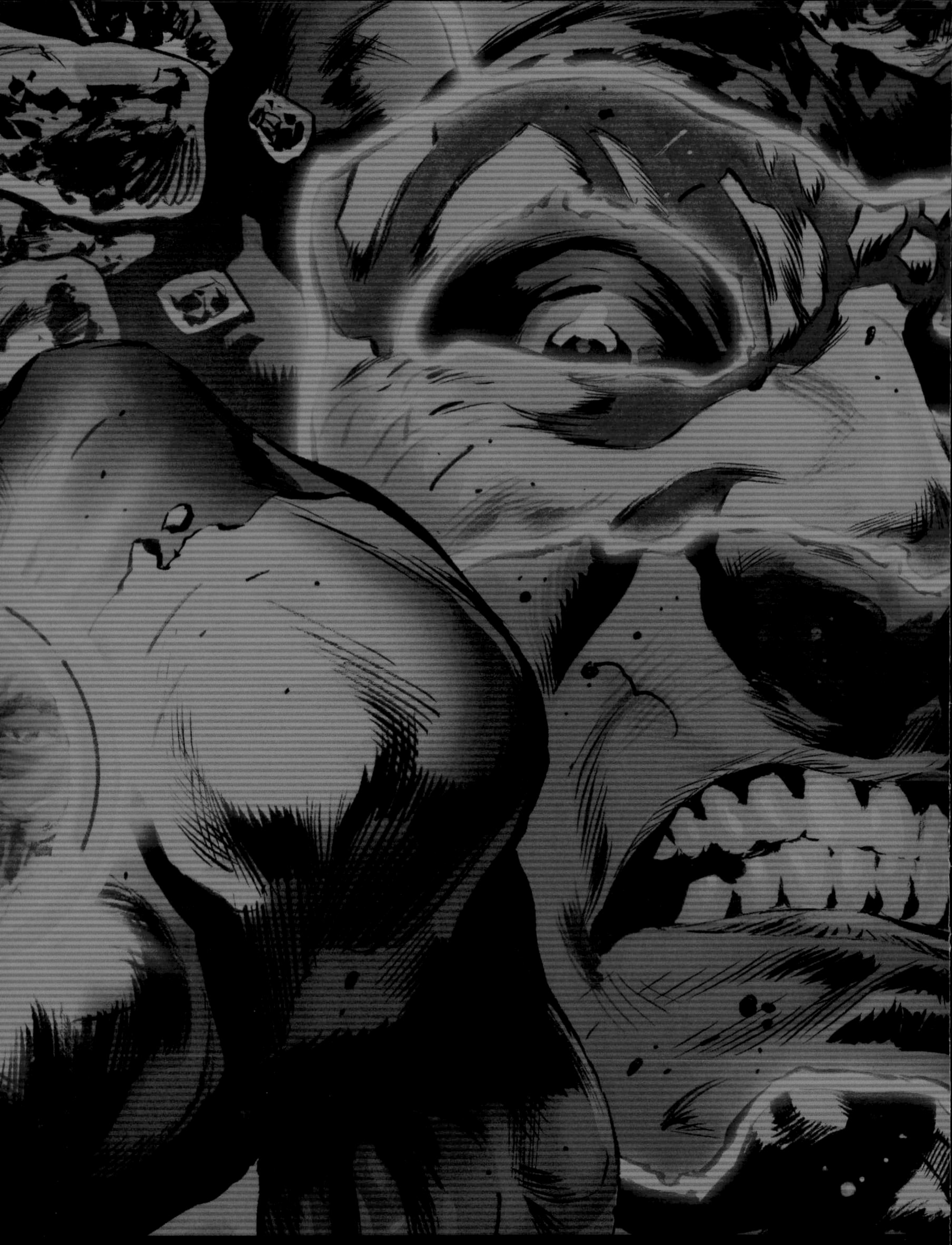

GREEN LANTERNS

#54

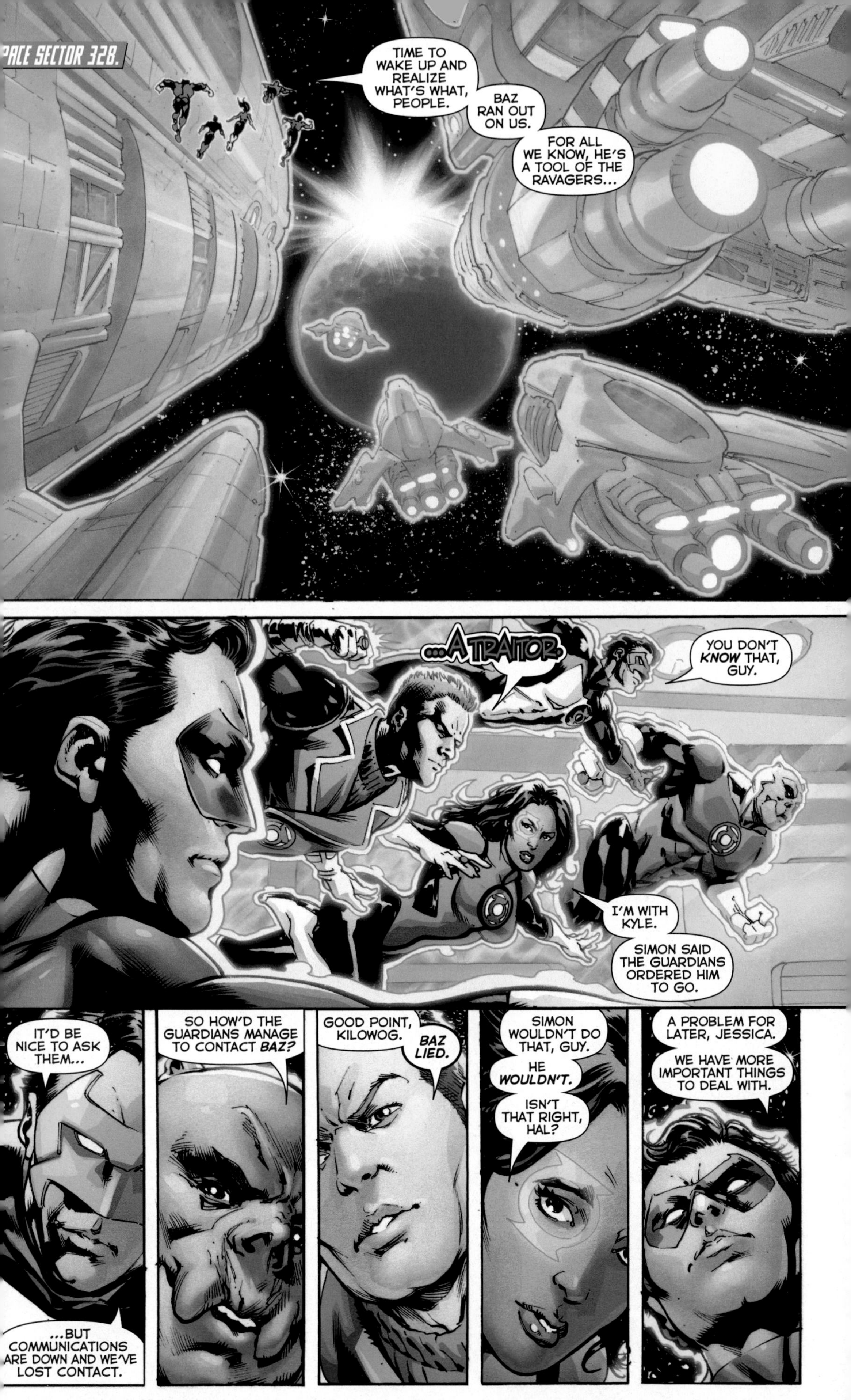
PACE SECTOR 328.
TIME TO WAKE UP AND REALIZE WHAT'S WHAT, PEOPLE.
BAZ RAN OUT ON US.
FOR ALL WE KNOW, HE'S A TOOL OF THE RAVAGERS...
...A TRAITOR.
YOU DON'T *KNOW* THAT, GUY.
I'M WITH KYLE.
SIMON SAID THE GUARDIANS ORDERED HIM TO GO.
IT'D BE NICE TO ASK THEM...
...BUT COMMUNICATIONS ARE DOWN AND WE'VE LOST CONTACT.
SO HOW'D THE GUARDIANS MANAGE TO CONTACT *BAZ?*
GOOD POINT, KILOWOG.
BAZ LIED.
SIMON WOULDN'T DO THAT, GUY.
HE *WOULDN'T.*
ISN'T THAT RIGHT, HAL?
A PROBLEM FOR LATER, JESSICA.
WE HAVE MORE IMPORTANT THINGS TO DEAL WITH.

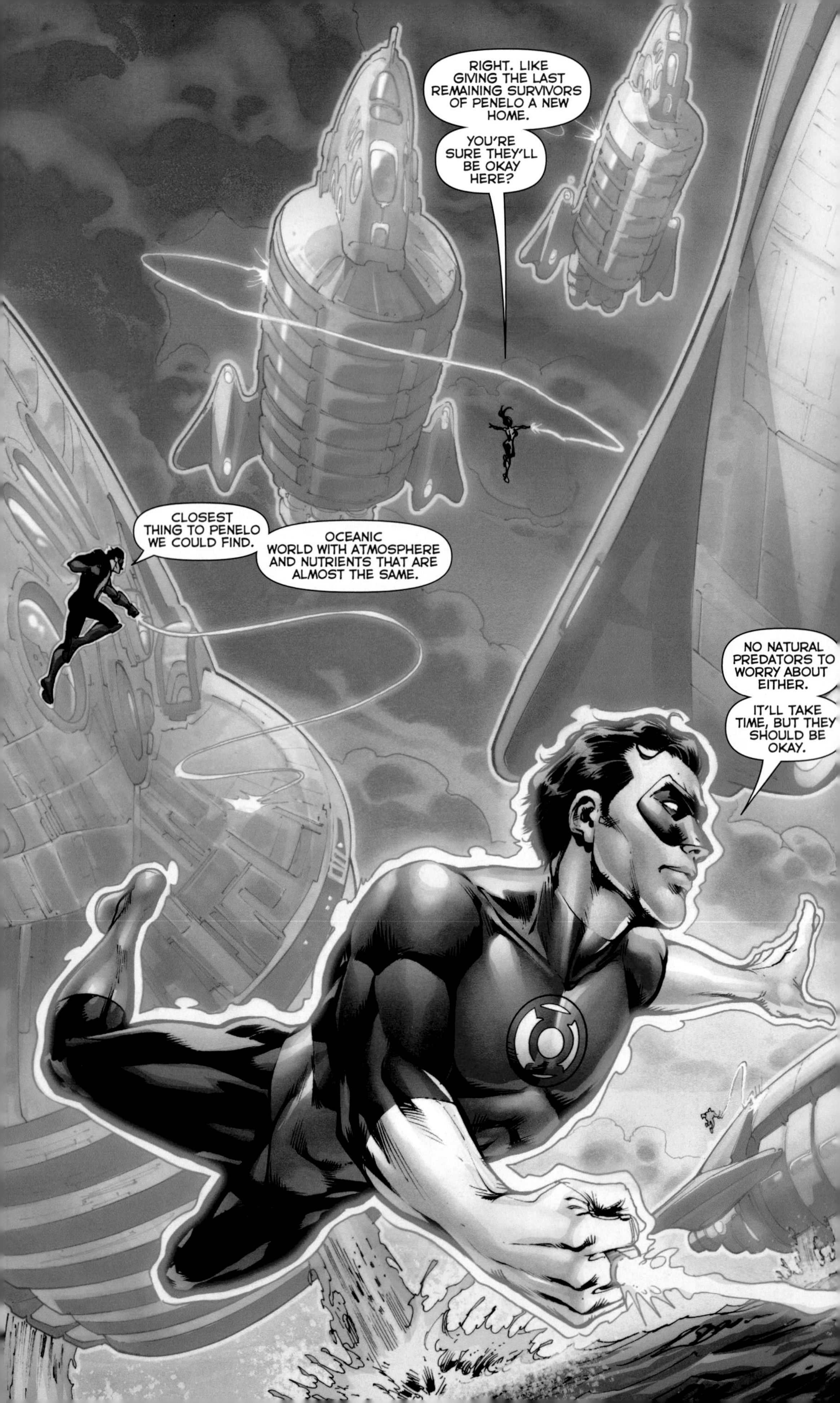
RIGHT. LIKE GIVING THE LAST REMAINING SURVIVORS OF PENELO A NEW HOME.
YOU'RE SURE THEY'LL BE OKAY HERE?
CLOSEST THING TO PENELO WE COULD FIND.
OCEANIC WORLD WITH ATMOSPHERE AND NUTRIENTS THAT ARE ALMOST THE SAME.
NO NATURAL PREDATORS TO WORRY ABOUT EITHER.
IT'LL TAKE TIME, BUT THEY SHOULD BE OKAY.

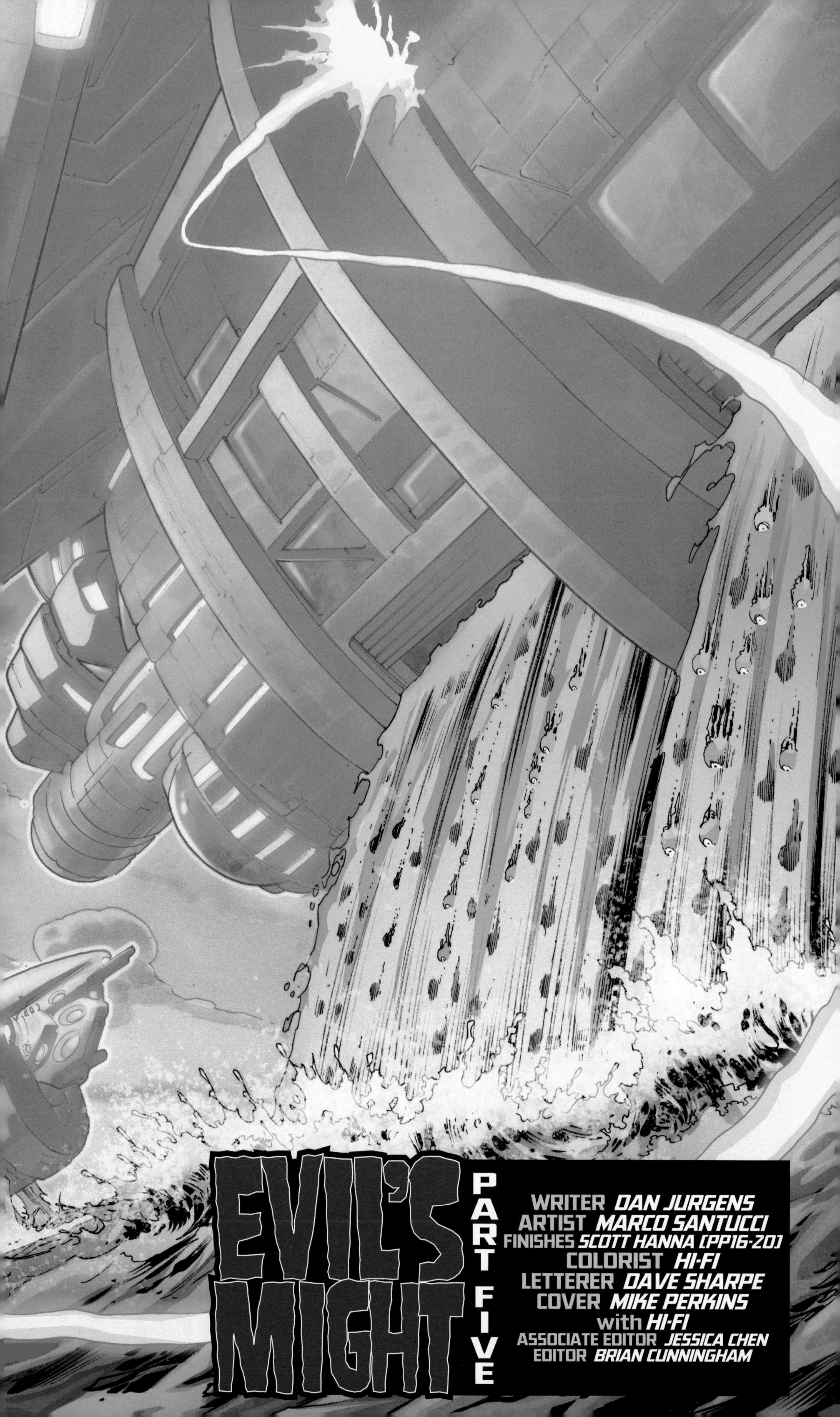

EVIL'S MIGHT
PART FIVE
WRITER DAN JURGENS
ARTIST MARCO SANTUCCI
FINISHES SCOTT HANNA [PP16-20]
COLORIST HI-FI
LETTERER DAVE SHARPE
COVER MIKE PERKINS
with HI-FI
ASSOCIATE EDITOR JESSICA CHEN
EDITOR BRIAN CUNNINGHAM

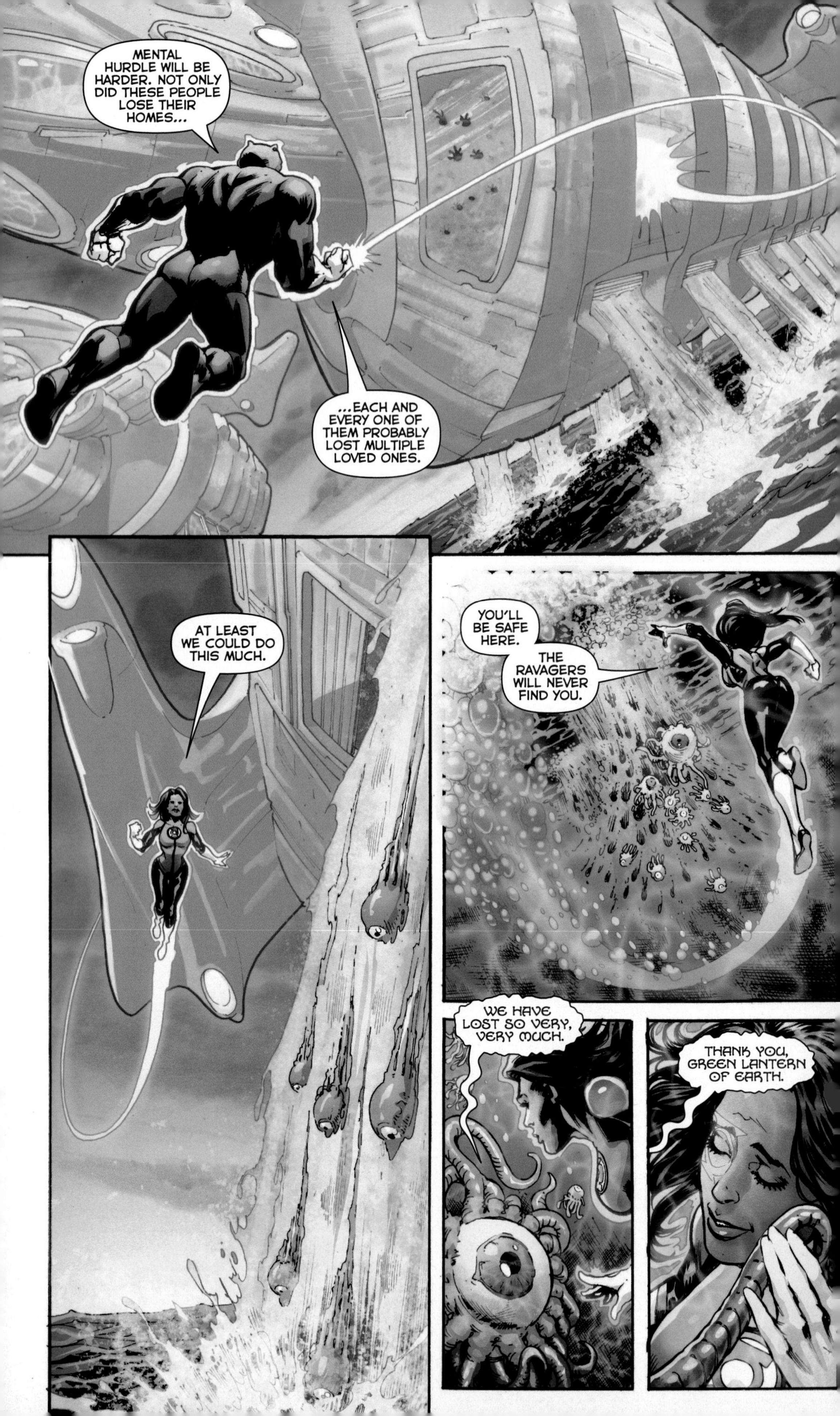
MENTAL HURDLE WILL BE HARDER. NOT ONLY DID THESE PEOPLE LOSE THEIR HOMES...
...EACH AND EVERY ONE OF THEM PROBABLY LOST MULTIPLE LOVED ONES.
AT LEAST WE COULD DO THIS MUCH.
YOU'LL BE SAFE HERE.
THE RAVAGERS WILL NEVER FIND YOU.
WE HAVE LOST SO VERY, VERY MUCH.
THANK YOU, GREEN LANTERN OF EARTH.

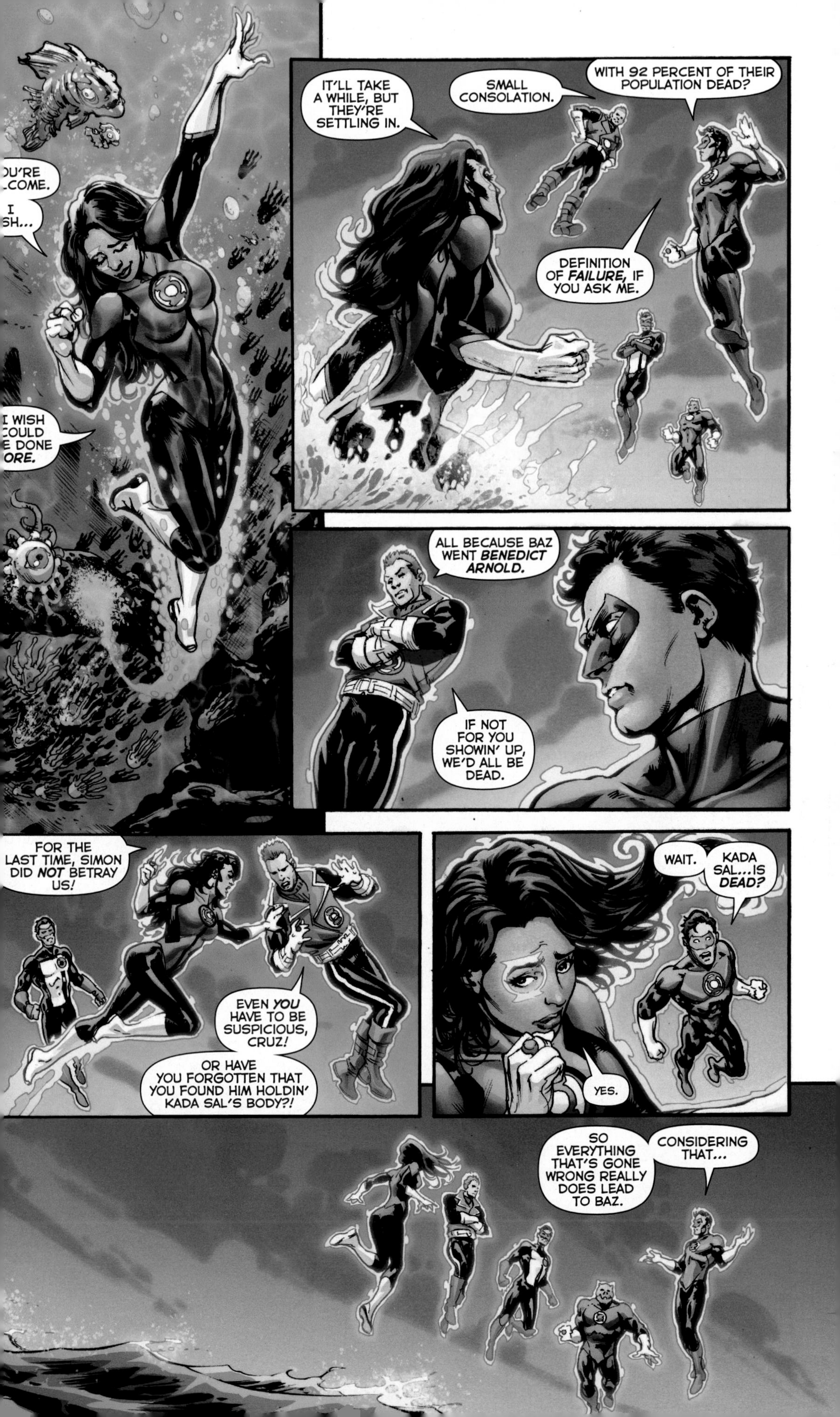

OU'RE
LCOME.
I
SH...
I WISH
COULD
E DONE
ORE.
IT'LL TAKE A WHILE, BUT THEY'RE SETTLING IN.
SMALL CONSOLATION.
WITH 92 PERCENT OF THEIR POPULATION DEAD?
DEFINITION OF *FAILURE,* IF YOU ASK ME.
ALL BECAUSE BAZ WENT *BENEDICT ARNOLD.*
IF NOT FOR YOU SHOWIN' UP, WE'D ALL BE DEAD.
FOR THE LAST TIME, SIMON DID *NOT* BETRAY US!
EVEN *YOU* HAVE TO BE SUSPICIOUS, CRUZ!
OR HAVE YOU FORGOTTEN THAT YOU FOUND HIM HOLDIN' KADA SAL'S BODY?!
WAIT.
KADA SAL...IS *DEAD?*
YES.
SO EVERYTHING THAT'S GONE WRONG REALLY DOES LEAD TO BAZ.
CONSIDERING THAT...

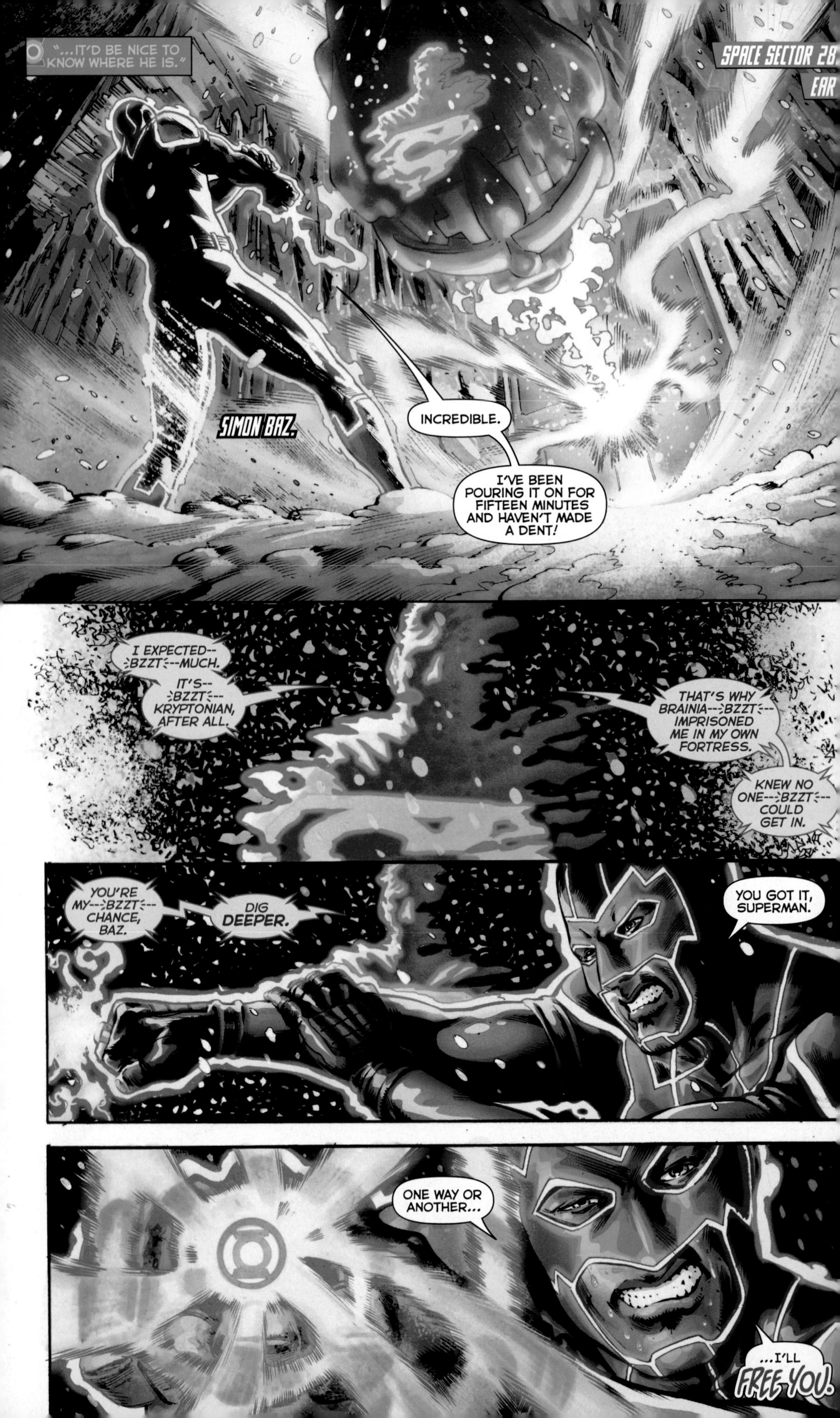
"...IT'D BE NICE TO KNOW WHERE HE IS."
SPACE SECTOR 28
EAR
SIMON BAZ.
INCREDIBLE.
I'VE BEEN POURING IT ON FOR FIFTEEN MINUTES AND HAVEN'T MADE A DENT!
I EXPECTED-- BZZT --MUCH.
IT'S-- BZZT -- KRYPTONIAN, AFTER ALL.
THAT'S WHY BRAINIA-- BZZT -- IMPRISONED ME IN MY OWN FORTRESS.
KNEW NO ONE-- BZZT -- COULD GET IN.
YOU'RE MY-- BZZT -- CHANCE, BAZ.
DIG DEEPER.
YOU GOT IT, SUPERMAN.
ONE WAY OR ANOTHER...
...I'LL FREE YOU.

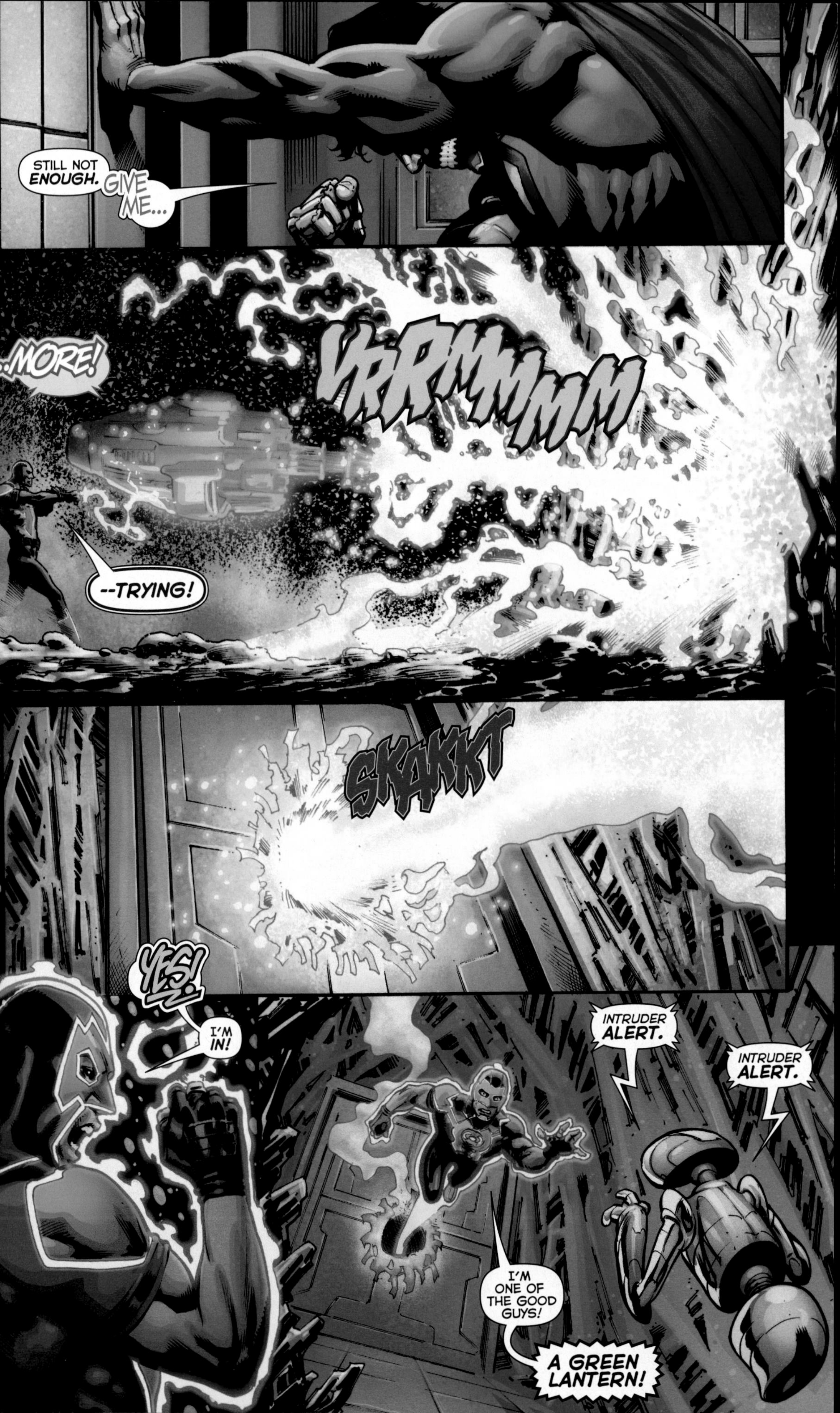
STILL NOT ENOUGH. GIVE ME...
...MORE!
VRRMMMMM
--TRYING!
SKAKKT
YES!
I'M IN!
INTRUDER ALERT.
INTRUDER ALERT.
I'M ONE OF THE GOOD GUYS!
A GREEN LANTERN!

IDENTITY CONFIRMED.

AUTHORIZATION NOT GRANTED.

KELEX IS PROGRAMMED TO DEFEND THE FOR--BZZT--AT ALL COSTS.

DO WHAT YOU MUST.

TAKE OUT YOUR OWN--

WELL, IF YOU SAY S SUPERMA

SSKASSSH

SORRY, BUDDY.

ON MY WAY!

THIS IS IT?

YES.

OPEN IT.

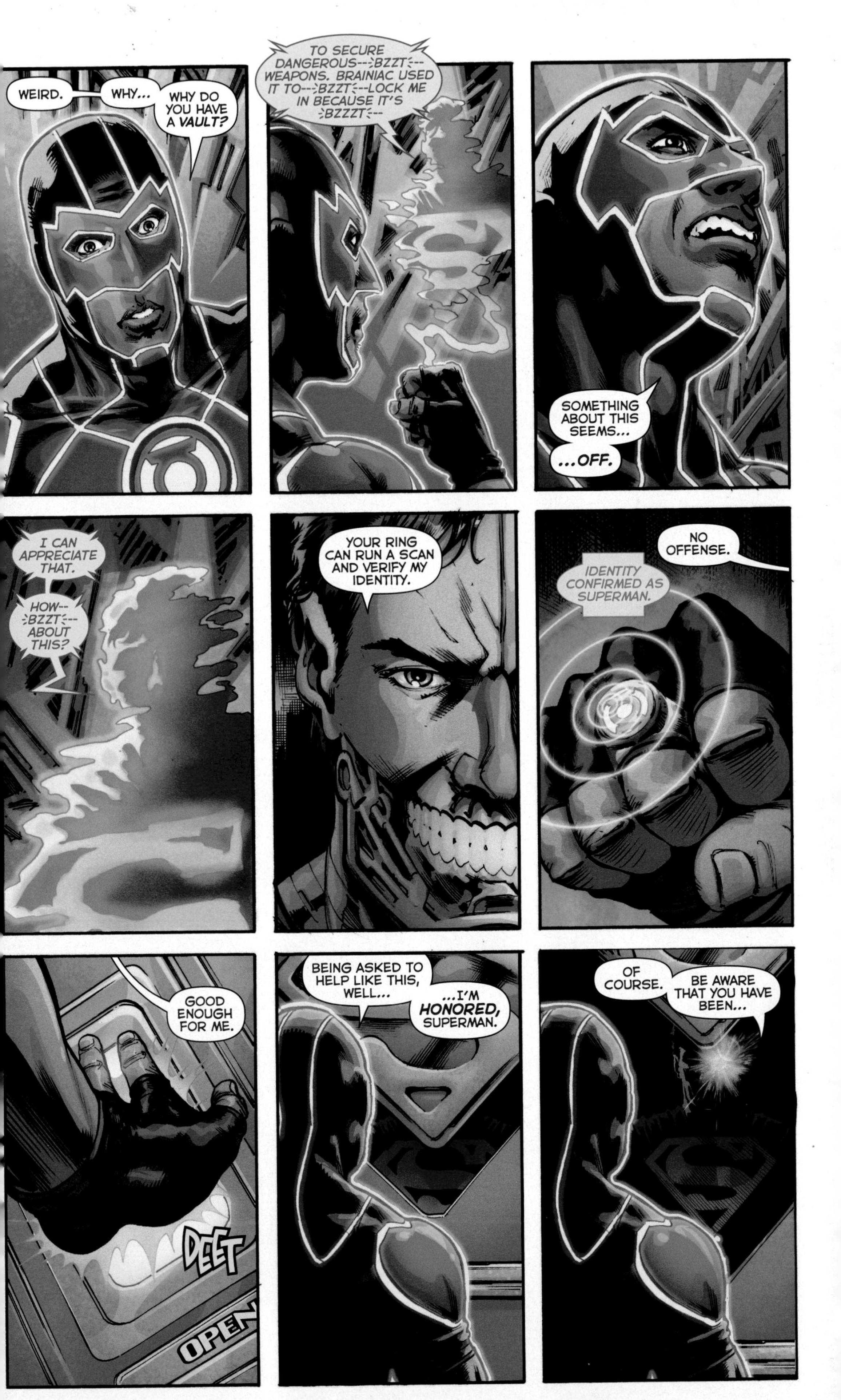
WEIRD.
WHY...
WHY DO YOU HAVE A VAULT?
TO SECURE DANGEROUS--BZZT--WEAPONS. BRAINIAC USED IT TO--BZZT--LOCK ME IN BECAUSE IT'S BZZZT--
SOMETHING ABOUT THIS SEEMS...
...OFF.
I CAN APPRECIATE THAT.
HOW--BZZT--ABOUT THIS?
YOUR RING CAN RUN A SCAN AND VERIFY MY IDENTITY.
NO OFFENSE.
IDENTITY CONFIRMED AS SUPERMAN.
GOOD ENOUGH FOR ME.
DEET
OPEN
BEING ASKED TO HELP LIKE THIS, WELL...
...I'M HONORED, SUPERMAN.
OF COURSE.
BE AWARE THAT YOU HAVE BEEN...

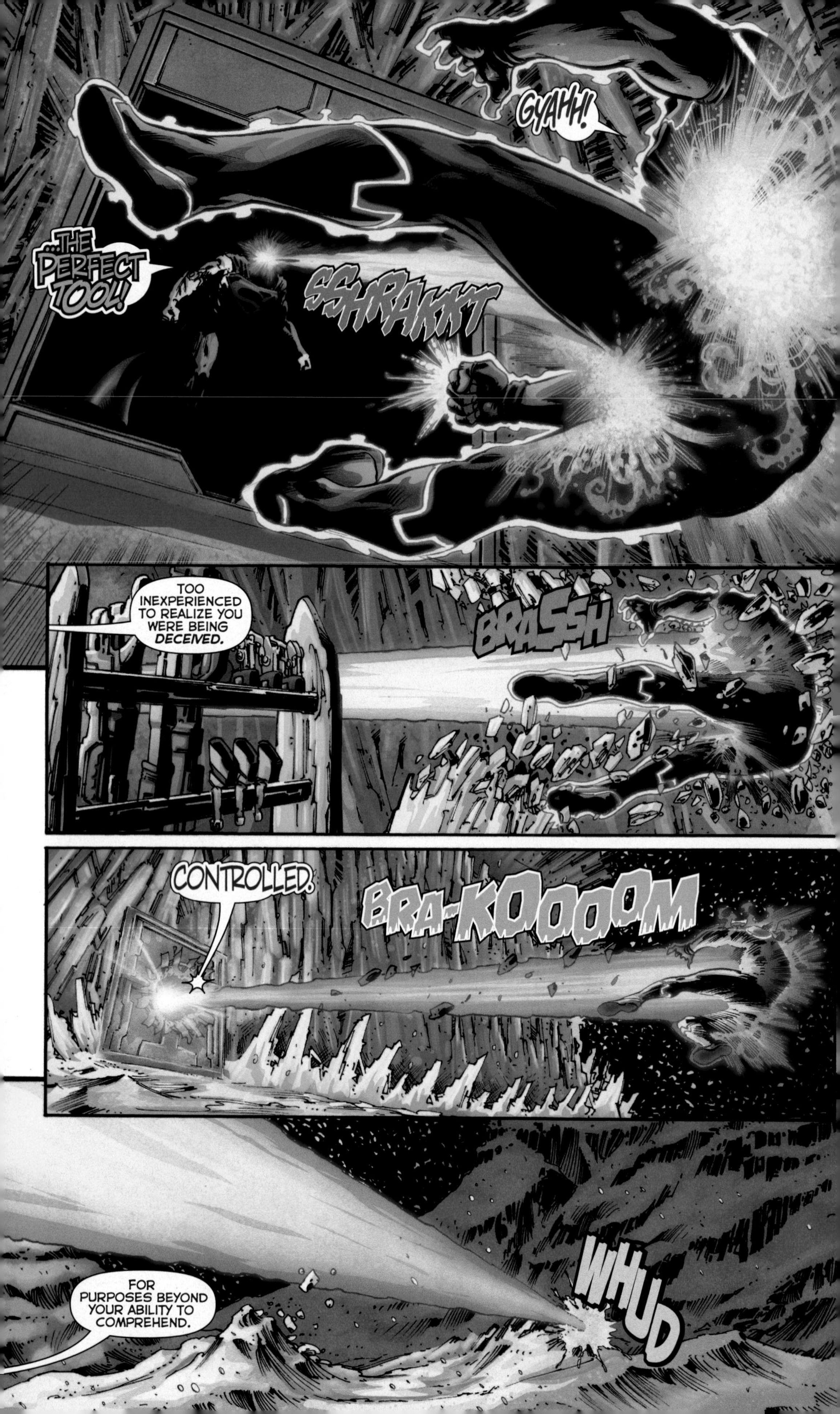
GYAHH!
...THE PERFECT TOOL!
SSHRAKKT
TOO INEXPERIENCED TO REALIZE YOU WERE BEING DECEIVED.
BRASSH
CONTROLLED.
BRA-KOOOOM
FOR PURPOSES BEYOND YOUR ABILITY TO COMPREHEND.
WHUD

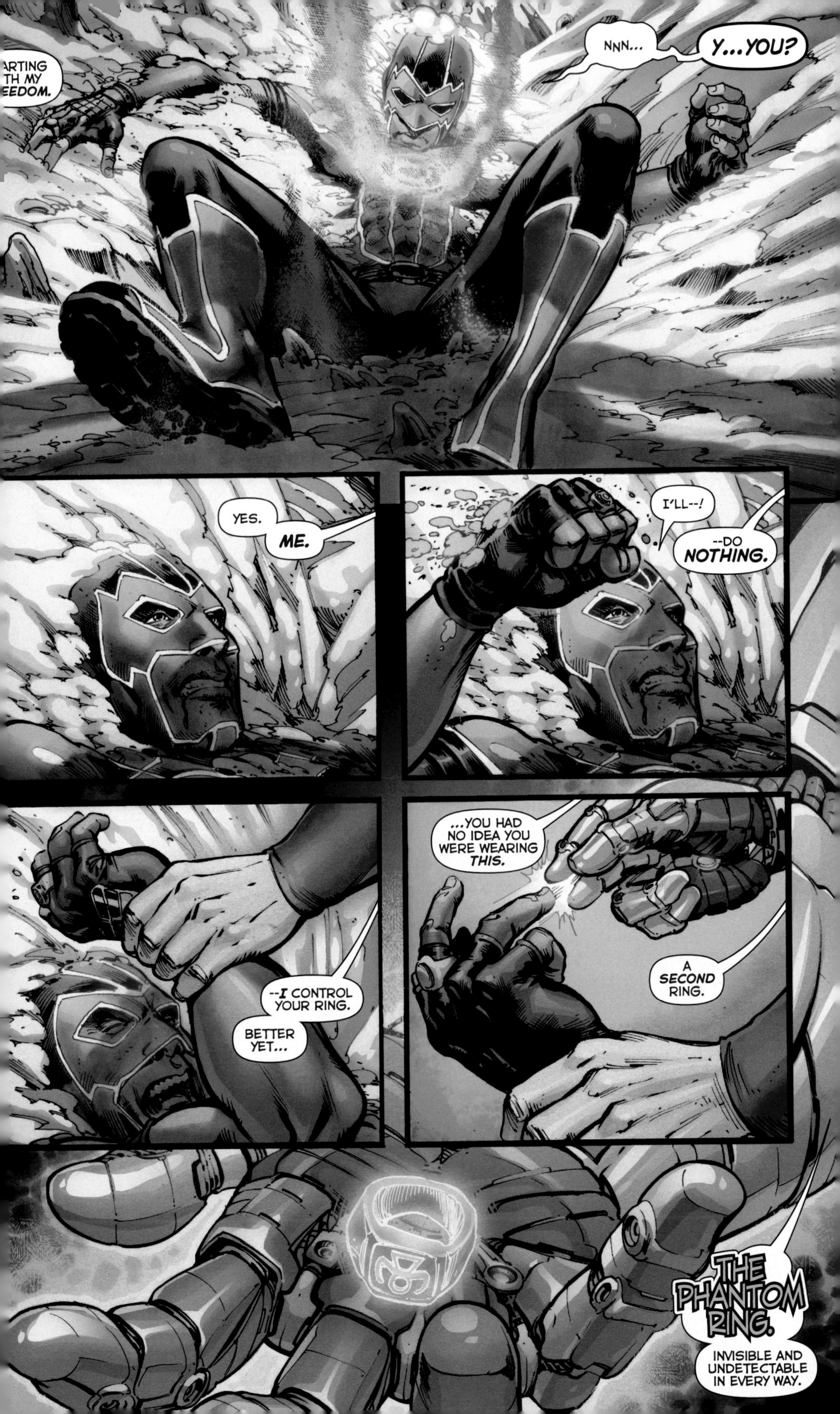

ARTING
TH MY
EEDOM.
NNN...
Y...YOU?
YES.
ME.
I'LL--!
--DO
NOTHING.
--I CONTROL
YOUR RING.
BETTER
YET...
...YOU HAD
NO IDEA YOU
WERE WEARING
THIS.
A
SECOND
RING.
THE
PHANTOM
RING.
INVISIBLE AND
UNDETECTABLE
IN EVERY WAY.

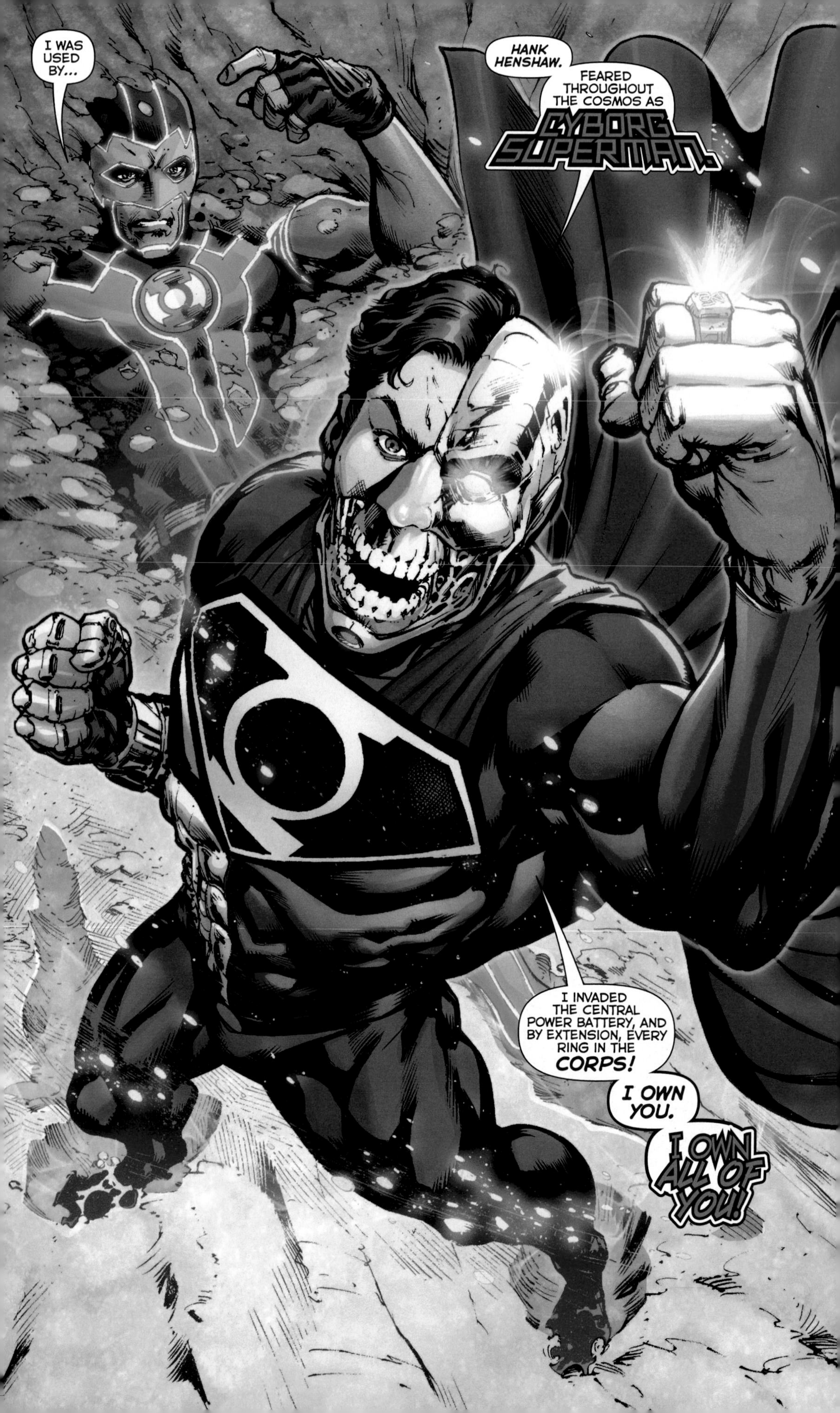
I WAS USED BY...
HANK HENSHAW.
FEARED THROUGHOUT THE COSMOS AS CYBORG SUPERMAN.
I INVADED THE CENTRAL POWER BATTERY, AND BY EXTENSION, EVERY RING IN THE CORPS!
I OWN YOU.
I OWN ALL OF YOU!

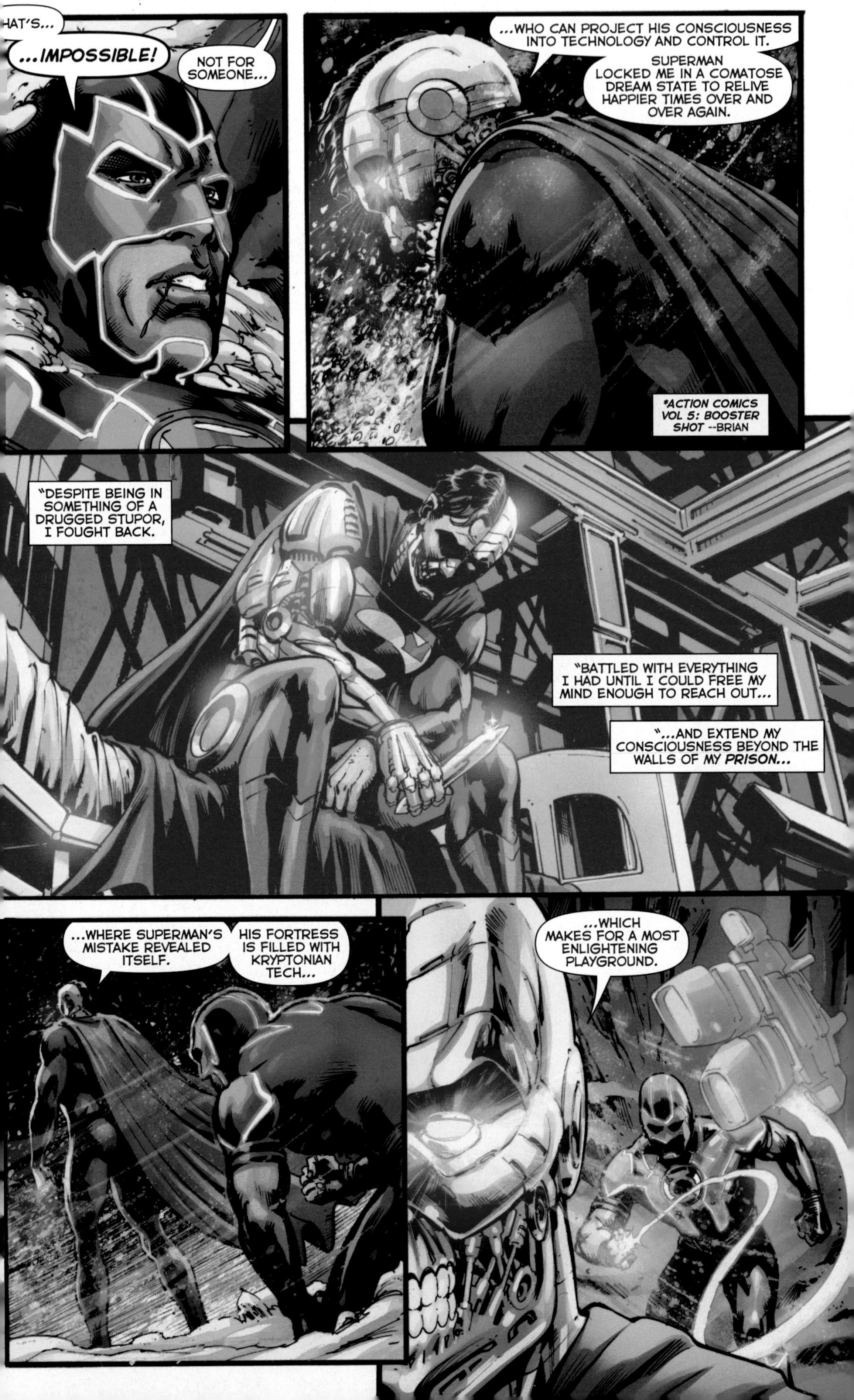
HAT'S...
...IMPOSSIBLE!
NOT FOR SOMEONE...
...WHO CAN PROJECT HIS CONSCIOUSNESS INTO TECHNOLOGY AND CONTROL IT.
SUPERMAN LOCKED ME IN A COMATOSE DREAM STATE TO RELIVE HAPPIER TIMES OVER AND OVER AGAIN.
*ACTION COMICS VOL 5: BOOSTER SHOT --BRIAN
"DESPITE BEING IN SOMETHING OF A DRUGGED STUPOR, I FOUGHT BACK.
"BATTLED WITH EVERYTHING I HAD UNTIL I COULD FREE MY MIND ENOUGH TO REACH OUT...
"...AND EXTEND MY CONSCIOUSNESS BEYOND THE WALLS OF MY PRISON...
...WHERE SUPERMAN'S MISTAKE REVEALED ITSELF.
HIS FORTRESS IS FILLED WITH KRYPTONIAN TECH...
...WHICH MAKES FOR A MOST ENLIGHTENING PLAYGROUND.

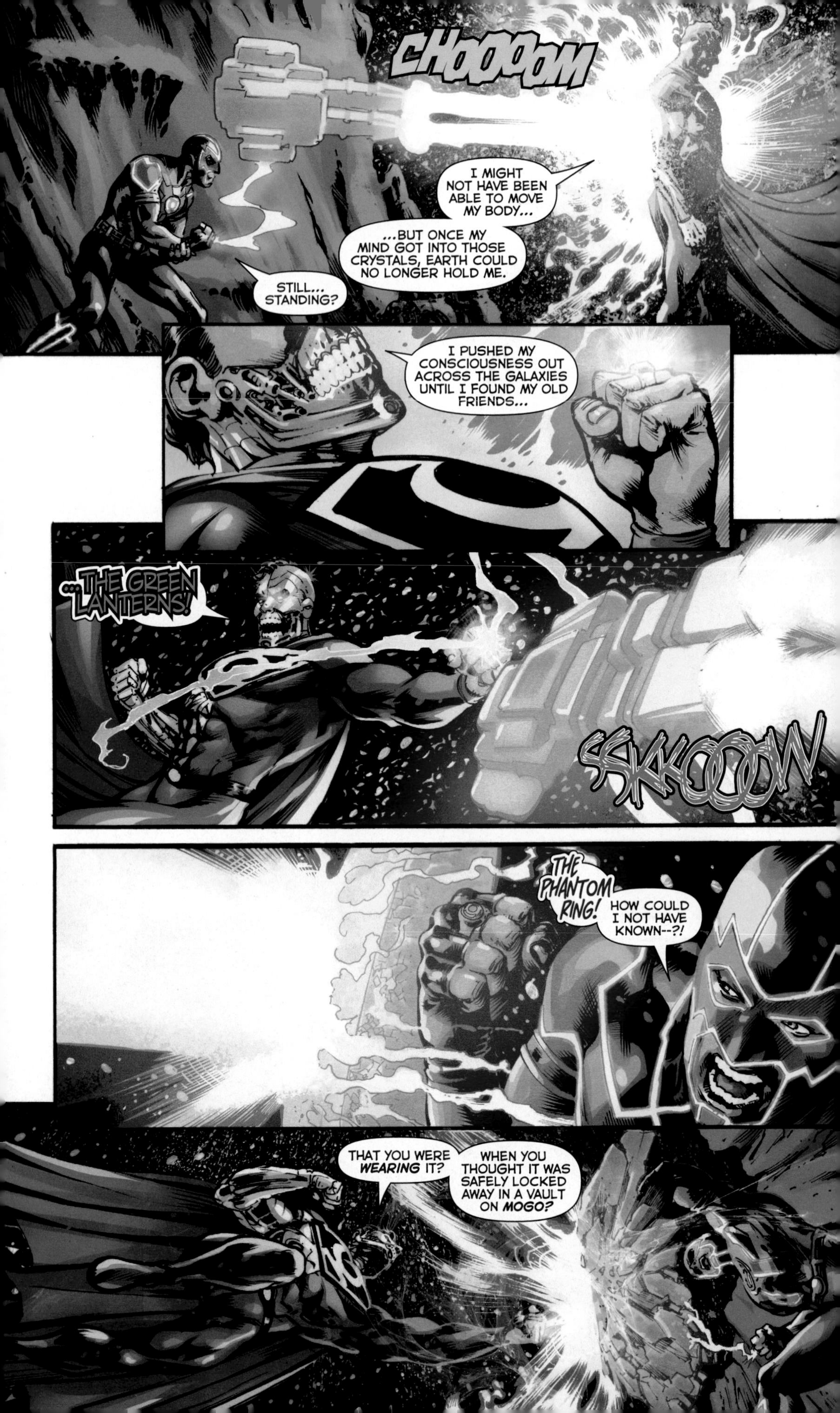
CHOOOOOM
I MIGHT NOT HAVE BEEN ABLE TO MOVE MY BODY...
...BUT ONCE MY MIND GOT INTO THOSE CRYSTALS, EARTH COULD NO LONGER HOLD ME.
STILL... STANDING?
I PUSHED MY CONSCIOUSNESS OUT ACROSS THE GALAXIES UNTIL I FOUND MY OLD FRIENDS...
...THE GREEN LANTERNS!
SSKKOOOOW
THE PHANTOM RING!
HOW COULD I NOT HAVE KNOWN--?!
THAT YOU WERE *WEARING* IT?
WHEN YOU THOUGHT IT WAS SAFELY LOCKED AWAY IN A VAULT ON *MOGO?*

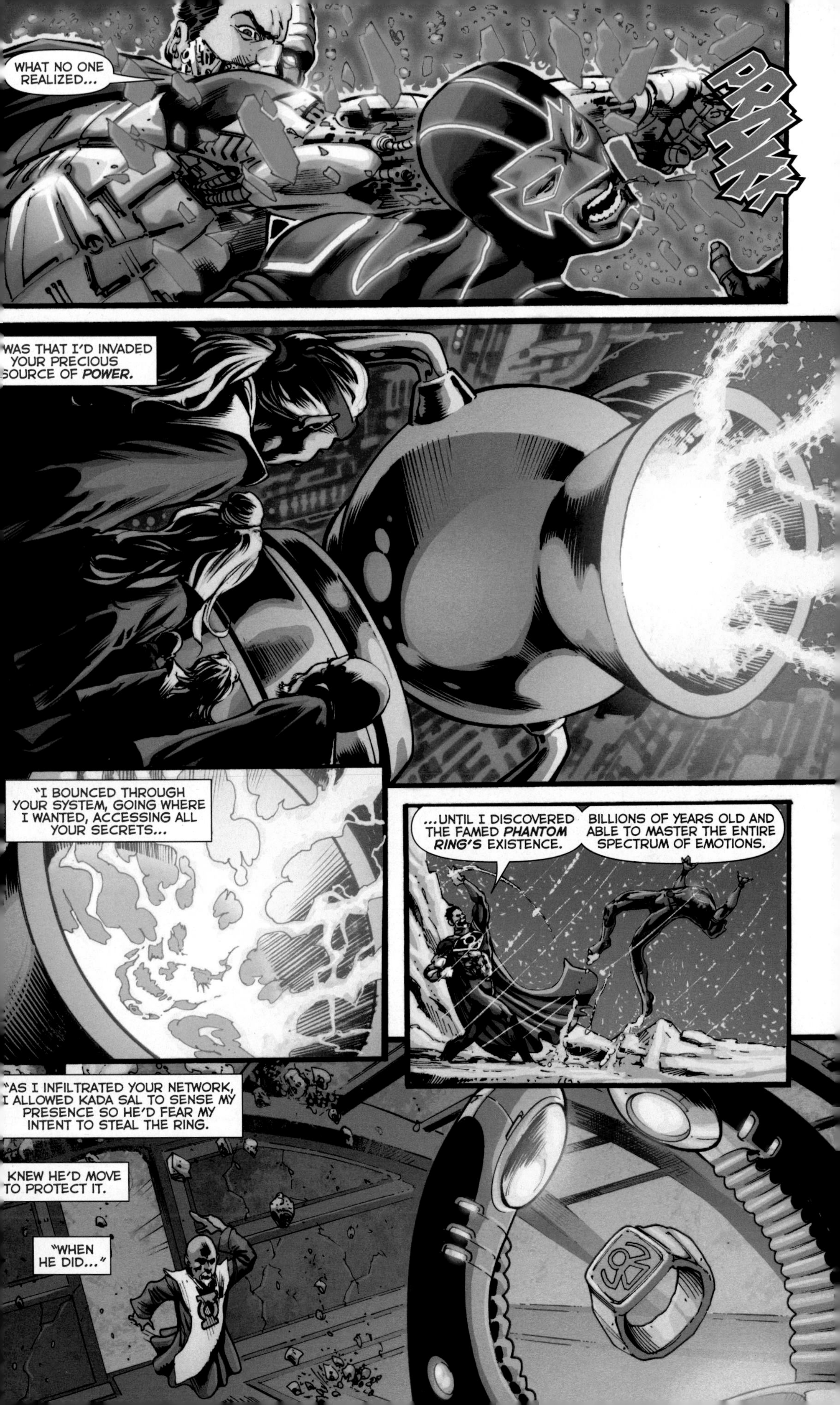
WHAT NO ONE REALIZED...
PRAKK
WAS THAT I'D INVADED YOUR PRECIOUS SOURCE OF *POWER.*
"I BOUNCED THROUGH YOUR SYSTEM, GOING WHERE I WANTED, ACCESSING ALL YOUR SECRETS...
...UNTIL I DISCOVERED THE FAMED *PHANTOM RING'S* EXISTENCE.
BILLIONS OF YEARS OLD AND ABLE TO MASTER THE ENTIRE SPECTRUM OF EMOTIONS.
"AS I INFILTRATED YOUR NETWORK, I ALLOWED KADA SAL TO SENSE MY PRESENCE SO HE'D FEAR MY INTENT TO STEAL THE RING.
KNEW HE'D MOVE TO PROTECT IT.
"WHEN HE DID..."

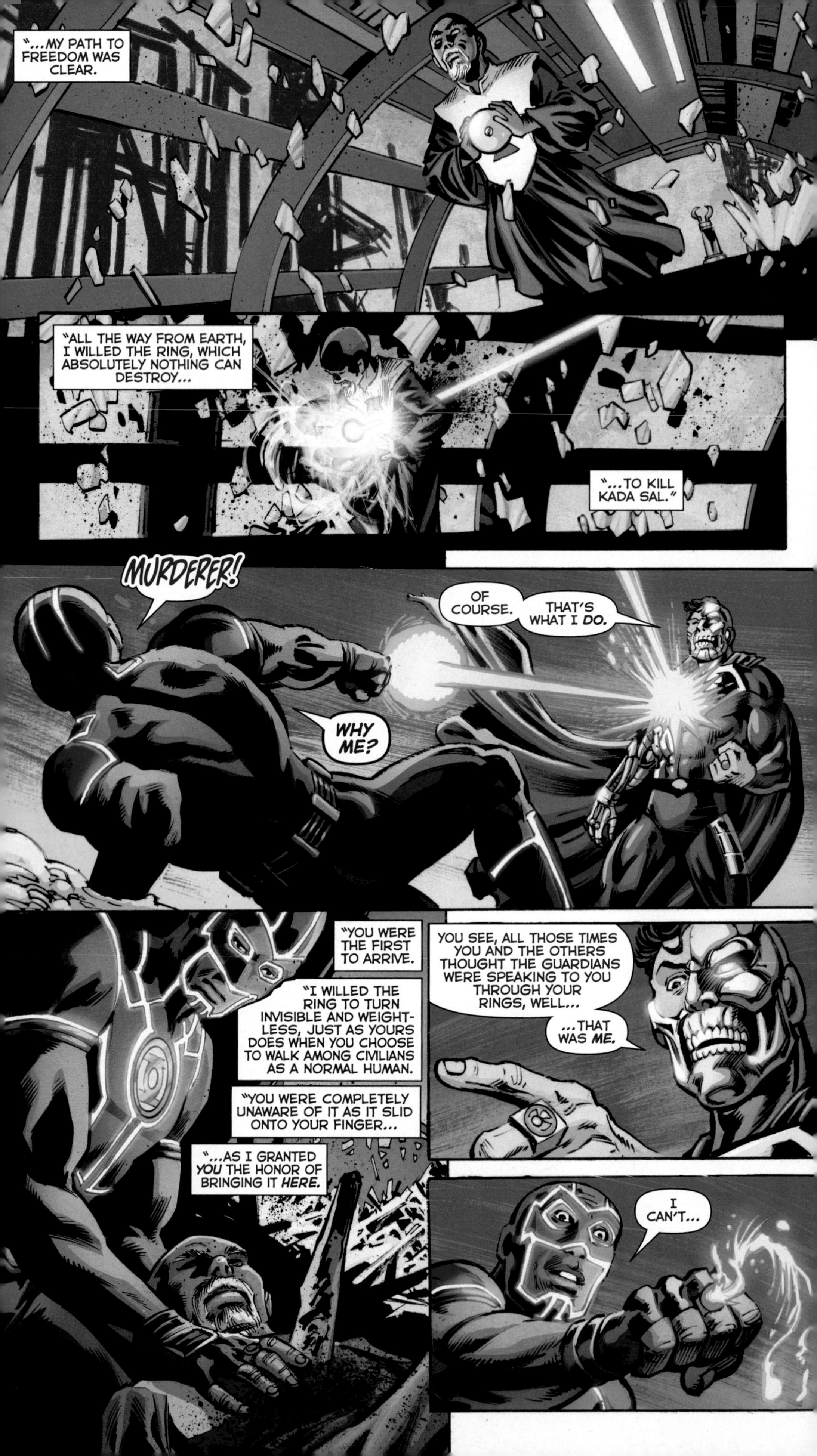
"...MY PATH TO FREEDOM WAS CLEAR.
"ALL THE WAY FROM EARTH, I WILLED THE RING, WHICH ABSOLUTELY NOTHING CAN DESTROY...
"...TO KILL KADA SAL."
MURDERER!
WHY ME?
OF COURSE.
THAT'S WHAT I DO.
"YOU WERE THE FIRST TO ARRIVE.
"I WILLED THE RING TO TURN INVISIBLE AND WEIGHTLESS, JUST AS YOURS DOES WHEN YOU CHOOSE TO WALK AMONG CIVILIANS AS A NORMAL HUMAN.
"YOU WERE COMPLETELY UNAWARE OF IT AS IT SLID ONTO YOUR FINGER...
"...AS I GRANTED YOU THE HONOR OF BRINGING IT HERE.
YOU SEE, ALL THOSE TIMES YOU AND THE OTHERS THOUGHT THE GUARDIANS WERE SPEAKING TO YOU THROUGH YOUR RINGS, WELL...
...THAT WAS ME.
I CAN'T...

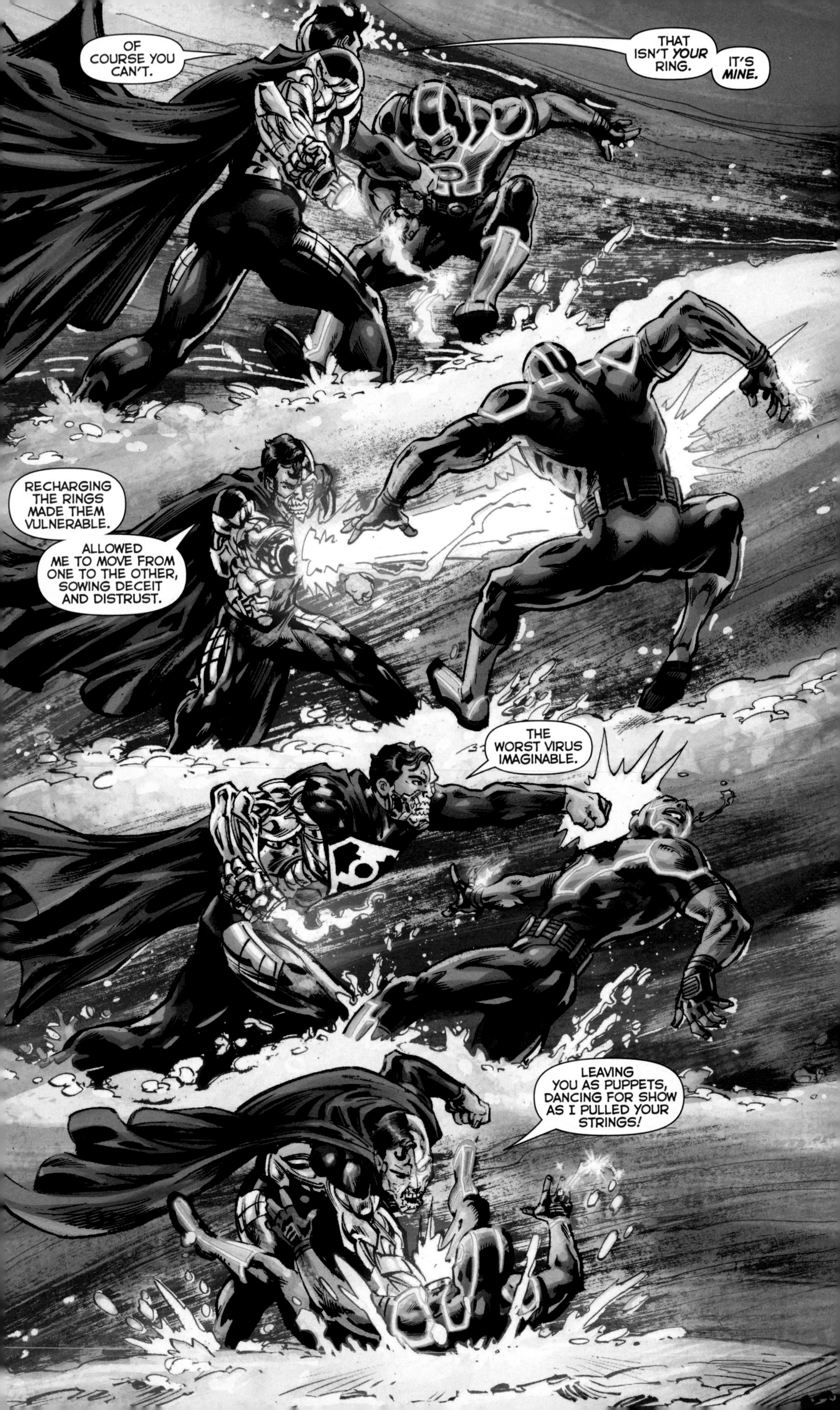

OF COURSE YOU CAN'T.
THAT ISN'T *YOUR* RING.
IT'S *MINE.*
RECHARGING THE RINGS MADE THEM VULNERABLE.
ALLOWED ME TO MOVE FROM ONE TO THE OTHER, SOWING DECEIT AND DISTRUST.
THE WORST VIRUS IMAGINABLE.
LEAVING YOU AS PUPPETS, DANCING FOR SHOW AS I PULLED YOUR STRINGS!

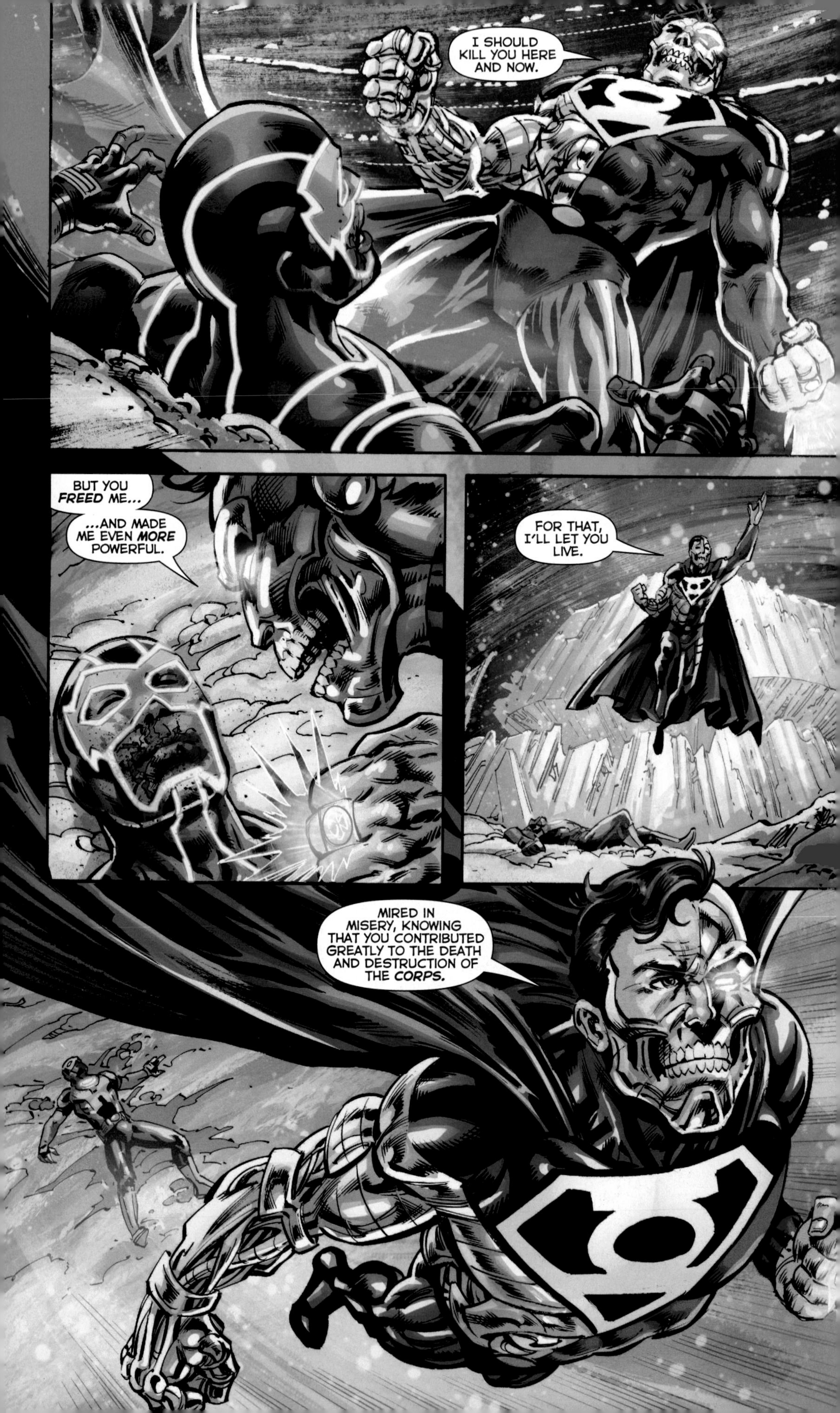
I SHOULD KILL YOU HERE AND NOW.
BUT YOU *FREED* ME...
...AND MADE ME EVEN *MORE* POWERFUL.
FOR THAT, I'LL LET YOU LIVE.
MIRED IN MISERY, KNOWING THAT YOU CONTRIBUTED GREATLY TO THE DEATH AND DESTRUCTION OF THE *CORPS*.

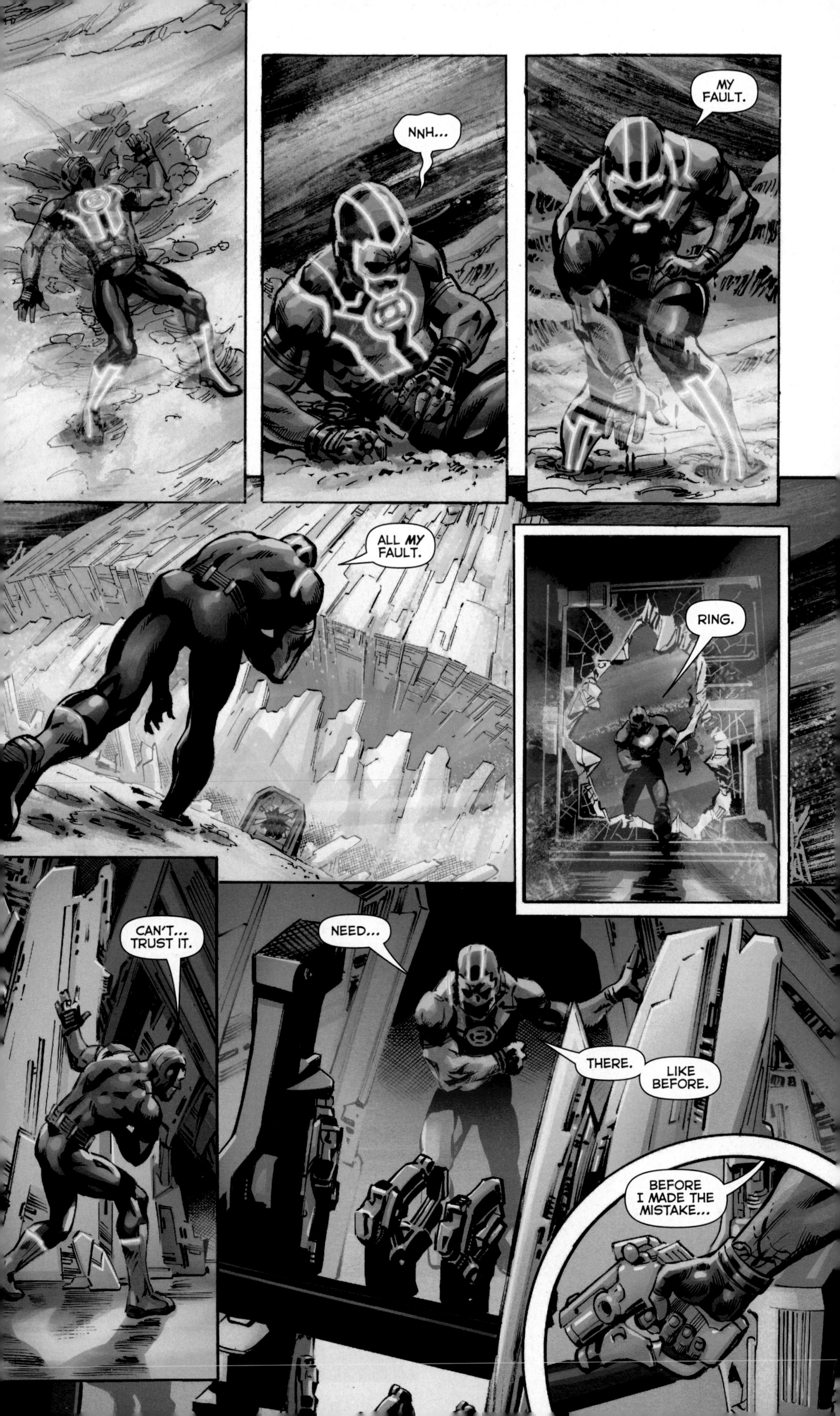
NNH...
MY FAULT.
ALL MY FAULT.
RING.
CAN'T... TRUST IT.
NEED...
THERE.
LIKE BEFORE.
BEFORE I MADE THE MISTAKE...

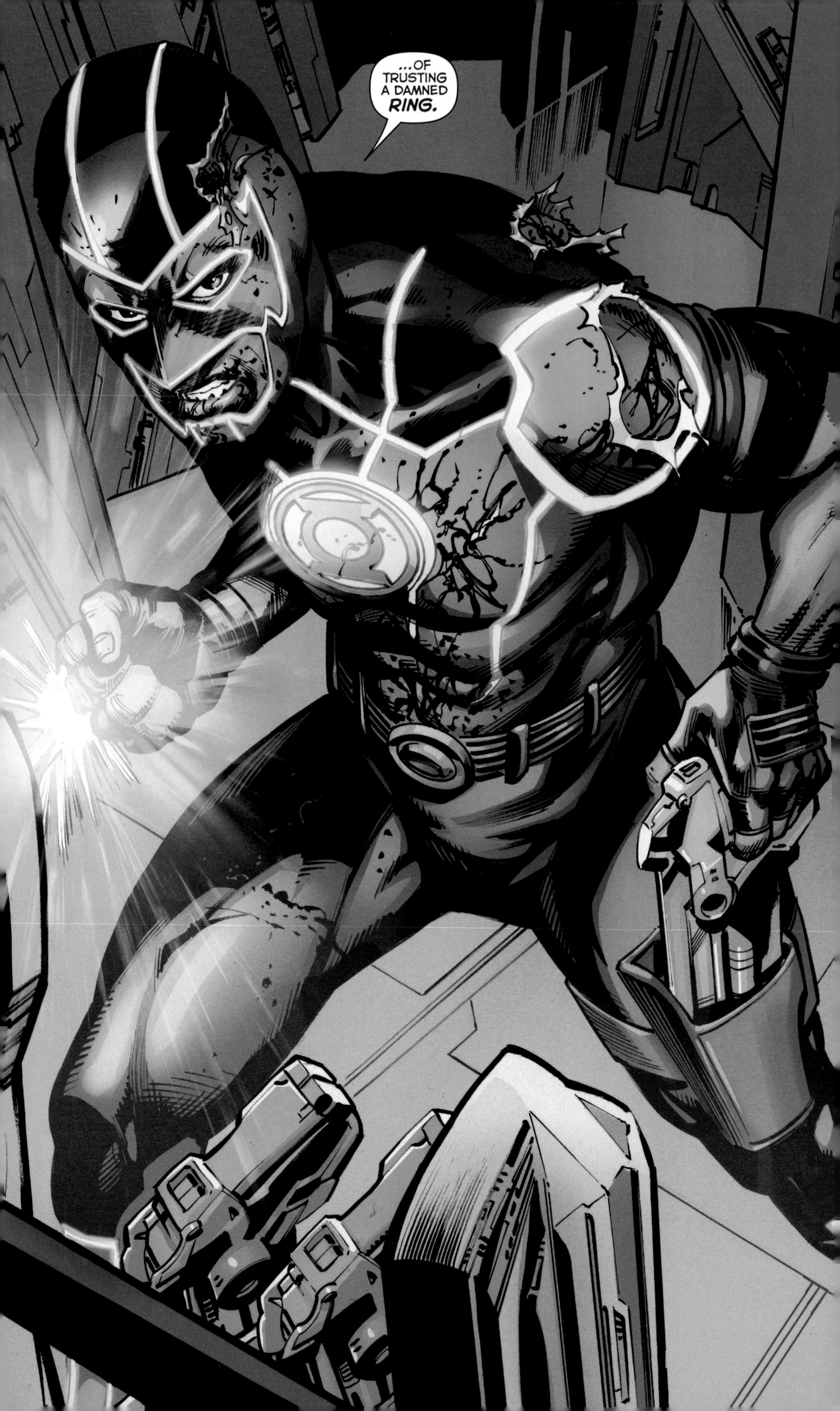
...OF TRUSTING A DAMNED RING.

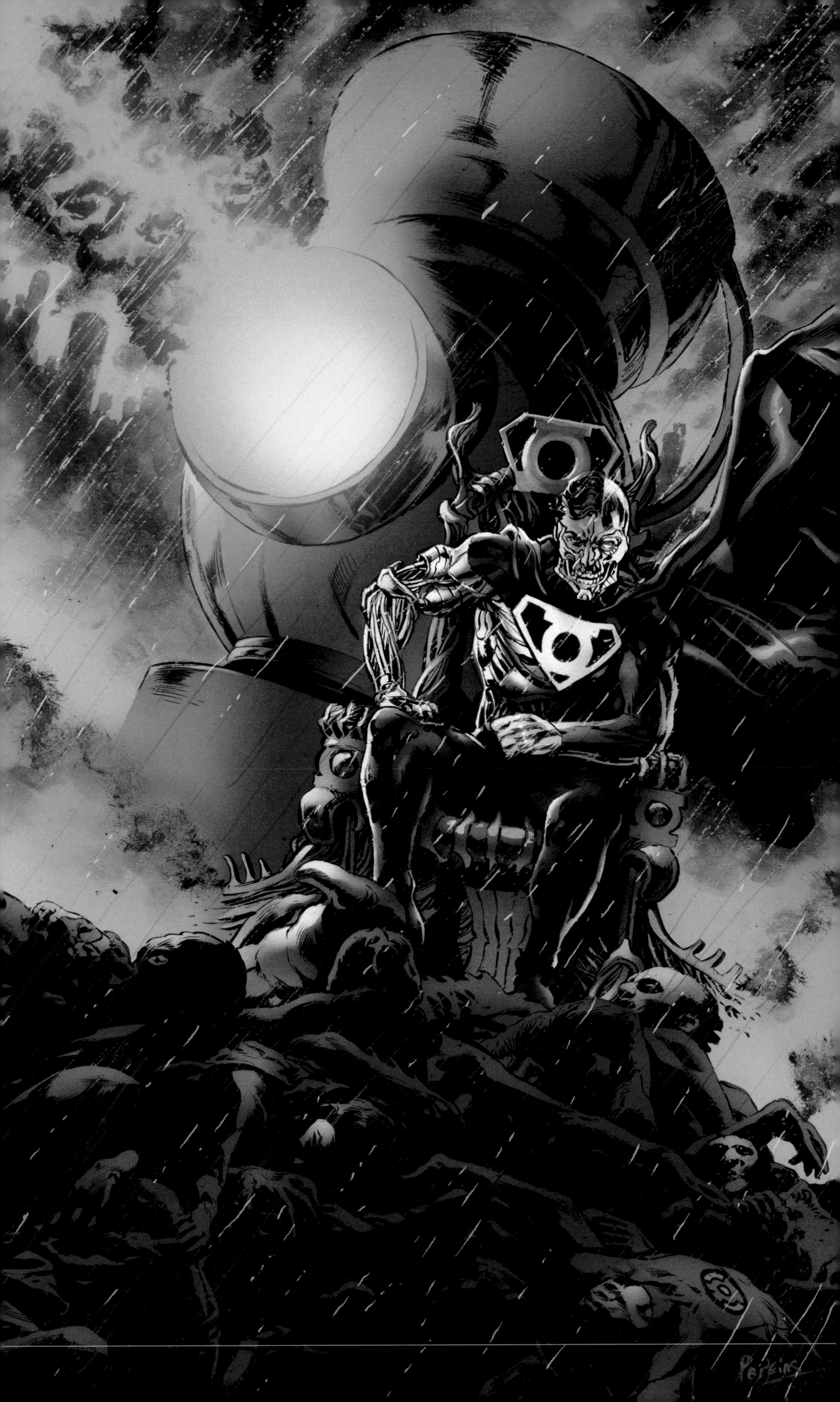
Perkins

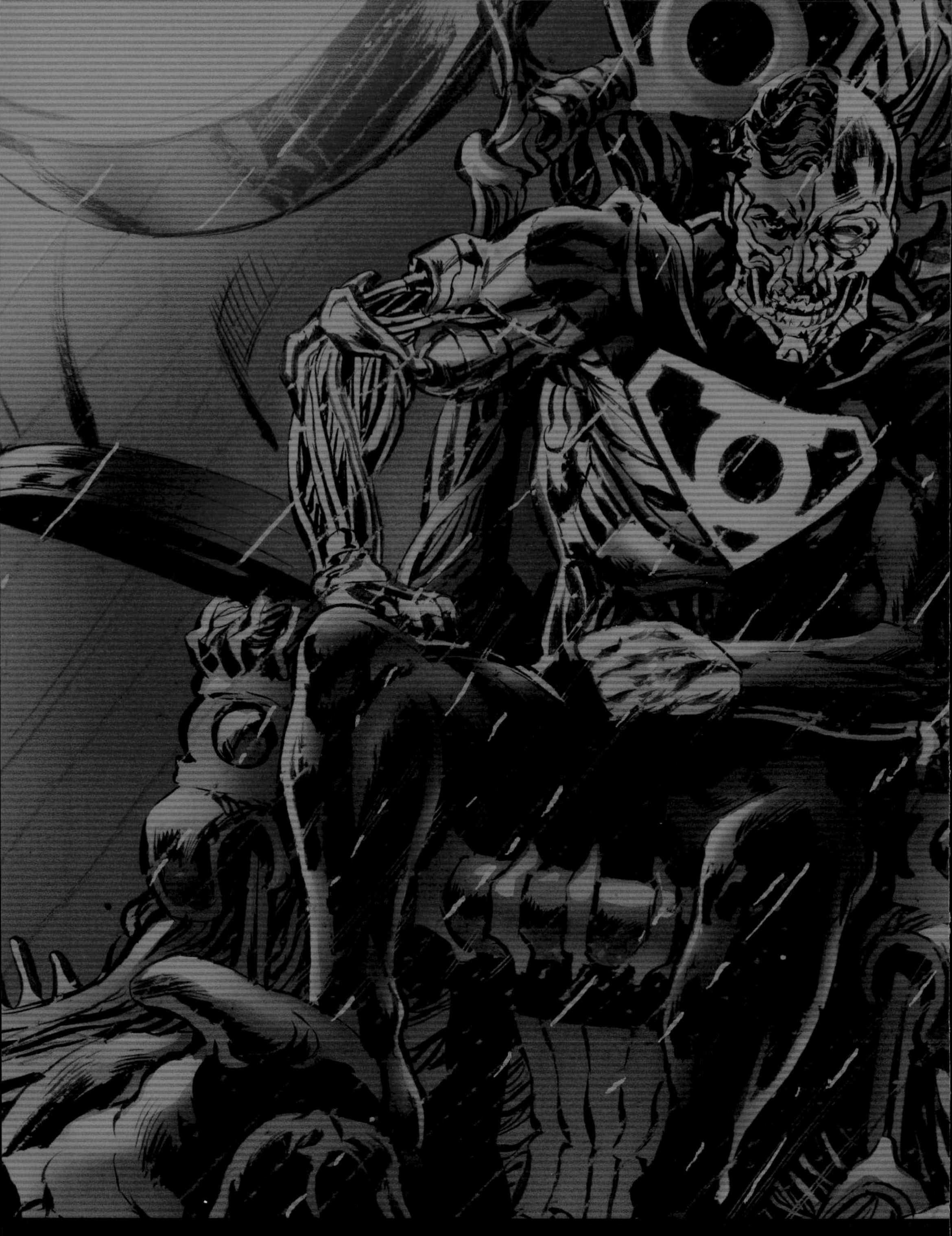

GREEN LANTERNS

#55

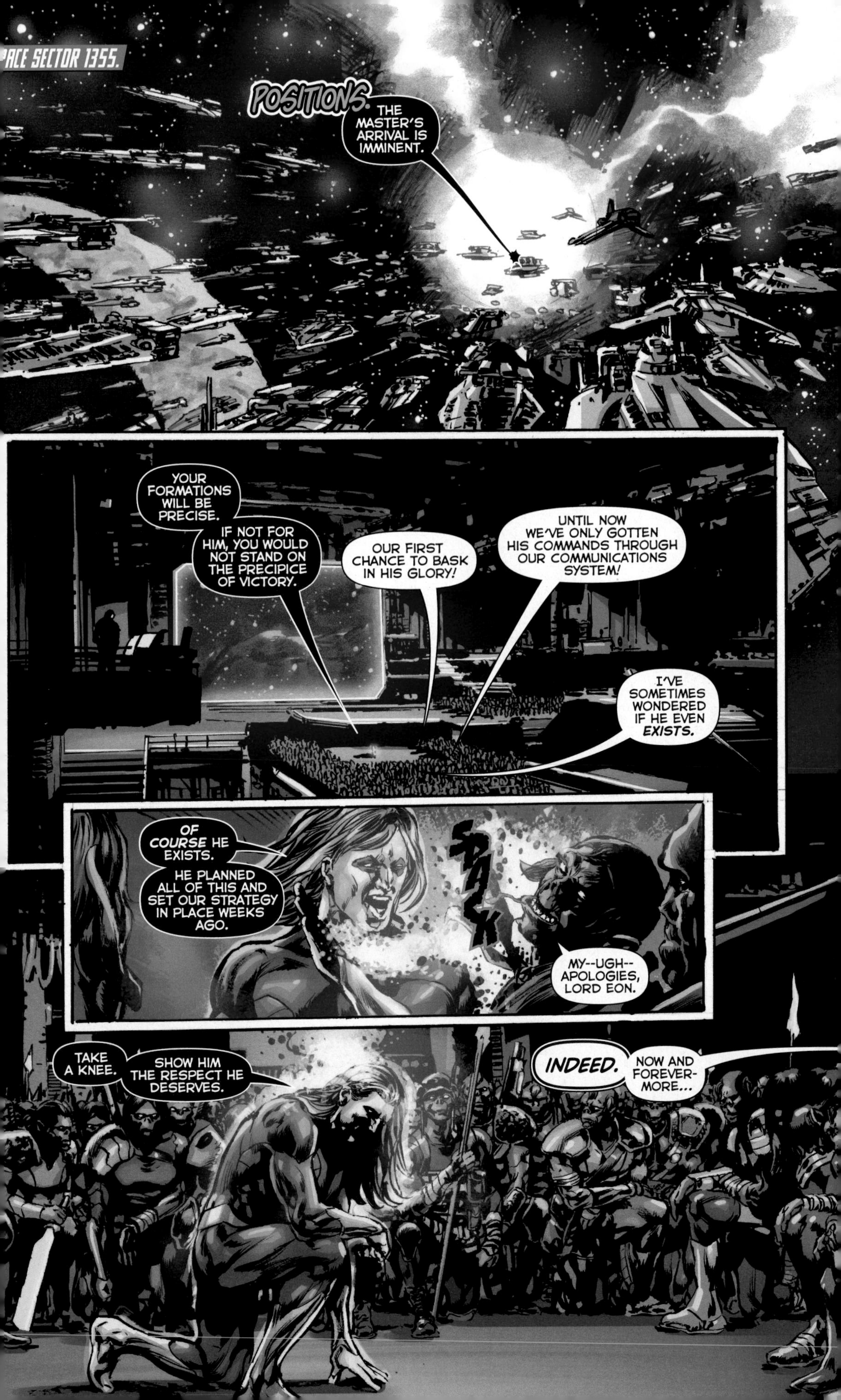

ACE SECTOR 1355.
POSITIONS.
THE MASTER'S ARRIVAL IS IMMINENT.
YOUR FORMATIONS WILL BE PRECISE.
IF NOT FOR HIM, YOU WOULD NOT STAND ON THE PRECIPICE OF VICTORY.
OUR FIRST CHANCE TO BASK IN HIS GLORY!
UNTIL NOW WE'VE ONLY GOTTEN HIS COMMANDS THROUGH OUR COMMUNICATIONS SYSTEM!
I'VE SOMETIMES WONDERED IF HE EVEN *EXISTS.*
OF COURSE HE EXISTS.
HE PLANNED ALL OF THIS AND SET OUR STRATEGY IN PLACE WEEKS AGO.
SPAK
MY--UGH--APOLOGIES, LORD EON.
TAKE A KNEE.
SHOW HIM THE RESPECT HE DESERVES.
INDEED.
NOW AND FOREVER-MORE...

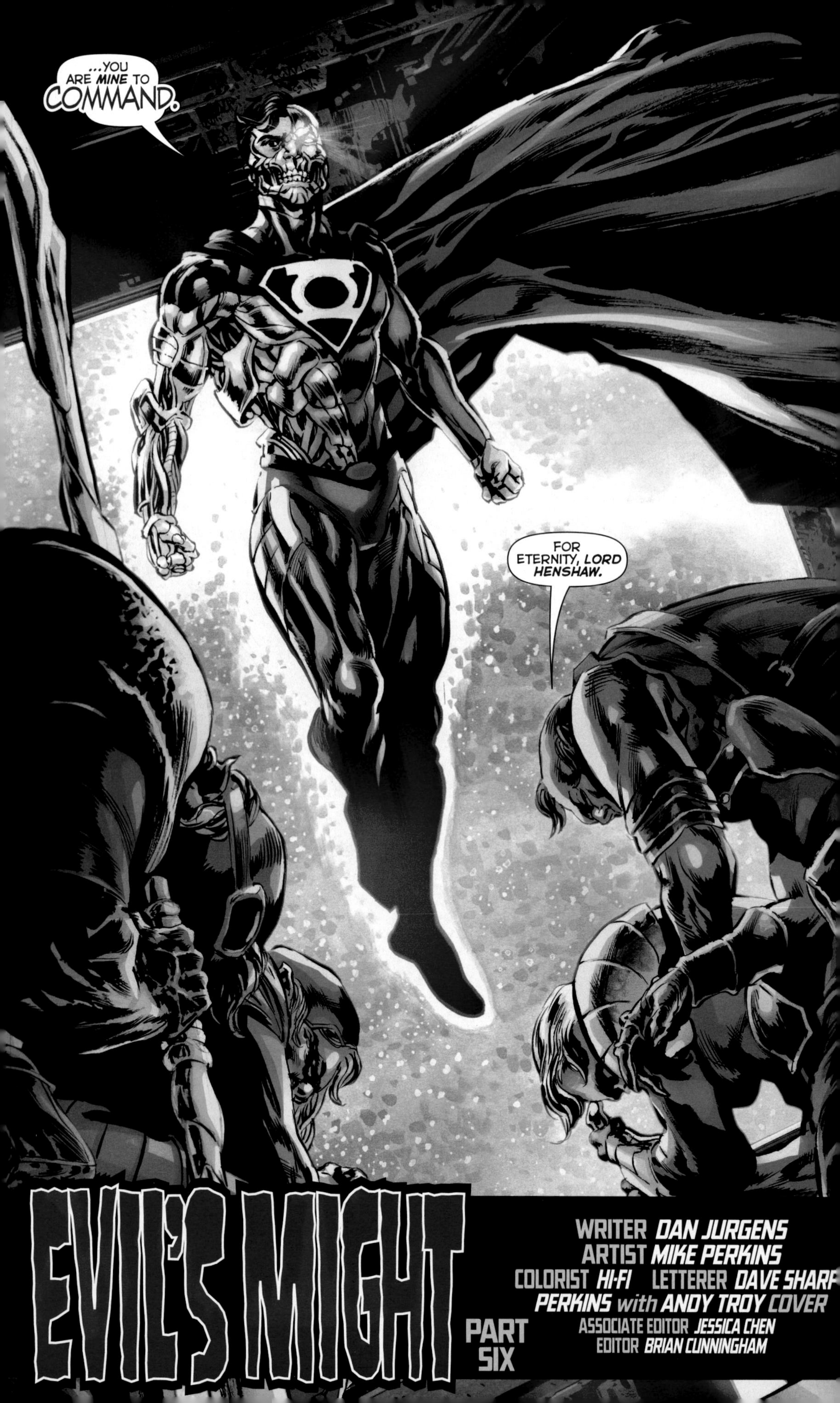

...YOU ARE MINE TO COMMAND.
FOR ETERNITY, LORD HENSHAW.
EVIL'S MIGHT
PART SIX
WRITER DAN JURGENS
ARTIST MIKE PERKINS
COLORIST HI-FI LETTERER DAVE SHARPE
PERKINS with ANDY TROY COVER
ASSOCIATE EDITOR JESSICA CHEN
EDITOR BRIAN CUNNINGHAM

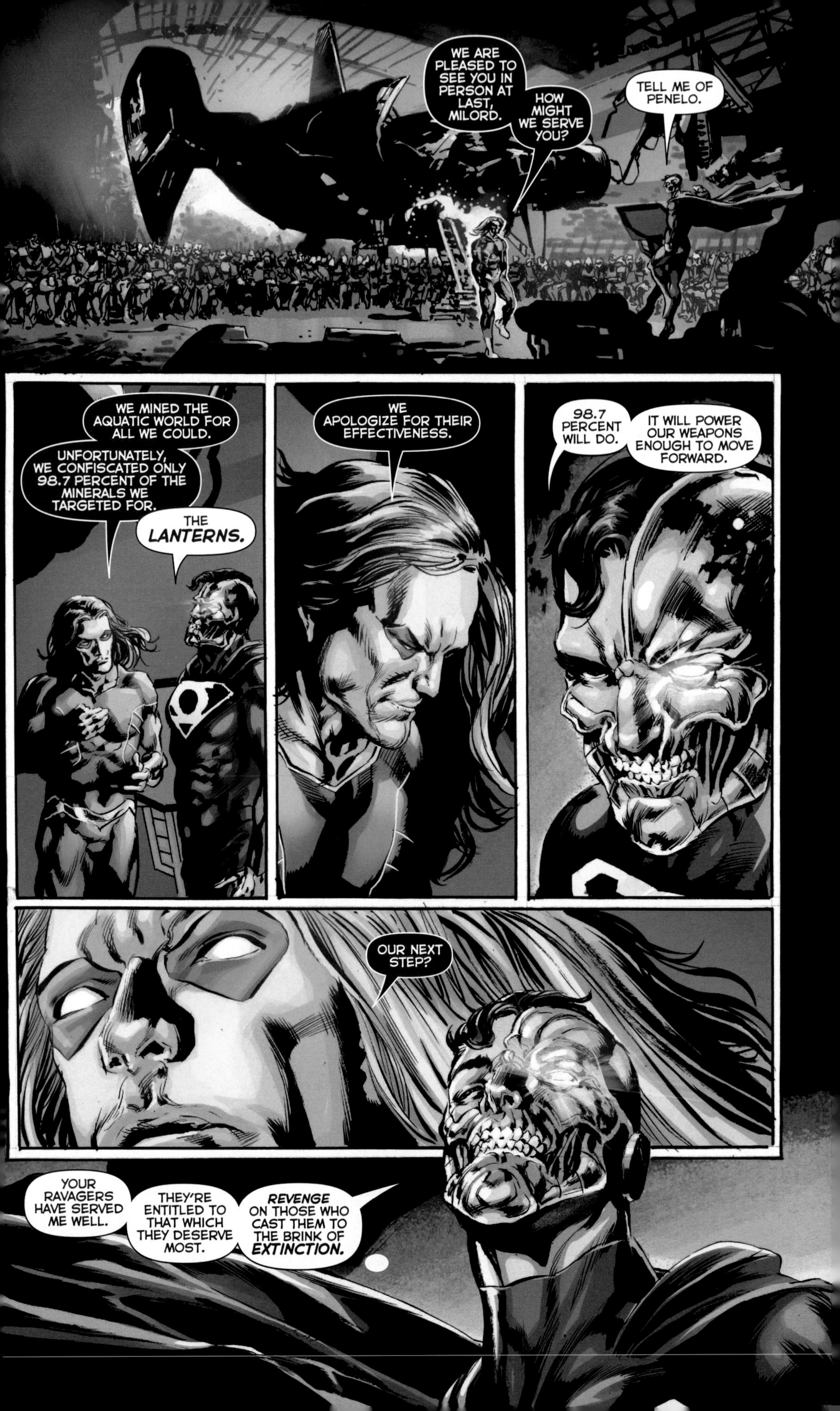
WE ARE PLEASED TO SEE YOU IN PERSON AT LAST, MILORD.
HOW MIGHT WE SERVE YOU?
TELL ME OF PENELO.
WE MINED THE AQUATIC WORLD FOR ALL WE COULD.
UNFORTUNATELY, WE CONFISCATED ONLY 98.7 PERCENT OF THE MINERALS WE TARGETED FOR.
THE LANTERNS.
WE APOLOGIZE FOR THEIR EFFECTIVENESS.
98.7 PERCENT WILL DO.
IT WILL POWER OUR WEAPONS ENOUGH TO MOVE FORWARD.
OUR NEXT STEP?
YOUR RAVAGERS HAVE SERVED ME WELL.
THEY'RE ENTITLED TO THAT WHICH THEY DESERVE MOST.
REVENGE ON THOSE WHO CAST THEM TO THE BRINK OF EXTINCTION.

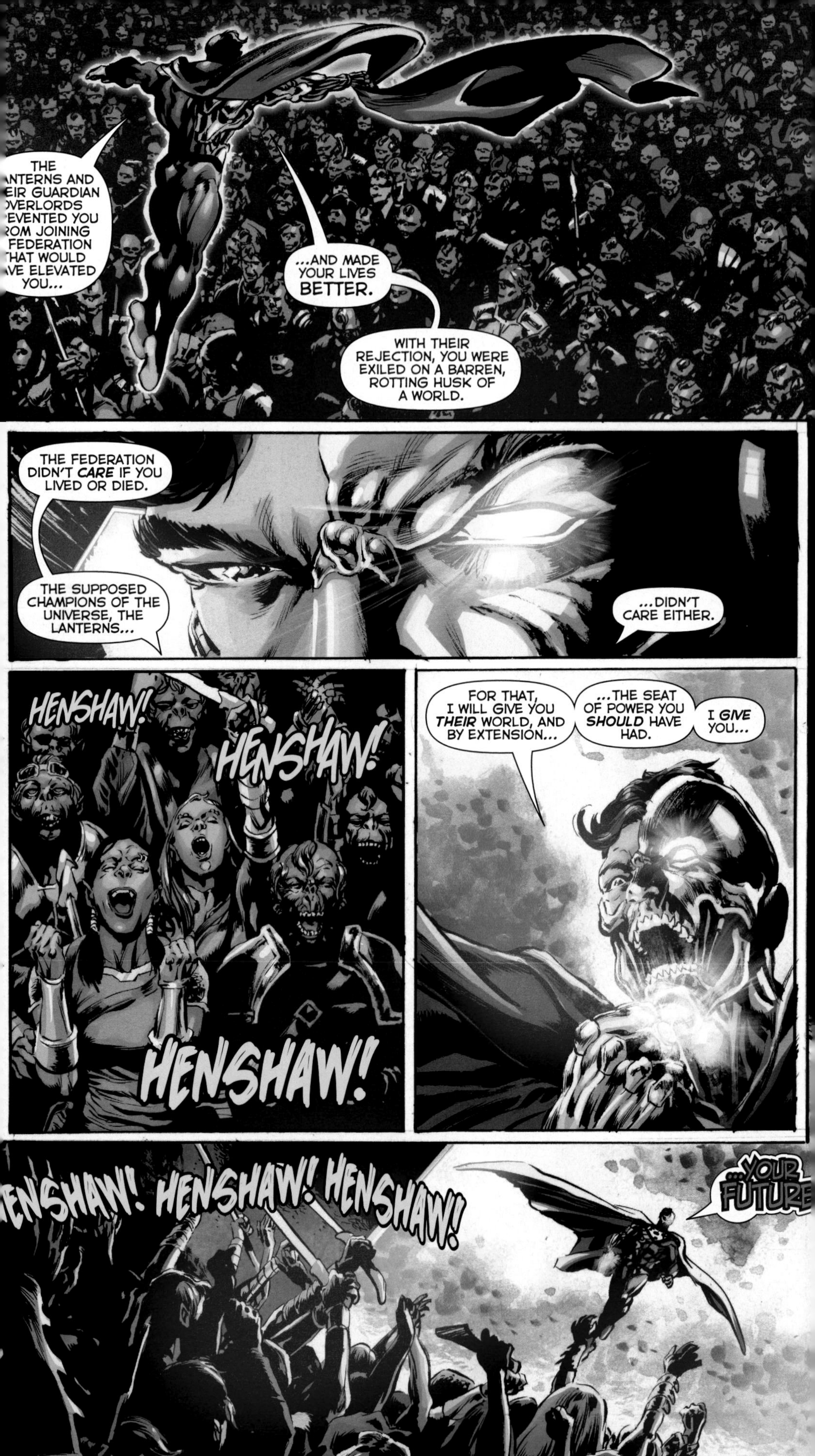
THE ANTERNS AND EIR GUARDIAN OVERLORDS EVENTED YOU ROM JOINING FEDERATION THAT WOULD VE ELEVATED YOU...
...AND MADE YOUR LIVES BETTER.
WITH THEIR REJECTION, YOU WERE EXILED ON A BARREN, ROTTING HUSK OF A WORLD.
THE FEDERATION DIDN'T CARE IF YOU LIVED OR DIED.
THE SUPPOSED CHAMPIONS OF THE UNIVERSE, THE LANTERNS...
...DIDN'T CARE EITHER.
HENSHAW!
HENSHAW!
HENSHAW!
FOR THAT, I WILL GIVE YOU THEIR WORLD, AND BY EXTENSION...
...THE SEAT OF POWER YOU SHOULD HAVE HAD.
I GIVE YOU...
ENSHAW! HENSHAW! HENSHAW!
...YOUR FUTURE!

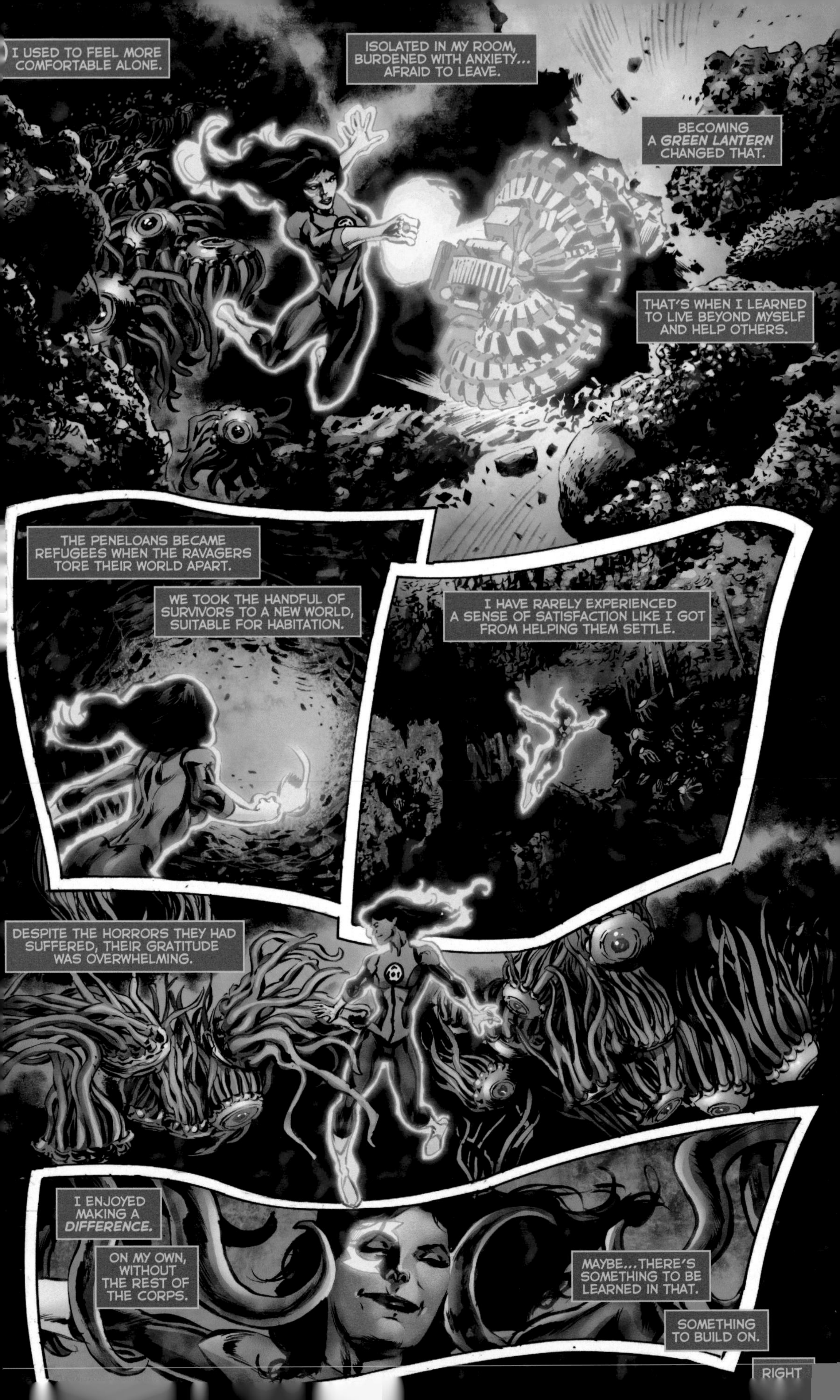

I USED TO FEEL MORE COMFORTABLE ALONE.
ISOLATED IN MY ROOM, BURDENED WITH ANXIETY... AFRAID TO LEAVE.
BECOMING A *GREEN LANTERN* CHANGED THAT.
THAT'S WHEN I LEARNED TO LIVE BEYOND MYSELF AND HELP OTHERS.
THE PENELOANS BECAME REFUGEES WHEN THE RAVAGERS TORE THEIR WORLD APART.
WE TOOK THE HANDFUL OF SURVIVORS TO A NEW WORLD, SUITABLE FOR HABITATION.
I HAVE RARELY EXPERIENCED A SENSE OF SATISFACTION LIKE I GOT FROM HELPING THEM SETTLE.
DESPITE THE HORRORS THEY HAD SUFFERED, THEIR GRATITUDE WAS OVERWHELMING.
I ENJOYED MAKING A *DIFFERENCE.*
ON MY OWN, WITHOUT THE REST OF THE CORPS.
MAYBE...THERE'S SOMETHING TO BE LEARNED IN THAT.
SOMETHING TO BUILD ON.
RIGHT

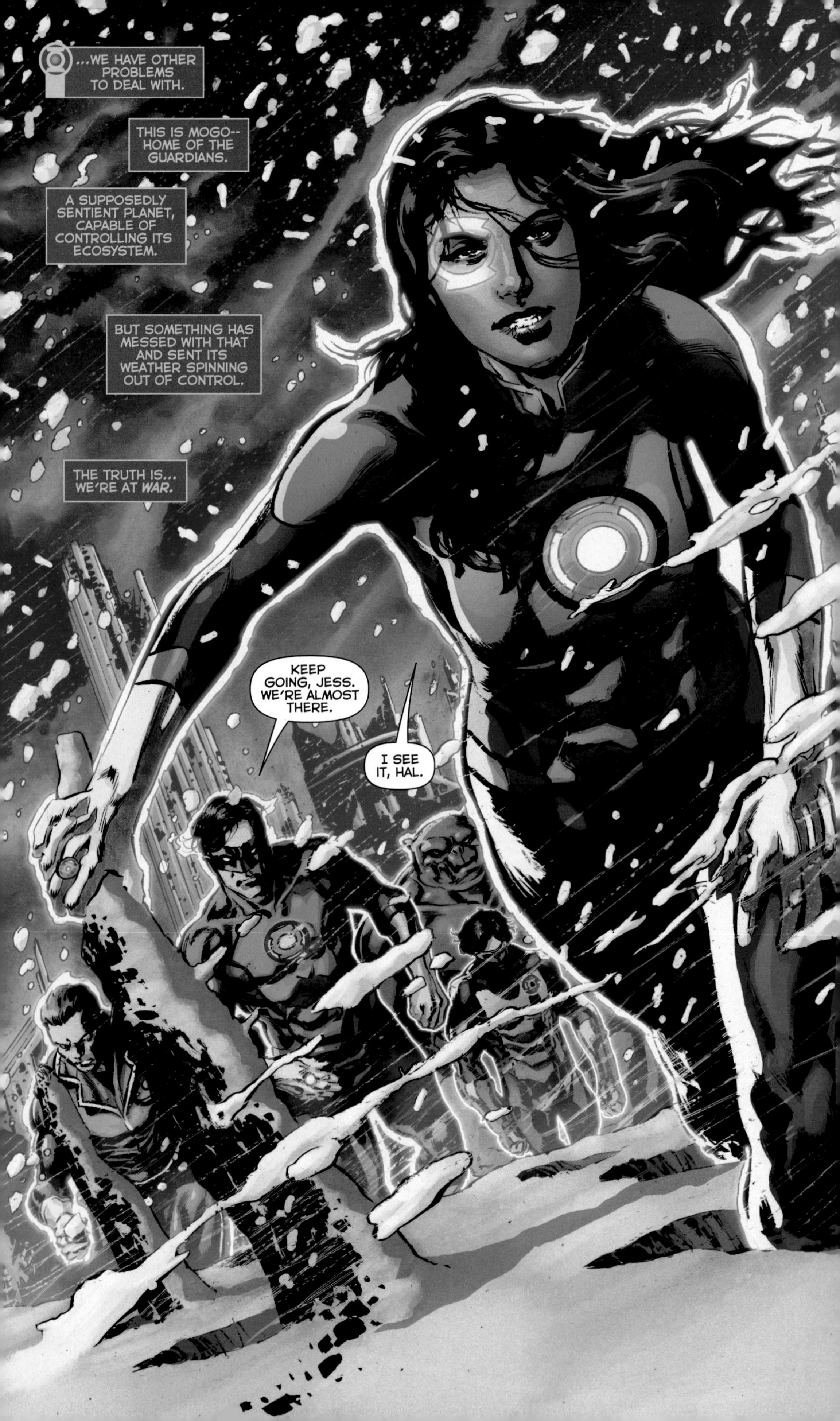
...WE HAVE OTHER PROBLEMS TO DEAL WITH.
THIS IS MOGO-- HOME OF THE GUARDIANS.
A SUPPOSEDLY SENTIENT PLANET, CAPABLE OF CONTROLLING ITS ECOSYSTEM.
BUT SOMETHING HAS MESSED WITH THAT AND SENT ITS WEATHER SPINNING OUT OF CONTROL.
THE TRUTH IS... WE'RE AT *WAR*.
KEEP GOING, JESS. WE'RE ALMOST THERE.
I SEE IT, HAL.

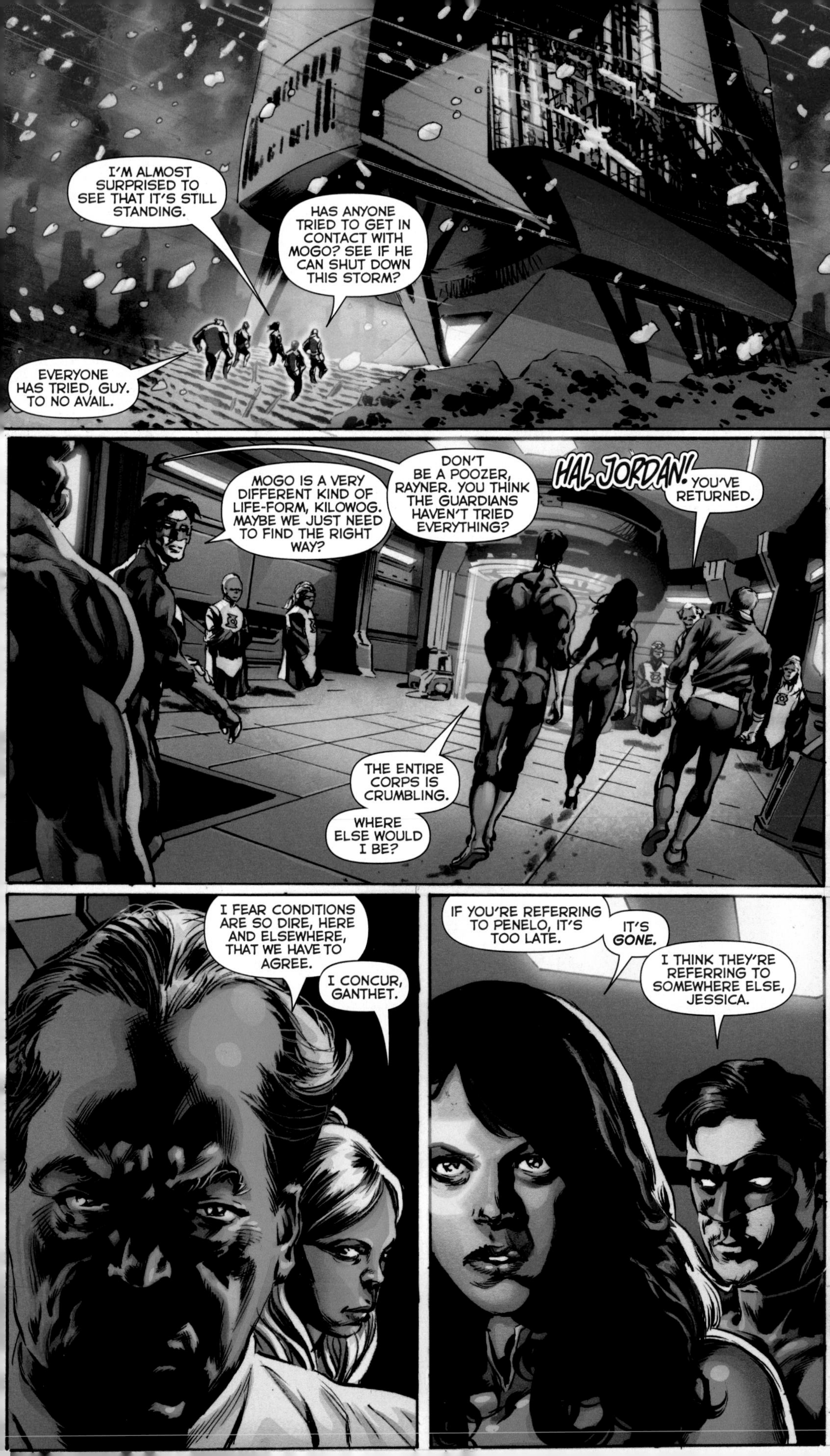
I'M ALMOST SURPRISED TO SEE THAT IT'S STILL STANDING.
HAS ANYONE TRIED TO GET IN CONTACT WITH MOGO? SEE IF HE CAN SHUT DOWN THIS STORM?
EVERYONE HAS TRIED, GUY. TO NO AVAIL.
MOGO IS A VERY DIFFERENT KIND OF LIFE-FORM, KILOWOG. MAYBE WE JUST NEED TO FIND THE RIGHT WAY?
DON'T BE A POOZER, RAYNER. YOU THINK THE GUARDIANS HAVEN'T TRIED EVERYTHING?
HAL JORDAN! YOU'VE RETURNED.
THE ENTIRE CORPS IS CRUMBLING.
WHERE ELSE WOULD I BE?
I FEAR CONDITIONS ARE SO DIRE, HERE AND ELSEWHERE, THAT WE HAVE TO AGREE.
I CONCUR, GANTHET.
IF YOU'RE REFERRING TO PENELO, IT'S TOO LATE.
IT'S GONE.
I THINK THEY'RE REFERRING TO SOMEWHERE ELSE, JESSICA.

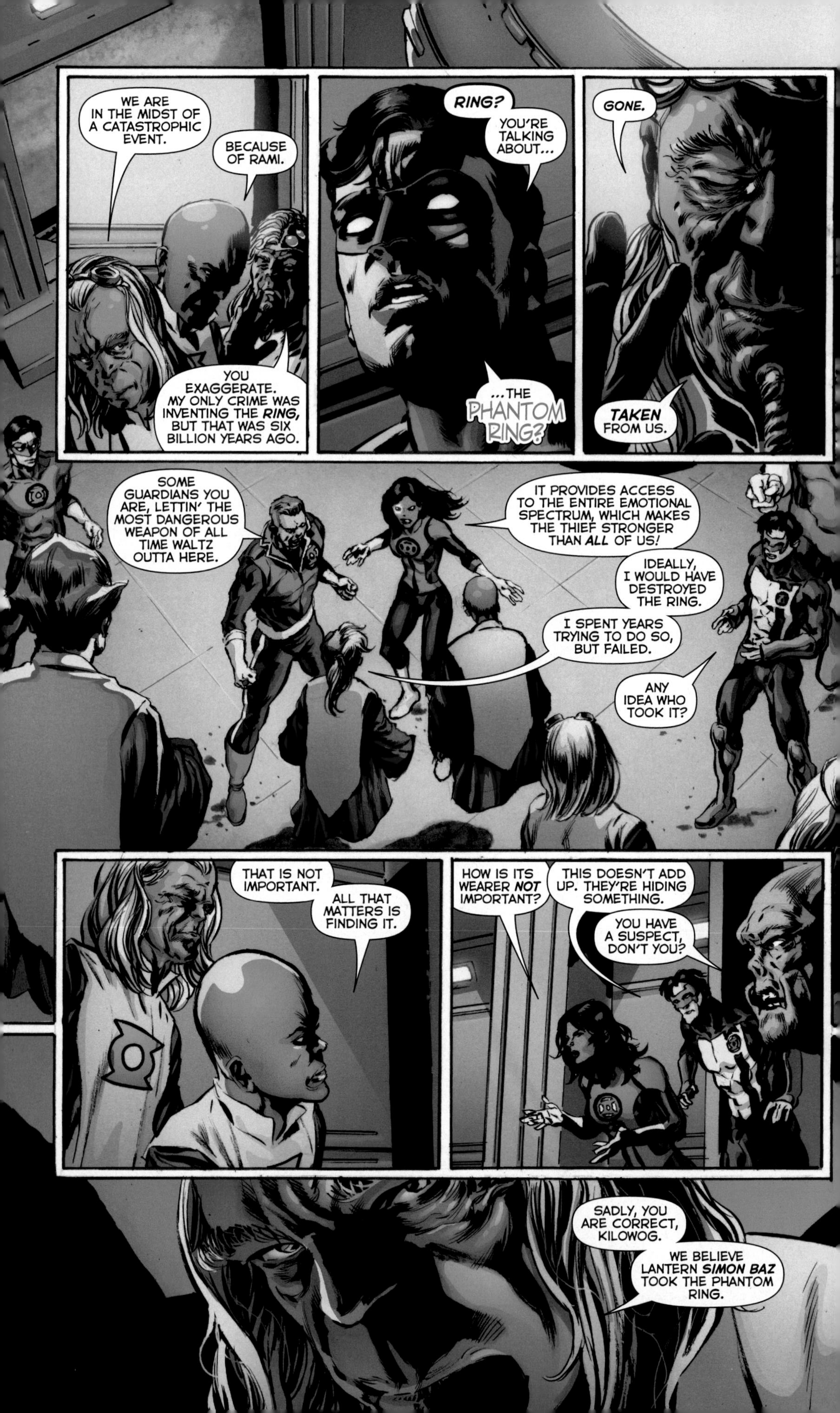
WE ARE IN THE MIDST OF A CATASTROPHIC EVENT.
BECAUSE OF RAMI.
YOU EXAGGERATE. MY ONLY CRIME WAS INVENTING THE RING, BUT THAT WAS SIX BILLION YEARS AGO.
RING?
YOU'RE TALKING ABOUT...
...THE PHANTOM RING?
GONE.
TAKEN FROM US.
SOME GUARDIANS YOU ARE, LETTIN' THE MOST DANGEROUS WEAPON OF ALL TIME WALTZ OUTTA HERE.
IT PROVIDES ACCESS TO THE ENTIRE EMOTIONAL SPECTRUM, WHICH MAKES THE THIEF STRONGER THAN ALL OF US!
IDEALLY, I WOULD HAVE DESTROYED THE RING.
I SPENT YEARS TRYING TO DO SO, BUT FAILED.
ANY IDEA WHO TOOK IT?
THAT IS NOT IMPORTANT.
ALL THAT MATTERS IS FINDING IT.
HOW IS ITS WEARER NOT IMPORTANT?
THIS DOESN'T ADD UP. THEY'RE HIDING SOMETHING.
YOU HAVE A SUSPECT, DON'T YOU?
SADLY, YOU ARE CORRECT, KILOWOG.
WE BELIEVE LANTERN SIMON BAZ TOOK THE PHANTOM RING.

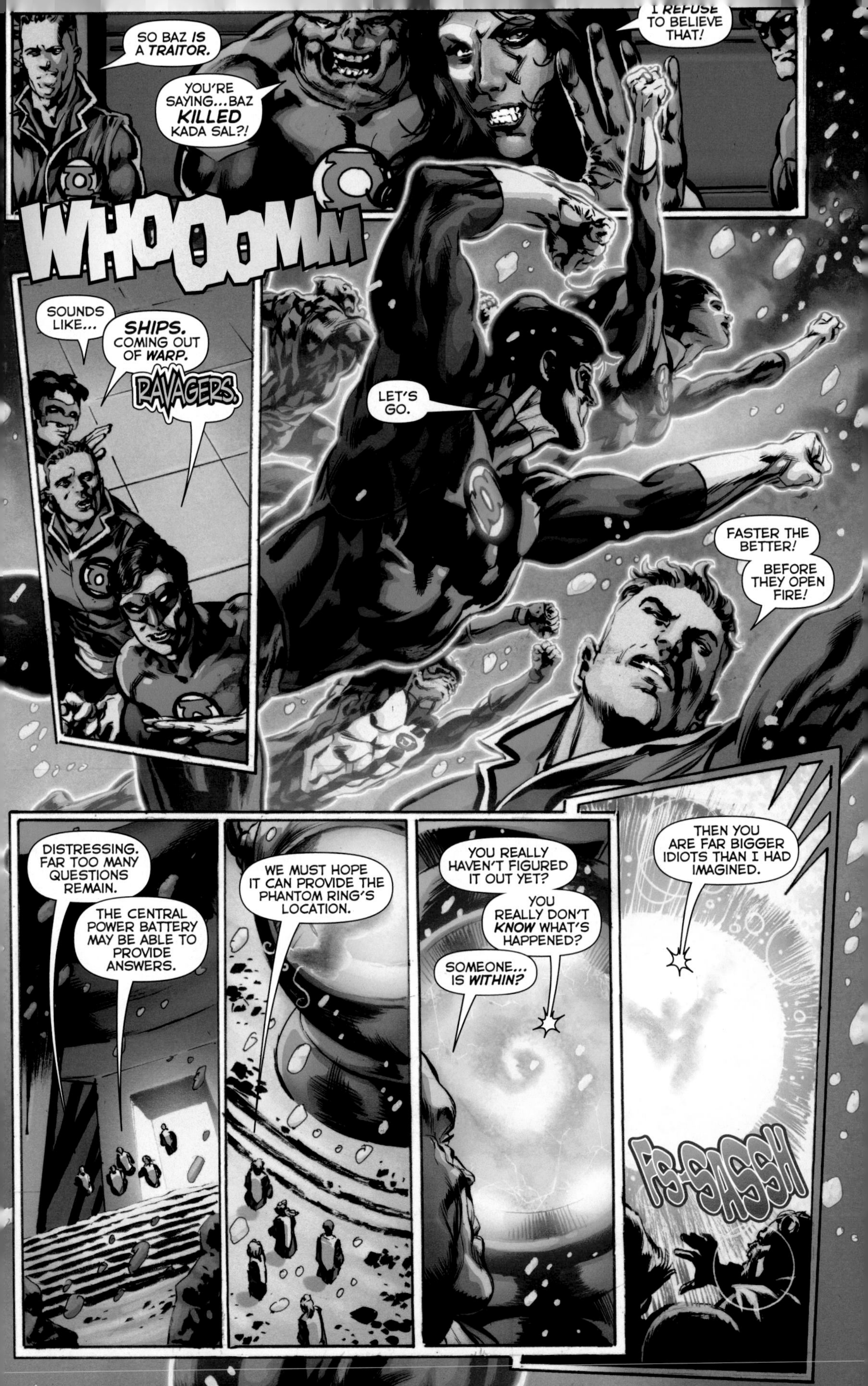
SO BAZ IS A TRAITOR.
YOU'RE SAYING...BAZ KILLED KADA SAL?!
I REFUSE TO BELIEVE THAT!
WHOOOOMM
SOUNDS LIKE...
SHIPS. COMING OUT OF WARP.
RAVAGERS.
LET'S GO.
FASTER THE BETTER!
BEFORE THEY OPEN FIRE!
DISTRESSING. FAR TOO MANY QUESTIONS REMAIN.
THE CENTRAL POWER BATTERY MAY BE ABLE TO PROVIDE ANSWERS.
WE MUST HOPE IT CAN PROVIDE THE PHANTOM RING'S LOCATION.
YOU REALLY HAVEN'T FIGURED IT OUT YET?
YOU REALLY DON'T KNOW WHAT'S HAPPENED?
SOMEONE... IS WITHIN?
THEN YOU ARE FAR BIGGER IDIOTS THAN I HAD IMAGINED.
FS-SASSH

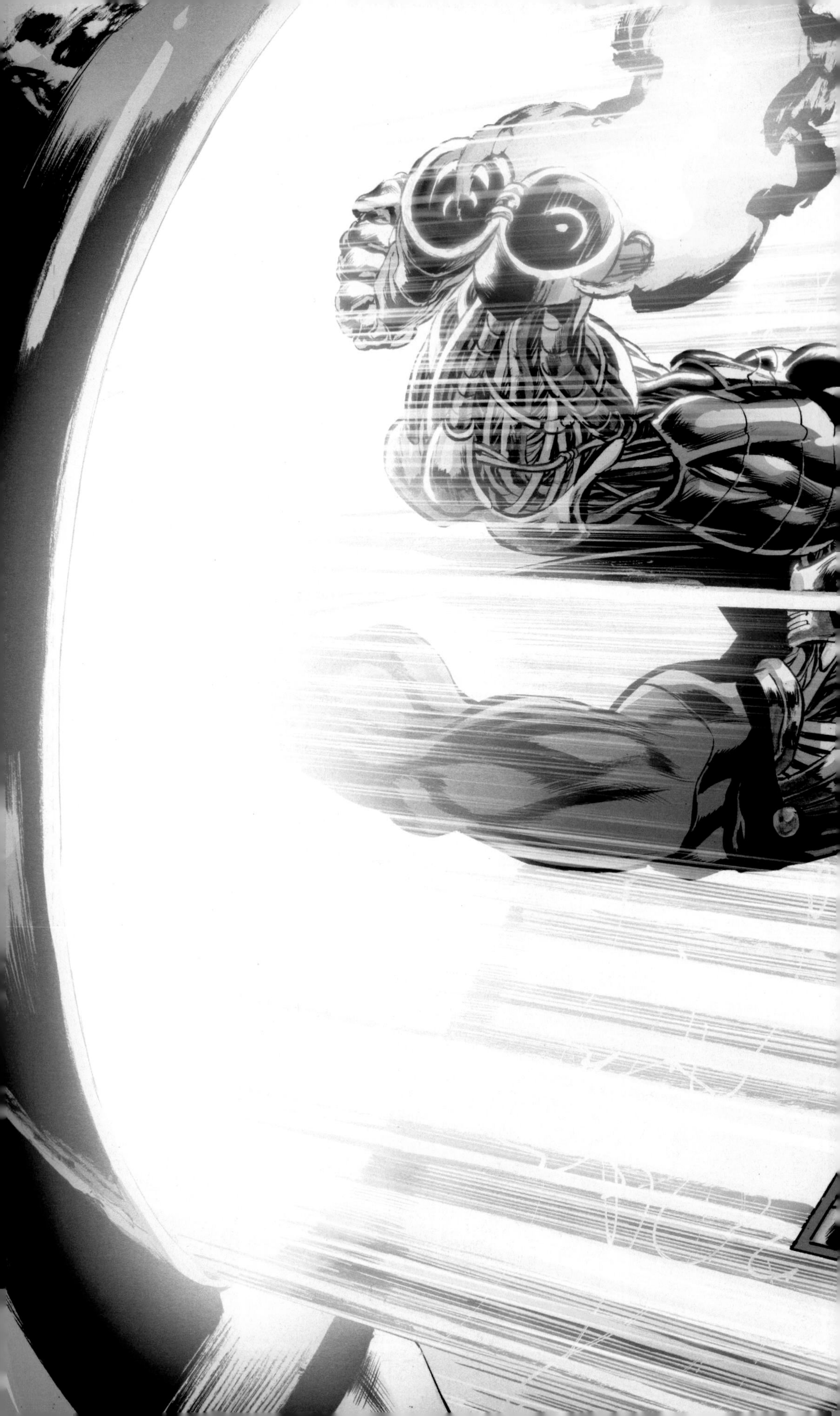

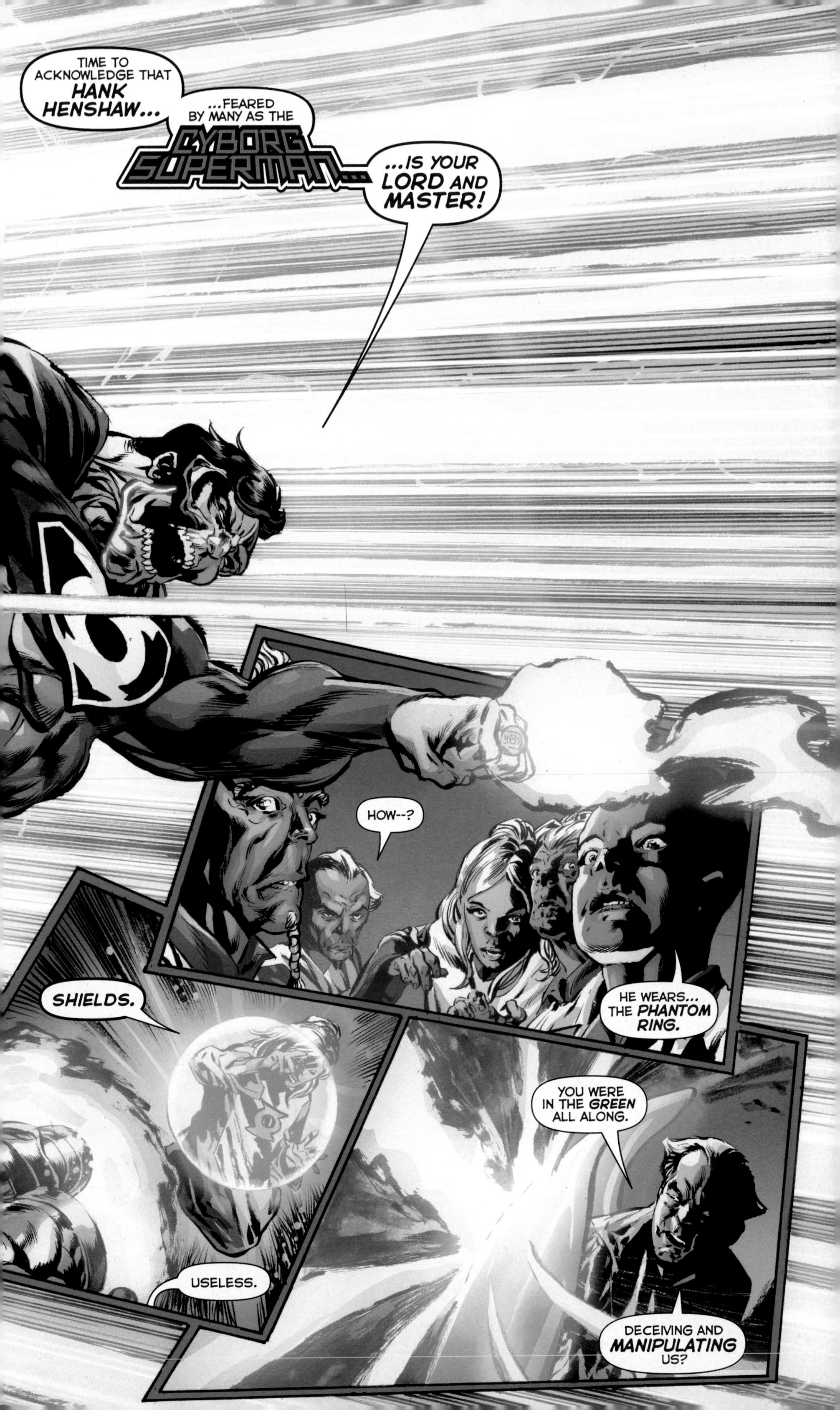
TIME TO ACKNOWLEDGE THAT HANK HENSHAW...
...FEARED BY MANY AS THE
CYBORG SUPERMAN...
...IS YOUR LORD AND MASTER!
HOW--?
HE WEARS... THE PHANTOM RING.
SHIELDS.
USELESS.
YOU WERE IN THE GREEN ALL ALONG.
DECEIVING AND MANIPULATING US?

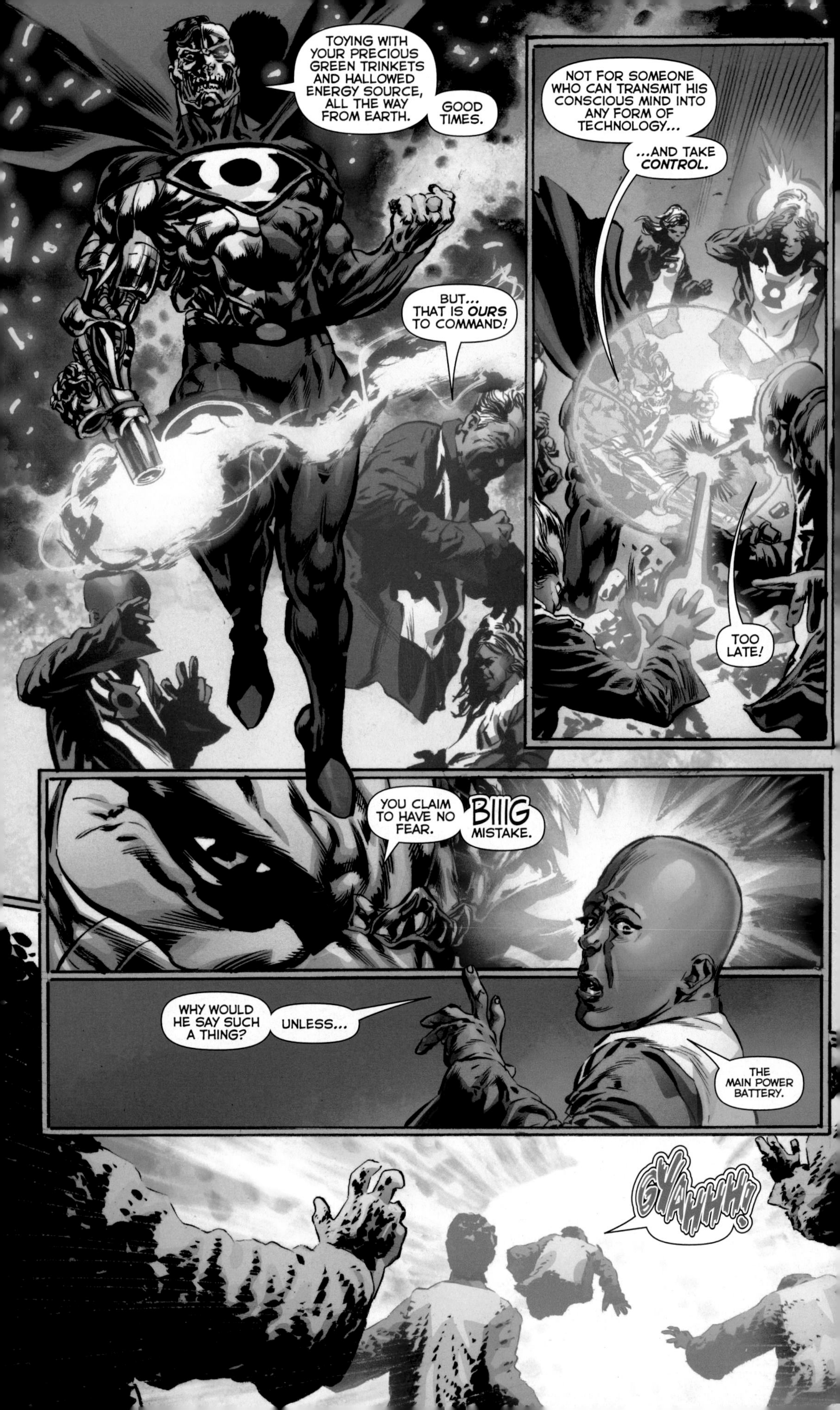
TOYING WITH YOUR PRECIOUS GREEN TRINKETS AND HALLOWED ENERGY SOURCE, ALL THE WAY FROM EARTH.
GOOD TIMES.
BUT... THAT IS OURS TO COMMAND!
NOT FOR SOMEONE WHO CAN TRANSMIT HIS CONSCIOUS MIND INTO ANY FORM OF TECHNOLOGY...
...AND TAKE CONTROL.
TOO LATE!
YOU CLAIM TO HAVE NO FEAR.
BIIIG MISTAKE.
WHY WOULD HE SAY SUCH A THING?
UNLESS...
THE MAIN POWER BATTERY.
GYAHHHH!

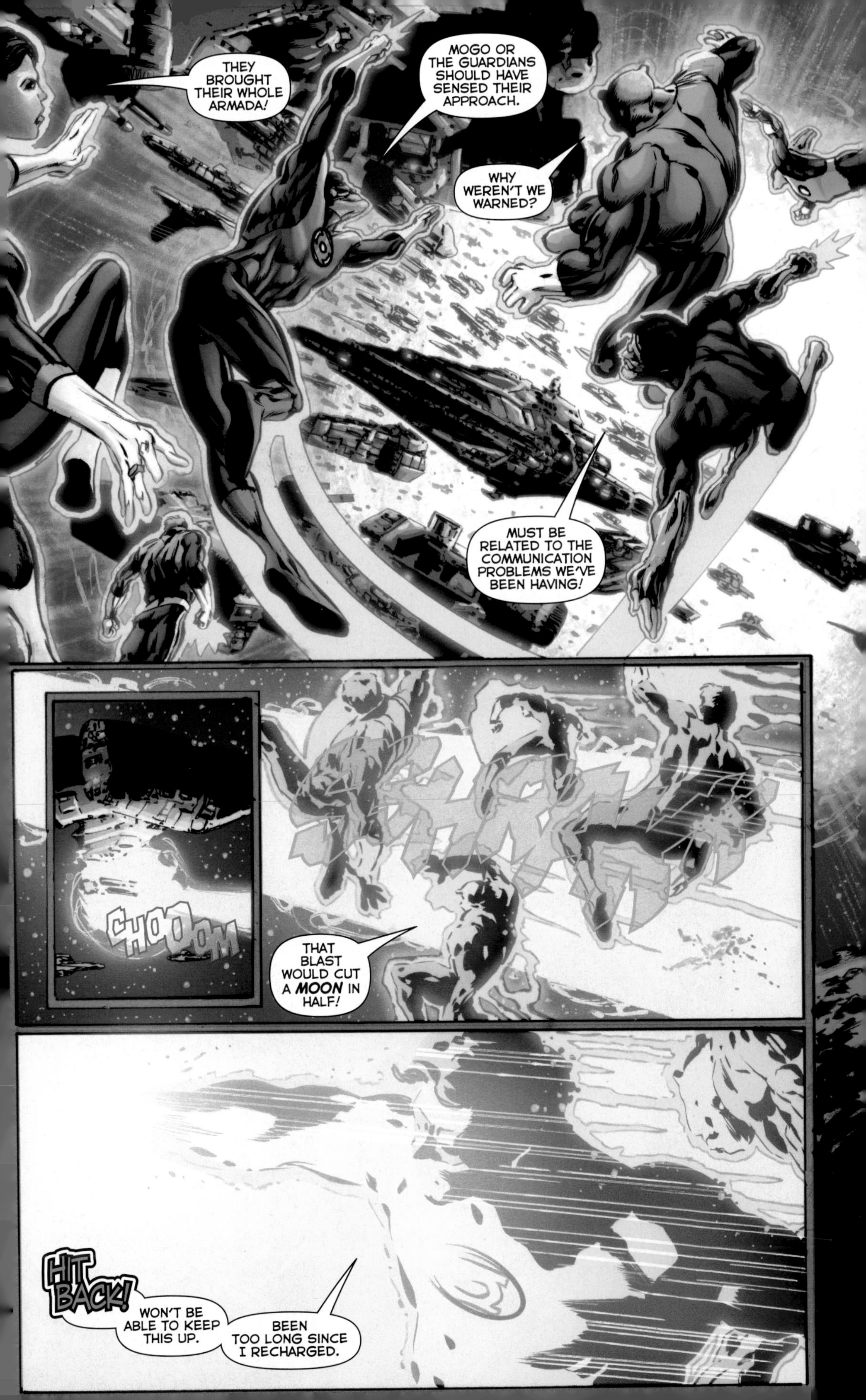
THEY BROUGHT THEIR WHOLE ARMADA!
MOGO OR THE GUARDIANS SHOULD HAVE SENSED THEIR APPROACH.
WHY WEREN'T WE WARNED?
MUST BE RELATED TO THE COMMUNICATION PROBLEMS WE'VE BEEN HAVING!
CHOOOM
THAT BLAST WOULD CUT A MOON IN HALF!
HIT BACK!
WON'T BE ABLE TO KEEP THIS UP.
BEEN TOO LONG SINCE I RECHARGED.

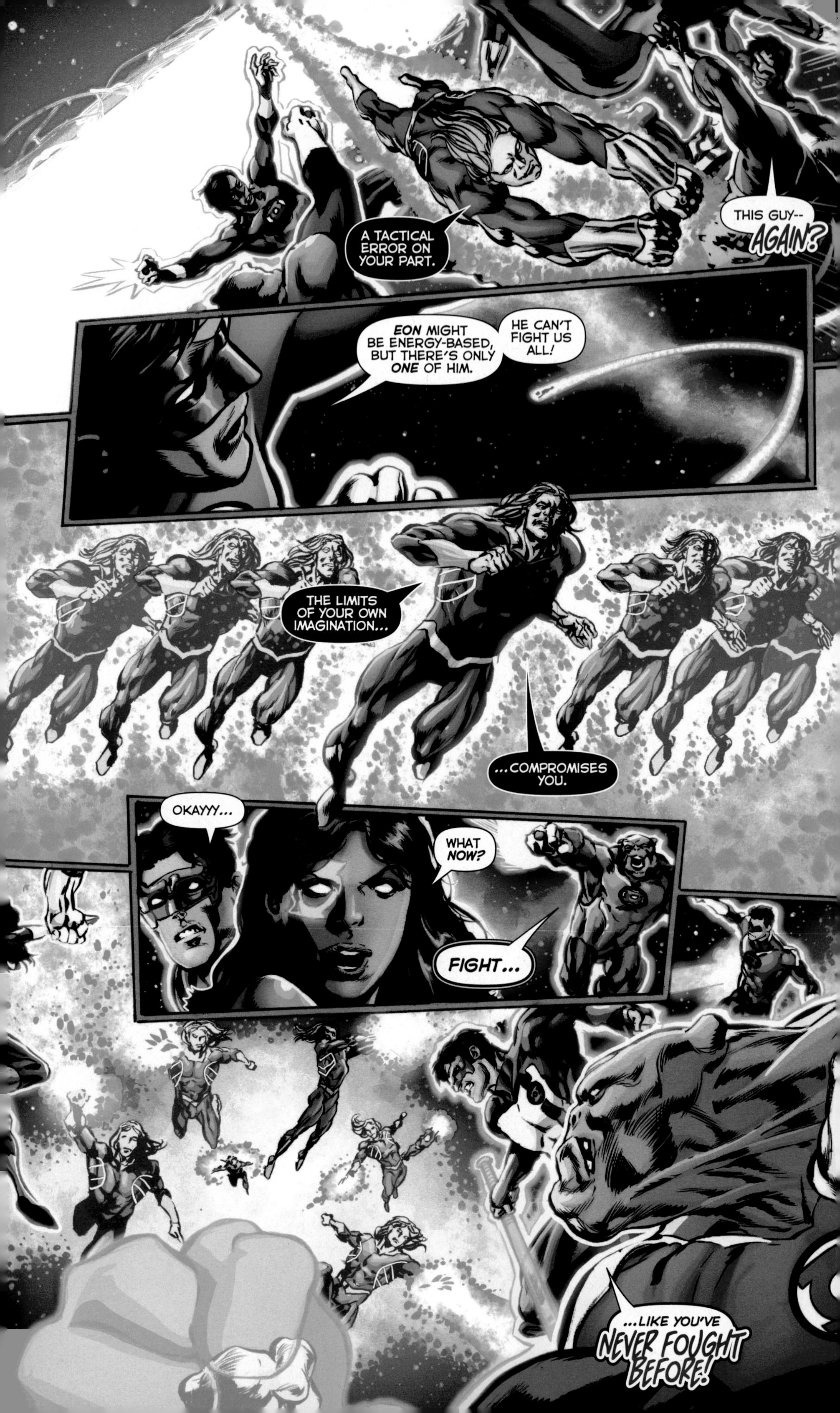
A TACTICAL ERROR ON YOUR PART.
THIS GUY-- AGAIN?
EON MIGHT BE ENERGY-BASED, BUT THERE'S ONLY ONE OF HIM.
HE CAN'T FIGHT US ALL!
THE LIMITS OF YOUR OWN IMAGINATION...
...COMPROMISES YOU.
OKAYYY...
WHAT NOW?
FIGHT...
...LIKE YOU'VE NEVER FOUGHT BEFORE!

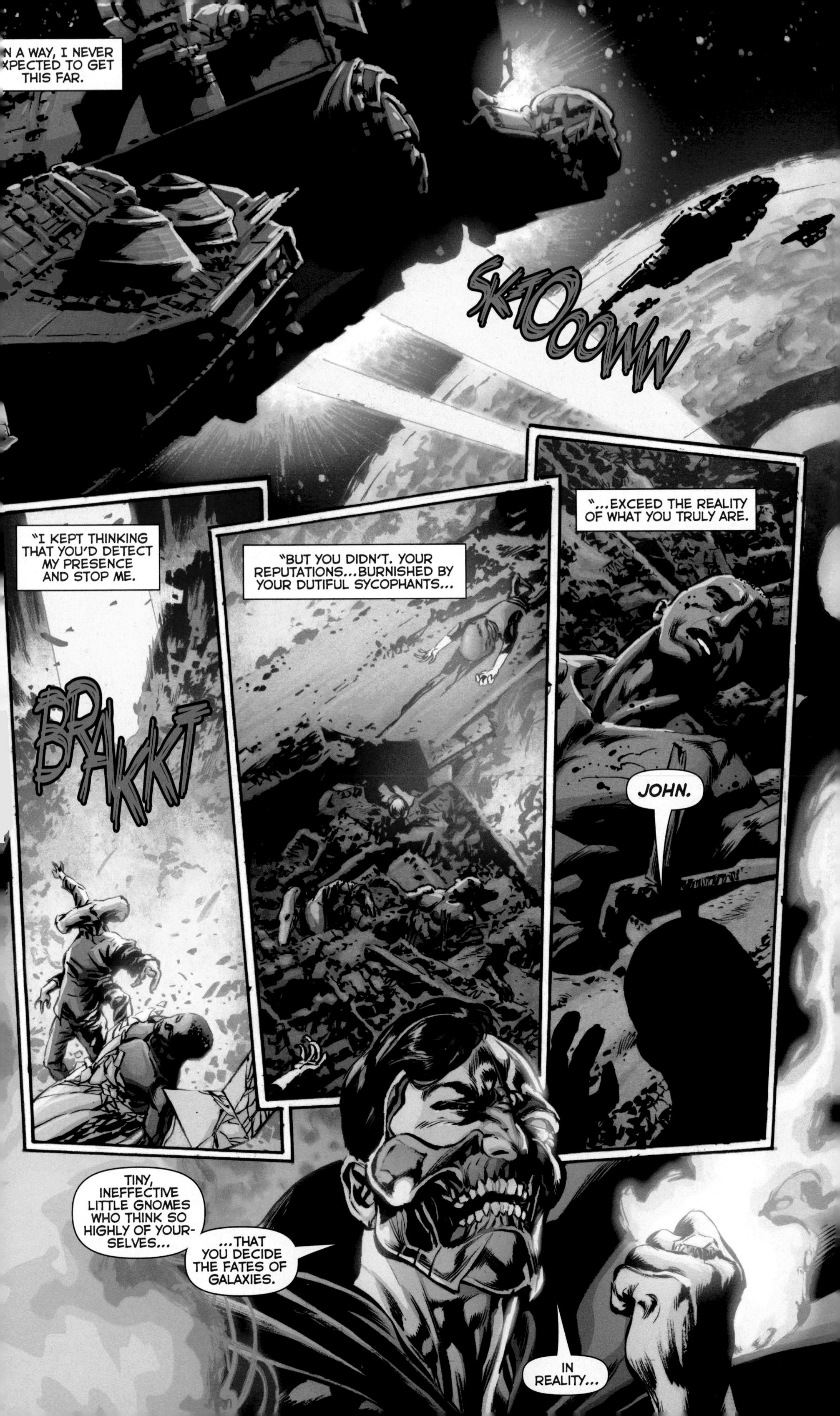
N A WAY, I NEVER XPECTED TO GET THIS FAR.
SKTOOOWW
"I KEPT THINKING THAT YOU'D DETECT MY PRESENCE AND STOP ME.
BRAKKT
"BUT YOU DIDN'T. YOUR REPUTATIONS...BURNISHED BY YOUR DUTIFUL SYCOPHANTS...
"...EXCEED THE REALITY OF WHAT YOU TRULY ARE.
JOHN.
TINY, INEFFECTIVE LITTLE GNOMES WHO THINK SO HIGHLY OF YOURSELVES...
...THAT YOU DECIDE THE FATES OF GALAXIES.
IN REALITY...

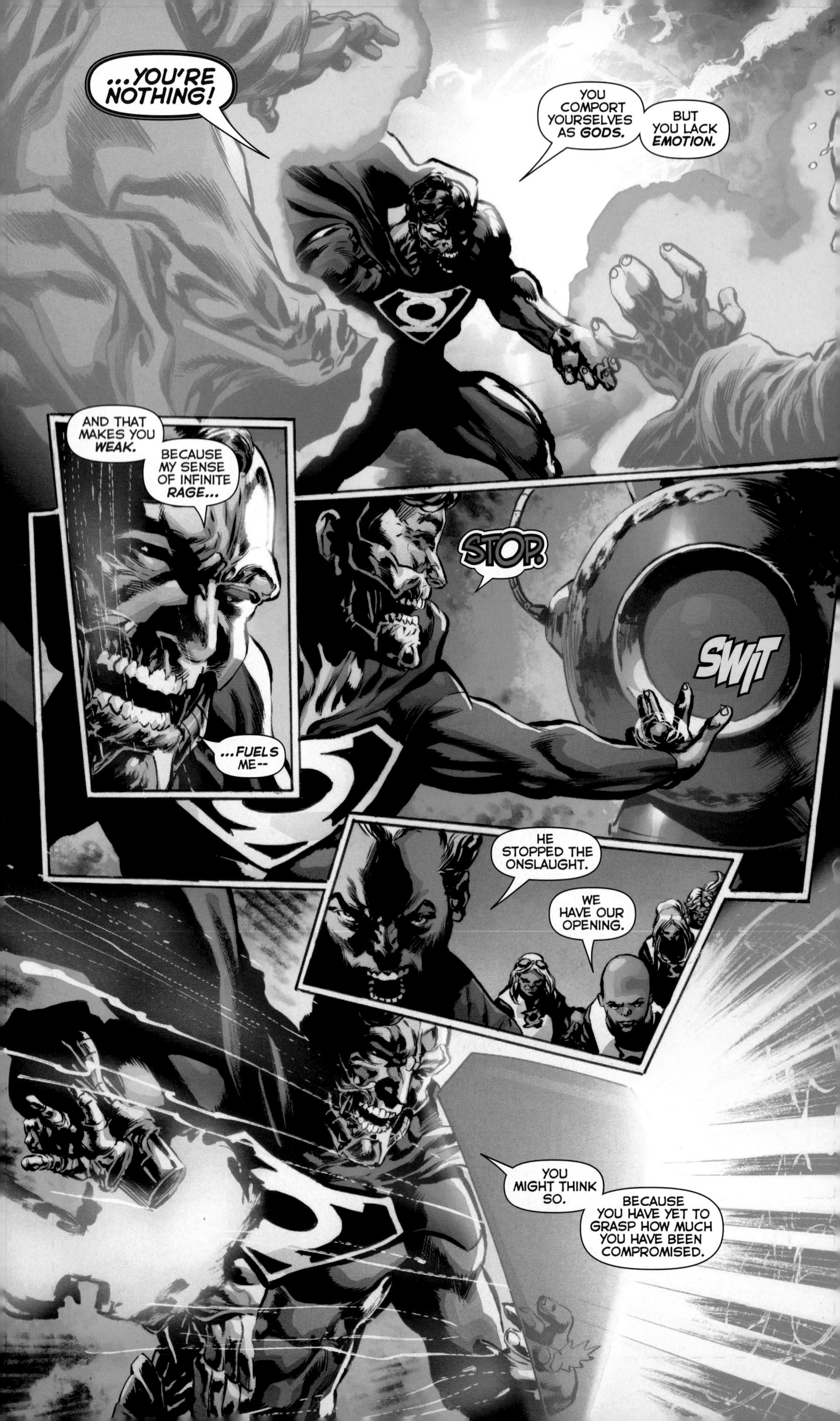
...YOU'RE NOTHING!
YOU COMPORT YOURSELVES AS GODS.
BUT YOU LACK EMOTION.
AND THAT MAKES YOU WEAK.
BECAUSE MY SENSE OF INFINITE RAGE...
...FUELS ME--
STOP.
SWIT
HE STOPPED THE ONSLAUGHT.
WE HAVE OUR OPENING.
YOU MIGHT THINK SO.
BECAUSE YOU HAVE YET TO GRASP HOW MUCH YOU HAVE BEEN COMPROMISED.

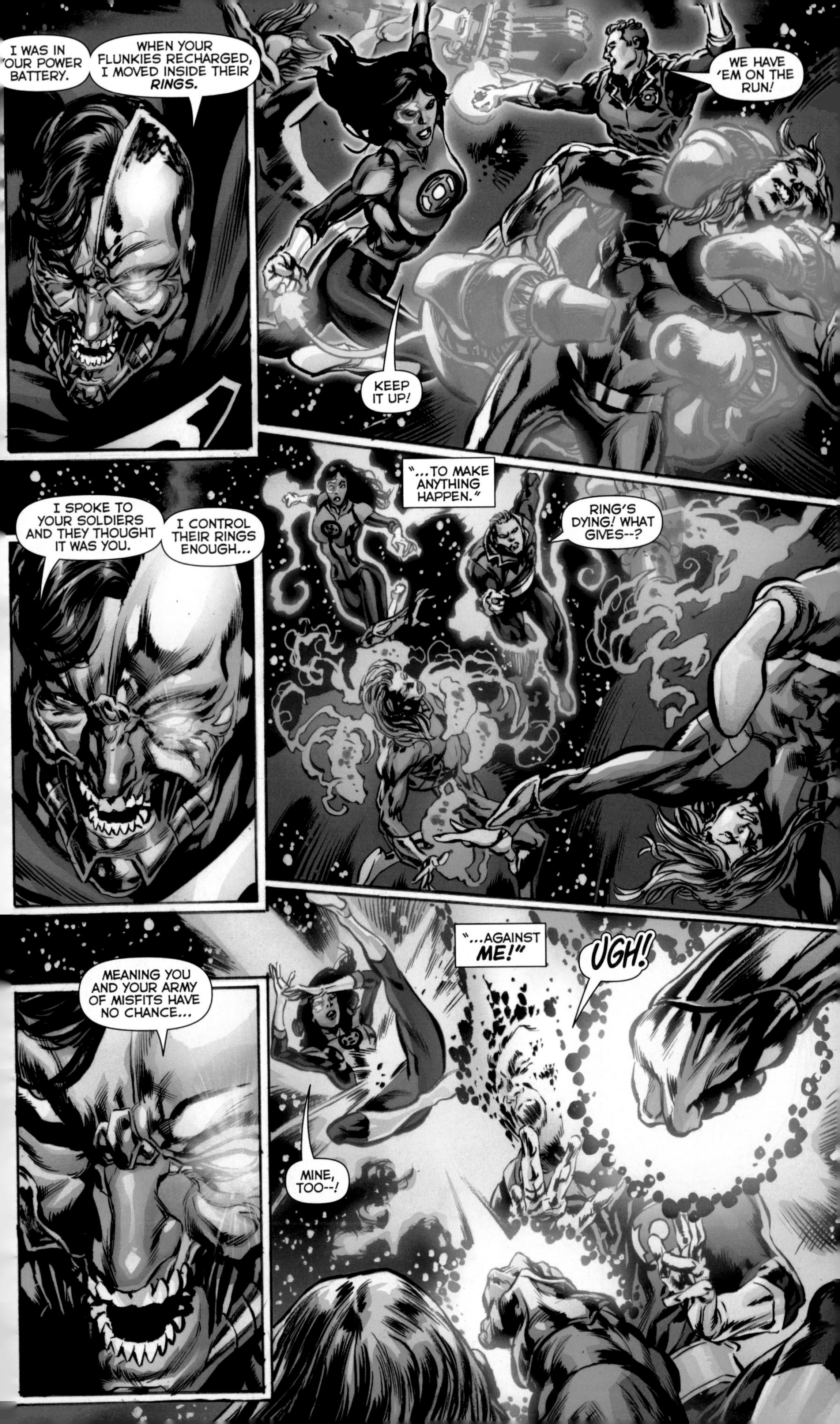
I WAS IN YOUR POWER BATTERY.
WHEN YOUR FLUNKIES RECHARGED, I MOVED INSIDE THEIR RINGS.
WE HAVE 'EM ON THE RUN!
KEEP IT UP!
I SPOKE TO YOUR SOLDIERS AND THEY THOUGHT IT WAS YOU.
I CONTROL THEIR RINGS ENOUGH...
"...TO MAKE ANYTHING HAPPEN."
RING'S DYING! WHAT GIVES--?
MEANING YOU AND YOUR ARMY OF MISFITS HAVE NO CHANCE...
"...AGAINST ME!"
UGH!
MINE, TOO--!

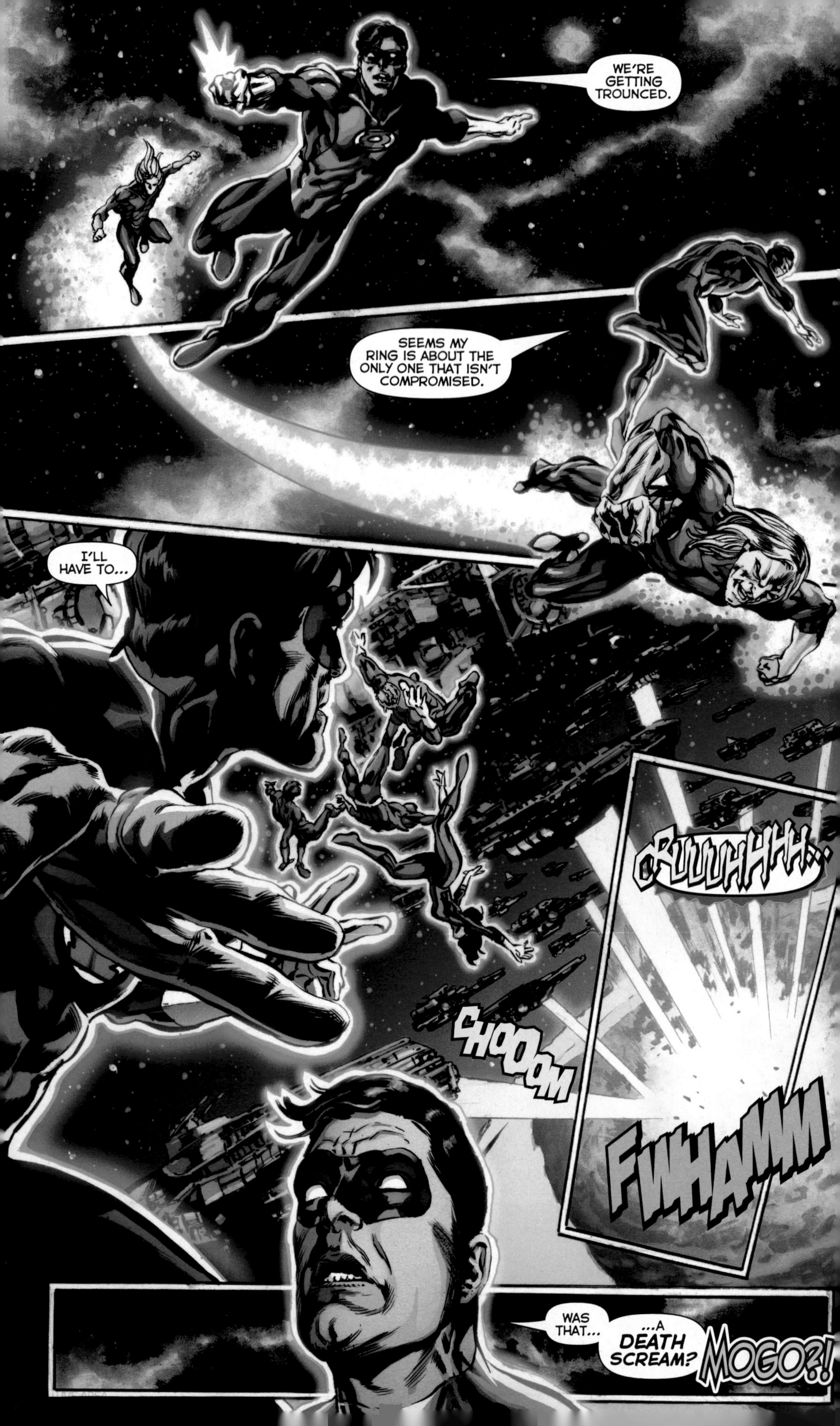
WE'RE GETTING TROUNCED.
SEEMS MY RING IS ABOUT THE ONLY ONE THAT ISN'T COMPROMISED.
I'LL HAVE TO...
CRUUUHHH...
CHOOOOM
FWHAMM
WAS THAT...
...A DEATH SCREAM?
MOGO?!

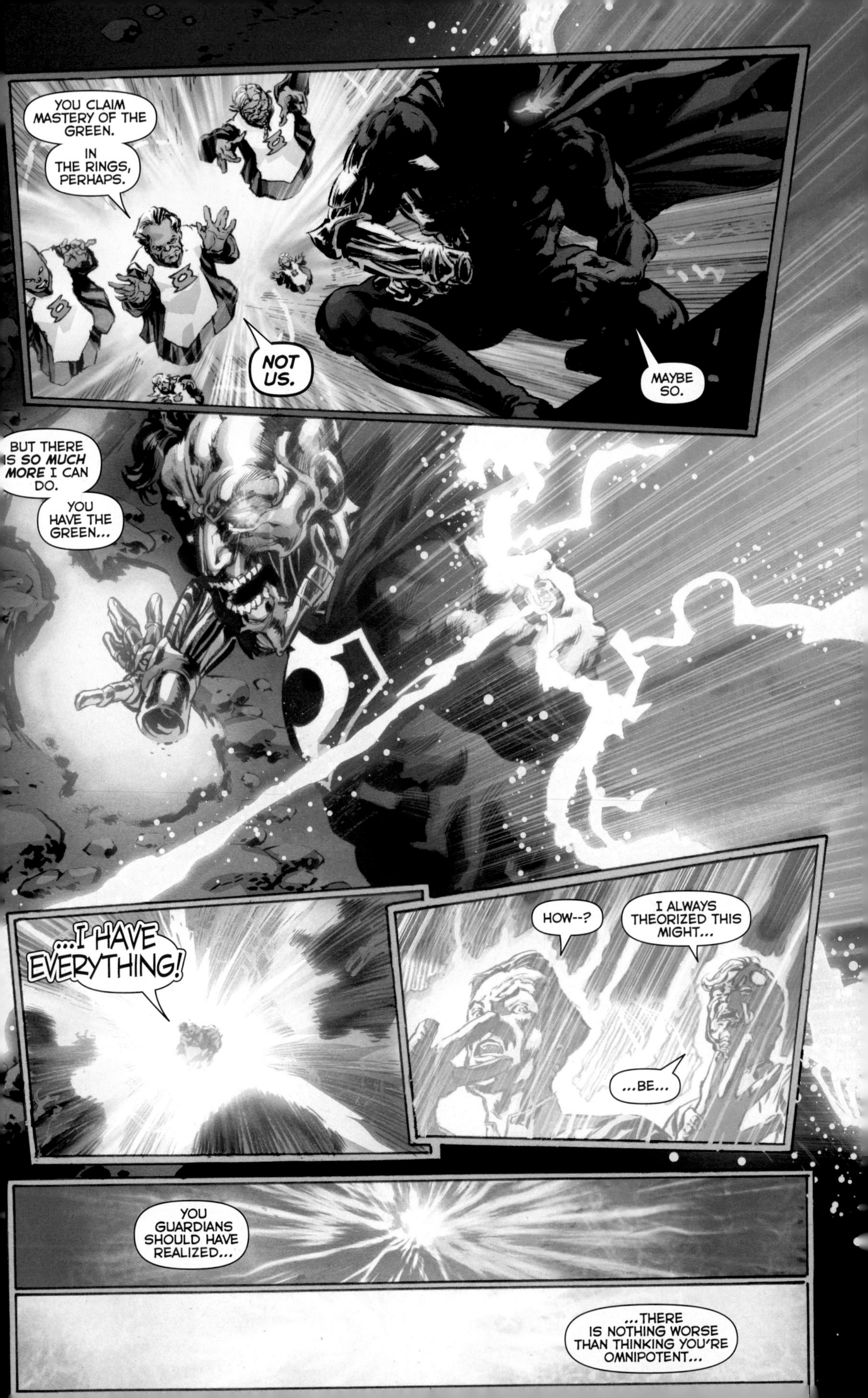
YOU CLAIM MASTERY OF THE GREEN.
IN THE RINGS, PERHAPS.
NOT US.
MAYBE SO.
BUT THERE IS SO MUCH MORE I CAN DO.
YOU HAVE THE GREEN...
...I HAVE EVERYTHING!
HOW--?
I ALWAYS THEORIZED THIS MIGHT...
...BE...
YOU GUARDIANS SHOULD HAVE REALIZED...
...THERE IS NOTHING WORSE THAN THINKING YOU'RE OMNIPOTENT...

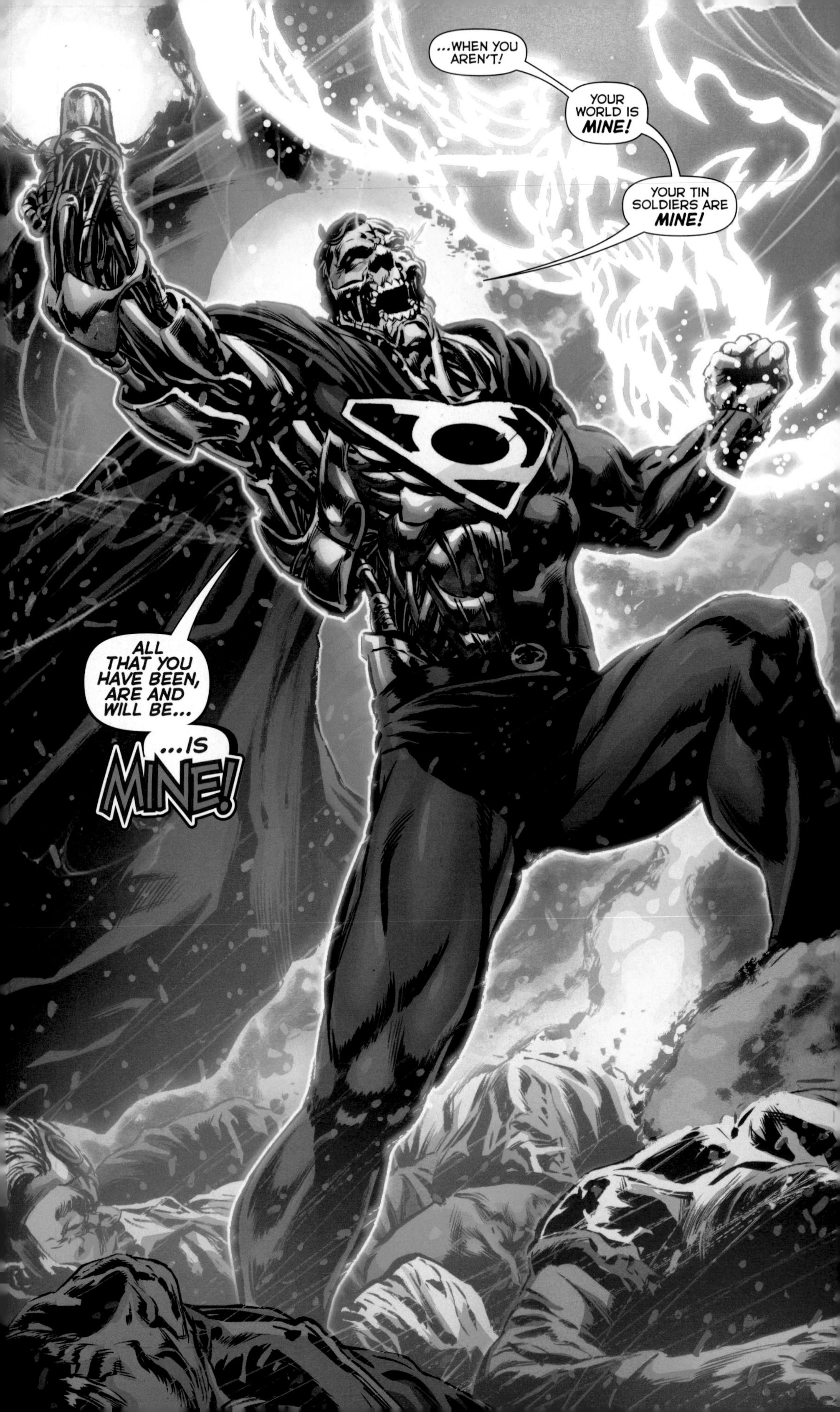
...WHEN YOU AREN'T!
YOUR WORLD IS MINE!
YOUR TIN SOLDIERS ARE MINE!
ALL THAT YOU HAVE BEEN, ARE AND WILL BE...
...IS MINE!

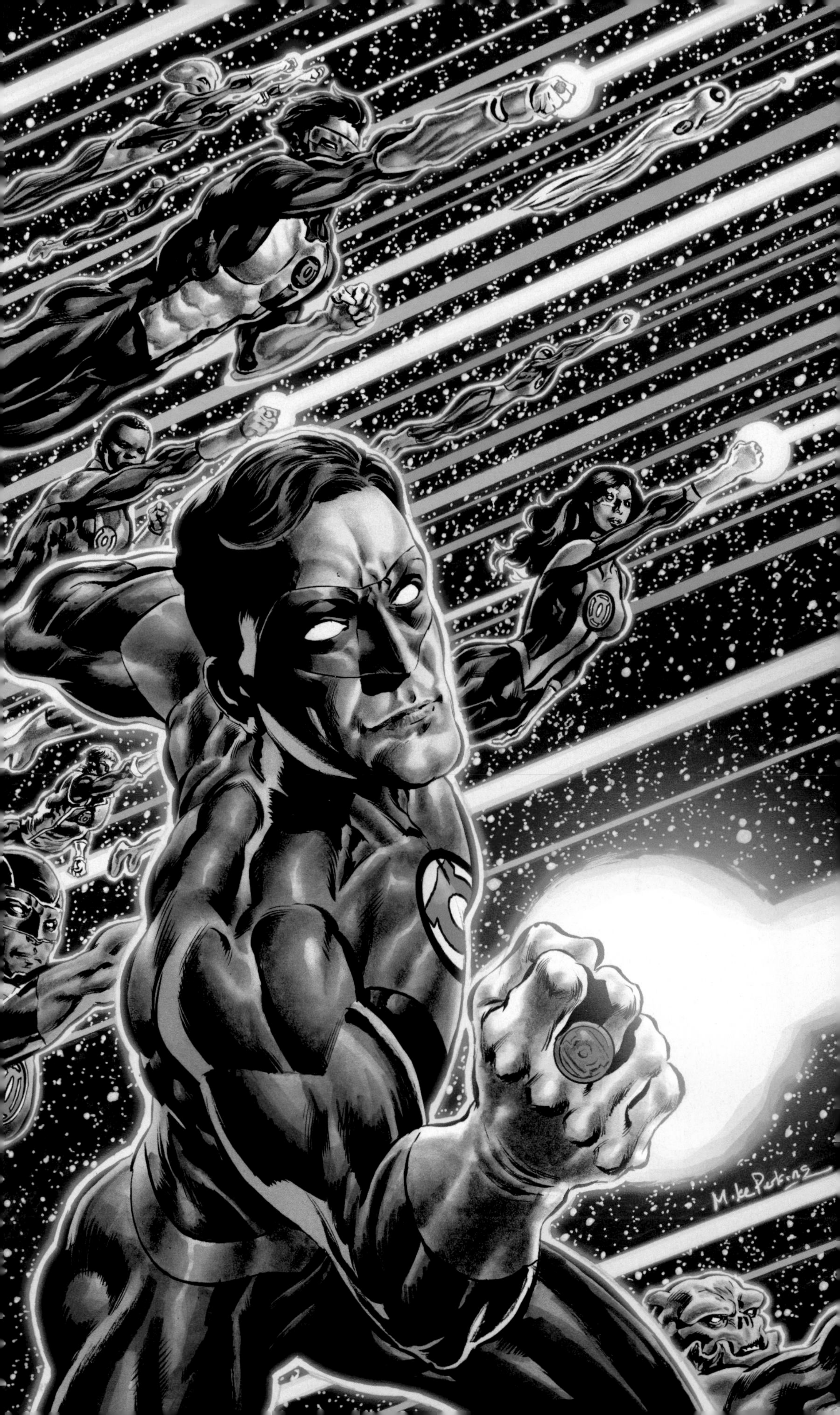
Mike Perkins

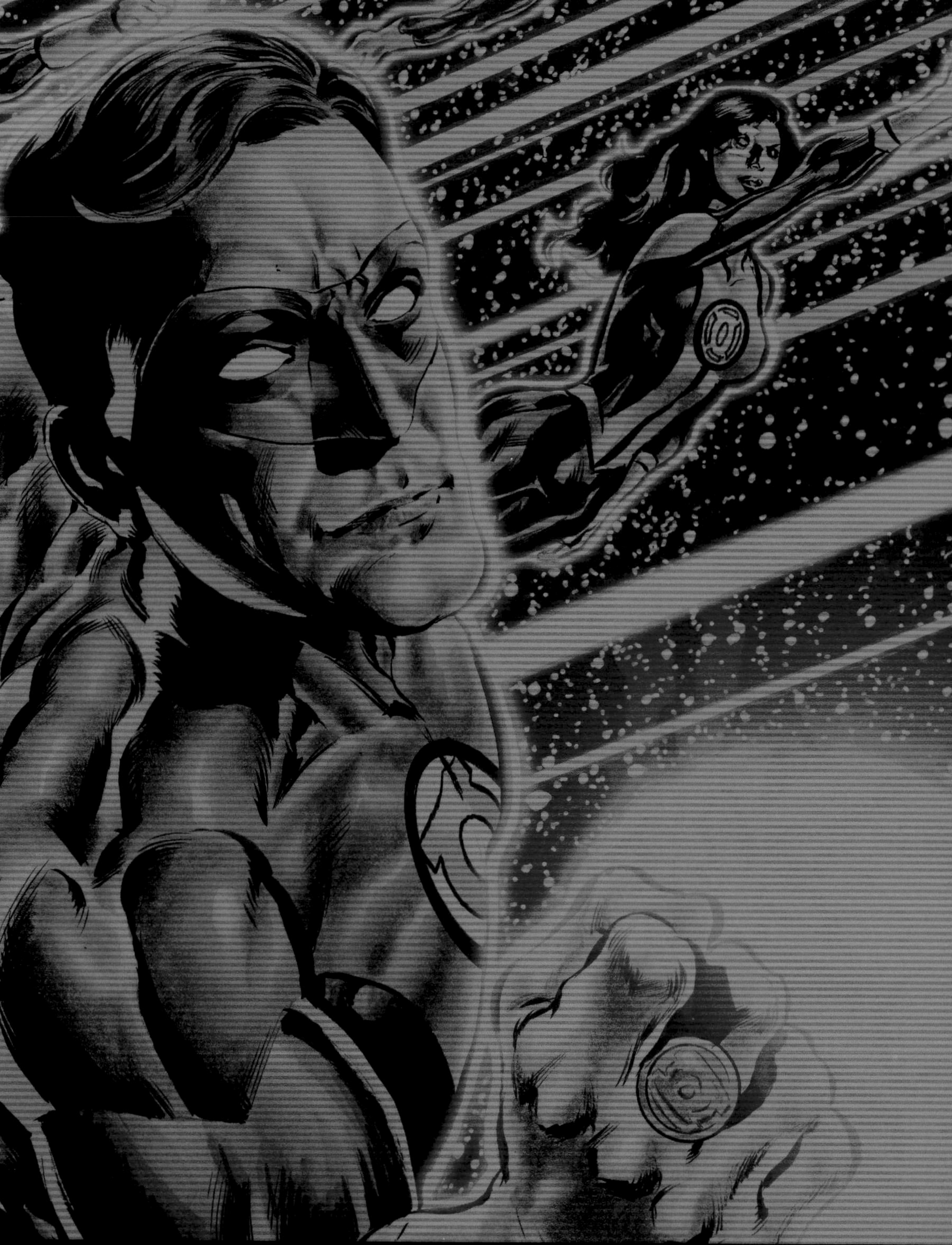

GREEN LANTERNS

#56

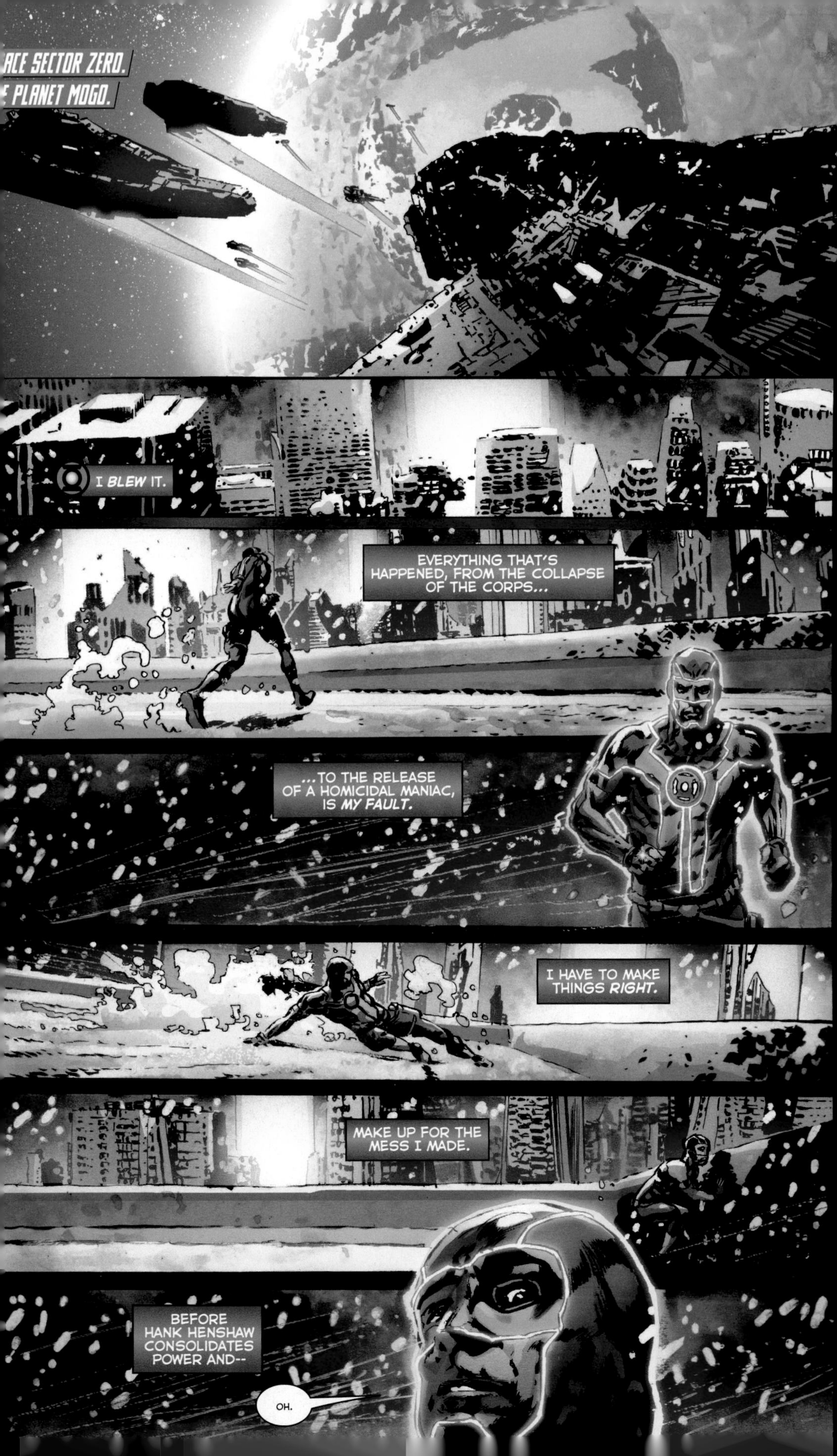
ACE SECTOR ZERO.
PLANET MOGO.
I BLEW IT.
EVERYTHING THAT'S HAPPENED, FROM THE COLLAPSE OF THE CORPS...
...TO THE RELEASE OF A HOMICIDAL MANIAC, IS MY FAULT.
I HAVE TO MAKE THINGS RIGHT.
MAKE UP FOR THE MESS I MADE.
BEFORE HANK HENSHAW CONSOLIDATES POWER AND--
OH.

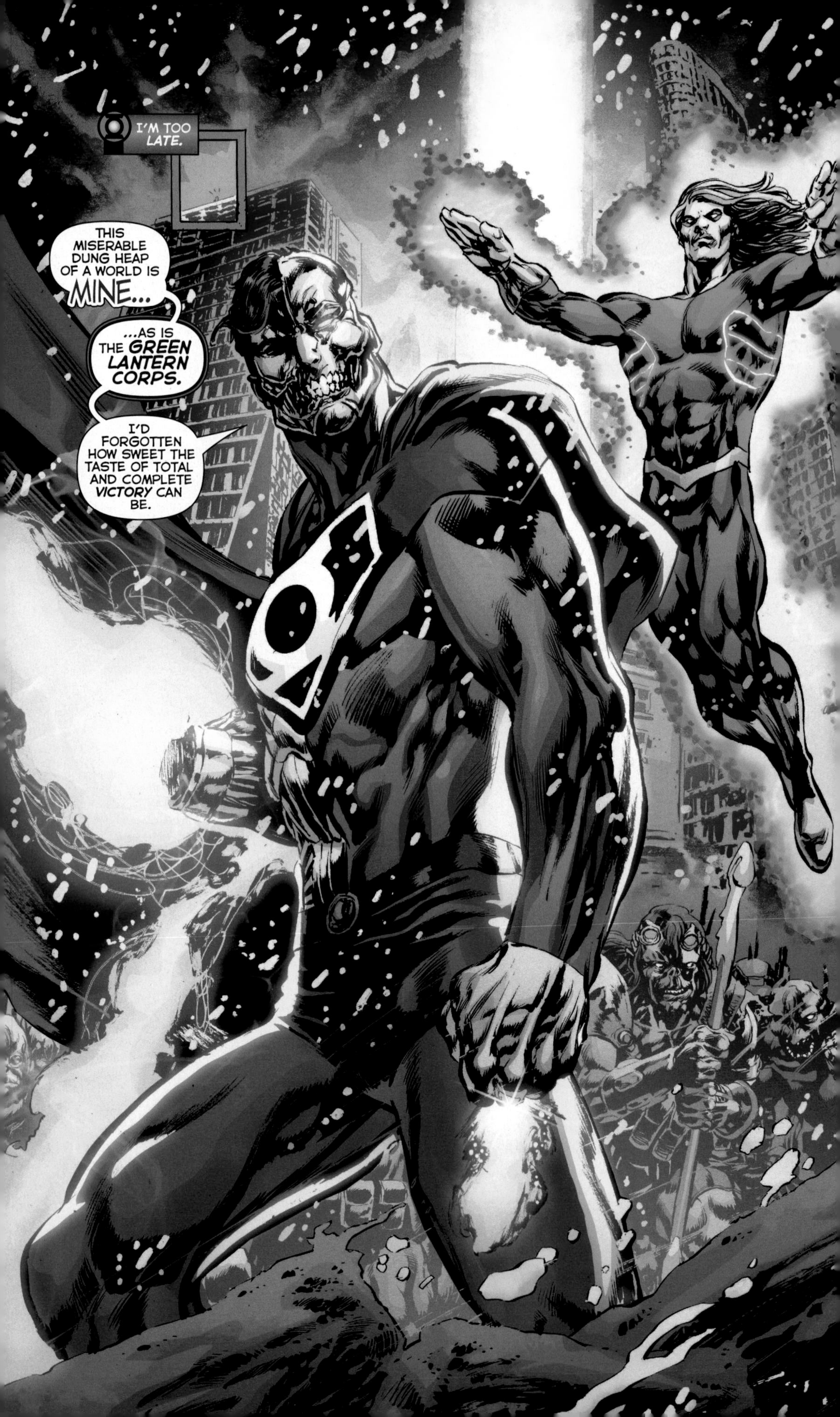
I'M TOO LATE.
THIS MISERABLE DUNG HEAP OF A WORLD IS MINE...
...AS IS THE GREEN LANTERN CORPS.
I'D FORGOTTEN HOW SWEET THE TASTE OF TOTAL AND COMPLETE VICTORY CAN BE.

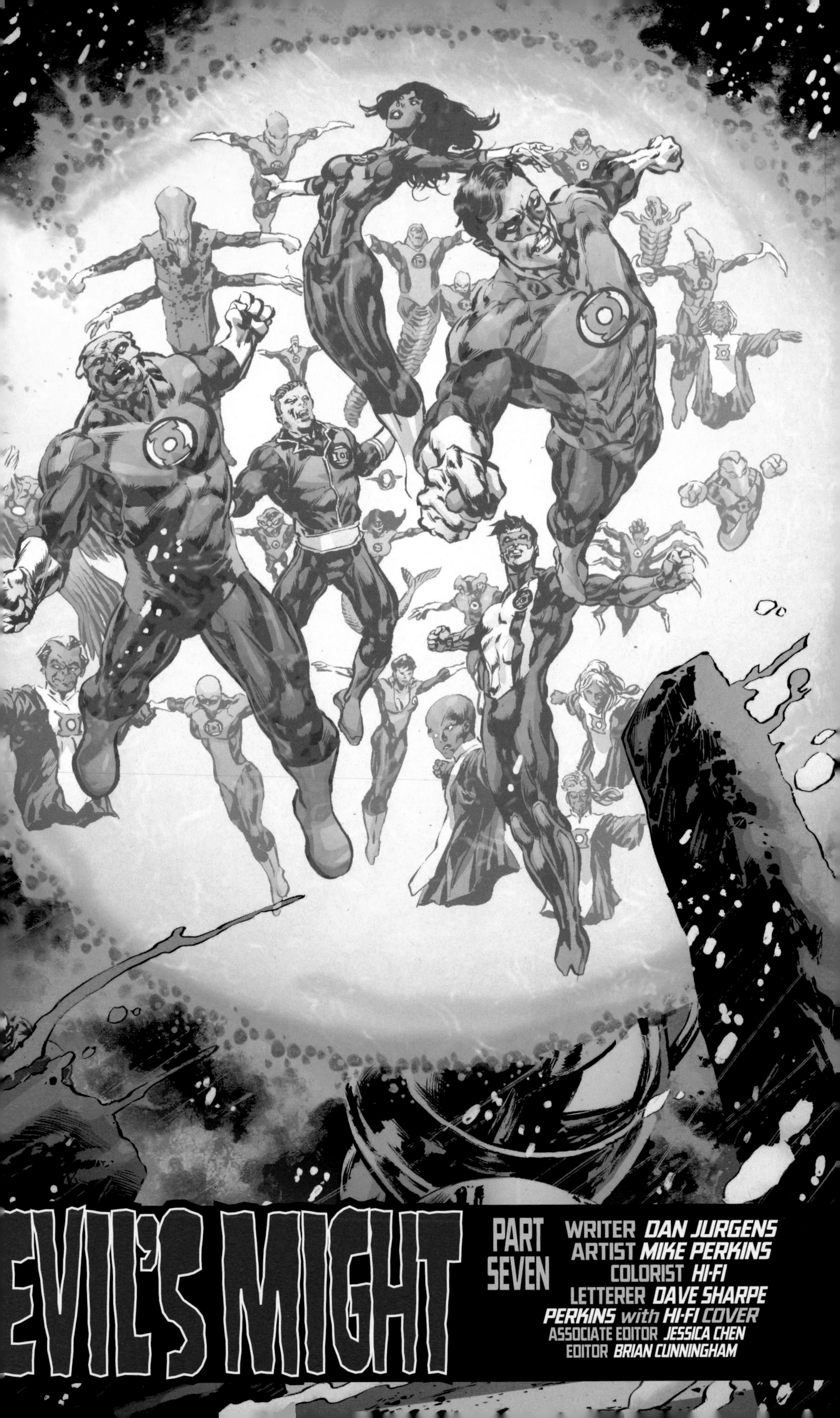
EVIL'S MIGHT
PART SEVEN
WRITER DAN JURGENS
ARTIST MIKE PERKINS
COLORIST HI-FI
LETTERER DAVE SHARPE
PERKINS with HI-FI COVER
ASSOCIATE EDITOR JESSICA CHEN
EDITOR BRIAN CUNNINGHAM

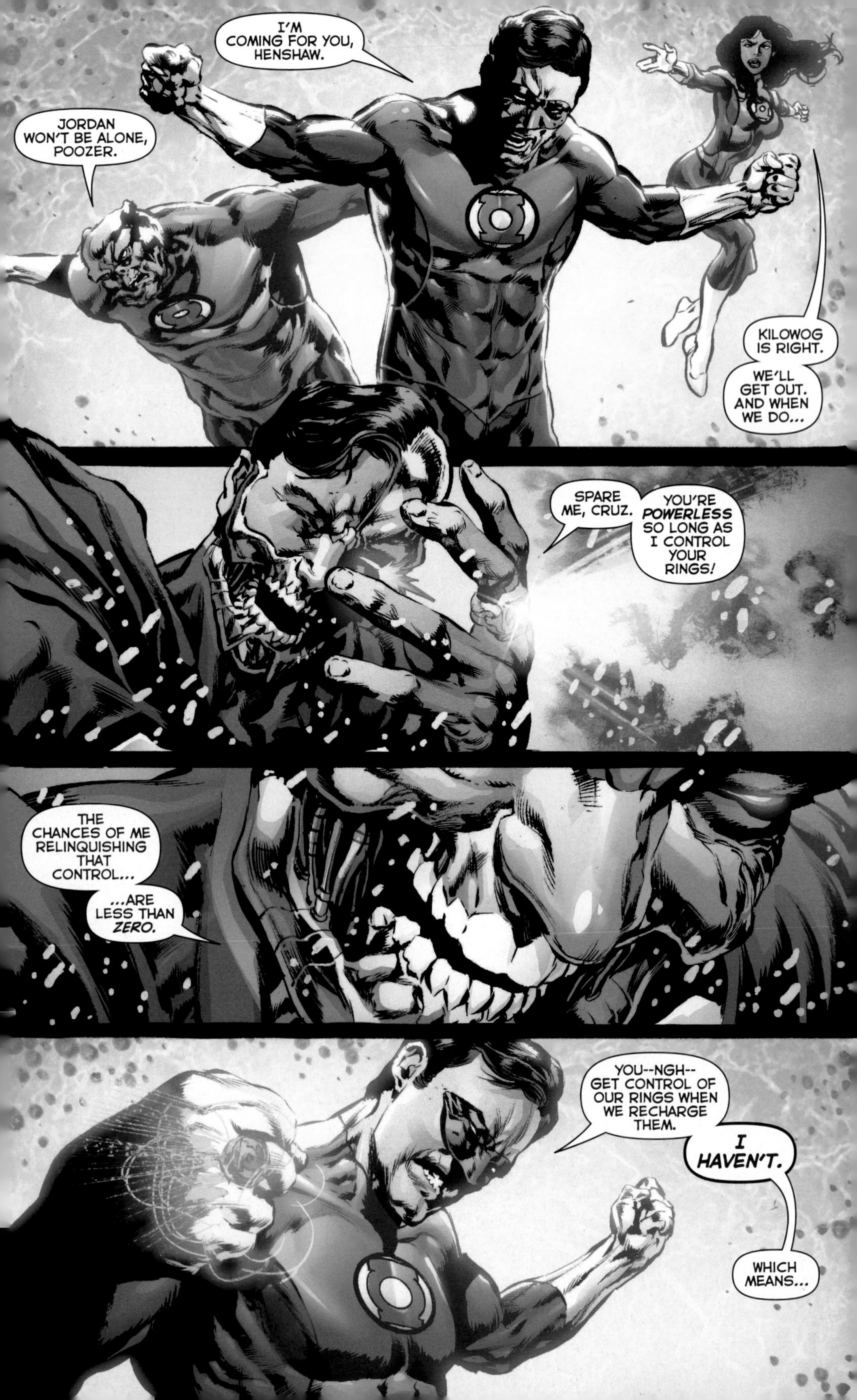
I'M COMING FOR YOU, HENSHAW.
JORDAN WON'T BE ALONE, POOZER.
KILOWOG IS RIGHT.
WE'LL GET OUT. AND WHEN WE DO...
SPARE ME, CRUZ.
YOU'RE POWERLESS SO LONG AS I CONTROL YOUR RINGS!
THE CHANCES OF ME RELINQUISHING THAT CONTROL...
...ARE LESS THAN ZERO.
YOU--NGH-- GET CONTROL OF OUR RINGS WHEN WE RECHARGE THEM.
I HAVEN'T.
WHICH MEANS...

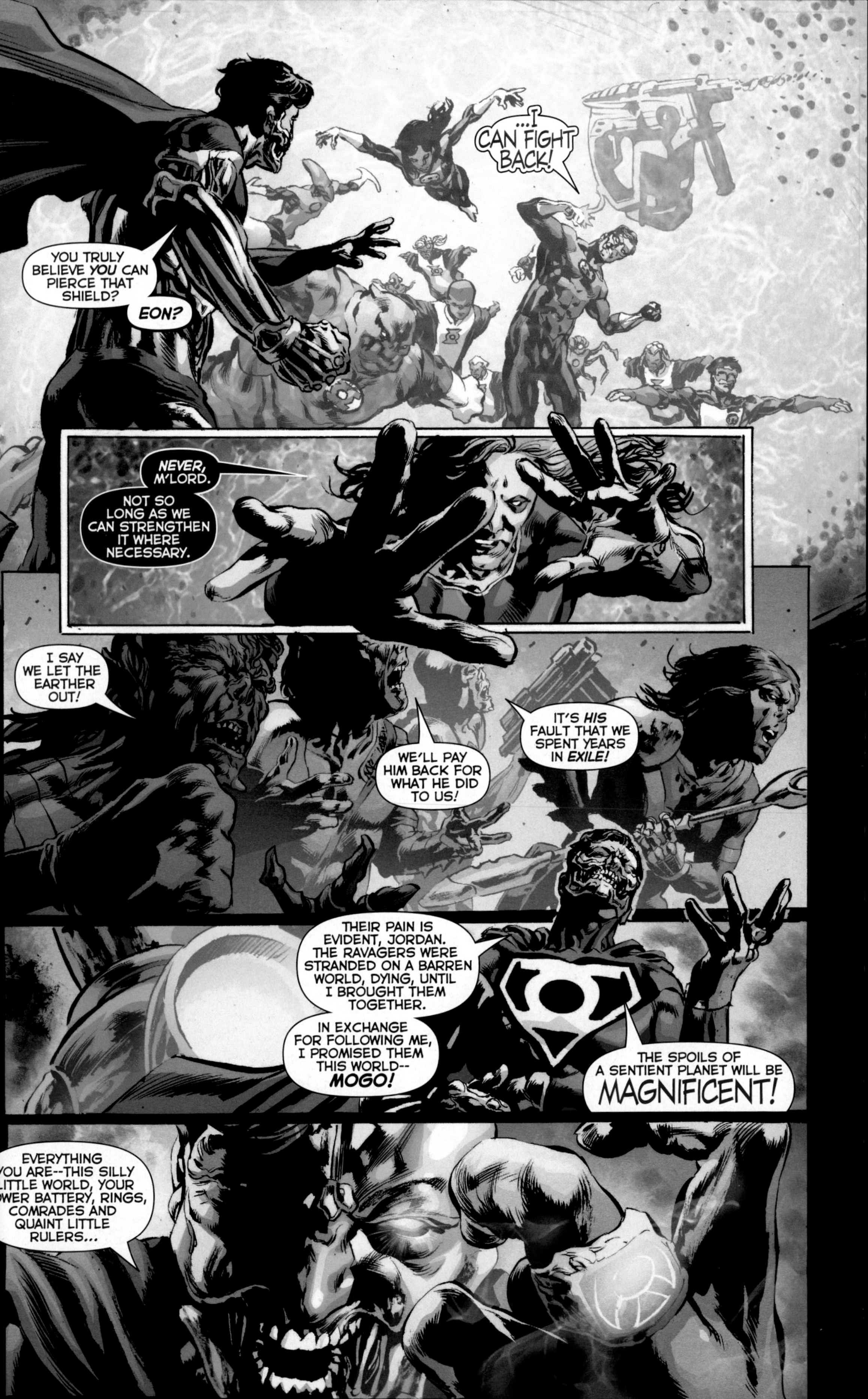

...I CAN FIGHT BACK!
YOU TRULY BELIEVE YOU CAN PIERCE THAT SHIELD?
EON?
NEVER, M'LORD.
NOT SO LONG AS WE CAN STRENGTHEN IT WHERE NECESSARY.
I SAY WE LET THE EARTHER OUT!
WE'LL PAY HIM BACK FOR WHAT HE DID TO US!
IT'S HIS FAULT THAT WE SPENT YEARS IN EXILE!
THEIR PAIN IS EVIDENT, JORDAN. THE RAVAGERS WERE STRANDED ON A BARREN WORLD, DYING, UNTIL I BROUGHT THEM TOGETHER.
IN EXCHANGE FOR FOLLOWING ME, I PROMISED THEM THIS WORLD--MOGO!
THE SPOILS OF A SENTIENT PLANET WILL BE MAGNIFICENT!
EVERYTHING YOU ARE--THIS SILLY LITTLE WORLD, YOUR POWER BATTERY, RINGS, COMRADES AND QUAINT LITTLE RULERS...

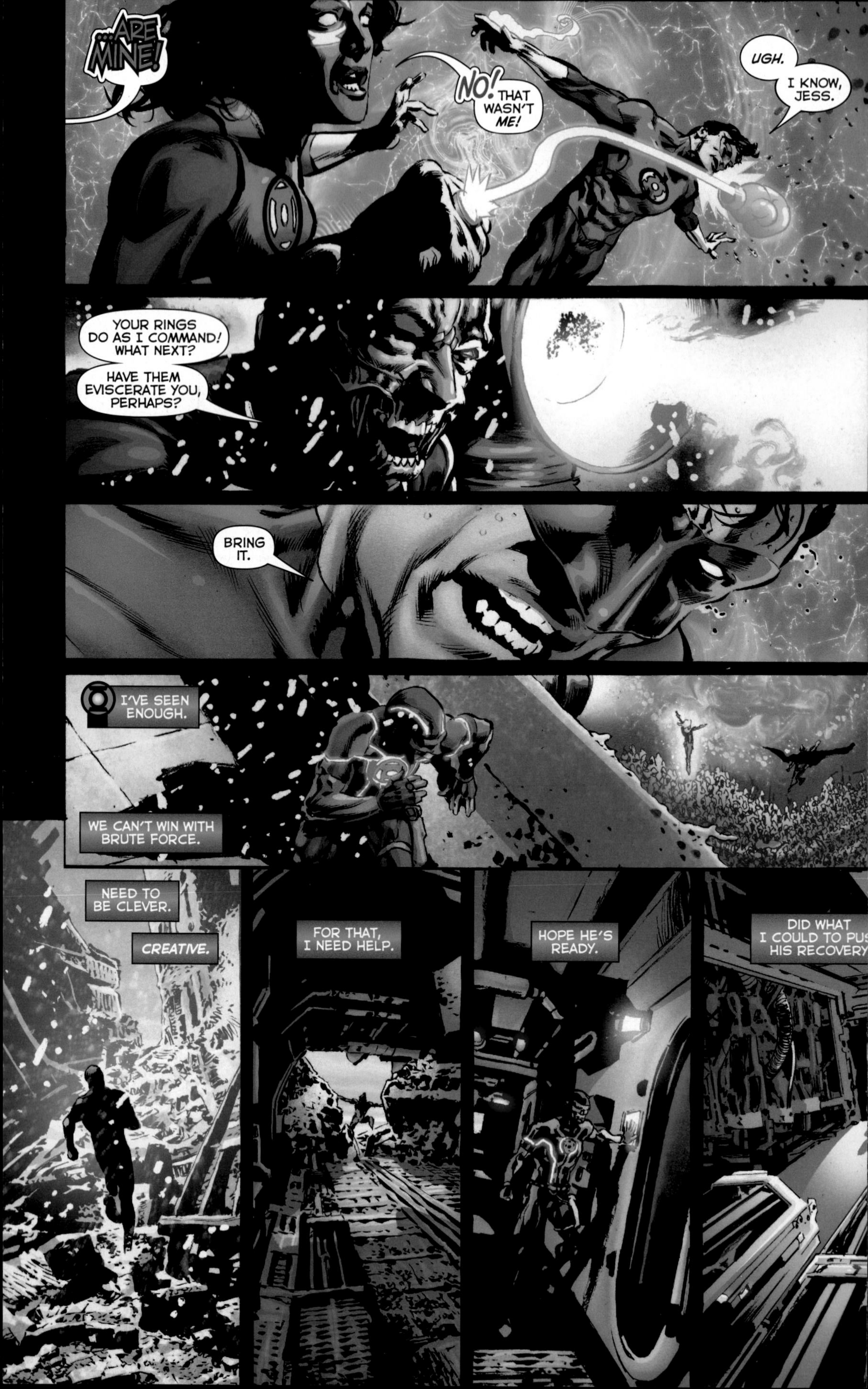
...ARE MINE!
NO! THAT WASN'T ME!
UGH.
I KNOW, JESS.
YOUR RINGS DO AS I COMMAND! WHAT NEXT?
HAVE THEM EVISCERATE YOU, PERHAPS?
BRING IT.
I'VE SEEN ENOUGH.
WE CAN'T WIN WITH BRUTE FORCE.
NEED TO BE CLEVER.
CREATIVE.
FOR THAT, I NEED HELP.
HOPE HE'S READY.
DID WHAT I COULD TO PUS HIS RECOVERY

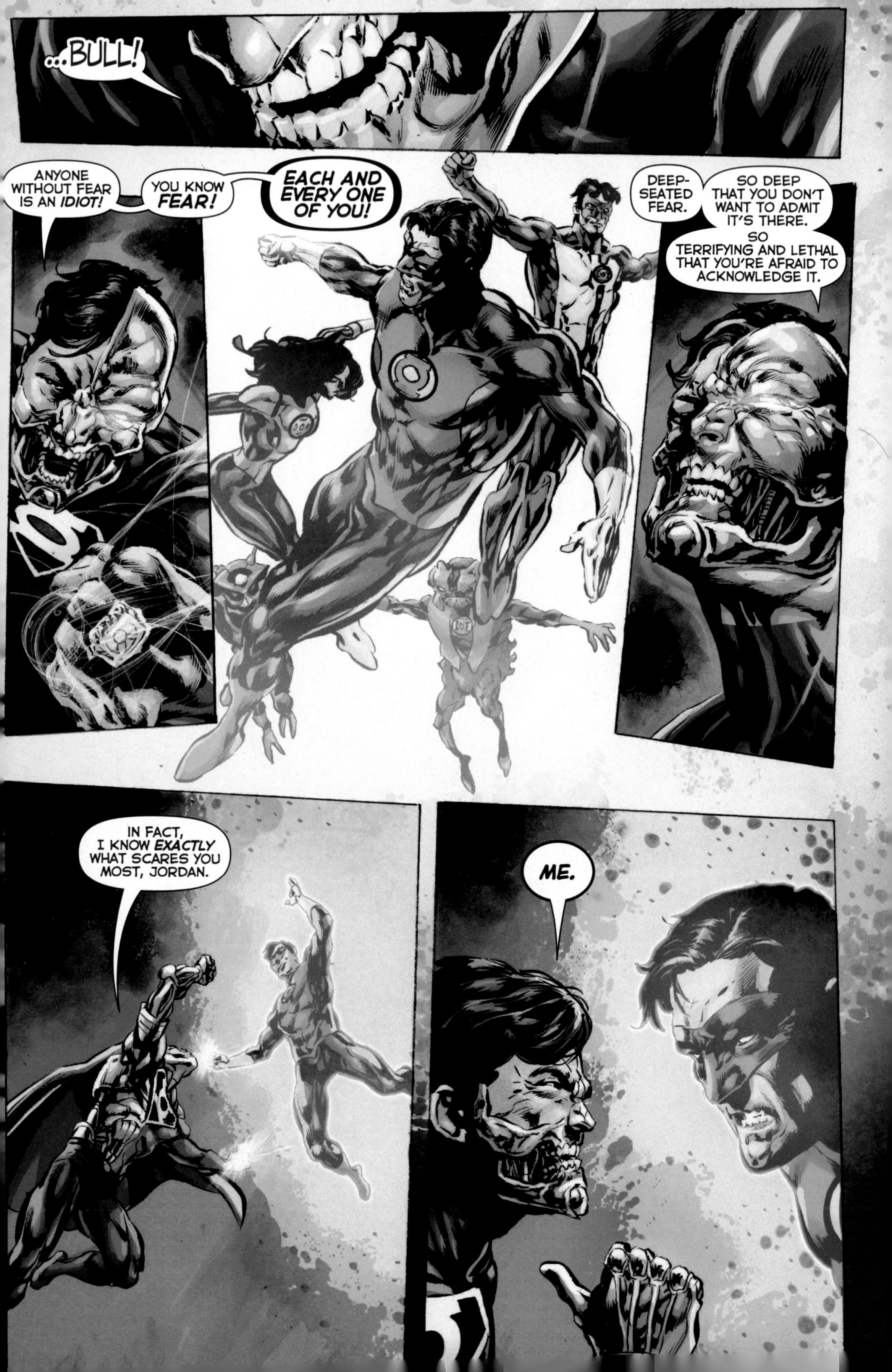
...BULL!
ANYONE WITHOUT FEAR IS AN *IDIOT!*
YOU KNOW **FEAR!**
EACH AND EVERY ONE OF YOU!
DEEP-SEATED FEAR.
SO DEEP THAT YOU DON'T WANT TO ADMIT IT'S THERE.
SO TERRIFYING AND LETHAL THAT YOU'RE AFRAID TO ACKNOWLEDGE IT.
IN FACT, I KNOW *EXACTLY* WHAT SCARES YOU MOST, JORDAN.
ME.

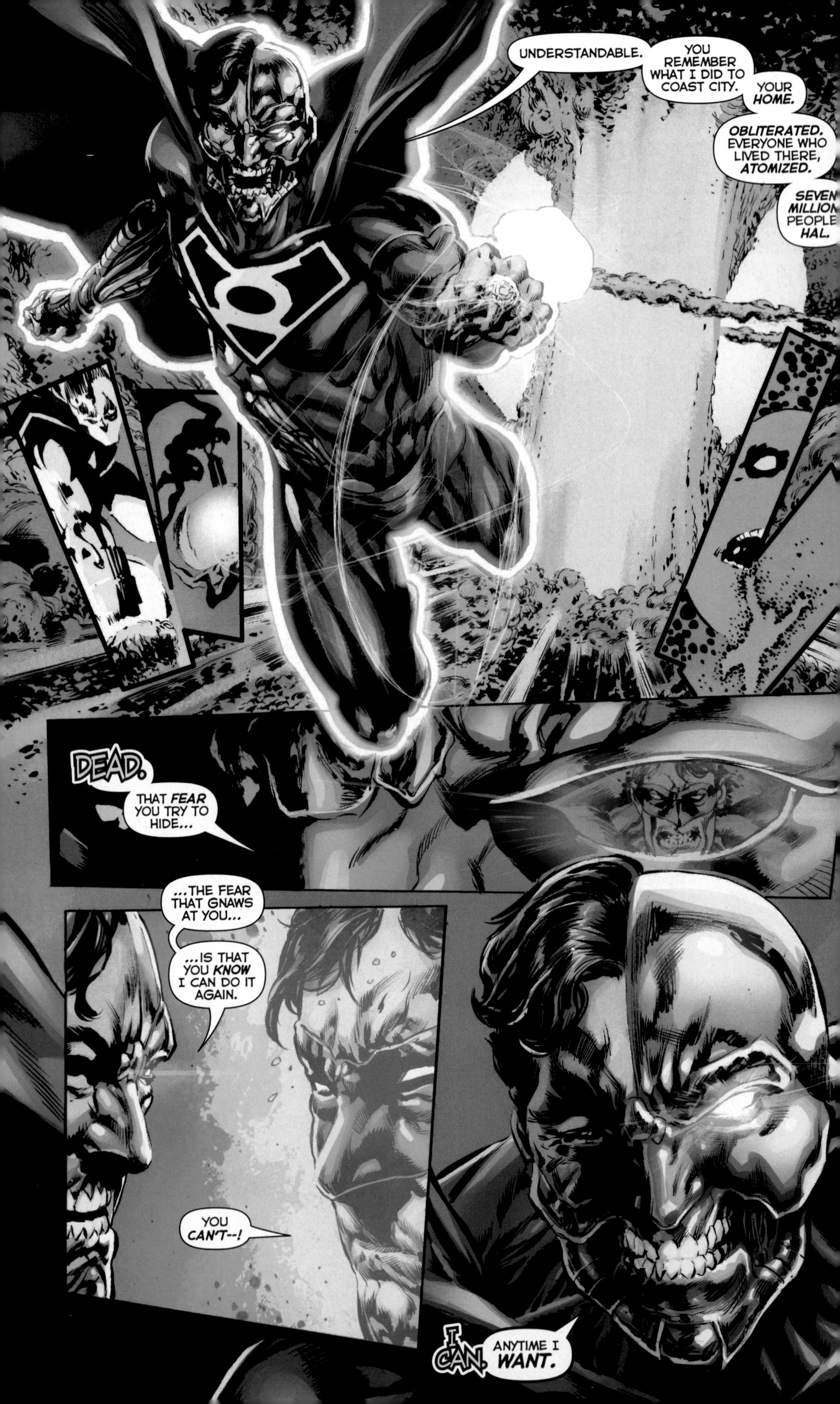
UNDERSTANDABLE.
YOU REMEMBER WHAT I DID TO COAST CITY.
YOUR HOME.
OBLITERATED. EVERYONE WHO LIVED THERE, ATOMIZED.
SEVEN MILLION PEOPLE HAL.
DEAD.
THAT FEAR YOU TRY TO HIDE...
...THE FEAR THAT GNAWS AT YOU...
...IS THAT YOU KNOW I CAN DO IT AGAIN.
YOU CAN'T--!
I CAN. ANYTIME I WANT.

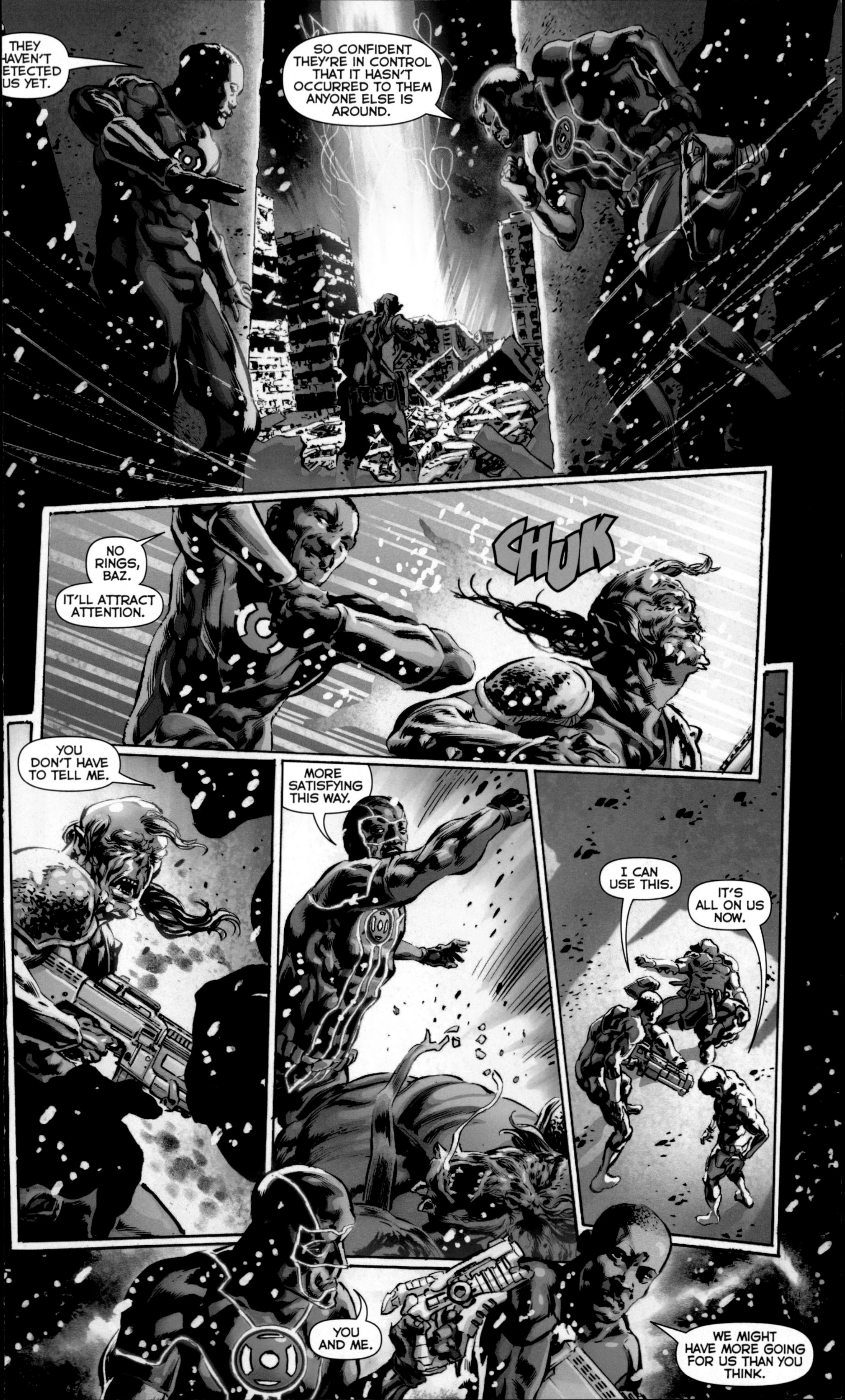
THEY HAVEN'T DETECTED US YET.
SO CONFIDENT THEY'RE IN CONTROL THAT IT HASN'T OCCURRED TO THEM ANYONE ELSE IS AROUND.
NO RINGS, BAZ.
IT'LL ATTRACT ATTENTION.
CHUK
YOU DON'T HAVE TO TELL ME.
MORE SATISFYING THIS WAY.
I CAN USE THIS.
IT'S ALL ON US NOW.
YOU AND ME.
WE MIGHT HAVE MORE GOING FOR US THAN YOU THINK.

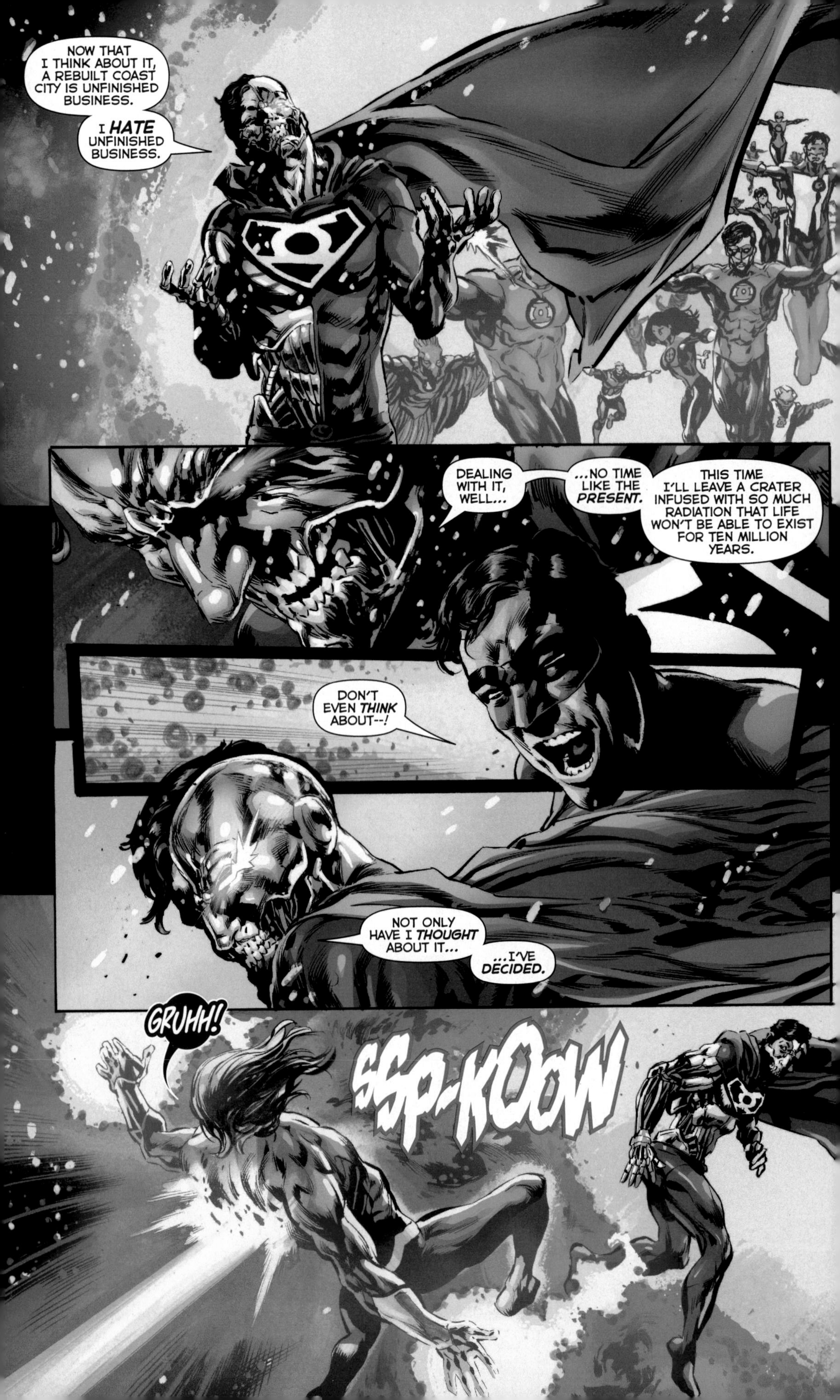
NOW THAT I THINK ABOUT IT, A REBUILT COAST CITY IS UNFINISHED BUSINESS.
I *HATE* UNFINISHED BUSINESS.
DEALING WITH IT, WELL...
...NO TIME LIKE THE *PRESENT.*
THIS TIME I'LL LEAVE A CRATER INFUSED WITH SO MUCH RADIATION THAT LIFE WON'T BE ABLE TO EXIST FOR TEN MILLION YEARS.
DON'T EVEN *THINK* ABOUT--!
NOT ONLY HAVE I *THOUGHT* ABOUT IT...
...I'VE *DECIDED.*
GRUHH!
SSP-KOOW

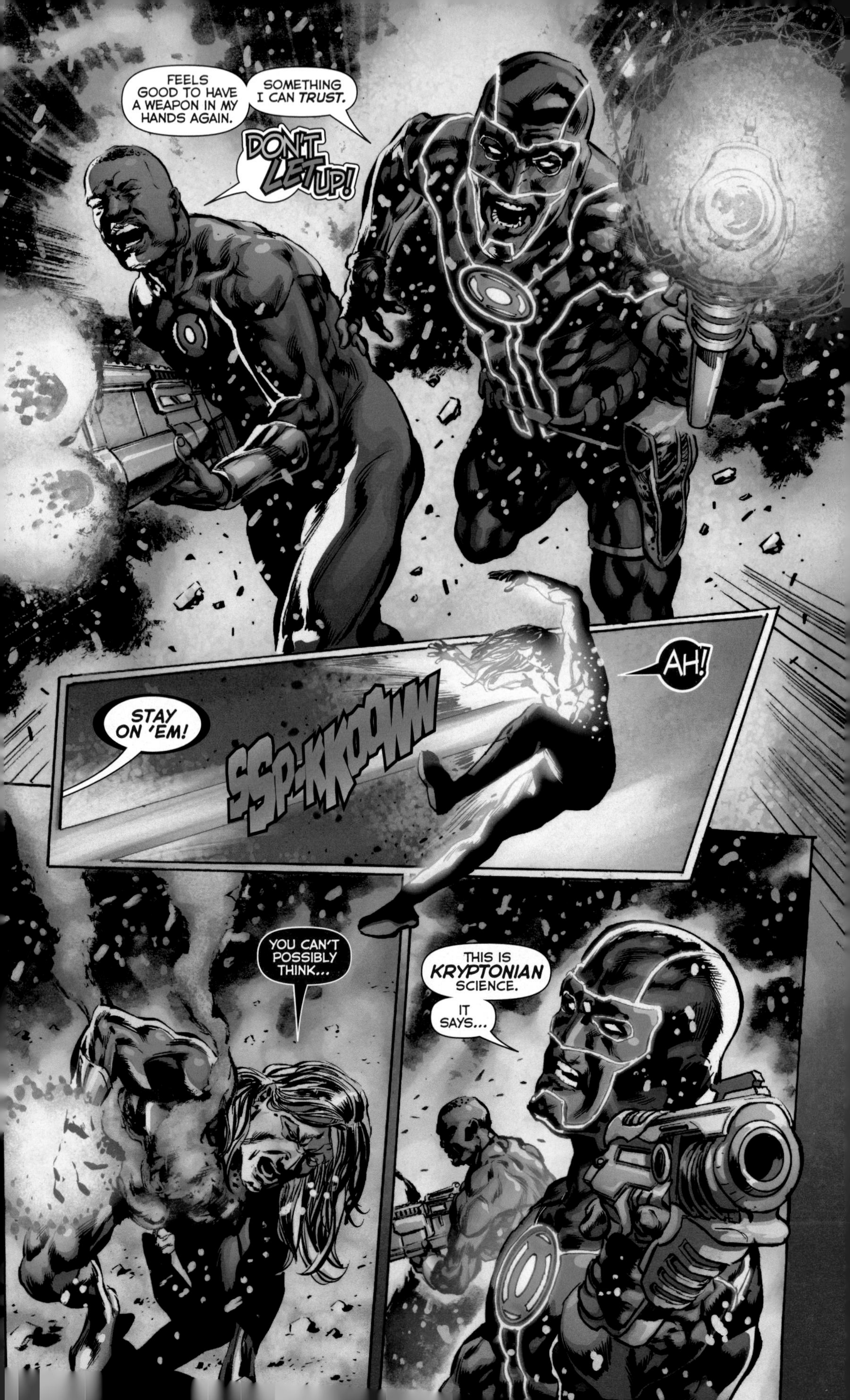
FEELS GOOD TO HAVE A WEAPON IN MY HANDS AGAIN.
SOMETHING I CAN TRUST.
DON'T LET UP!
AH!
STAY ON 'EM!
SSP-KKOOWW
YOU CAN'T POSSIBLY THINK...
THIS IS KRYPTONIAN SCIENCE.
IT SAYS...

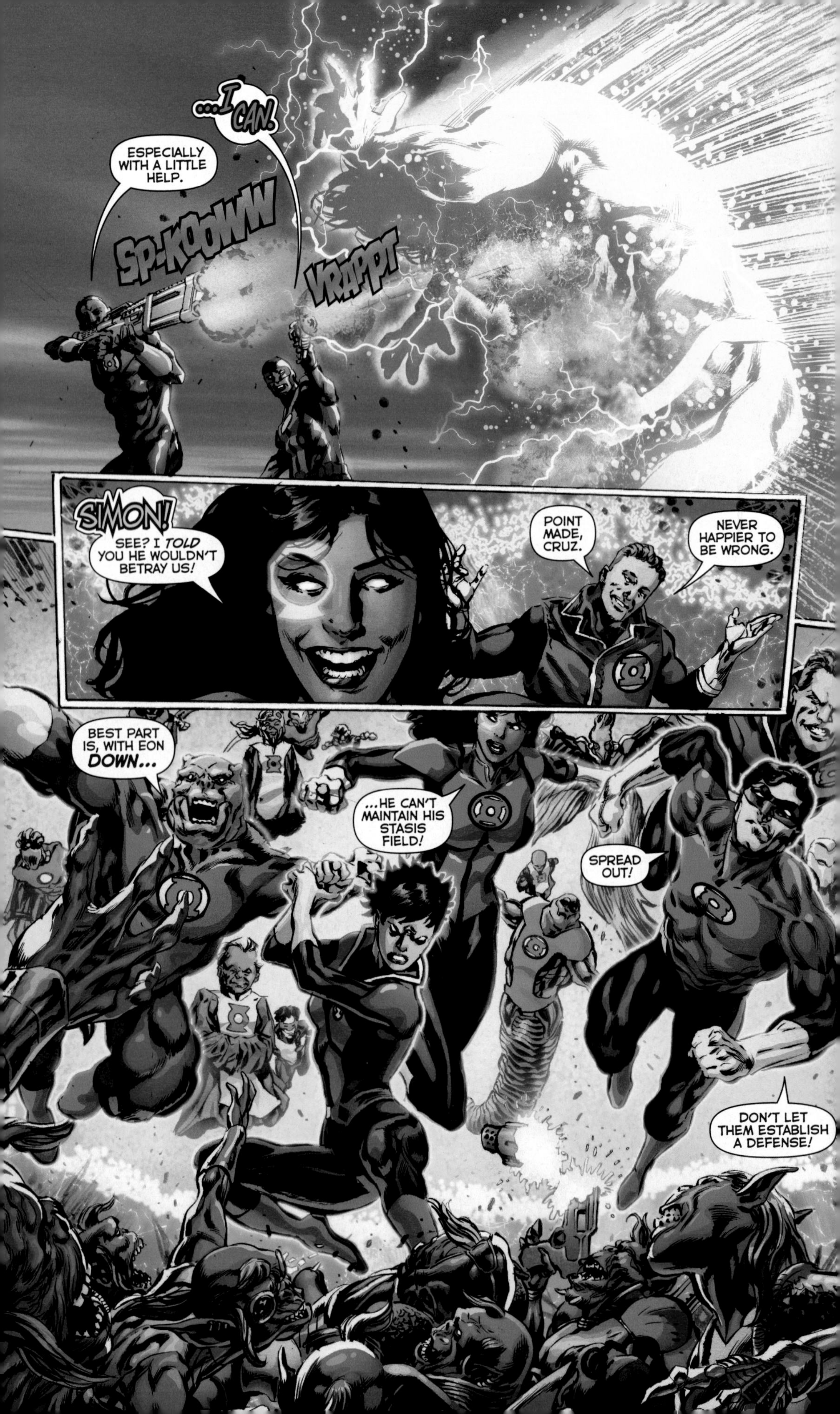
ESPECIALLY WITH A LITTLE HELP.
...I CAN.
SP-KOOWN
VRAPPT
SIMON!
SEE? I TOLD YOU HE WOULDN'T BETRAY US!
POINT MADE, CRUZ.
NEVER HAPPIER TO BE WRONG.
BEST PART IS, WITH EON DOWN...
...HE CAN'T MAINTAIN HIS STASIS FIELD!
SPREAD OUT!
DON'T LET THEM ESTABLISH A DEFENSE!

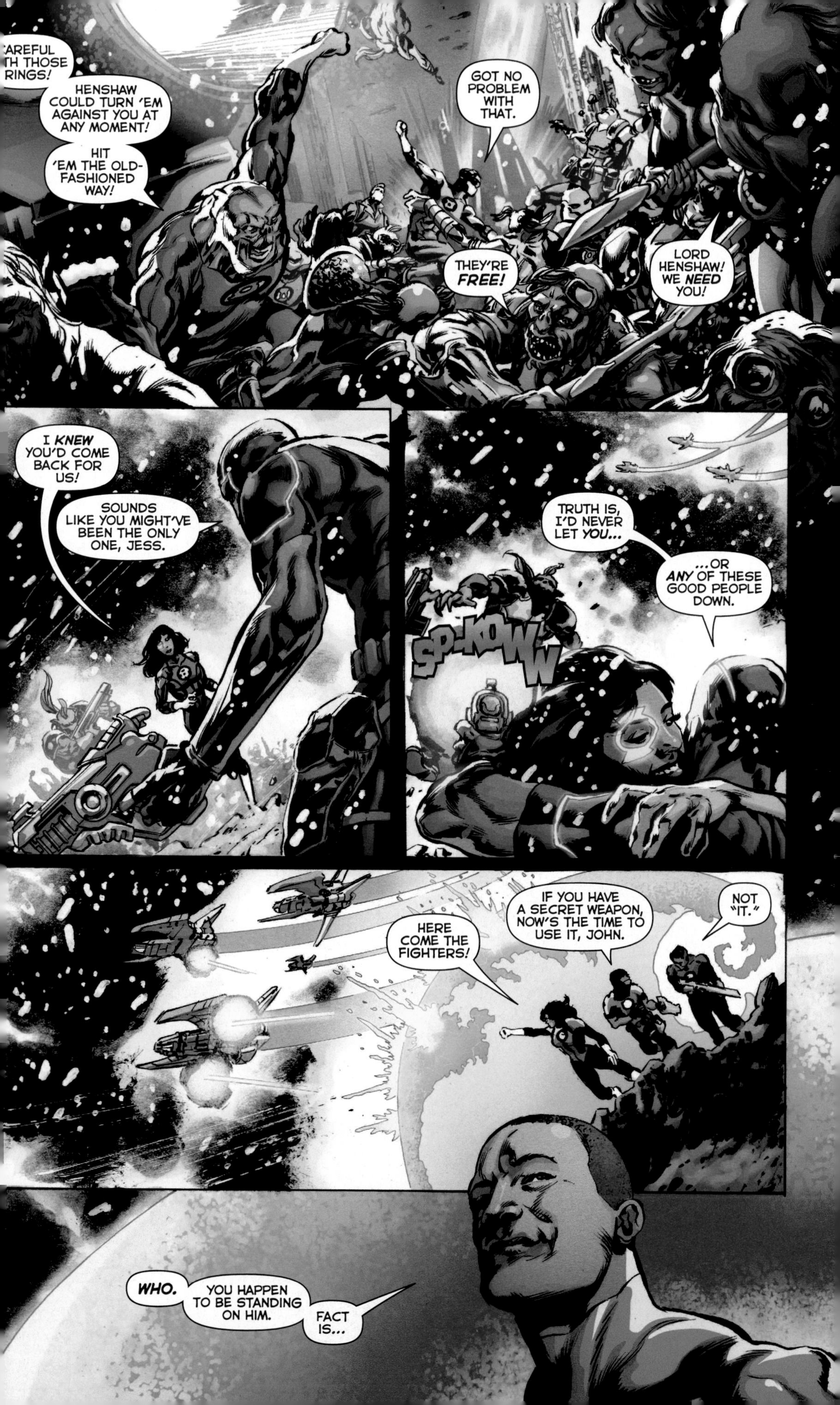

AREFUL
TH THOSE
RINGS!
HENSHAW COULD TURN 'EM AGAINST YOU AT ANY MOMENT!
HIT 'EM THE OLD-FASHIONED WAY!
GOT NO PROBLEM WITH THAT.
THEY'RE FREE!
LORD HENSHAW! WE NEED YOU!
I KNEW YOU'D COME BACK FOR US!
SOUNDS LIKE YOU MIGHT'VE BEEN THE ONLY ONE, JESS.
TRUTH IS, I'D NEVER LET YOU...
...OR ANY OF THESE GOOD PEOPLE DOWN.
SP-KOWW
HERE COME THE FIGHTERS!
IF YOU HAVE A SECRET WEAPON, NOW'S THE TIME TO USE IT, JOHN.
NOT "IT."
WHO.
YOU HAPPEN TO BE STANDING ON HIM.
FACT IS...

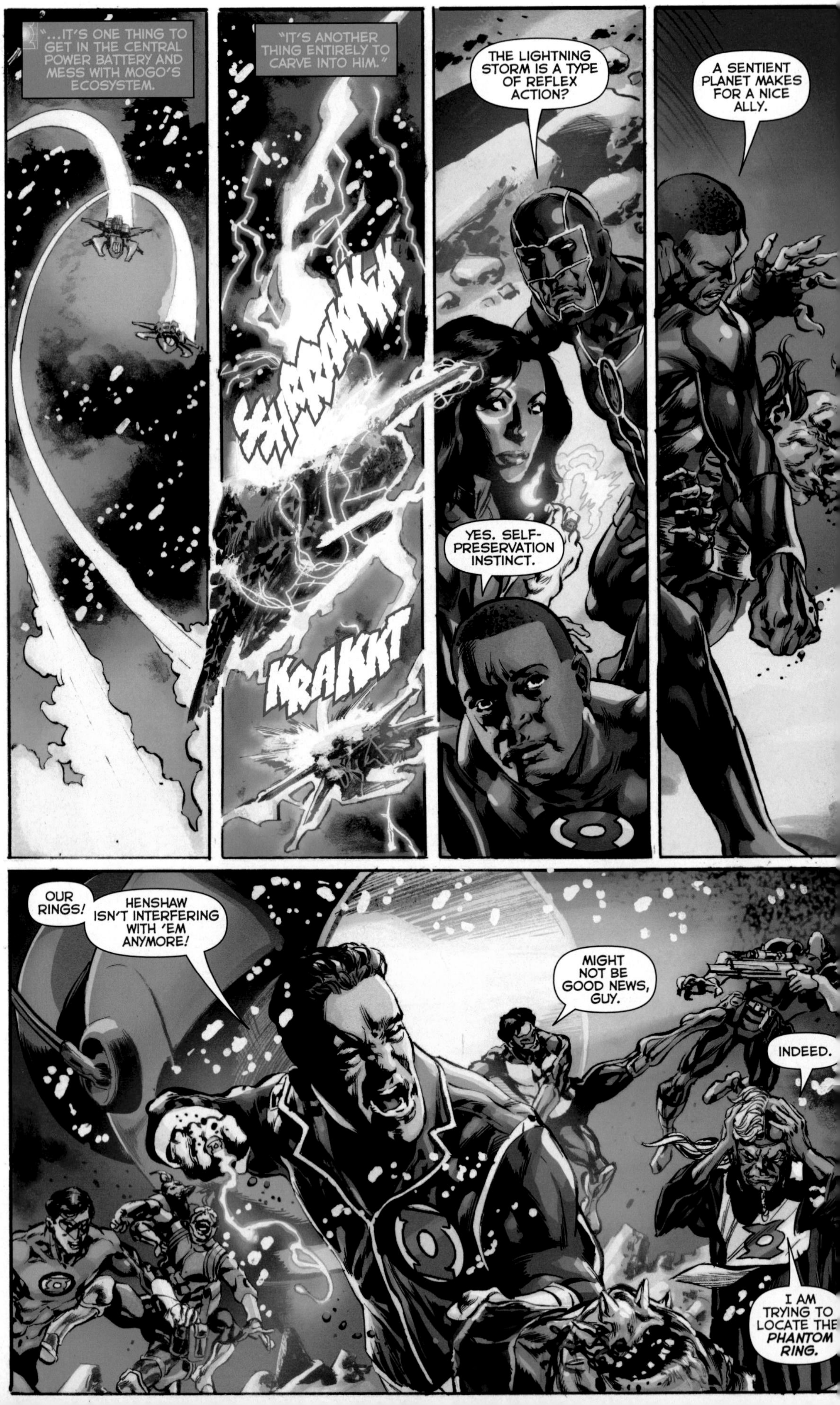
"...IT'S ONE THING TO GET IN THE CENTRAL POWER BATTERY AND MESS WITH MOGO'S ECOSYSTEM.
"IT'S ANOTHER THING ENTIRELY TO CARVE INTO HIM."
SHRAKKK
KRAKKT
THE LIGHTNING STORM IS A TYPE OF REFLEX ACTION?
YES. SELF-PRESERVATION INSTINCT.
A SENTIENT PLANET MAKES FOR A NICE ALLY.
OUR RINGS!
HENSHAW ISN'T INTERFERING WITH 'EM ANYMORE!
MIGHT NOT BE GOOD NEWS, GUY.
INDEED.
I AM TRYING TO LOCATE THE *PHANTOM RING.*

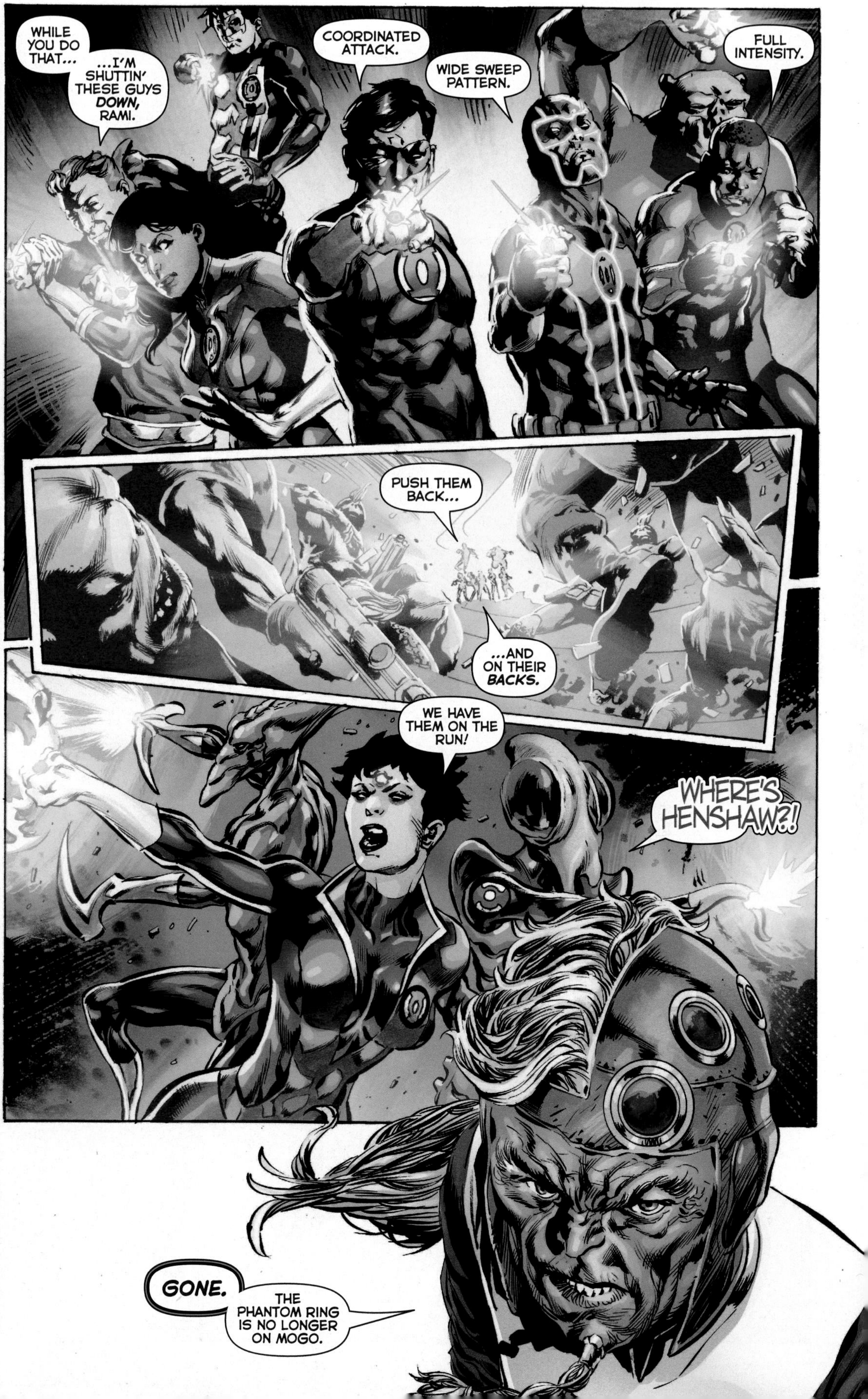
WHILE YOU DO THAT...
...I'M SHUTTIN' THESE GUYS DOWN, RAMI.
COORDINATED ATTACK.
WIDE SWEEP PATTERN.
FULL INTENSITY.
PUSH THEM BACK...
...AND ON THEIR BACKS.
WE HAVE THEM ON THE RUN!
WHERE'S HENSHAW?!
GONE.
THE PHANTOM RING IS NO LONGER ON MOGO.

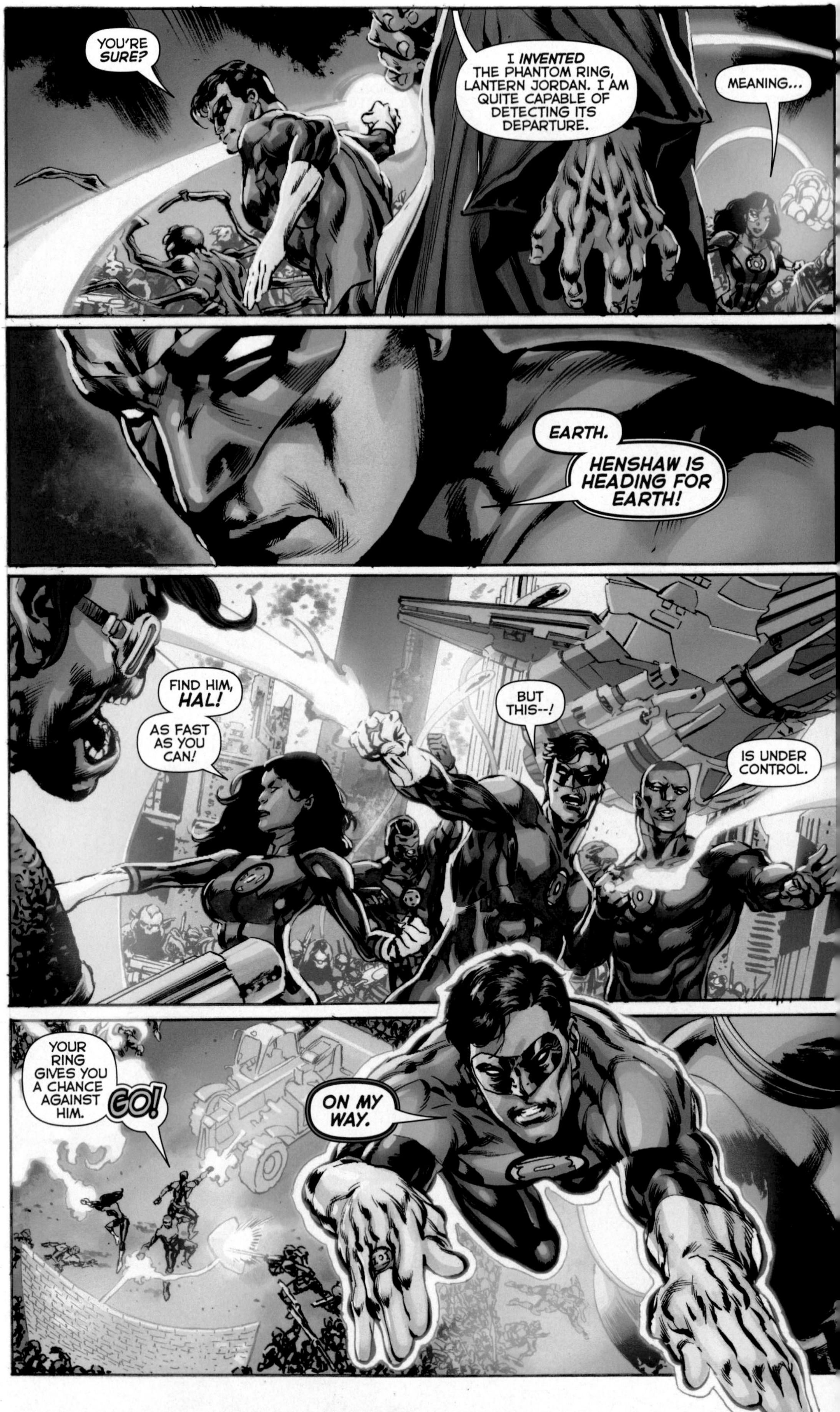
YOU'RE SURE?
I INVENTED THE PHANTOM RING, LANTERN JORDAN. I AM QUITE CAPABLE OF DETECTING ITS DEPARTURE.
MEANING...
EARTH.
HENSHAW IS HEADING FOR EARTH!
FIND HIM, HAL!
AS FAST AS YOU CAN!
BUT THIS--!
IS UNDER CONTROL.
YOUR RING GIVES YOU A CHANCE AGAINST HIM.
GO!
ON MY WAY.

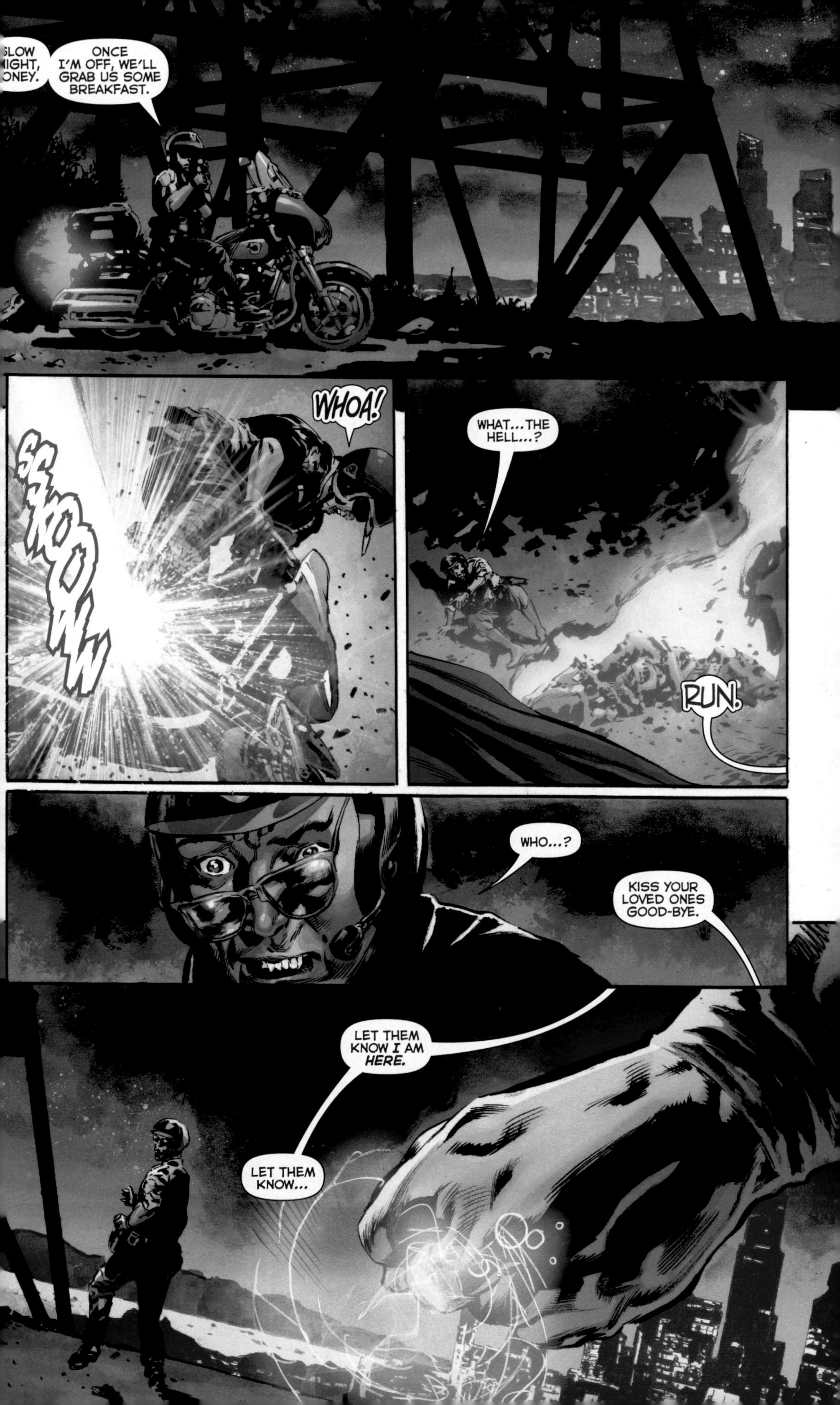
SLOW
NIGHT,
ONEY.
ONCE I'M OFF, WE'LL GRAB US SOME BREAKFAST.
WHOA!
SKROOWW
WHAT... THE HELL...?
RUN.
WHO...?
KISS YOUR LOVED ONES GOOD-BYE.
LET THEM KNOW I AM HERE.
LET THEM KNOW...

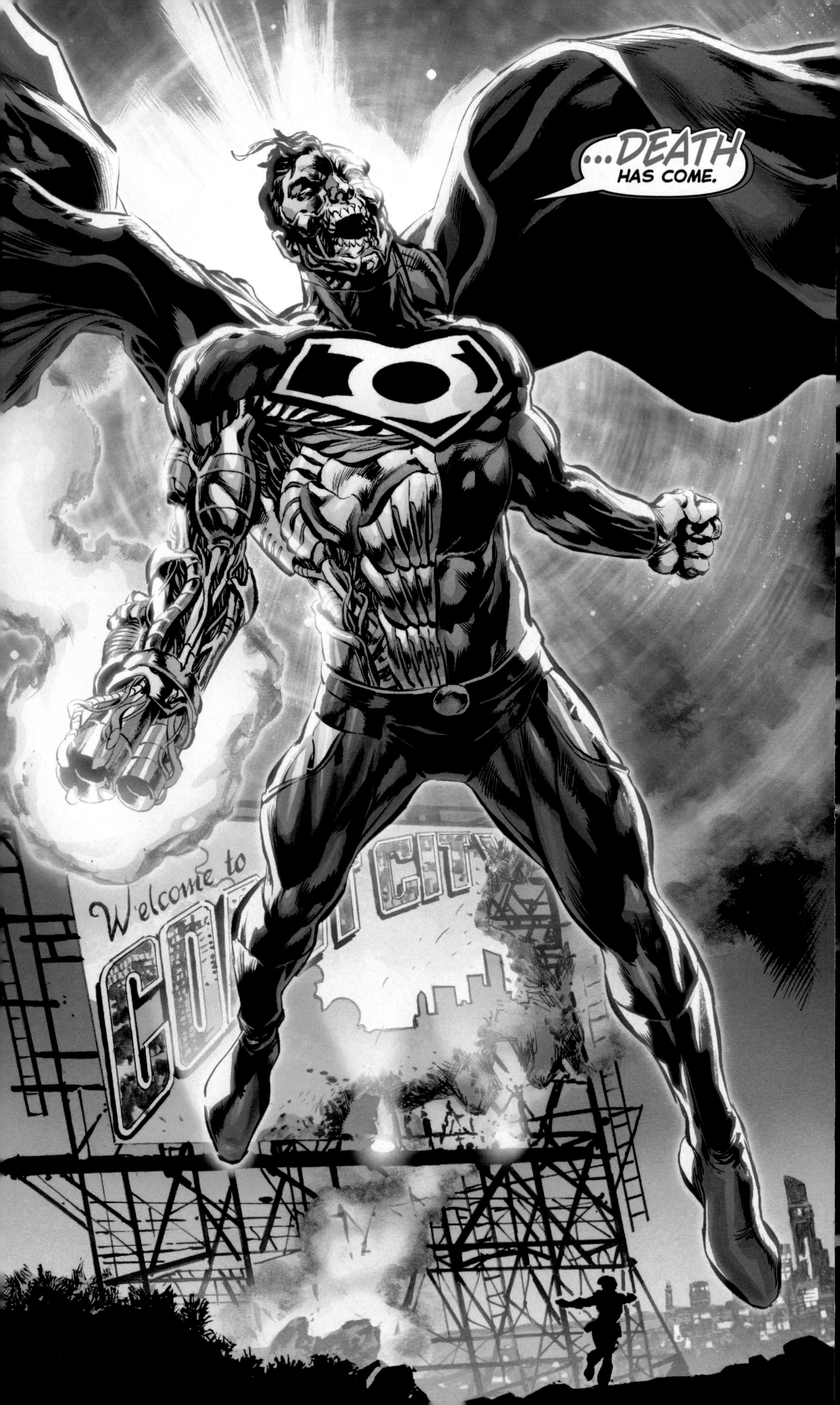
...DEATH HAS COME.
Welcome to

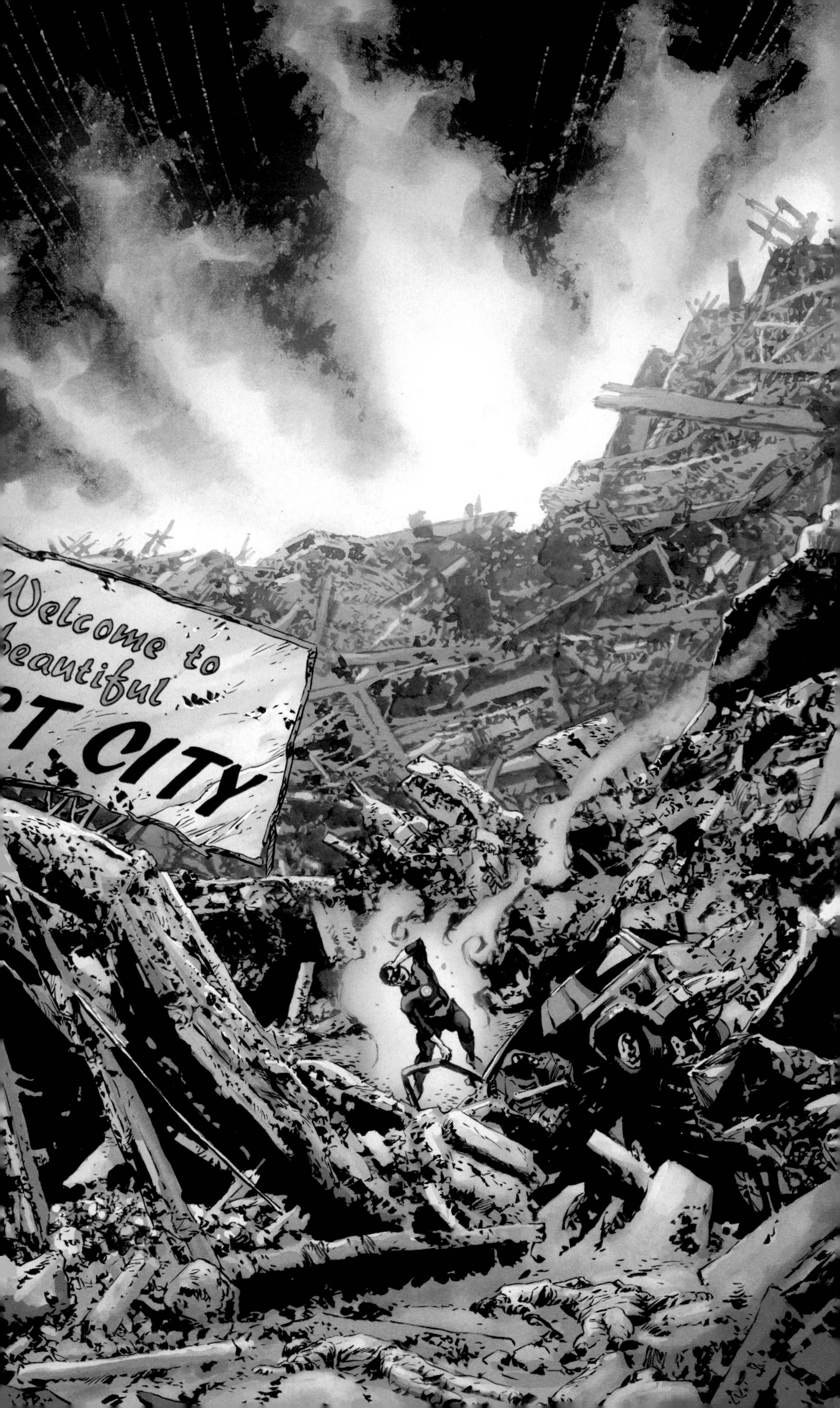

Welcome to
beautiful
...T CITY

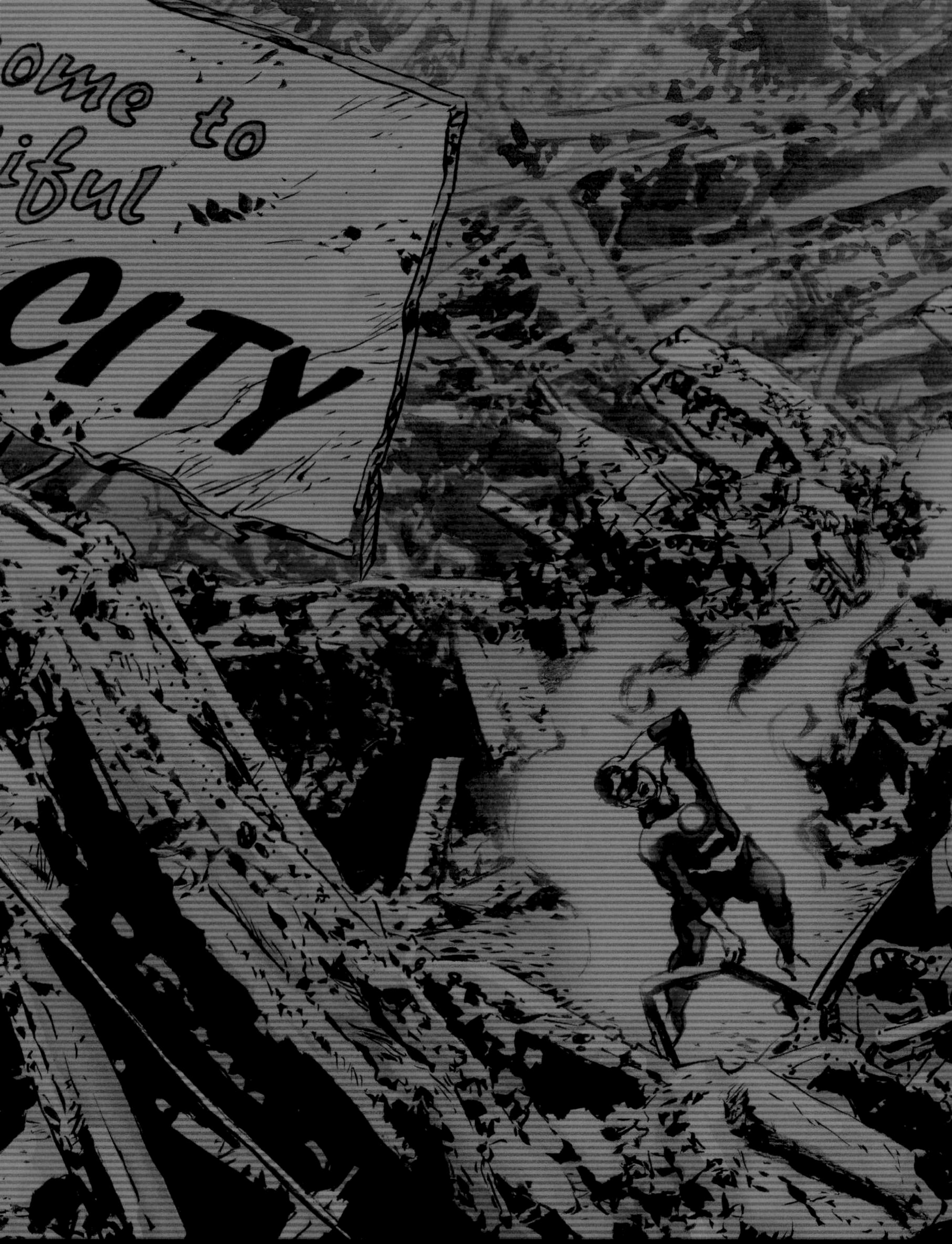
ome to
iful
CITY

GREEN LANTERNS
#57

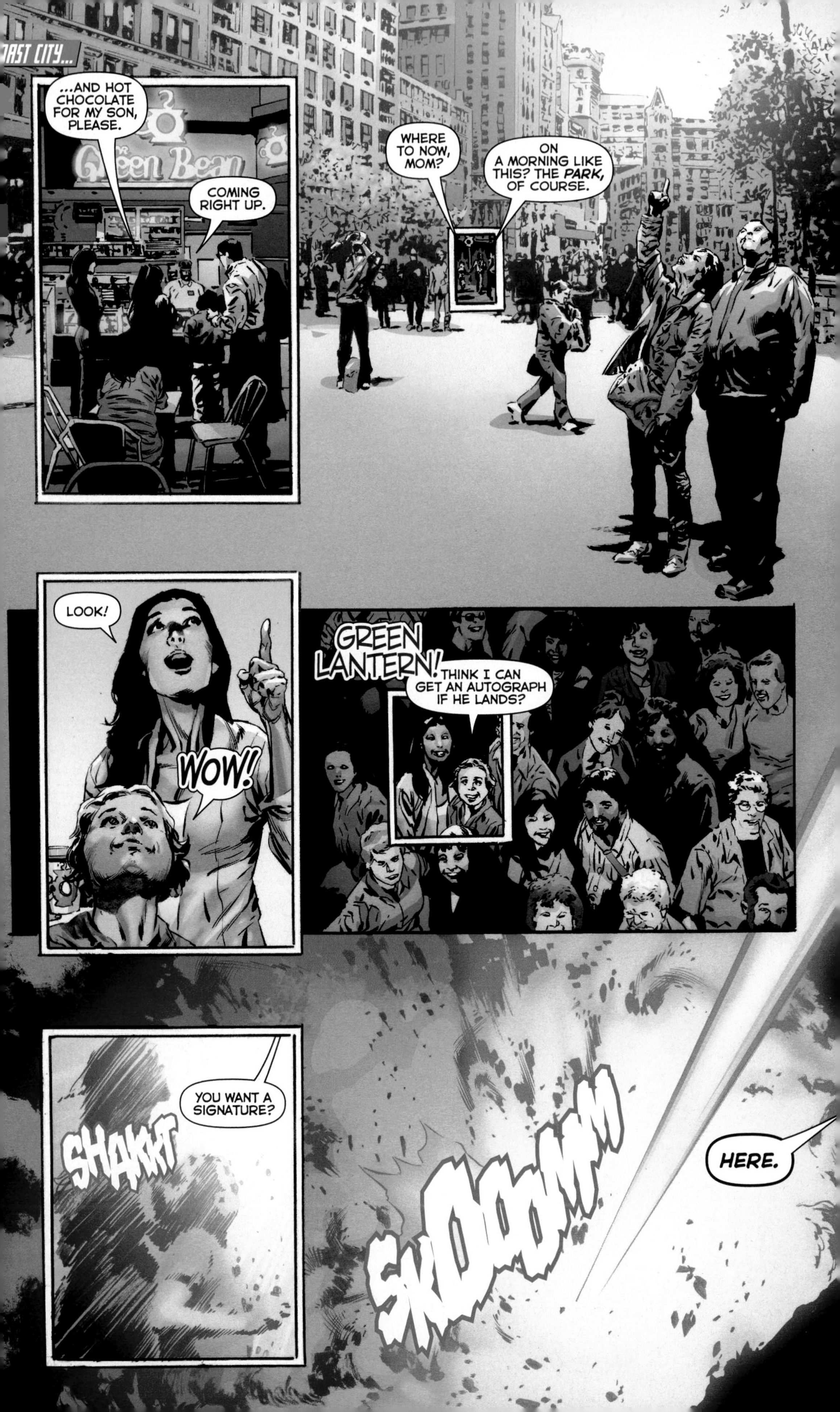

...AND HOT CHOCOLATE FOR MY SON, PLEASE.
COMING RIGHT UP.
WHERE TO NOW, MOM?
ON A MORNING LIKE THIS? THE *PARK,* OF COURSE.
LOOK!
WOW!
GREEN LANTERN!
THINK I CAN GET AN AUTOGRAPH IF HE LANDS?
YOU WANT A SIGNATURE?
SHAKKT
SKOOMM
HERE.

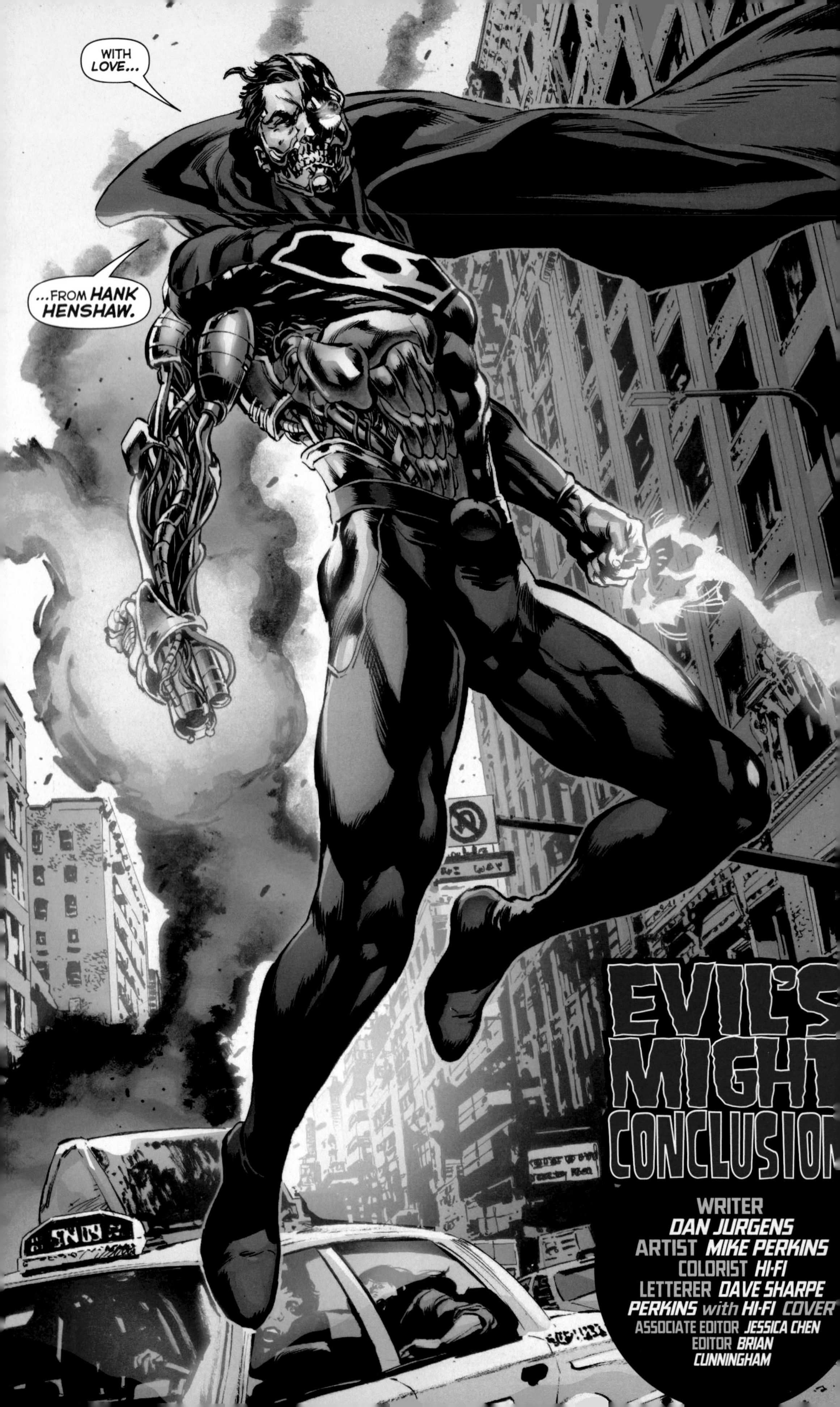
WITH LOVE...
...FROM HANK HENSHAW.
EVIL'S MIGHT CONCLUSION
WRITER DAN JURGENS
ARTIST MIKE PERKINS
COLORIST HI-FI
LETTERER DAVE SHARPE
PERKINS with HI-FI COVER
ASSOCIATE EDITOR JESSICA CHEN
EDITOR BRIAN CUNNINGHAM

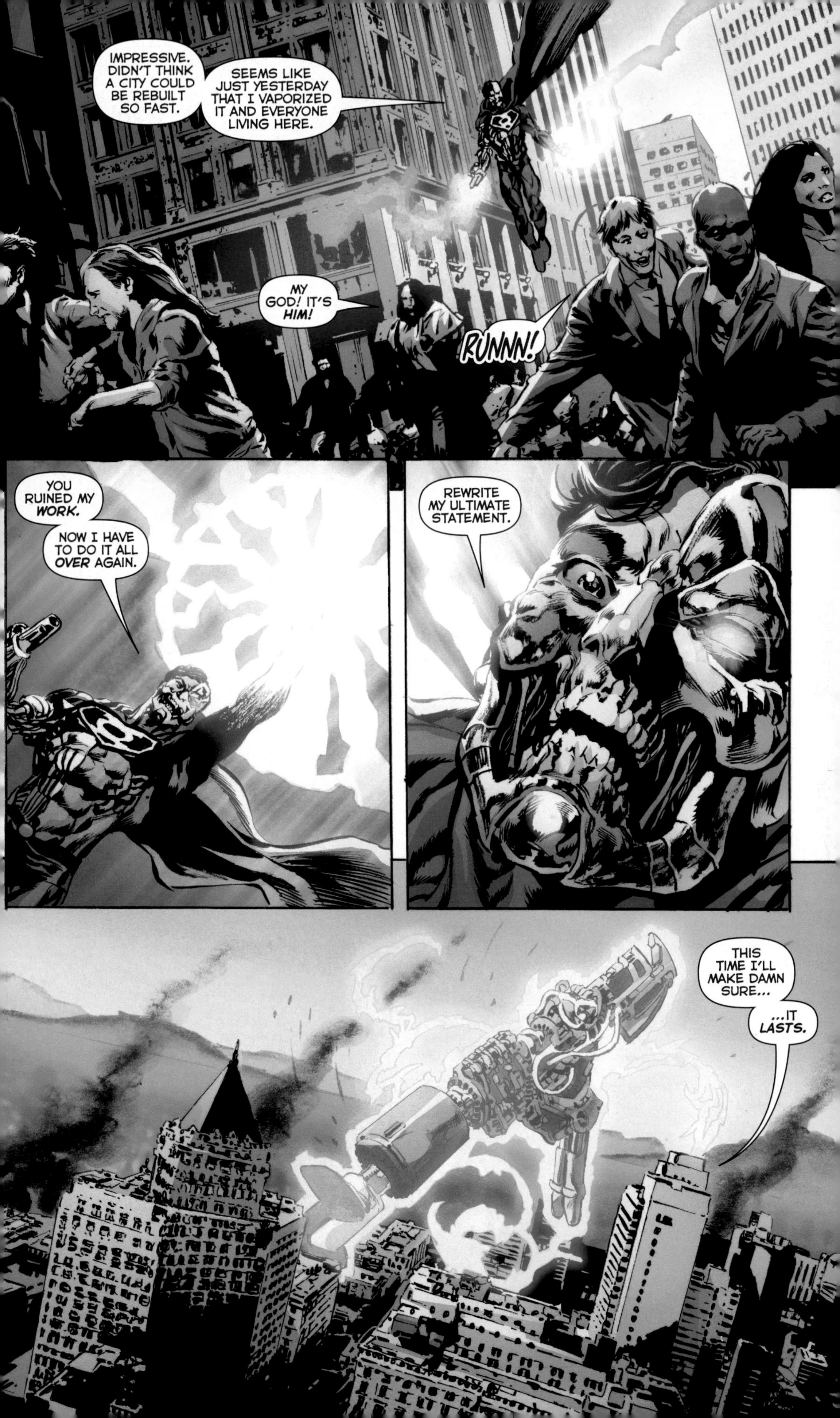
IMPRESSIVE. DIDN'T THINK A CITY COULD BE REBUILT SO FAST.
SEEMS LIKE JUST YESTERDAY THAT I VAPORIZED IT AND EVERYONE LIVING HERE.
MY GOD! IT'S *HIM!*
RUNNN!
YOU RUINED MY *WORK.*
NOW I HAVE TO DO IT ALL *OVER* AGAIN.
REWRITE MY ULTIMATE STATEMENT.
THIS TIME I'LL MAKE DAMN SURE...
...IT *LASTS.*

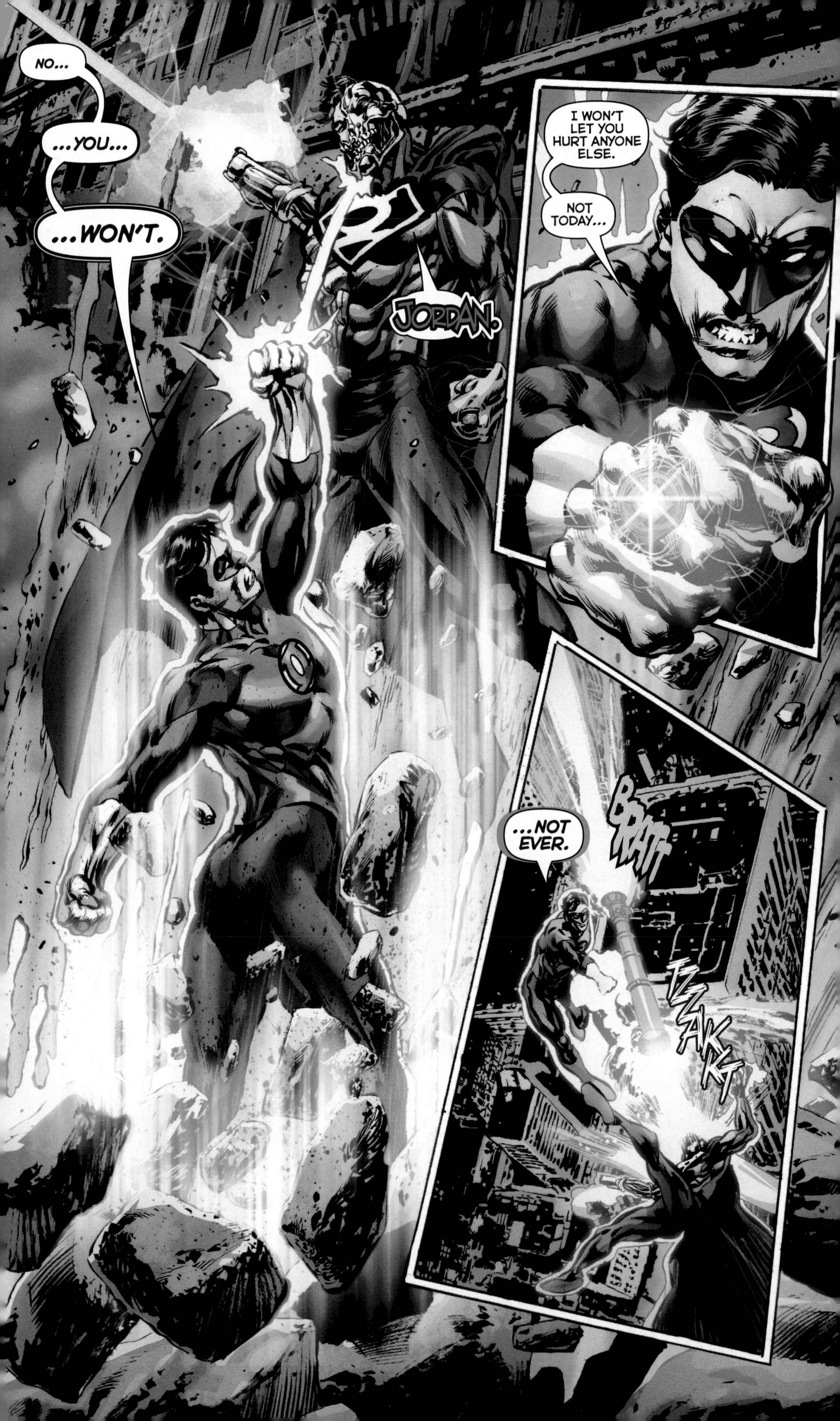
NO...
...YOU...
...WON'T.
JORDAN.
I WON'T LET YOU HURT ANYONE ELSE.
NOT TODAY...
...NOT EVER.
BRATT
FZZAKT

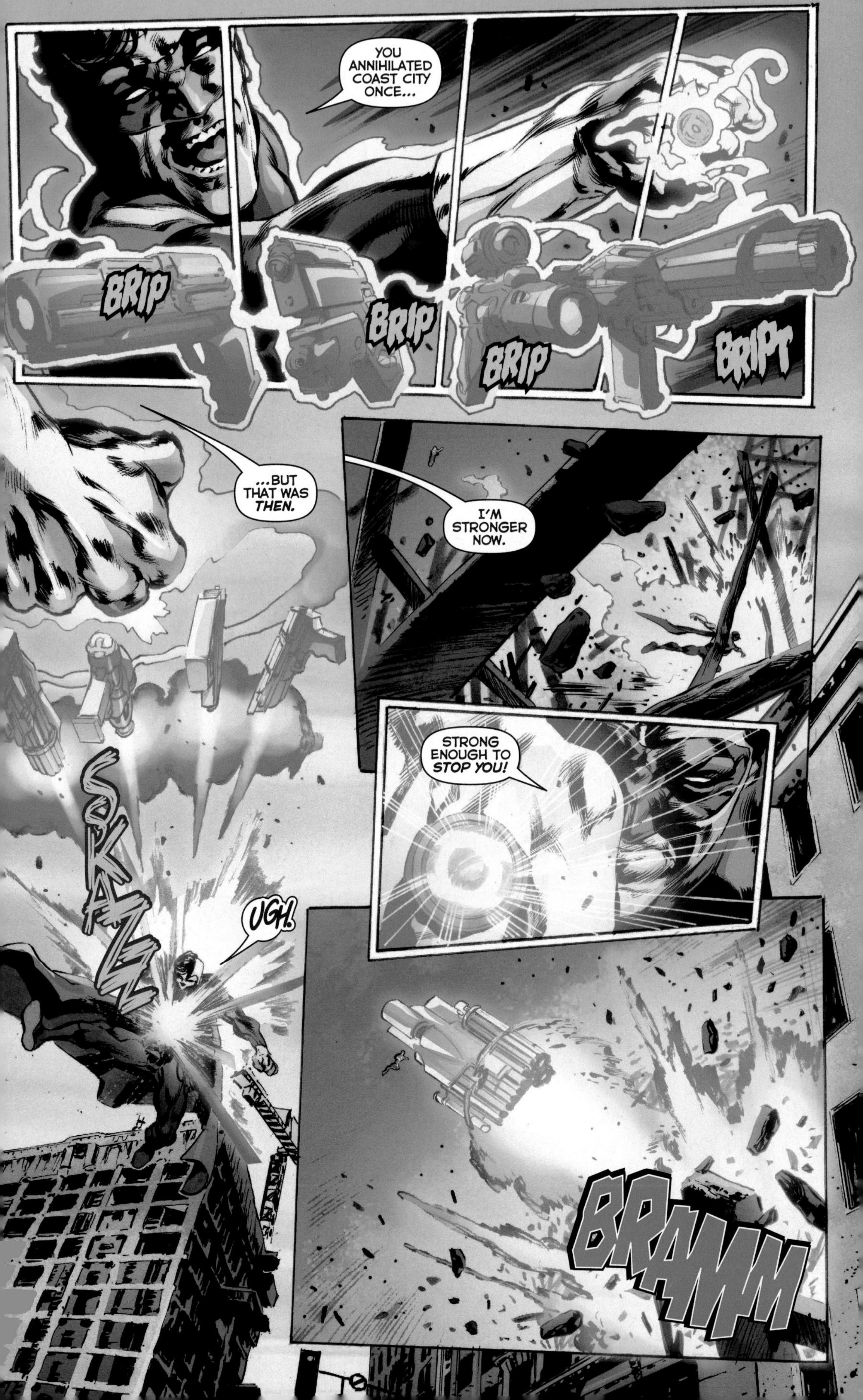
YOU ANNIHILATED COAST CITY ONCE...
BRIP
BRIP
BRIP
BRIPT
...BUT THAT WAS *THEN.*
I'M STRONGER NOW.
STRONG ENOUGH TO *STOP YOU!*
UGH!
BRAMMM

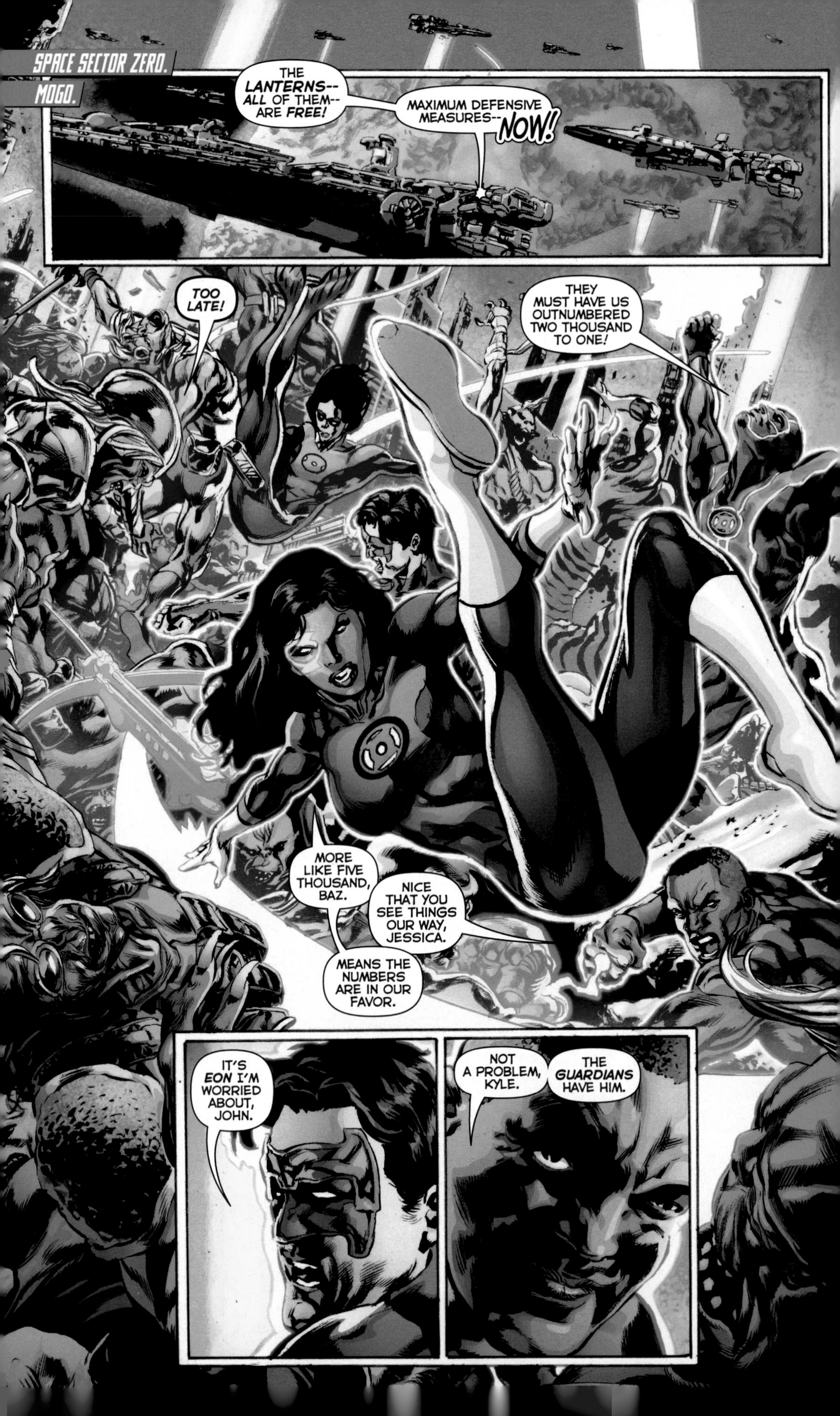

SPACE SECTOR ZERO.
MOGO.
THE LANTERNS-- ALL OF THEM-- ARE FREE!
MAXIMUM DEFENSIVE MEASURES--NOW!
TOO LATE!
THEY MUST HAVE US OUTNUMBERED TWO THOUSAND TO ONE!
MORE LIKE FIVE THOUSAND, BAZ.
MEANS THE NUMBERS ARE IN OUR FAVOR.
NICE THAT YOU SEE THINGS OUR WAY, JESSICA.
IT'S EON I'M WORRIED ABOUT, JOHN.
NOT A PROBLEM, KYLE.
THE GUARDIANS HAVE HIM.

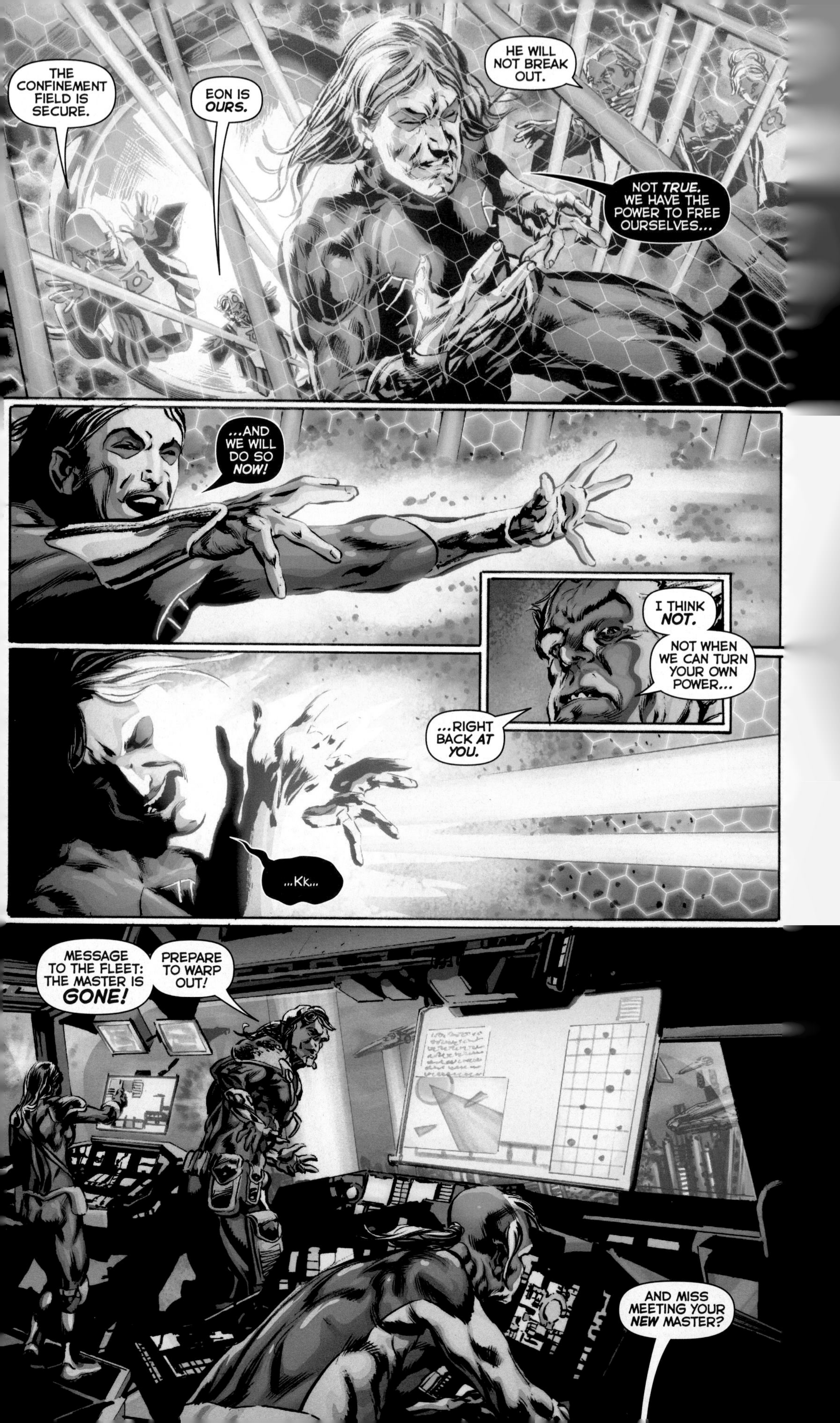
THE CONFINEMENT FIELD IS SECURE.
EON IS *OURS.*
HE WILL NOT BREAK OUT.
NOT *TRUE.* WE HAVE THE POWER TO FREE OURSELVES...
...AND WE WILL DO SO *NOW!*
I THINK *NOT.*
NOT WHEN WE CAN TURN YOUR OWN POWER...
...RIGHT BACK *AT YOU.*
...Kk...
MESSAGE TO THE FLEET: THE MASTER IS *GONE!*
PREPARE TO WARP OUT!
AND MISS MEETING YOUR *NEW* MASTER?

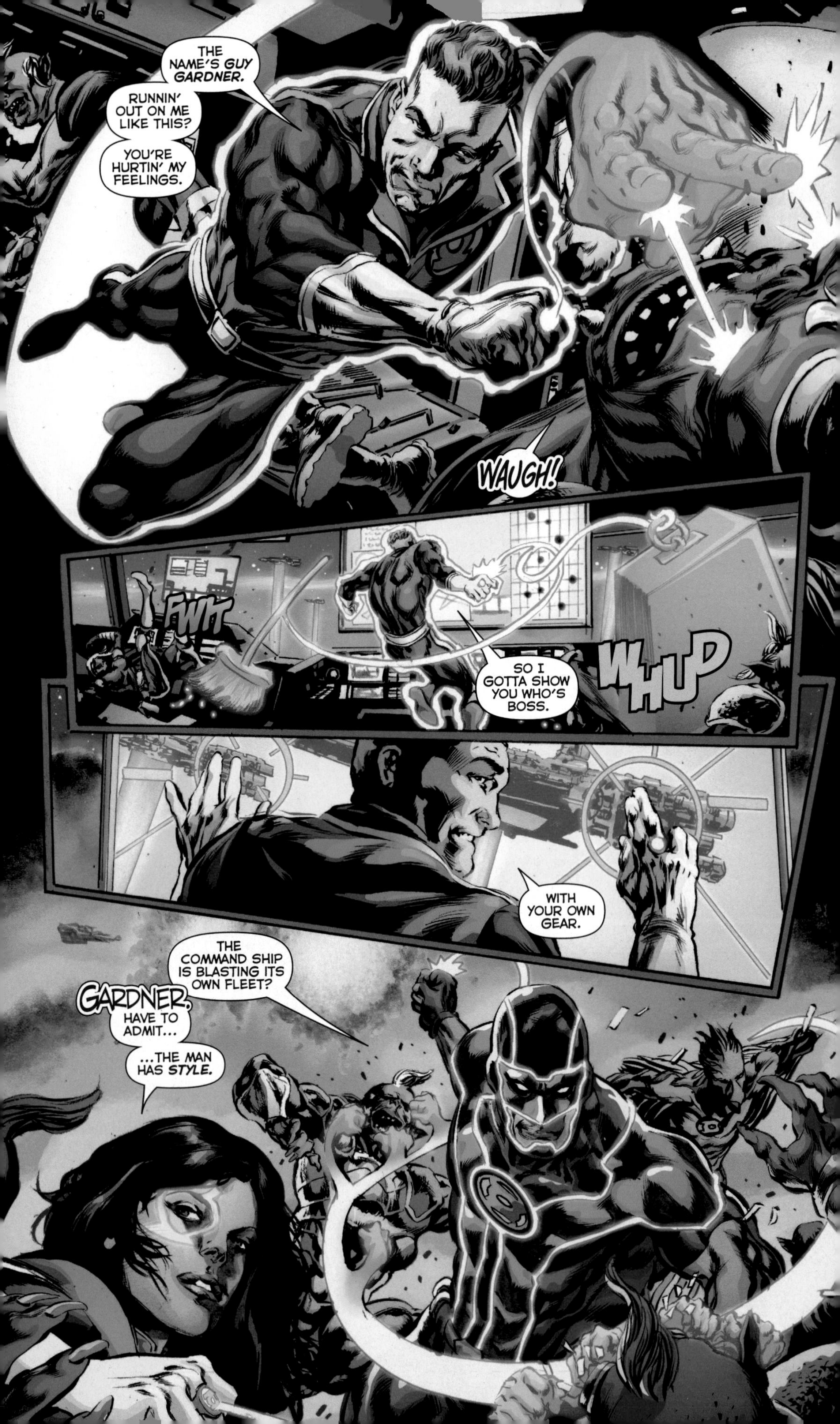
THE NAME'S GUY GARDNER.
RUNNIN' OUT ON ME LIKE THIS?
YOU'RE HURTIN' MY FEELINGS.
WAUGH!
FWIT
SO I GOTTA SHOW YOU WHO'S BOSS.
WHUD
WITH YOUR OWN GEAR.
THE COMMAND SHIP IS BLASTING ITS OWN FLEET?
GARDNER.
HAVE TO ADMIT...
...THE MAN HAS STYLE.

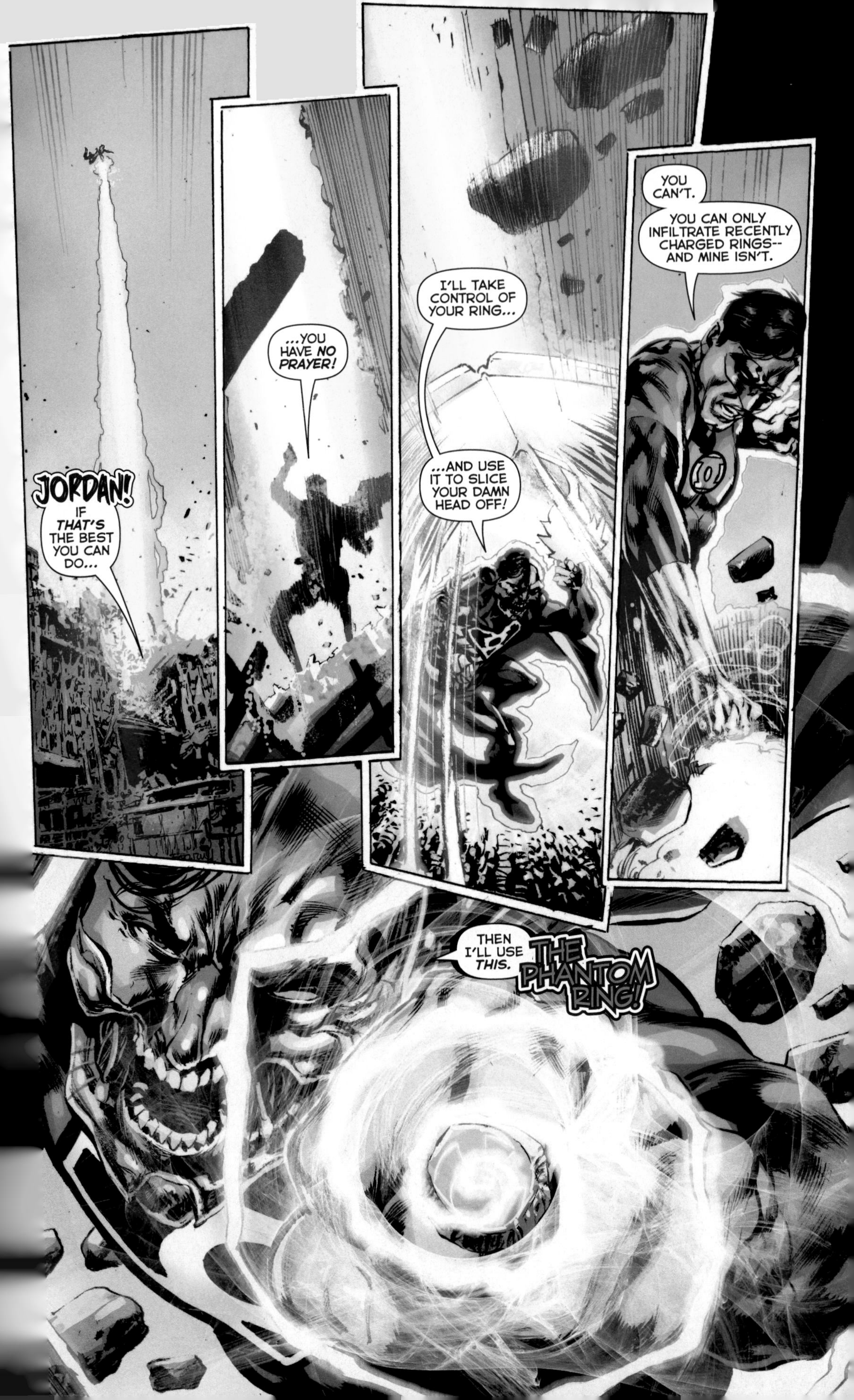
JORDAN! IF THAT'S THE BEST YOU CAN DO...
...YOU HAVE NO PRAYER!
I'LL TAKE CONTROL OF YOUR RING...
...AND USE IT TO SLICE YOUR DAMN HEAD OFF!
YOU CAN'T.
YOU CAN ONLY INFILTRATE RECENTLY CHARGED RINGS-- AND MINE ISN'T.
THEN I'LL USE THIS.
THE PHANTOM RING!

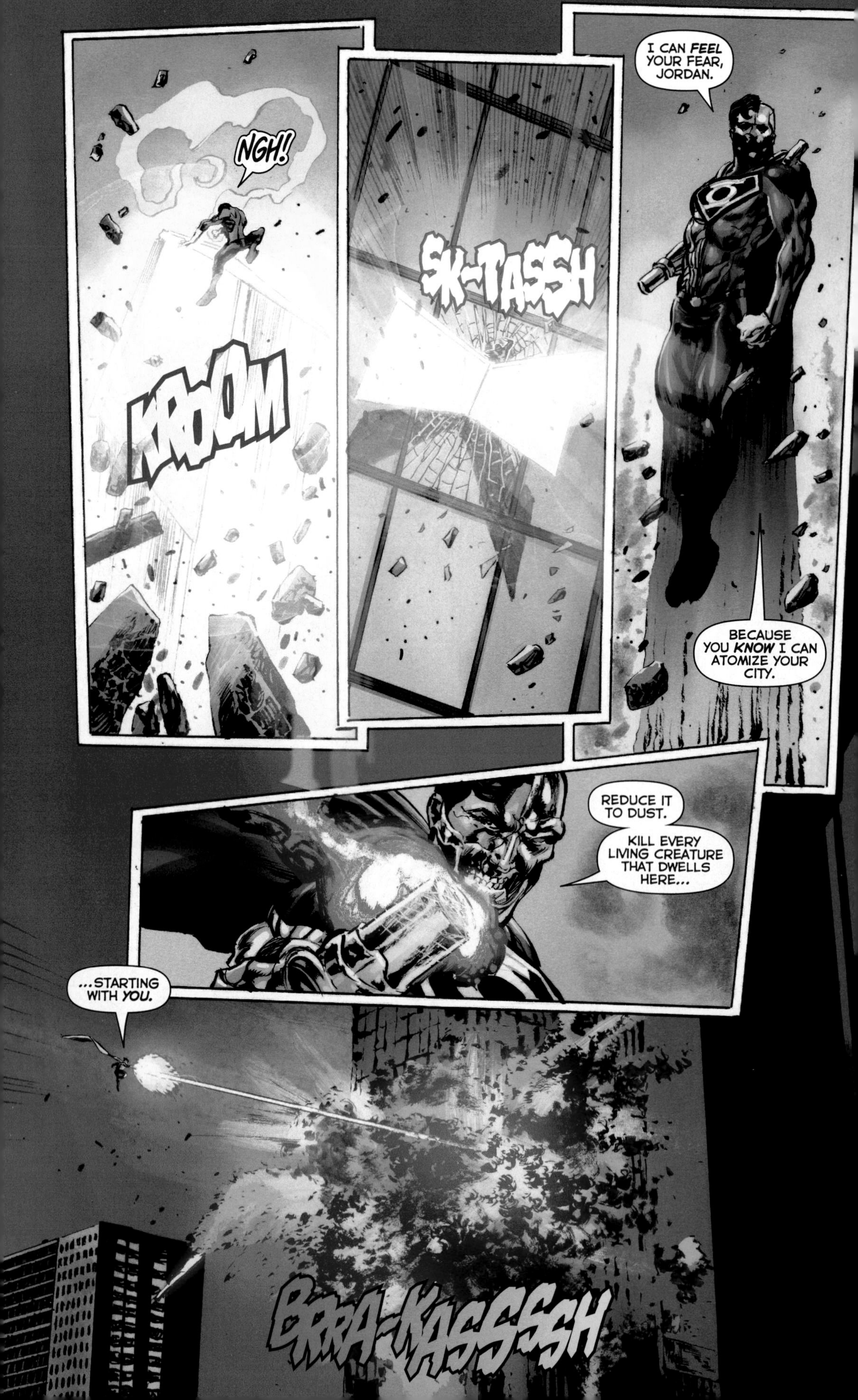
NGH!
KROOM
SK-TASSH
I CAN *FEEL* YOUR FEAR, JORDAN.
BECAUSE YOU *KNOW* I CAN ATOMIZE YOUR CITY.
REDUCE IT TO DUST.
KILL EVERY LIVING CREATURE THAT DWELLS HERE...
...STARTING WITH *YOU.*
BRRA-KASSSSH

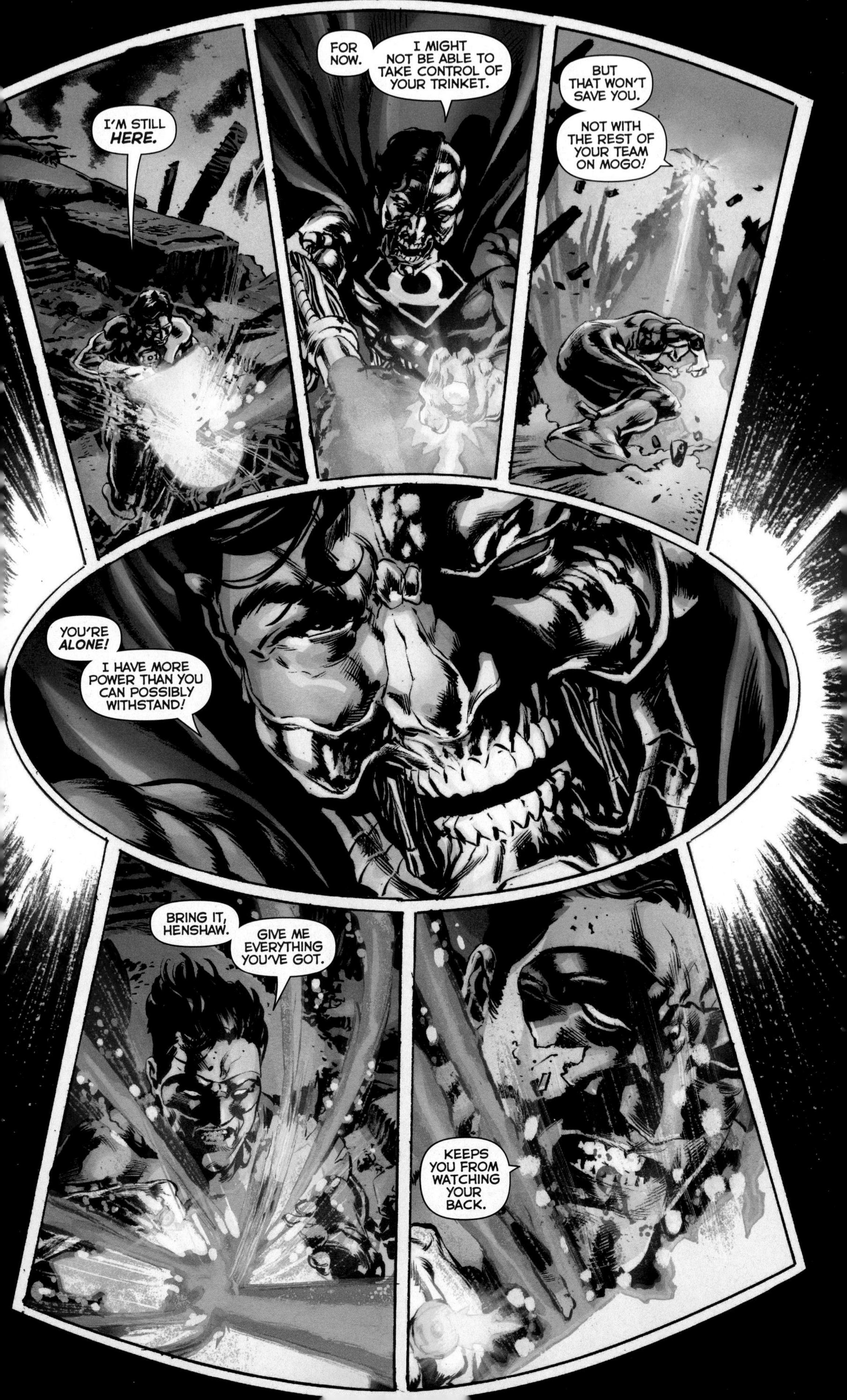
I'M STILL HERE.
FOR NOW.
I MIGHT NOT BE ABLE TO TAKE CONTROL OF YOUR TRINKET.
BUT THAT WON'T SAVE YOU.
NOT WITH THE REST OF YOUR TEAM ON MOGO!
YOU'RE ALONE!
I HAVE MORE POWER THAN YOU CAN POSSIBLY WITHSTAND!
BRING IT, HENSHAW.
GIVE ME EVERYTHING YOU'VE GOT.
KEEPS YOU FROM WATCHING YOUR BACK.

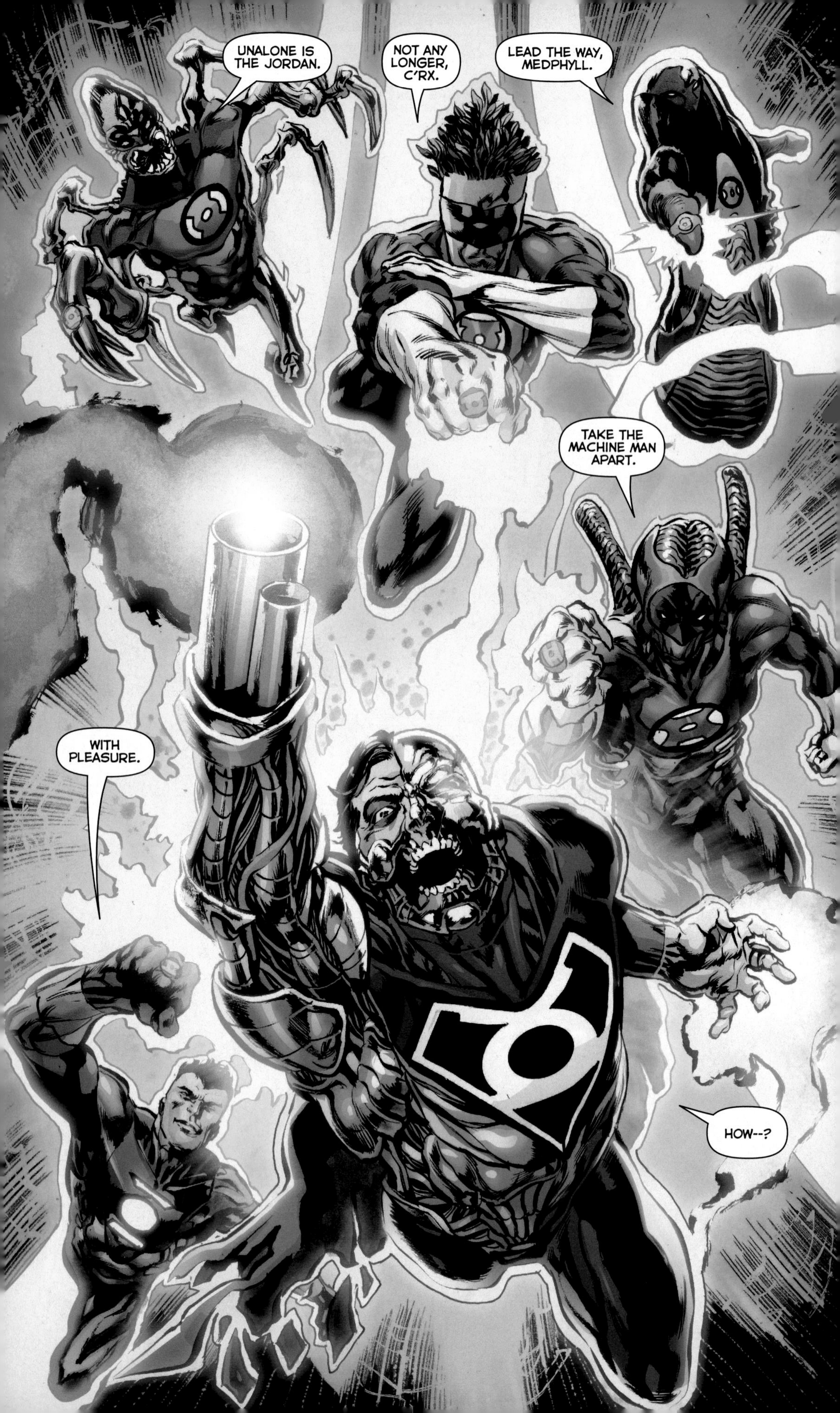
UNALONE IS THE JORDAN.
NOT ANY LONGER, C'RX.
LEAD THE WAY, MEDPHYLL.
TAKE THE MACHINE MAN APART.
WITH PLEASURE.
HOW--?

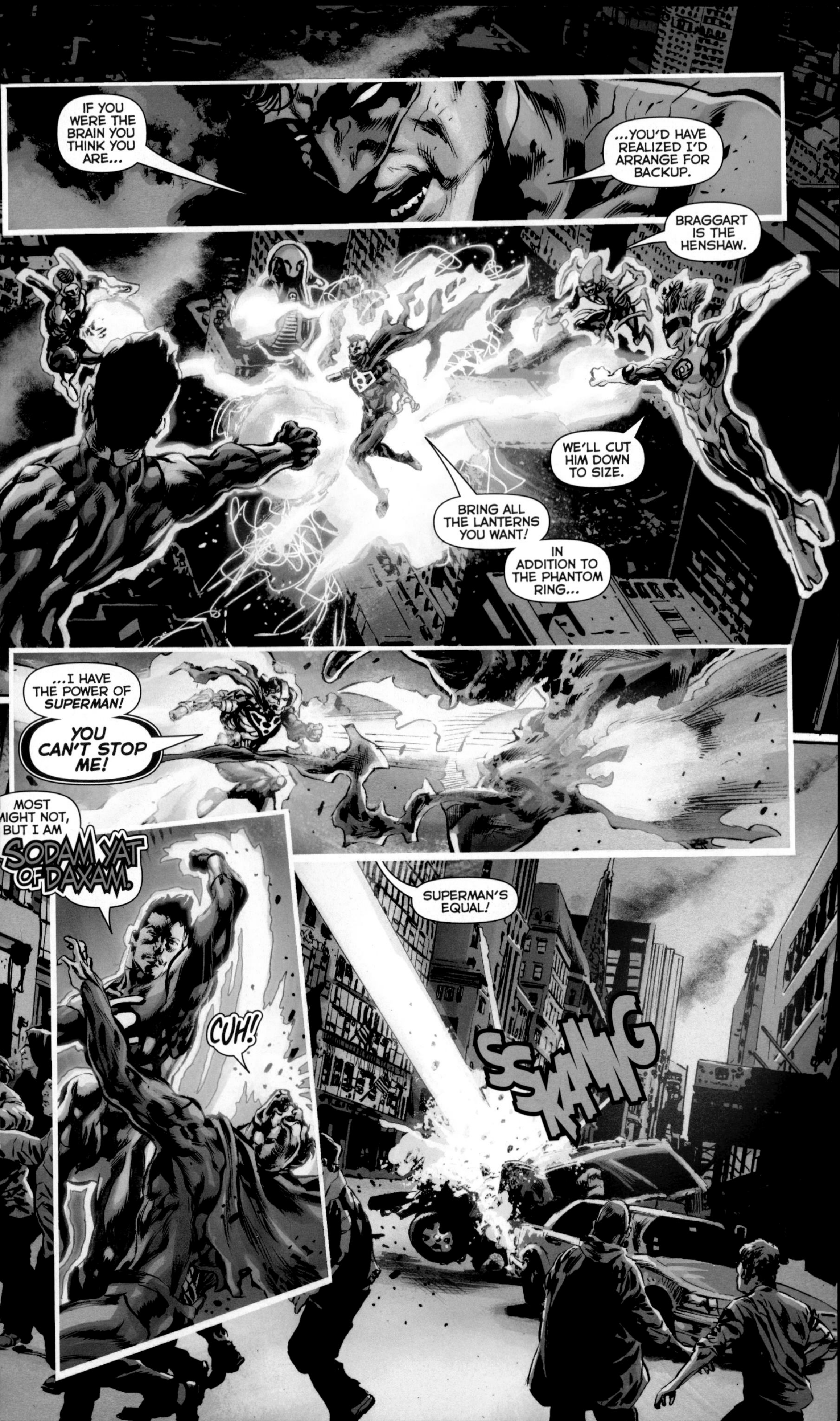

IF YOU WERE THE BRAIN YOU THINK YOU ARE...
...YOU'D HAVE REALIZED I'D ARRANGE FOR BACKUP.
BRAGGART IS THE HENSHAW.
WE'LL CUT HIM DOWN TO SIZE.
BRING ALL THE LANTERNS YOU WANT!
IN ADDITION TO THE PHANTOM RING...
...I HAVE THE POWER OF SUPERMAN!
YOU CAN'T STOP ME!
MOST MIGHT NOT, BUT I AM
SODAM YAT OF DAXAM.
SUPERMAN'S EQUAL!
CUH!
SSKAHHG

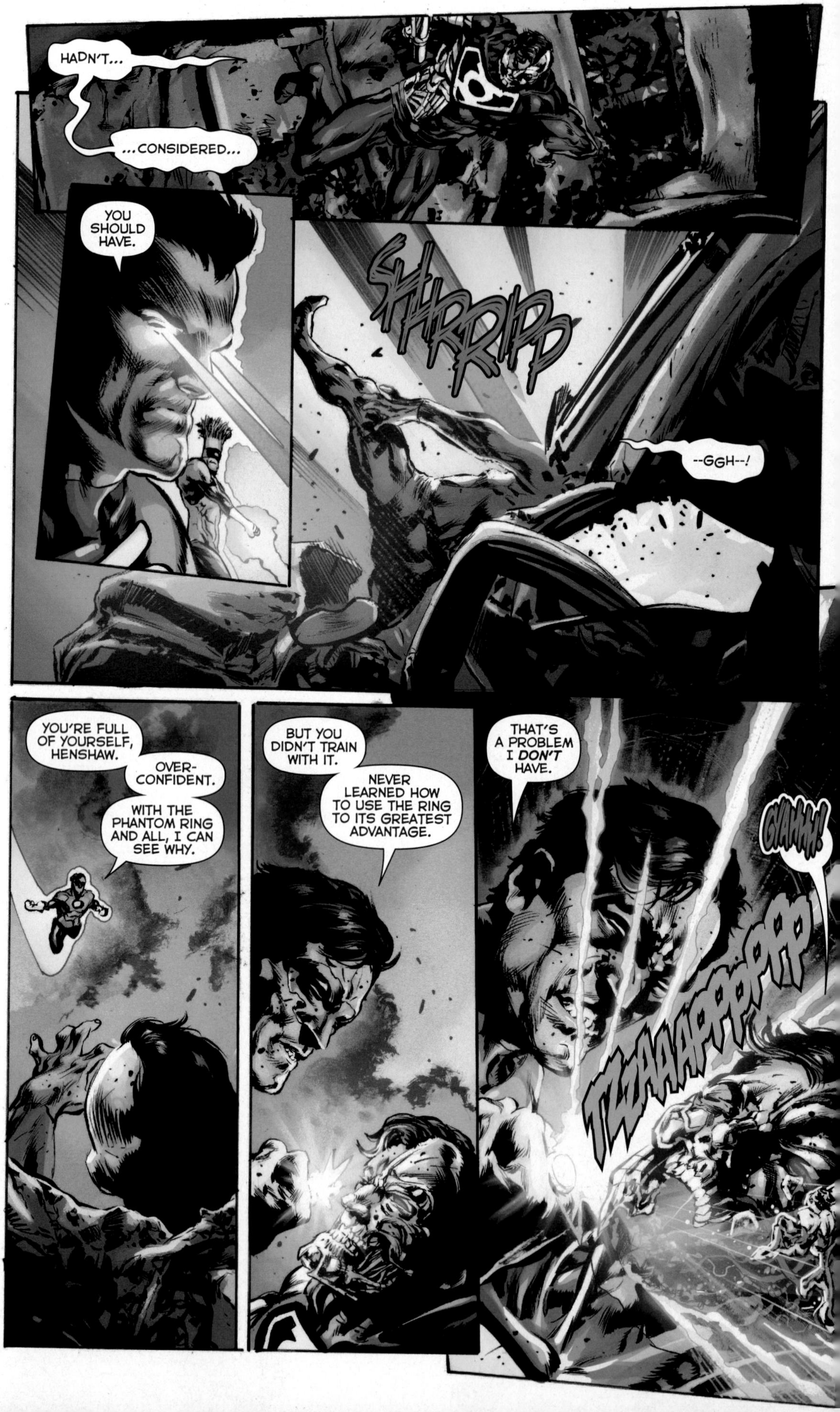
HADN'T...
...CONSIDERED...
YOU SHOULD HAVE.
SHHRIPP
--GGH--!
YOU'RE FULL OF YOURSELF, HENSHAW.
OVER-CONFIDENT.
WITH THE PHANTOM RING AND ALL, I CAN SEE WHY.
BUT YOU DIDN'T TRAIN WITH IT.
NEVER LEARNED HOW TO USE THE RING TO ITS GREATEST ADVANTAGE.
THAT'S A PROBLEM I *DON'T* HAVE.
GYAHHH!
TZZAAAPPPPPP

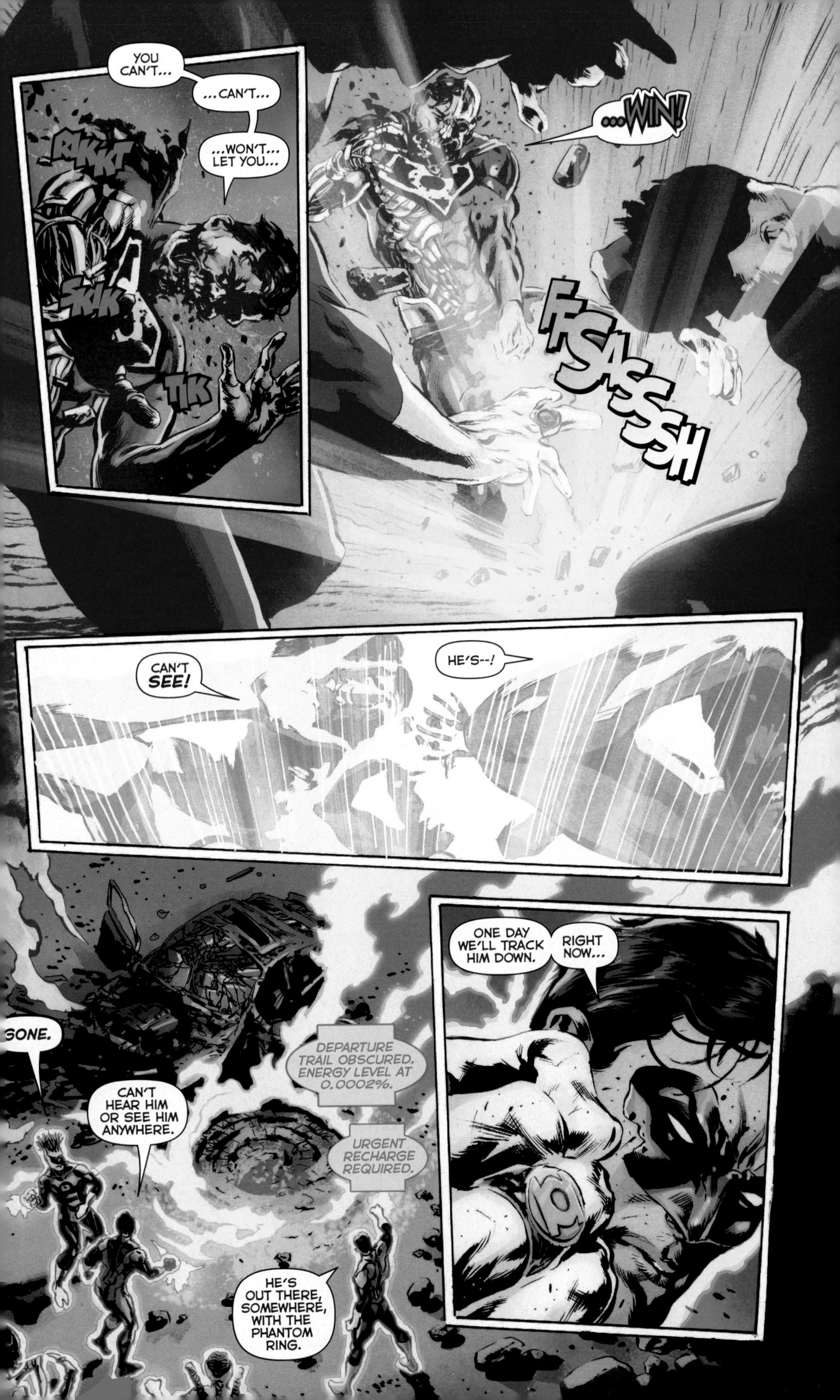
YOU CAN'T...
...CAN'T...
...WON'T... LET YOU...
RIKKKT
SKIK
TIK
...WIN!
FFSASSSH
CAN'T SEE!
HE'S--!
GONE.
CAN'T HEAR HIM OR SEE HIM ANYWHERE.
DEPARTURE TRAIL OBSCURED. ENERGY LEVEL AT 0.0002%.
URGENT RECHARGE REQUIRED.
HE'S OUT THERE, SOMEWHERE, WITH THE PHANTOM RING.
ONE DAY WE'LL TRACK HIM DOWN.
RIGHT NOW...

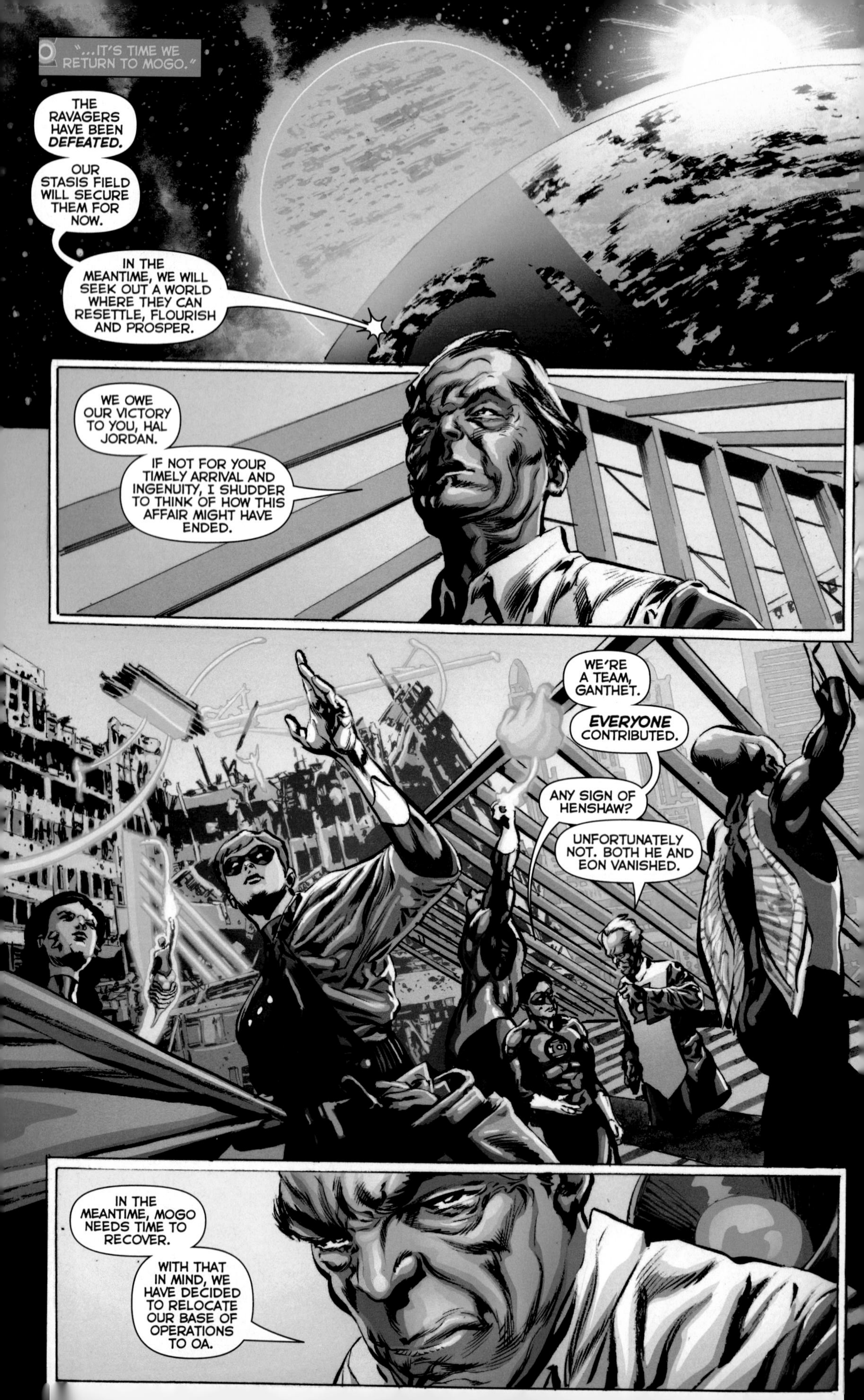
"...IT'S TIME WE RETURN TO MOGO."
THE RAVAGERS HAVE BEEN *DEFEATED.*
OUR STASIS FIELD WILL SECURE THEM FOR NOW.
IN THE MEANTIME, WE WILL SEEK OUT A WORLD WHERE THEY CAN RESETTLE, FLOURISH AND PROSPER.
WE OWE OUR VICTORY TO YOU, HAL JORDAN.
IF NOT FOR YOUR TIMELY ARRIVAL AND INGENUITY, I SHUDDER TO THINK OF HOW THIS AFFAIR MIGHT HAVE ENDED.
WE'RE A TEAM, GANTHET.
EVERYONE CONTRIBUTED.
ANY SIGN OF HENSHAW?
UNFORTUNATELY NOT. BOTH HE AND EON VANISHED.
IN THE MEANTIME, MOGO NEEDS TIME TO RECOVER.
WITH THAT IN MIND, WE HAVE DECIDED TO RELOCATE OUR BASE OF OPERATIONS TO OA.

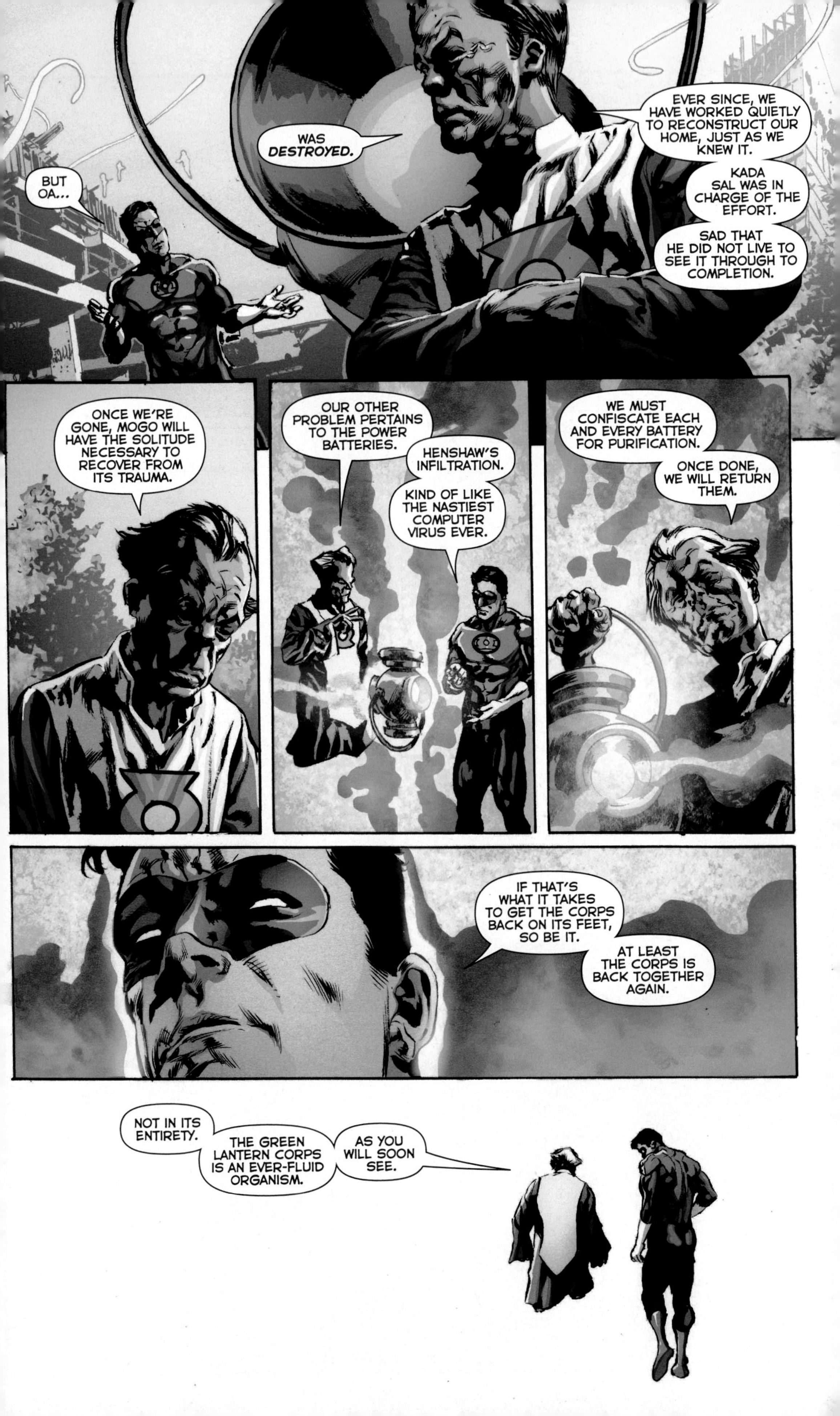

BUT OA...
WAS *DESTROYED.*
EVER SINCE, WE HAVE WORKED QUIETLY TO RECONSTRUCT OUR HOME, JUST AS WE KNEW IT.
KADA SAL WAS IN CHARGE OF THE EFFORT.
SAD THAT HE DID NOT LIVE TO SEE IT THROUGH TO COMPLETION.
ONCE WE'RE GONE, MOGO WILL HAVE THE SOLITUDE NECESSARY TO RECOVER FROM ITS TRAUMA.
OUR OTHER PROBLEM PERTAINS TO THE POWER BATTERIES.
HENSHAW'S INFILTRATION.
KIND OF LIKE THE NASTIEST COMPUTER VIRUS EVER.
WE MUST CONFISCATE EACH AND EVERY BATTERY FOR PURIFICATION.
ONCE DONE, WE WILL RETURN THEM.
IF THAT'S WHAT IT TAKES TO GET THE CORPS BACK ON ITS FEET, SO BE IT.
AT LEAST THE CORPS IS BACK TOGETHER AGAIN.
NOT IN ITS ENTIRETY.
THE GREEN LANTERN CORPS IS AN EVER-FLUID ORGANISM.
AS YOU WILL SOON SEE.

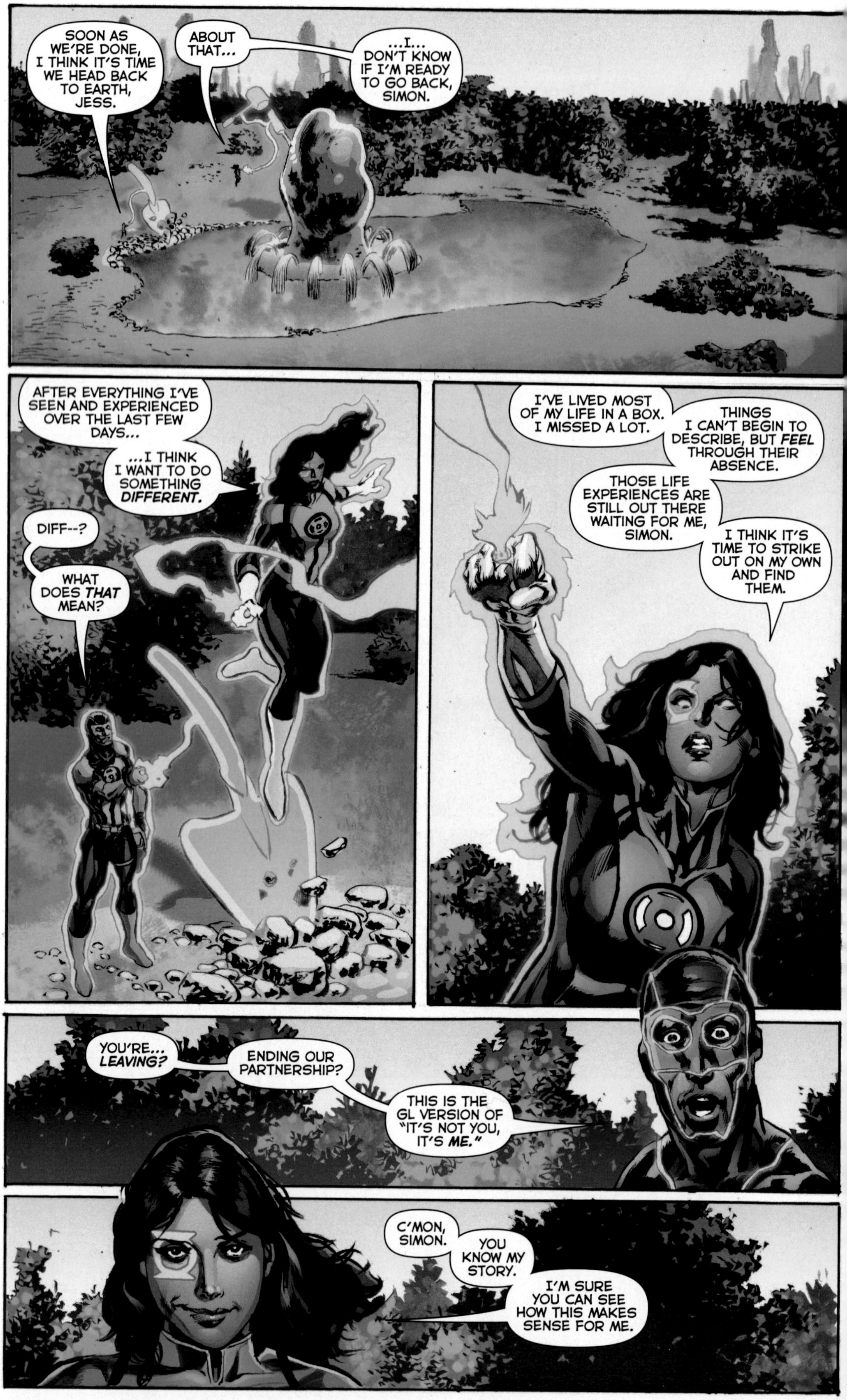

SOON AS WE'RE DONE, I THINK IT'S TIME WE HEAD BACK TO EARTH, JESS.
ABOUT THAT...
...I... DON'T KNOW IF I'M READY TO GO BACK, SIMON.
AFTER EVERYTHING I'VE SEEN AND EXPERIENCED OVER THE LAST FEW DAYS...
...I THINK I WANT TO DO SOMETHING *DIFFERENT.*
DIFF--?
WHAT DOES *THAT* MEAN?
I'VE LIVED MOST OF MY LIFE IN A BOX. I MISSED A LOT.
THINGS I CAN'T BEGIN TO DESCRIBE, BUT *FEEL* THROUGH THEIR ABSENCE.
THOSE LIFE EXPERIENCES ARE STILL OUT THERE WAITING FOR ME, SIMON.
I THINK IT'S TIME TO STRIKE OUT ON MY OWN AND FIND THEM.
YOU'RE... *LEAVING?*
ENDING OUR PARTNERSHIP?
THIS IS THE GL VERSION OF "IT'S NOT YOU, IT'S *ME.*"
C'MON, SIMON.
YOU KNOW MY STORY.
I'M SURE YOU CAN SEE HOW THIS MAKES SENSE FOR ME.

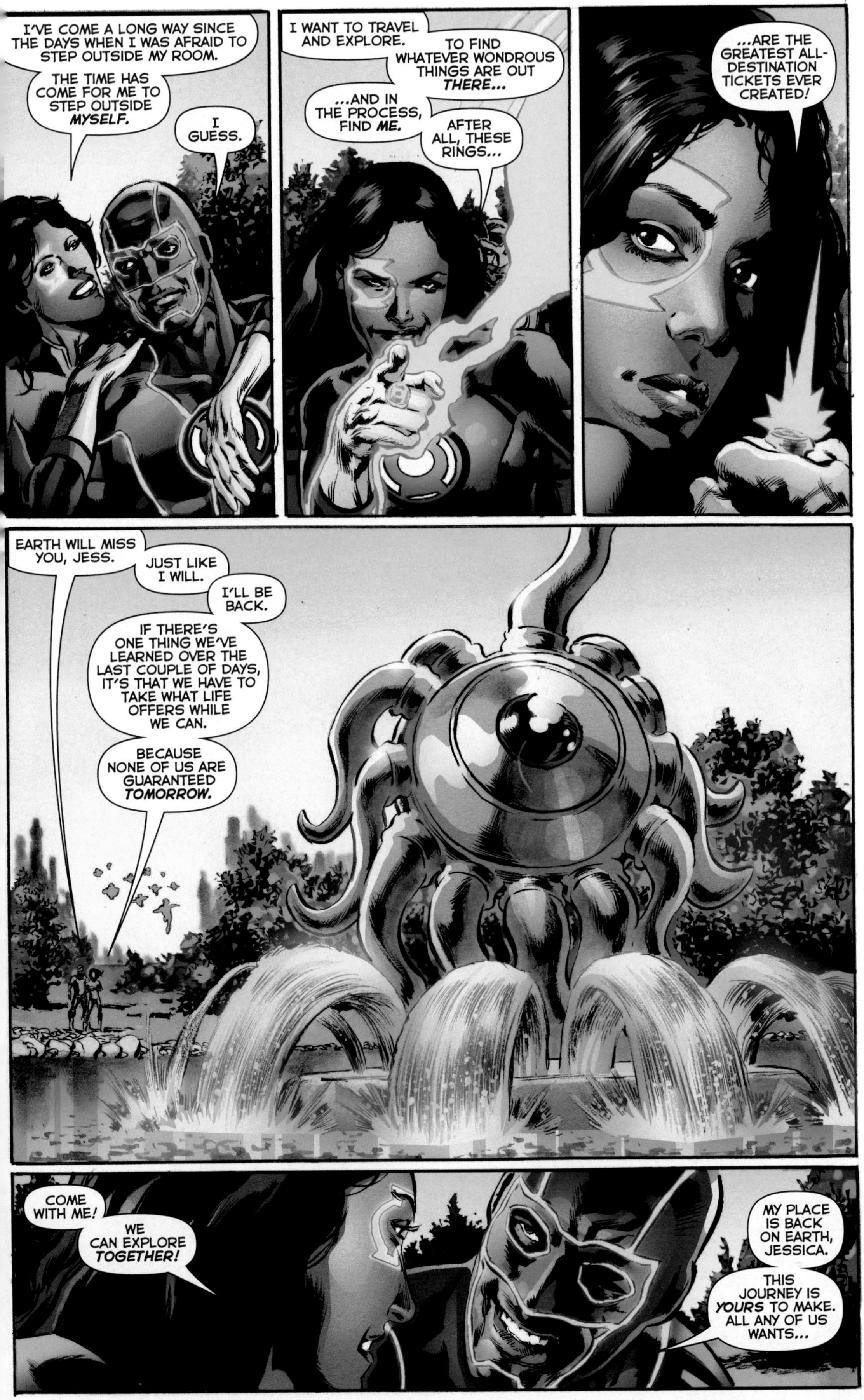
I'VE COME A LONG WAY SINCE THE DAYS WHEN I WAS AFRAID TO STEP OUTSIDE MY ROOM.
THE TIME HAS COME FOR ME TO STEP OUTSIDE MYSELF.
I GUESS.
I WANT TO TRAVEL AND EXPLORE.
TO FIND WHATEVER WONDROUS THINGS ARE OUT THERE...
...AND IN THE PROCESS, FIND ME.
AFTER ALL, THESE RINGS...
...ARE THE GREATEST ALL-DESTINATION TICKETS EVER CREATED!
EARTH WILL MISS YOU, JESS.
JUST LIKE I WILL.
I'LL BE BACK.
IF THERE'S ONE THING WE'VE LEARNED OVER THE LAST COUPLE OF DAYS, IT'S THAT WE HAVE TO TAKE WHAT LIFE OFFERS WHILE WE CAN.
BECAUSE NONE OF US ARE GUARANTEED TOMORROW.
COME WITH ME!
WE CAN EXPLORE TOGETHER!
MY PLACE IS BACK ON EARTH, JESSICA.
THIS JOURNEY IS YOURS TO MAKE. ALL ANY OF US WANTS...

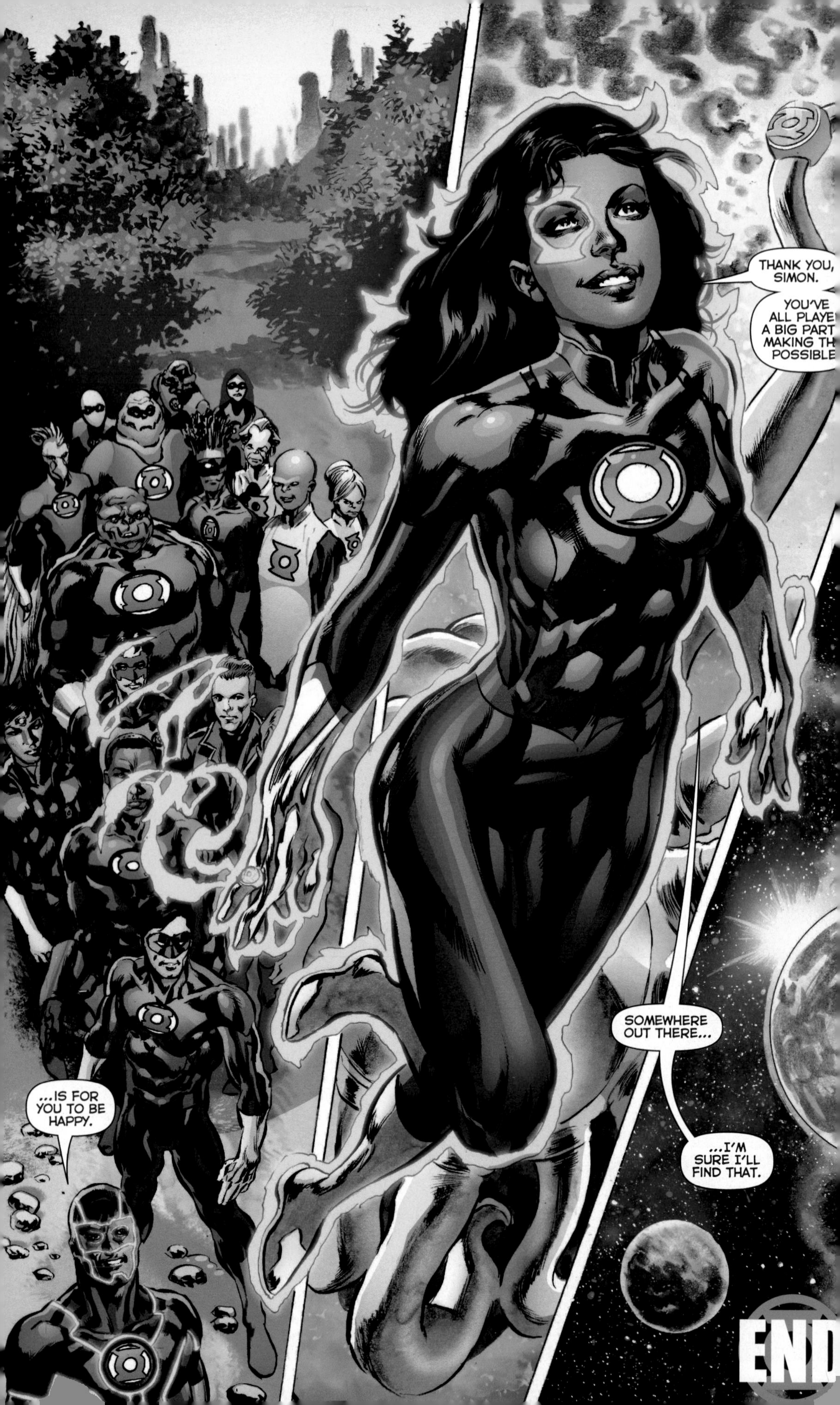
...IS FOR YOU TO BE HAPPY.
THANK YOU, SIMON.
YOU'VE ALL PLAYE A BIG PART MAKING TH POSSIBLE
SOMEWHERE OUT THERE...
...I'M SURE I'LL FIND THAT.
END

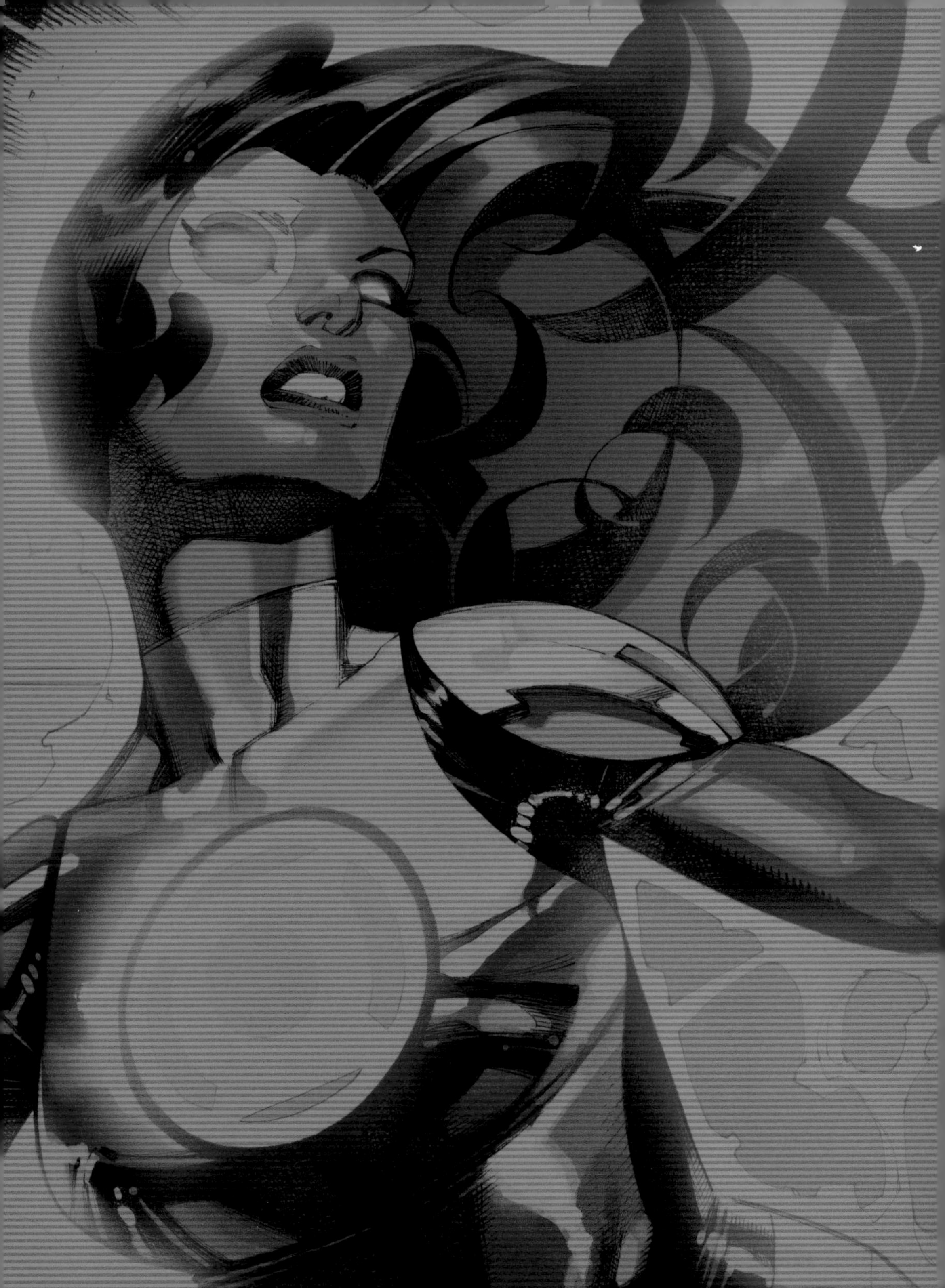

VARIANT COVER GALLERY

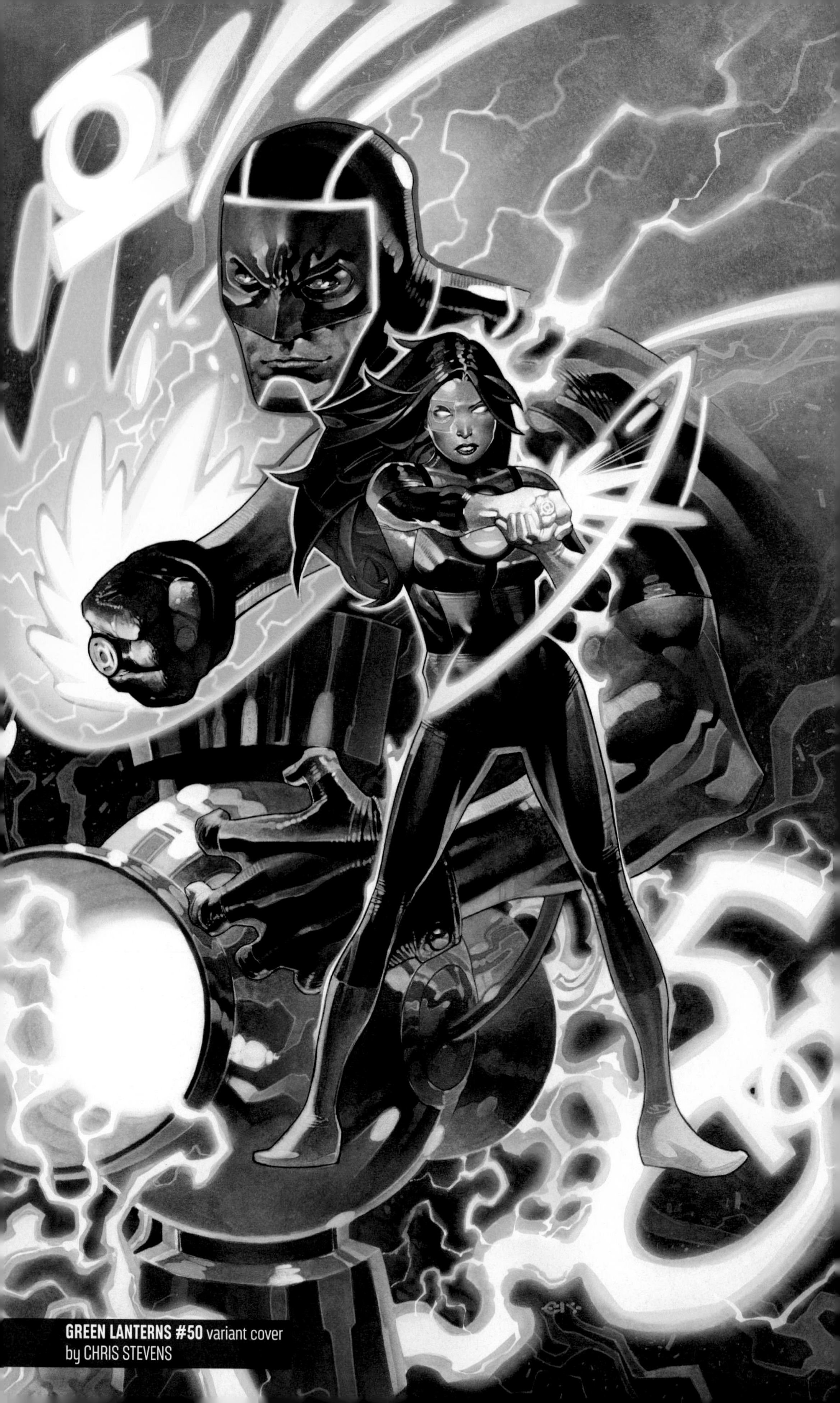

GREEN LANTERNS #50 variant cover
by CHRIS STEVENS

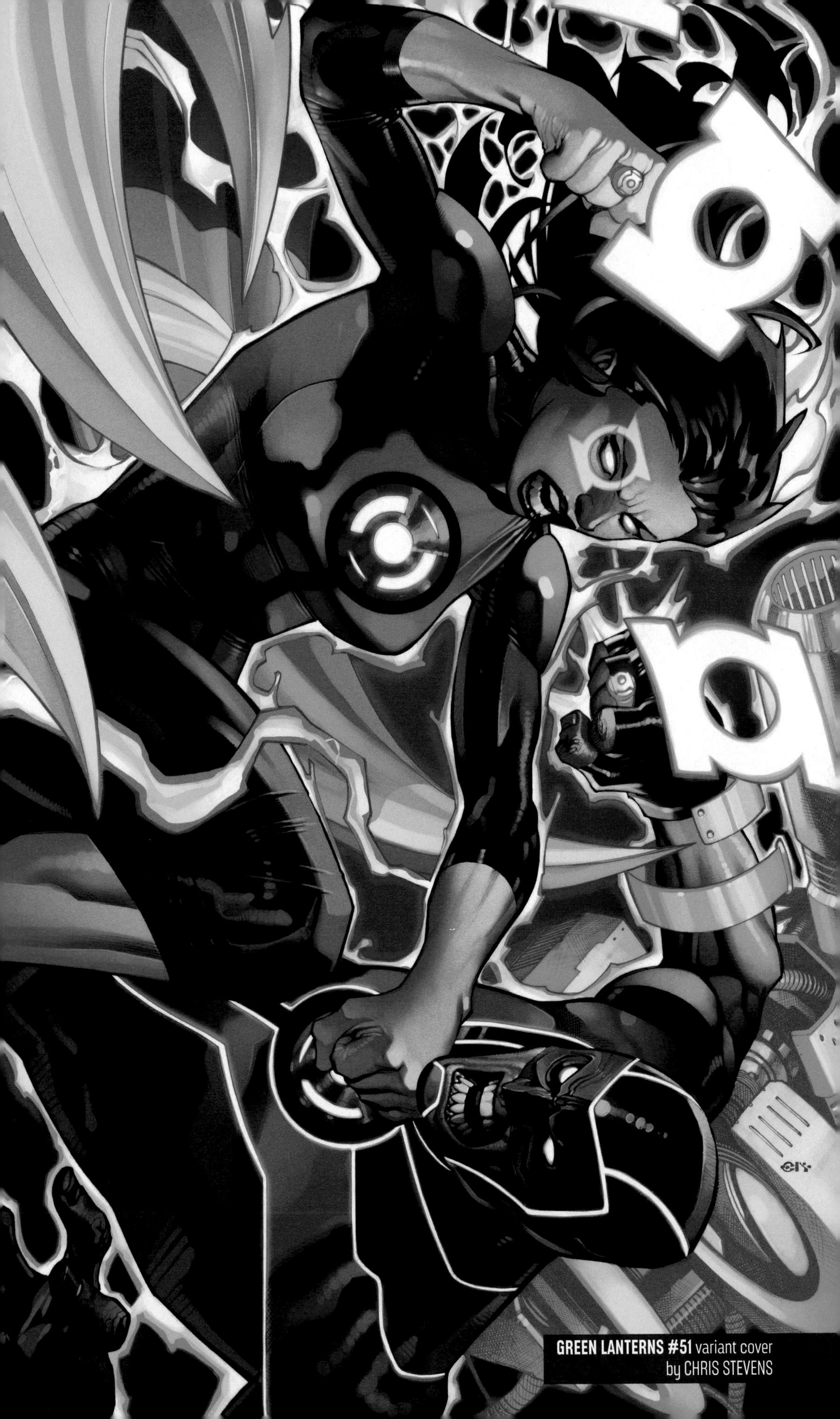

GREEN LANTERNS #51 variant cover
by CHRIS STEVENS

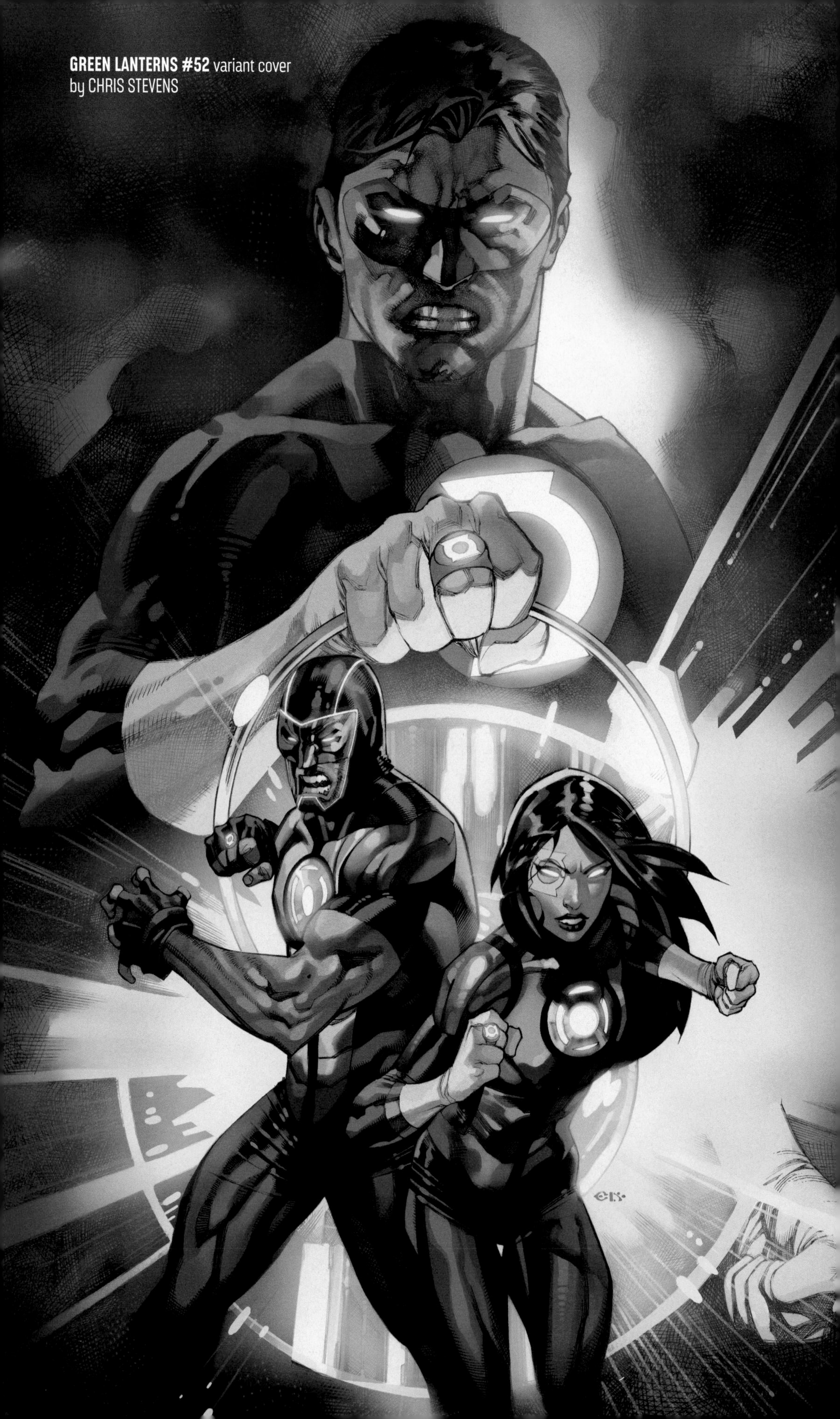

GREEN LANTERNS #52 variant cover
by CHRIS STEVENS

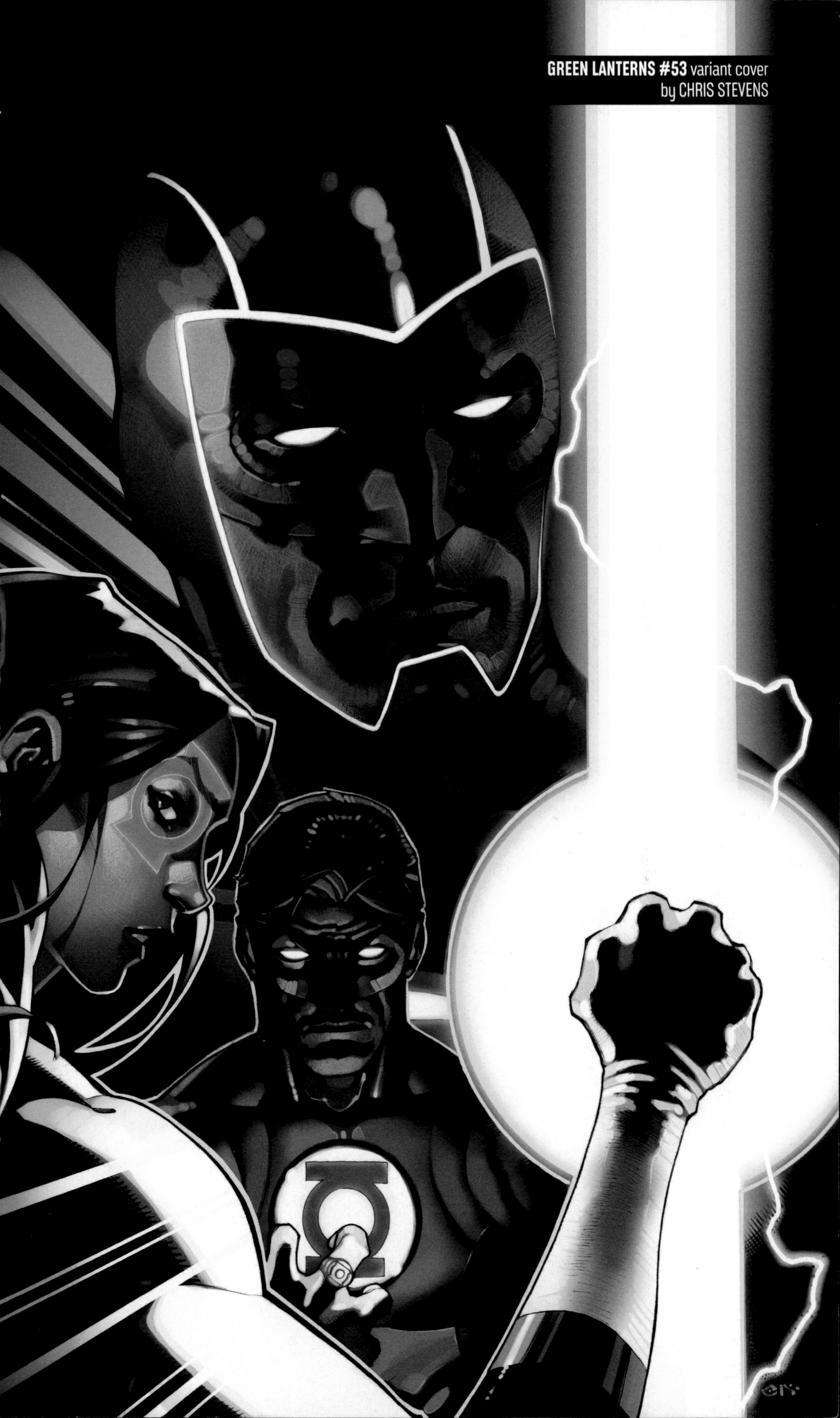

GREEN LANTERNS #53 variant cover
by CHRIS STEVENS

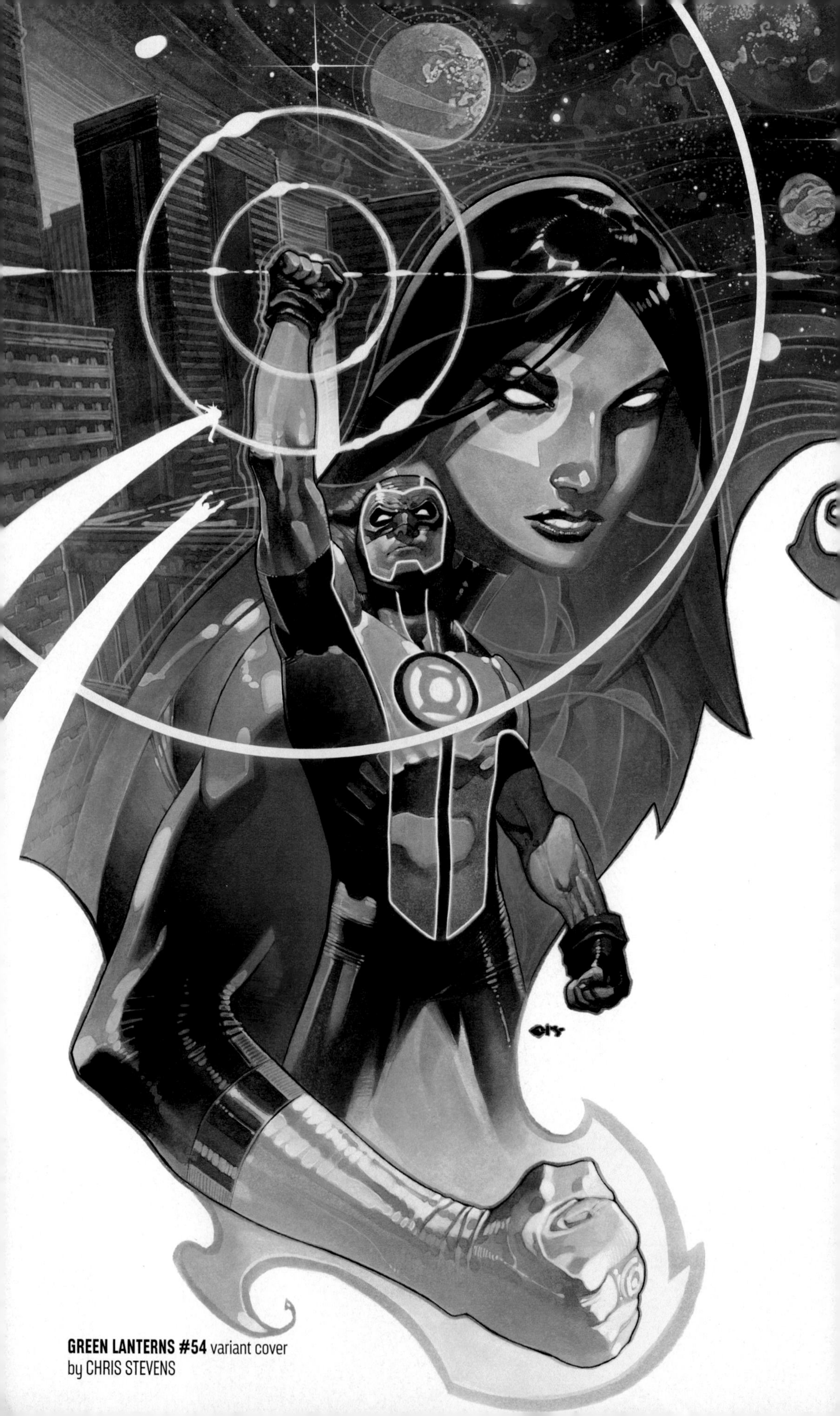

GREEN LANTERNS #54 variant cover
by CHRIS STEVENS

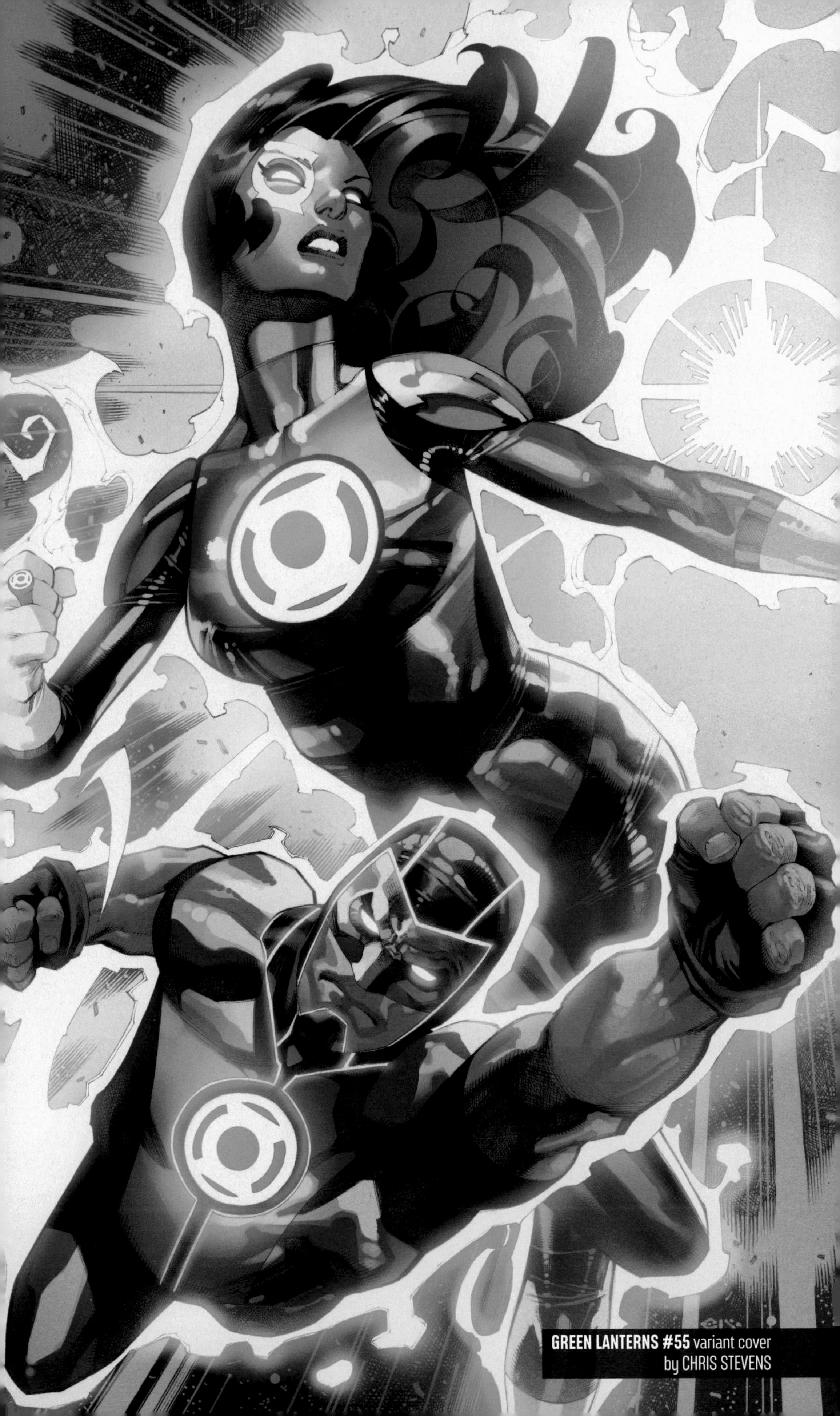

GREEN LANTERNS #55 variant cover
by CHRIS STEVENS

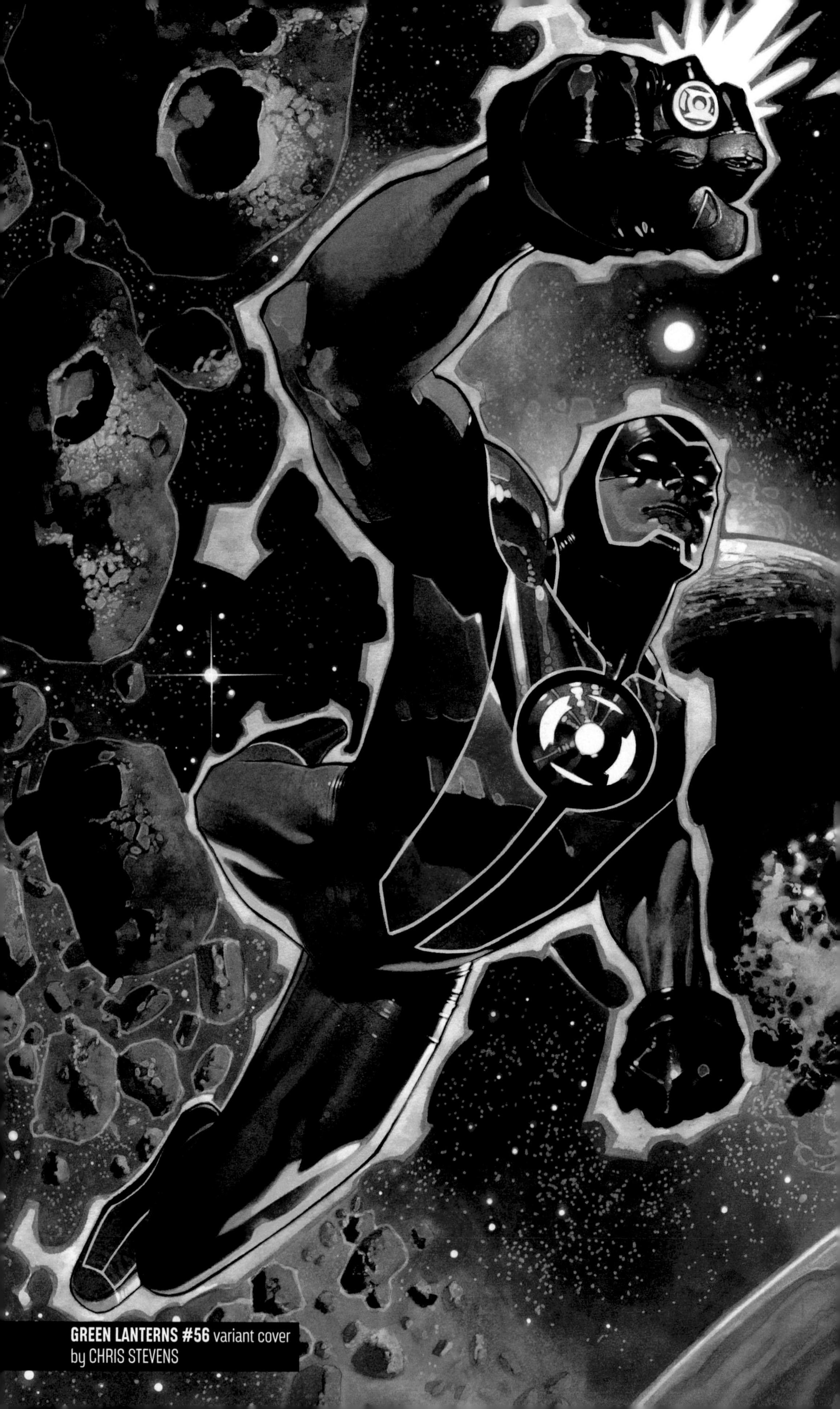

GREEN LANTERNS #56 variant cover
by CHRIS STEVENS

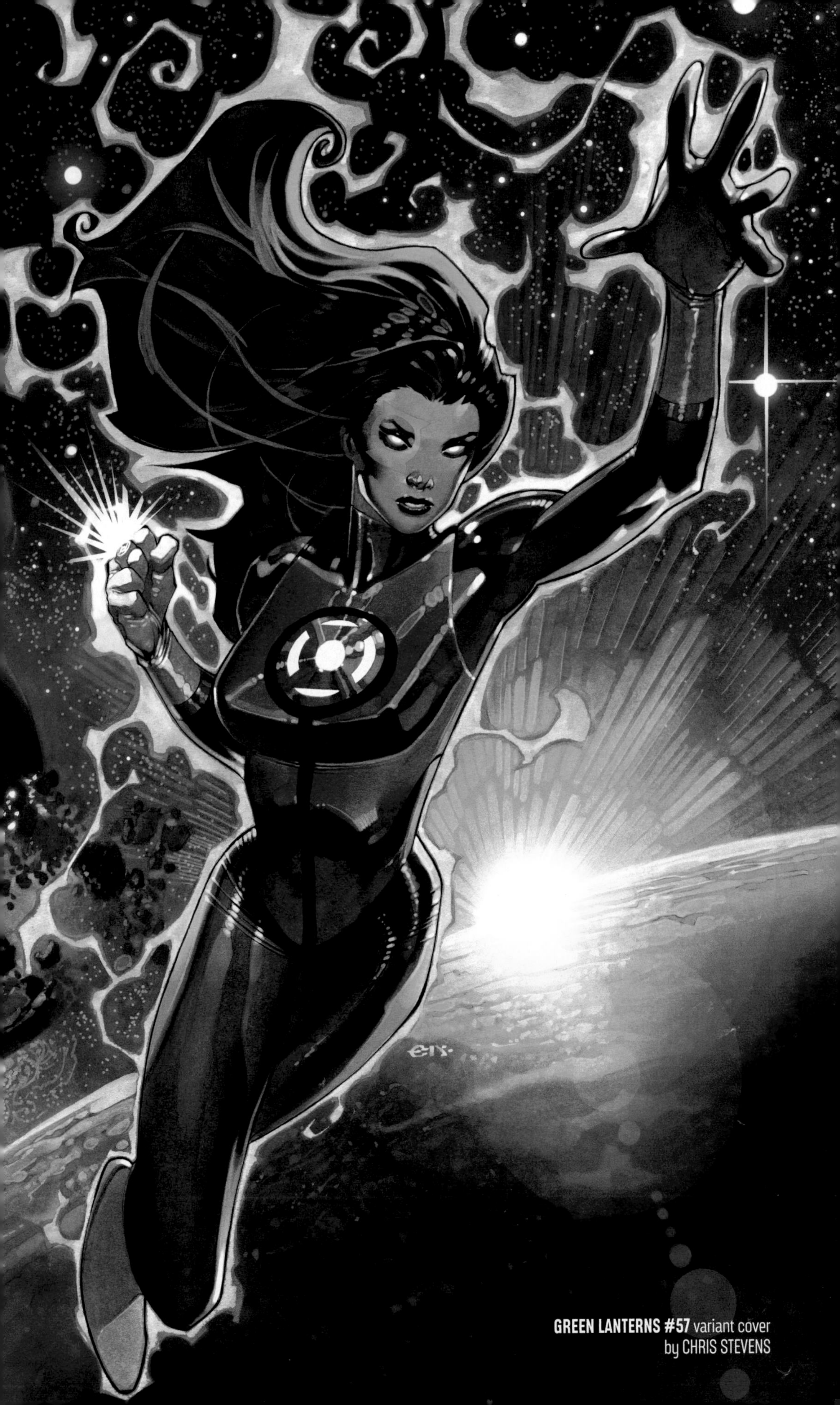

GREEN LANTERNS #57 variant cover
by CHRIS STEVENS

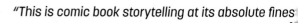

FROM THE WRITER OF
JUSTICE LEAGUE AND *THE FLASH*

GEOFF JOHNS
GREEN LANTERN: REBIRTH

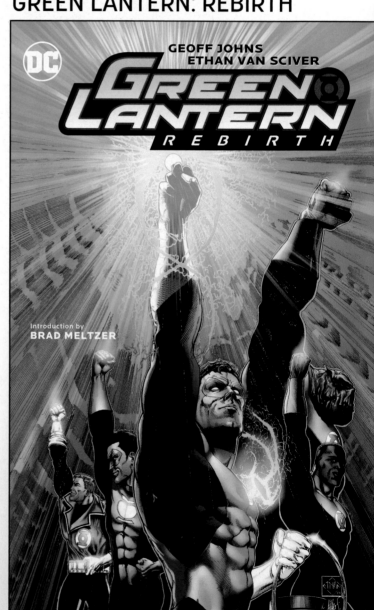

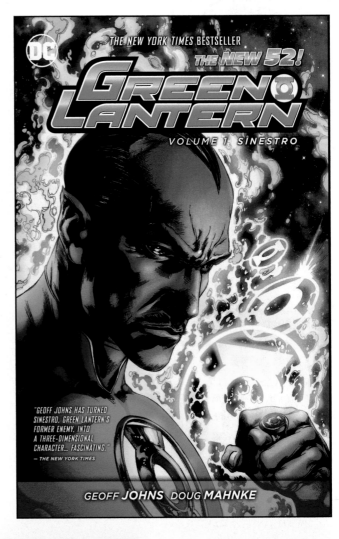

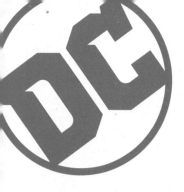

"Sam Humphries and artist Ethan Van Sciver debut a new era of emerald greatness!"
– COMIC BOOK RESOURCES

"...it's hard not to walk away impressed."
– IGN

DC UNIVERSE REBIRTH

GREEN LANTERNS

VOL. 1: RAGE PLANET

SAM HUMPHRIES
with ETHAN VAN SCIVER

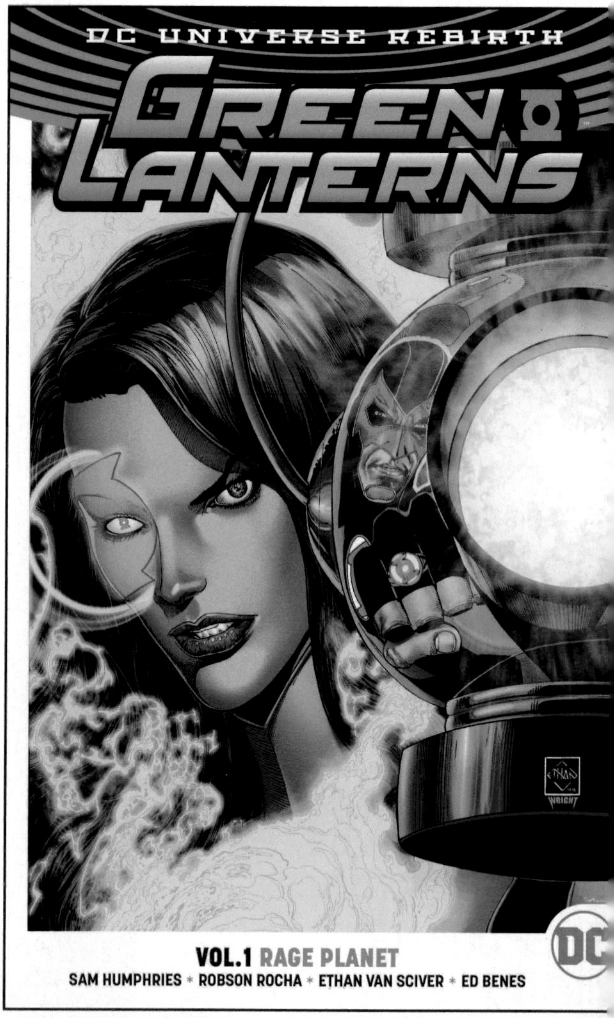
DC UNIVERSE REBIRTH
GREEN LANTERNS
VOL.1 RAGE PLANET
SAM HUMPHRIES * ROBSON ROCHA * ETHAN VAN SCIVER * ED BENES

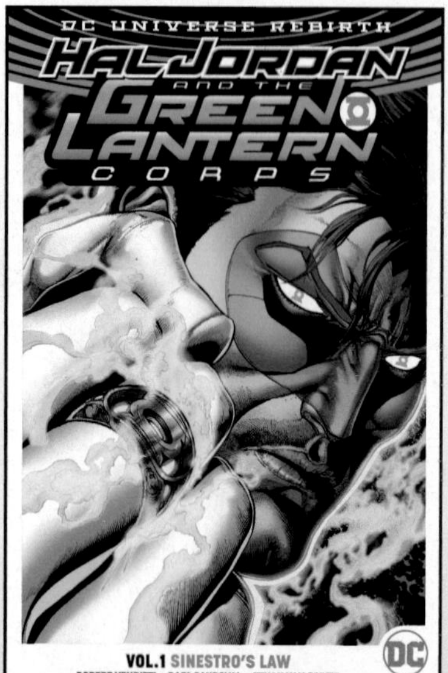
DC UNIVERSE REBIRTH
HAL JORDAN AND THE GREEN LANTERN CORPS
VOL.1 SINESTRO'S LAW
ROBERT VENDITTI * RAFA SANDOVAL * ETHAN VAN SCIVER

HAL JORDAN AND THE GREEN LANTERN CORPS VOL. 1: SINESTRO'S LAW

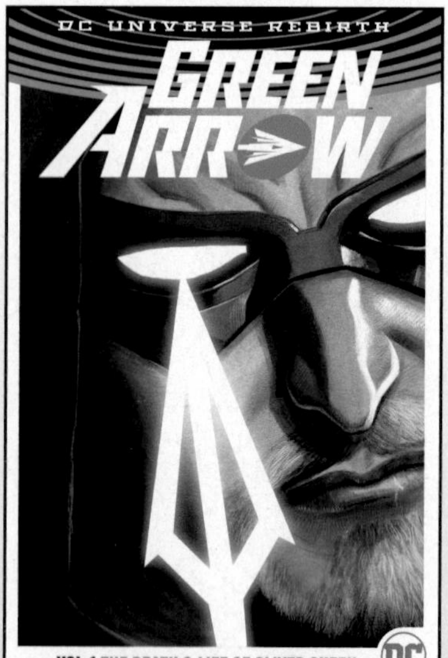
DC UNIVERSE REBIRTH
GREEN ARROW
VOL.1 THE DEATH & LIFE OF OLIVER QUEEN
BENJAMIN PERCY * OTTO SCHMIDT * JUAN FERREYRA

GREEN ARROW VOL. 1: THE DEATH & LIFE OF OLIVER QUEEN

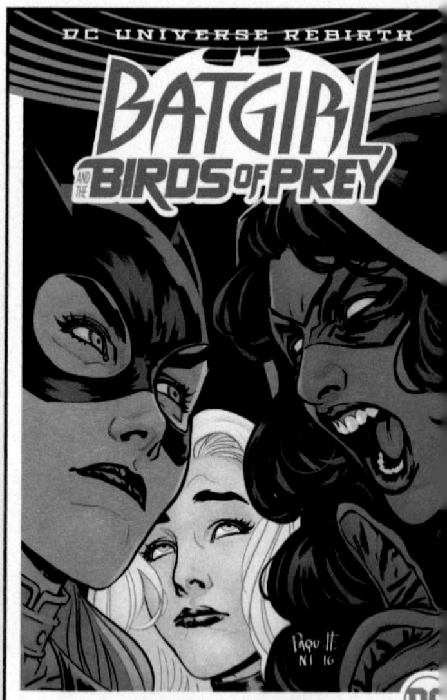
DC UNIVERSE REBIRTH
BATGIRL AND THE BIRDS OF PREY
VOL.1 WHO IS ORACLE?
JULIE BENSON * SHAWNA BENSON * CLAIRE ROE

BATGIRL AND THE BIRDS OF PREY VOL. 1: WHO IS ORACLE?

Get more DC graphic novels wherever comics and books are sold!